Inside
Case-based
Reasoning

Inside
Case-based
Reasoning

Christopher K. Riesbeck
Roger C. Schank

The Institute for the Learning Sciences
Northwestern University
Evanston, Illinois

 LAWRENCE ERLBAUM ASSOCIATES, PUBLISHERS
1989   Hillsdale, New Jersey   Hove and London

Lawrence Erlbaum Associates, Inc., Publishers
365 Broadway
Hillsdale, New Jersey 07642

Library of Congress Cataloging in Publication Data

Riesbeck, Christopher K.
  Inside case-based reasoning.

  Bibliography: p.
  Includes index.
  1. Artificial intelligence--Data processing.
2. Reasoning (Psychology) 3. Microprogramming.
4. LISP (Computer program language) I. Schank,
Roger C. 1948-   . II Title.
Q336.R54 1989   006.3   89-11961
ISBN 0-89859-767-6

Printed in the United States of America
10 9 8 7 6 5 4 3 2 1

Contents

Preface   **xxi**

1 Case-based Reasoning: An Introduction   **1**
  1.1 AI and Cognition   1
  1.2 Does Thinking really involve Thinking?   2
     1.2.1 Understanding Depends Upon Explanation   3
     1.2.2 Scripts   4
  1.3 The Basic Planning Algorithm   5
  1.4 Cases versus Rules   9
     1.4.1 Ossified Cases 12
     1.4.2 Paradigmatic Cases 12
     1.4.3 Stories 13
  1.5 Reminding 15
     1.5.1 Goal-based Reminding 19
     1.5.2 Plan-based Reminding 20
     1.5.3 Reminding across Multiple Contexts 21
     1.5.4 Morals 22
     1.5.5 Intentional Reminding 22
     1.5.6 A Perspective on Reminding 23

2 Case-based Reasoners   **25**
  2.1 Introduction 25
  2.2 Case Studies in Case-based Reasoning 26
     2.2.1 IPP 27
     2.2.2 CYRUS 27
     2.2.3 JUDGE 27
     2.2.4 CHEF 28
     2.2.5 COACH 28
     2.2.6 MEDIATOR 29
     2.2.7 HYPO 29
     2.2.8 PLEXUS 29

        2.2.9   PERSUADER 29

        2.2.10 CASEY 30

        2.2.11 SWALE 30

  2.3   Rule-based Reasoning 30

  2.4   Case-based Reasoning 32

  2.5   Memory Organization 33

        2.5.1   Memory Organization Packages (MOPs) 34

        2.5.2   Case-based Learning and Memory Organization 36

        2.5.3   Thematic Organization Packets 40

  2.6   Adapting Cases 41

        2.6.1   Types of Adaptation 43

        2.6.2   Adaptation Techniques 44

  2.7   Explanation and Repair 52

        2.7.1   Repair 53

3 Implementing Micro MOPS   55

  3.1   Introduction 55

  3.2   Some Basic Lisp Utilities 55

        3.2.1   Catching Errors 55

  3.3   Tables 56

  3.4   Iteration with the FOR Macro 59

  3.5   MOP-based Memory 61

  3.6   Implementation 67

  3.7   Extensions 87

        3.7.1   Structures versus Tables 88

        3.7.2   Debugging Tools 88

        3.7.3   Memory Statistics 89

        3.7.4   Improving Efficiency 89

        3.7.5   Indexing MOPs 90

        3.7.6   Generalization 91

4 Judge   93

  4.1   Protocol Data: What A Judge Does 93

  4.2   Case of the 16-year-old offender 94

        4.2.1   Prior Record 98

        4.2.2   Forming Explanations 99

        4.2.3   The Victims 100

        4.2.4   Legal Constraints and the Plea 100

  4.3   The Case of the 16-year-old Molester Revisited 101

        4.3.1   Experience-based Generalizations 103

        4.3.2   Choosing a Structure for Sentencing 104

      4.3.3   Conditions on Choices 106
      4.3.4   Motivations of the Offender 106
4.4   Case-based Reasoning 106
      4.4.1   Rationalization 108
4.5   Indexing and Retrieval 109
4.6   Summary of Protocol Data 111
4.7   The JUDGE Program 113
4.8   Interpreting Motivations 115
      4.8.1   Interpretation in JUDGE 117
4.9   Retrieving Previous Instances from Memory 118
4.10 Differentiating Cases 122
4.11 Generalization 124
4.12 Rule Differentiation 125
4.13 Applying Previous Strategies 129
4.14 Assessing Differences between Crimes 133
4.15 Modifying a Stored Sentence 134
4.16 Explaining Rules 137
4.17 The Effect of Ordering on Learning 138
4.18 Extending JUDGE 139

5 Micro JUDGE   141
5.1   Introduction 141
5.2   Implementing Micro JUDGE 141
5.3   Running the JUDGE Demo 158
5.4   Extensions 161
      5.4.1   Ordering of Cases 161
      5.4.2   Frequency of Actions 161
      5.4.3   Outcomes of Actions 162
      5.4.4   Consistency of Sentences 162
      5.4.5   Adapting Closest Cases 162

6 CHEF   165
6.1   Case-based Planning 165
6.2   A New Theory of Planning 166
      6.2.1   Building an Initial Plan 167
      6.2.2   Debugging Failed Plans 168
      6.2.3   Storing Plans for Later Use 169
6.3   Learning from Planning 169
6.4   Building it from the Bottom 171
      6.4.1   Why Case-based? 171
      6.4.2   Plan Retrieval 171

6.4.3   Plan Modification 174
6.4.4   Plan Storage 176
6.4.5   Plan Repair 177
6.4.6   Learning from Failure 179
6.4.7   Problem Anticipation 181
6.4.8   The Final Package 182
6.5   CHEF: A Case-based Planner 184
6.5.1   When Plans Fail 186
6.5.2   Explaining Plan Failures 187
6.5.3   Plan Repair Strategies and TOPs 189
6.5.4   Anticipating Failures 193
6.6   Learning Plans 198
6.7   Learning to Predict Failures 201
6.8   Learning Critics 206
6.9   How Learning from Planning is Different 209
6.10 How Learning from Planning is Better 211

7 **Micro CHEF**   **213**
7.1   Introduction 213
7.2   Implementing Micro CHEF 213
7.3   Implementing Repair in Micro CHEF 226
7.4   Indexing Repairs in Micro CHEF 230
7.5   Running the CHEF Demo 233
7.6   Extensions 243
7.6.1   Constraints on Optional Fillers 243
7.6.2   MOP-SUBST 243
7.6.3   Merging Steps 243
7.6.4   Including Cooking Times 244
7.6.5   Adding New Kinds of Steps 244
7.6.6   Adapting Closest Cases 245
7.6.7   Simulation 246
7.6.8   Evaluation 247
7.6.9   Explanation 248
7.6.10 Other Kinds of Recipes 248

8 **Plan Creation**   **249**
8.1   Introduction 249
8.1.1   Examples of Plan Creation 250
8.1.2   Models of Plan Creation 252
8.2   Replanning and Planning 256
8.2.1   Planning as Decision Making 257

      8.2.2   Implicit Decisions 259
      8.2.3   Plan Repair and Learning 261
  8.3 Learning in a Competitive Domain 261
      8.3.1   Forced Choice and Generalized Problem Descriptions . . 262
      8.3.2   The Football Domain 263
      8.3.3   The Blitz 264
      8.3.4   Analyzing the Examples 265
      8.3.5   Applying Plan Transformations 268
      8.3.6   Problem Analysis 269
  8.4 A Catalog of Plan Transformations 271
      8.4.1   Scheduling Transformations 272
      8.4.2   Information Processing Transformations 277
  8.5 A Detailed Example 281
      8.5.1   The Design of the Play 282
      8.5.2   The Fork 283
      8.5.3   Representing Plans 284
      8.5.4   Recognizing the situation 286
      8.5.5   Applying the Fork 286
  8.6 Conclusions 289

9 Micro COACH   **291**
  9.1 Introduction 291
  9.2 Implementing Micro COACH 292
  9.3 Running the COACH Demo 309
  9.4 Extensions 315
      9.4.1   Correcting M-CB-DEFEND 315
      9.4.2   Recognizing Failing Plays 315
      9.4.3   A Football Play Simulator 315
      9.4.4   Generating the Option Play 316
      9.4.5   Adding States 317
      9.4.6   Representing Strategic Knowledge 318

10 Case-based Parsing   **319**
  10.1 Introduction 319
      10.1.1 Background 319
      10.1.2 Case-based Parsing 320
      10.1.3 Memory Organization 321
      10.1.4 Memory Search 323
      10.1.5 Understander Goals 325
      10.1.6 Output 326
      10.1.7 History 328

10.2 The Case-based Parser 329
10.3 A Theory of Case-based Parsing 329
    10.3.1 Linguistic Knowledge 330
    10.3.2 Integrating Knowledge Sources 332
    10.3.3 Dynamic Memory 332
10.4 Modifying Memory 333
    10.4.1 Opinion Formation in Economics 334
    10.4.2 Simple Memory Modification 335
    10.4.3 Complex Specialization Failures 337
    10.4.4 Repairing Failures 337
10.5 Word-sense Ambiguity 338
    10.5.1 Selectional Restrictions 339
    10.5.2 Scriptal Lexicons 339
    10.5.3 Beyond Word-sense Ambiguity 340
10.6 Implementing a Case-based Parser 341
    10.6.1 Marker Passing 341
    10.6.2 Activation Markers 342
    10.6.3 Prediction Markers 342
    10.6.4 Implementation and Theory 343
10.7 Theoretical Issues 343
10.8 An Example 346
    10.8.1 The Context for the Example 346
    10.8.2 Knowledge Representation 347
    10.8.3 Program Trace 347

11 Micro DMAP   353
11.1 Introduction 353
11.2 Implementing Micro DMAP 355
11.3 Running the DMAP Demo 365
11.4 Extensions 370
    11.4.1 Extending memory 370
    11.4.2 Parsing for Other Domains 370
    11.4.3 Pruning Predictions 370
    11.4.4 Handling Near Misses 370
    11.4.5 Representing Index Patterns 371
    11.4.6 Generation 371
    11.4.7 Adding Syntactic Knowledge 372

12 Cases and Intelligence   373

Bibliography   391

A Appendix **401**
   A.1 Common Lisp in Other Lisps 401
   A.2 Backquote (') 401
   A.3 COPY-LIST 403
   A.4 EQL 403
   A.5 ERROR 404
   A.6 #' and FUNCTION 404
   A.7 FORMAT for Output 404
   A.8 GENTEMP 405
   A.9 GETF 407
   A.10 REMOVE-DUPLICATES 408
   A.11 &REST 408
   A.12 SETF and DEFSETF 410

Author Index **413**

Lisp Index **415**

Index **419**

List of Figures

2.1 CBR Flow Chart 32
2.2 Parameterized Adaptation in PERSUADER 46
2.3 Abstraction and Respecialization in PERSUADER 48
2.4 Reinstantiation in MEDIATOR 51

3.1 Example Expansion of DEFINE-TABLE 58
3.2 Toy Abstraction Hierarchy 64
3.3 The Abstraction Hierarchy under M-MTRANS 65
3.4 The New Abstraction Hierarchy under M-MTRANS 66

4.1 Intention Interpretation Rules 116

6.1 The RETRIEVER 174
6.2 The MODIFIER 175
6.3 The STORER 176
6.4 The REPAIRER 178
6.5 The ASSIGNER 180
6.6 The ANTICIPATOR 181
6.7 Goals Satisfied by STRAWBERRY-SOUFFLE 200
6.8 Avoidance Goal under STRAWBERRY-SOUFFLE 201
6.9 Marking FRUIT and SOUFFLE as Predictive of Problems . . . 203
6.10 Marking LIQUID and SOUFFLE as Predictive of Problems . . 205
6.11 Repairing DUCK-DUMPLINGS with REMOVE-FEATURE . . 208
6.12 Storing New Critic under DUCK 208
6.13 Using New DUCK Critic 209

8.1 Sweep, Bootleg Run, and Option Play 282
8.2 The SWEEP Play 286
8.3 Choosing and Running Football Plays 287

10.1 Conceptual Analysis versus Case-based Parsing 322
10.2 Milton Friedman's Argument 324
10.3 Case-based Parsing Output 327

List of Tables

3.1   Rules for Final Value of FOR Forms 60

A.1   Primitive Printing Functions 405
A.2   Examples of Primitive Printing Functions 405

List of Listingss

3.1	`INSIST`	56
3.2	Definition of `DEFINE-TABLE`	58
3.3	Definition of `FOR`	62
3.4	Definition of `FOR` Keywords	63
3.5	MOP Access Functions	68
3.6	MOP Predicates	69
3.7	Basic Role Access Functions	71
3.8	Basic MOP Abstraction Functions	72
3.9	MOP Construction Functions	73
3.10	Memory Management Functions	74
3.11	Extended Role Access Functions	75
3.12	Extended MOP Abstraction Predicates	77
3.13	MOP Equality Functions	78
3.14	Refining Functions	78
3.15	Instance Installation Functions	79
3.16	Abstraction Installation Functions	80
3.17	Top-Level Memory Update Functions	81
3.18	Form to MOP Functions	82
3.19	Group MOP Functions	83
3.20	MOP Display Functions	85
3.21	Basic MOPS	86
3.22	Basic Abstraction and Calculation Functions	87
5.1	Top-Level Micro JUDGE Function	141
5.2	Micro JUDGE Basic MOPs	142
5.3	Range Constraints	143
5.4	Micro JUDGE Event MOPs	144
5.5	Micro JUDGE Top-Level MOP	145
5.6	Micro JUDGE Role Calculation Functions	146
5.7	Micro JUDGE Calculation MOPs	147
5.8	Micro JUDGE Adjustment Functions	148
5.9	Micro JUDGE Adaptation Functions	149

5.10 Comparison MOPs 150
5.11 Micro JUDGE MOPs for Adaptation 151
5.12 Micro JUDGE Force and Motive Adaptation MOPs 152
5.13 Micro JUDGE Mixed Comparison Adaptation MOPs 153
5.14 Micro JUDGE First Test Case 154
5.15 Micro JUDGE Second Test Case 155
5.16 Micro JUDGE Third Test Case 156
5.17 Micro JUDGE Demo 157
7.1   Top-Level Micro CHEF Function 214
7.2   Micro CHEF Basic MOPs 215
7.3   Micro CHEF Event MOPs 216
7.4   Micro CHEF Recipe Steps MOP 216
7.5   Substitution Functions 218
7.6   Dynamic MOP-making Functions 219
7.7   Calculating Preconditions 220
7.8   Precondition Functions 221
7.9   Micro CHEF Precondition Merging Functions 222
7.10 Micro CHEF Adaptation Functions 223
7.11 Micro CHEF Top-Level MOP 223
7.12 Micro CHEF Beef and Green Beans Recipe 224
7.13 Micro CHEF Chicken and Peanuts Recipe 225
7.14 Micro CHEF Top-Level Repair Function 226
7.15 Micro CHEF Explanation MOPs 227
7.16 Rule Mappings 228
7.17 Role Resetting Function 228
7.18 Micro CHEF Role Calculation Functions 229
7.19 Micro CHEF Top-Level Repair MOP 230
7.20 Micro CHEF Generalization Functions 231
7.21 MOP Instances for CHEF Examples 232
7.22 Micro CHEF Test Function 233
7.23 Micro CHEF Test Cases 234
7.24 Micro CHEF Demo 235
9.1   Top-Level Micro COACH Function 292
9.2   Micro COACH Basic MOPs 293
9.3   Extended Comparison MOPs 295
9.4   Micro COACH Event MOPs 296
9.5   Micro COACH Play MOPs 297
9.6   Micro COACH Execution Result MOPs 298
9.7   Micro COACH Failure and Explanation MOPs 299
9.8   Micro COACH Repair MOPs 300
9.9   Micro COACH Strategy MOPs 301

9.10   Micro COACH Exclusion Functions 302
9.11   Conjoined Constraints 303
9.12   Micro COACH Exclusion MOPs 304
9.13   Micro COACH Detected Event Function 305
9.14   Micro COACH Delay Functions 306
9.15   Micro COACH Enablement MOPs 307
9.16   Micro COACH Play Merging Functions 308
9.17   Micro COACH Delay Testing Functions 309
9.18   Micro COACH Deception Making Functions 310
9.19   Micro COACH Demo 311
11.1   Micro DMAP Top-Level Function 356
11.2   Micro DMAP Global Variables and Tables 357
11.3   Micro DMAP Prediction Role Access Functions 357
11.4   Micro DMAP Prediction Construction Functions 358
11.5   Micro DMAP Triggering Functions 359
11.6   Micro DMAP Prediction Triggering Functions 360
11.7   Micro DMAP Top-Level Functions 361
11.8   Micro DMAP Display Functions 362
11.9   Micro DMAP Basic MOPs 363
11.10 Micro DMAP Event and State Change MOPs 364
11.11 Micro DMAP Event and State Change MOPs 365
11.12 Micro DMAP Phrases 366
11.13 Micro DMAP Demo 367
A.1   Definitions for BACKQUOTE 402
A.2   Definitions for Backquote (') Readmacro 403
A.3   Definition of COPY-LIST 404
A.4   Definitions of GETF and REMF 409
A.5   Definition of REMOVE-DUPLICATES 410
A.6   Definitions of SETF and DEFSETF 411
A.7   Definitions of ESETF and DEFSETF 412

Preface

In 1981, we published a book called *Inside Computer Understanding.* That book contained two kinds of material. First, there were substantial chapters summarizing doctoral work on various models of knowledge-based understanding developed at Yale. These chapters were written by the original researchers and described both the theoretical aspects of their work and the practical details. Second, each chapter was accompanied by miniature or "micro" versions of each AI program discussed. These Lisp programs ranged from 5 to 15 pages long, including substantial commentary, and were augmented by a series of exercises for the reader. The intent was that the programs would capture the bare essentials of the doctoral work, while still be short enough and simple enough to be easily understood and modified by anyone with only a cursory introduction to AI programming.

We first developed this approach of substantial description plus micro program for a 4-week cognitive science summer school, given at Yale in 1978, with the support of the Sloan Foundation's program in Cognitive Science. Our students then were professors and graduate students from psychology, linguistics, and anthropology. After only one week of Lisp lessons and lectures on our models of understanding, they were capable of running, modifying, and extending the micro programs we had developed. From this hands-on experience, they gained a far richer and deeper understanding of our work than would have been possible in a whole semester of classroom lectures.

Inside Computer Understanding aimed for the same audience of knowledgable, motivated readers with an interest in AI and how it really works, but not an expertise in AI. *Inside Computer Understanding* reached an even larger audience than we expected, thanks to several events that occurred at the same time as the appearance of the book. First, there was the arrival of powerful personal computers that brought computer power to cognitive scientists who formerly had little or no access to computers. Happily, the fact that we'd chosen to use a very small subset of Lisp for pedagogical purposes meant that it was quite feasible to transfer our micro programs to personal computers.

Second, there was the explosion in interest in Artificial Intelligence, especially in the business world. Suddenly, almost every major corporation wanted to know what AI was all about, and a number of training programs in AI were begun.

Third, there was the dramatic appearance of the Japanese Fifth Generation project. A whole country suddenly became hungry for hands-on experience with the gamut of AI programming. The micro programs in *Inside Computer Understanding* have appeared in several different texts in Japan in the past few years.

Not only was there a larger audience than we'd expected, but the benefits of creating the micro program were greater than we'd expected. We believed then, and believe even more strongly now, that the only way really to understand any AI program, is to program it yourself. Programming is not sufficient to understanding a model, but it is about as central as one can get. The micro programs clarify what the original models were all about. By including only key elements and expressing in the simplest possible procedural terms, it was easier to see what was at the heart of a program like SAM or PAM, and what was "a grungy detail." Developing the micro programs was also an educational experience for us. We found we understood what made the real programs work much better after we had to re-implement them in micro form. Finally, the micro programs became a toolkit for prototyping initial applications into new domains. The micro ELI parser in particular was used in several published AI research efforts as a simple first-pass semantics-based natural language analyzer. The micro programs were significantly modified in each case, just as we'd intended them to be.

Meanwhile, things did not stand still at Yale. There has been a fundamental shift in our ideas, moving from static knowledge-based programs to dynamic memory-based programs, as described in Chapter 1. These new models of memory and learning are, at first glance, much more complex and difficult to grasp. The interaction of concepts such as memory organization, indexing, abstraction, specialization, and so on, are subtle and varied. The need for a new book to do for memory-based learning what *Inside Computer Understanding* did for knowledge-based understanding is obvious.

Following roughly the same format, this book introduces the issues in dynamic memory and case-based reasoning, followed by extended descriptions of four major programming efforts conducted in the past few years at Yale on case-based reasoning and understanding. These descriptions were written by the original researchers, and edited by us, primarily for space and notational consistency.

Following each descriptive chapter is a chapter with the micro program version. The Lisp code in the listings in these chapters was extracted directly from our on-line manuscript and executed in a standard Common Lisp to produce the accompanying printed output.

One major topic that our micro implementations do not address very well is learning. They all *remember*, in that they add cases to memory as they reason and understand, but, with the exception of one part of micro CHEF, none of them generalizes its experiences. In contrast, all of the real case-based systems have had some learning component. IPP and CYRUS, two early models of dynamic memory, had generalization as a core component of their memory organization processes, JUDGE learned rules to augment its case-based reasoning, and CHEF learned new indexes to organize its recipes. Cases can support learning as simple as rote memory, as in our micro programs, or as creative as explanation by analogy, as in the SWALE program, currently in development. Learning is very hard to get right, but we believe that case-based reasoning is the right foundation.

ACKNOWLEDGMENTS

We'd like to acknowledge William Bain, Kristian Hammond, Gregg Collins, and Charles Martin, whose research is reported in this book. We'd also like to thank Michael Lebowitz and Charles Martin for implementing the initial versions of micro MOPS and micro DMAP.

This book was prepared under the auspices of the Yale Artificial Intelligence Project. This work, and the research on which it was based, were funded under the following grants and contracts: the Air Force Office of Scientific Research contracts F49620-82-K-0010 and 85-0343, the Defense Advanced Research Projects Agency (DARPA) of the Department of Defense, monitored by the Office of Naval Research, contracts N00014-82-K-0149 and N00014-86-K-0310, the Office of Naval Research, contracts N00014-85-K-0108 and N00014-75-C-1111, and the National Science Foundation, grant IST-8120451.

Finally, we would like to acknowledge a current major DARPA effort in case-based reasoning, monitored by the Air Force Office of Scientific Research, contract F49620-88-C-0058, which is supporting the development of real-world applications in case-based reasoning, funding researchers at Cognitive Systems, Inc., Brandeis University, the Georgia Institute of Technology, the University of Chicago, the University of Illinois at Champagne-Urbana, the University of Massachusetts at Amherst, and Yale University. The efforts of Colonel Robert L. Simpson at DARPA and Dr. Abraham Waksman at AFOSR are particularly appreciated.

Christopher K. Riesbeck
Roger C. Schank

1

Case-based Reasoning: An Introduction

1.1 AI and Cognition

The concept of the general problem solver has always served as a kind of metaphor for the field of Artificial Intelligence. The search for general mechanisms underlying intelligence is surely what AI is about and the writing of programs that apply general mechanisms to specific new problems has always been viewed as the ultimate in AI. Embodied within this view of AI is the general conception of a computer as an answer-giving device. That is, the computer-based view of the world is that you present a problem to the computer and it gives you the answer. The AI part of that view is that while number crunching computers will give arithmetic answers to arithmetic problems, an AI computer would give verbal answers to verbal problems. So, intelligent computers would be ones which, armed with their general problem solver, would take any problem and find the answer.

A machine that operates from first principles and is able to solve any problem by reasoning from those principles is inherently appealing, and thus it is no surprise that AI should have adopted such a program as its ultimate fantasy. But, there is a heavy theoretical price to pay for such a system. Moreover, the conception of computers and the interaction with computers that it implies is from another era when computers were not as ubiquitous as they are now, nor as available to the general public. The realities of how people would prefer to interact with computers, now that they have interacted with them, as well as realities about the nature of human thinking would seem to be reasons to reconsider both the idea of a general problem solver and of a computer that tells you answers that you need to know.

A good example of both of the problems that I am referring to here can be found in work on expert systems. Expert systems are rule-based systems in actual practice. The premise is that the knowledge of an expert can be embodied in a set of rules. This premise was derived historically from Newell and Simon's pioneering work on the General Problem Solver (GPS) [Newell and Simon, 1972], one of the first AI programs, and came to fruition in the DENDRAL project, one of the first rule-based expert systems [Feigenbaum *et al.*, 1971].

If you accept that solving a problem means following a set of general rules about problem solving, then it is not a terrific leap of faith to imagine that particular domains of knowledge can be captured by a set of additional rules about solving problems in a particular domain. Thus, if you buy the idea that the mind is a collection of general rules that can be applied to any situation, you quickly adopt the idea that there also would exist a set of specific rules that apply only to certain situations. Such rules are called *domain knowledge* by AI people. In this view, AI becomes an attempt to code all the domain knowledge that can be found to into rules that will be used by an expert system. This view is, on the surface quite appealing. It is appealing commercially because the claim is that experts are collections of rules that can be extracted and executed systematically. Thus, the claim is that machines can be made more and more expert by getting more and more rules.

The idea is also appealing from an intellectual point of view. The appeal of a general problem solver was that human thought depends upon a set of reasoning principles that are independent of any given domain of knowledge. The premise is that we reason the same way no matter what we are reasoning about and that a computer can be taught to reason by giving it general principles and ways of applying those principles to any domain. It is such systematicity that scientists crave and it is this kind of rigor that computer scientists really appreciate. It is no wonder that the work of Newell and Simon attracted so much attention in both AI and psychology. And, by extension, it is no wonder that work in expert systems attracted so much attention in the commercial world. The problem is that the conception of the nature of human reasoning embodied in both the general problem solver and expert systems is wrong.

1.2   Does Thinking really involve Thinking?

On first examination, the task ahead of someone who is interested in building a machine that is an effective simulation of human mental processes seems formidable. And, as years of only small progress in AI can attest, that task is formidable. Not only can people talk and chew gum at the same time, they can also reason, extrapolate, induce, deduce, contradict, and complain. They can retrieve long-lost items from memory and create new ideas and thoughts at the drop of a hat. They can understand situations and ideas that they have never seen before, as well as criticize the ideas of others. In short, human mental ability is nothing short of phenomenal.

But is the process of generating novel answers to questions really one of tremendous brilliance and complexity, or is it straightforward and routine? What is it that differentiates people who give wise answers to such questions from those that give dull ones?

Certain aspects of human thought may be a simpler affair than many scientists have imagined. Certainly the overwhelming complexity of the thinking process seems startling when so many humans actually seem to do so little inventive thinking. Scientists who seek general principles upon which the mind is based might do better by observing the behavior of people and attempting to postulate the simplest possible mechanisms that might replicate that behavior. Many seemingly complex processes are simpler than first meets the eye.

1.2.1 Understanding Depends Upon Explanation

The central process in everyday understanding is explanation. An understander of the world is an explainer of the world. In order to understand a story, a sentence, a question, or a scene you have witnessed, you have to explain to yourself exactly why the people you are hearing about or viewing are doing what they're doing. You need to know, or figure out, the goals of people you interact with, their intentions, and just what you might expect next. Since people don't make a habit of telling you these things all the time, understanding entails, at least in part, figuring this out for yourself. In other words, everyday understanding is a process which requires you to construct explanations for behaviors and events that have occurred.

Now, this assumption that everyday understanding requires explanation might lead you to assume that understanding is, in principle, a rather complex process. After all, constructing an explanation for everything you see and hear requires real intelligence of presumably a very complex sort.

But, there is something wrong here. How can it be that everyday understanding is such a complex process. Some very unintelligent people manage to understand the world they live in fairly well. Can it really be all that difficult?

1.2.2   Scripts

The answer is no and the reason is scripts. In the mid-seventies, in our natural language processing work at Yale, we invented the concept of a *script*. Scripts expressed our view that people didn't have to figure out how to convince someone to feed them, every time they entered a restaurant. All they really had to know was the script for restaurants, and play their part. Scripts were a guide for acting in stereotypical situations that help normal events go smoothly if all players do their bit the way they are suppposed to.

Scripts are useful for understanding the actions of others, as long as they do what we expect them to do, and we know the script that they are following. They are also useful to give to computers to enable computers to understand stories about stereotypical situations. When a paragraph was about a restaurant, we could realize, with very little effort, that we need not wonder about why the waitress agreed to bring what was asked for, and we could assume that what was ordered was what was eaten. To put this another way, not everything in the world is worthy of equal amounts of thought, and restaurant stories were readily understandable by a computer armed with a good enough restaurant script. In fact, not too much thinking has to be done, by a computer or a person, if the right script is available. You just have to play your part and events usually transpire the way they are supposed to. To put this another way, scripts eliminate the need to think very deeply. You don't have to attempt to infer the intentions of a waitress if they are already well-known, or the need to know them at all is obviated by knowing what behavior will work. Why concentrate your mental time on the obvious?

Taken as a strong hypothesis about the nature of human thought, it is possible to imagine that thinking is no more than applying scripts, no matter what the situation. This hypothesis holds that everything is a script. At first glance this view of scripts seems too strong. Instead of having a few scripts such as restaurant, airplane, department store, and such, that you could assume as being more or less the same for most people, this view assumes that we have thousands of scripts we use on a daily basis, such as sitting in my chair, pouring my juice, and so on, that we normally perform. The hypothesis is that most scripts are highly personal and would not be shared across individuals. In other words, every mundane aspect of life that requires little or no thought can be assumed to be a script.

This view says, in essence, that you need do very little thinking at all, that everything is pre-packaged and thus subject to very little spontaneous thought. In other words, under this view of the world, thinking means finding the right script to use, rather than generating new ideas and questions to think about during the course of participating in an event.

Now consider our more recent work at Yale on explanation. People explain things that they do not understand all the time. Most of this explanation is to themselves rather than to others. When an event needs no explanation, it is because you have seen events just like it before. In other words, a mental structure like a script exists to help interpret the new event. But, when no script seems to be relevant, the event being processed must be explained.

At first glance, the process of explanation would seem to be a very difficult one, since it involves understanding brand new ideas. But explanation does not seem so complicated if we consider explanation to be a process of adaptation rather than creation. In other words, it is possible to explain something new by adapting a standard explanation from another situation. Maybe we don't ever generate new explanations. Maybe we just adapt old ones to new situations. From the script point of view, if we don't have a script that works exactly to help us understand and operate in a situation, we can look for an old situation similar to the new one and try using whatever script we used in the old situation, with minor modifications.

The claim is that, given a choice between thinking hard and adapting an old script, people will choose the script every time.

1.3 The Basic Planning Algorithm

Planning is a human activity normally associated with the highest levels of thought in the popular and scientific imagination, but even there, not all that much thought might be necessary. People do not construct plans from first principles. They do not reason about each problem they face as if they had never before faced a problem like it. Rather, they try to find the best plan they have heard of or previously used that is closest to the problem at hand, and attempt to adapt that plan to the current situation. When faced with a question about what plan to use, we shouldn't be surprised to find people thinking of the most similar case they have heard of, and reasoning from it. Here are some examples of normal human thinking, that appeared in a radio "man in the street" interview:

What do you think of our increased assistance in El Salvador?

1. I'm against it. I don't want to see us get involved anymore. I think we have to start taking care of things at home first.

2. It makes me fairly nervous. I look at it as a sort of Viet Nam. I thinks it's great for the U.S. when a country does indeed need help, but I also think we should be very careful about

how we spend our money, the way the economy is here in the states ourselves.

3. What happened in Viet Nam should have taught the American people a lesson.

4. I'm fearful that it might lead to a situation similar to what we faced in Viet Nam 15 years ago, and therefore I would examine carefully anything we did before we got ourselves stuck into a situation we can't get ourselves out of.

Note that the question here is not whether reasoning from prior cases is what you *ought* to do. The question is whether it is what people do do. Virtually whenever there is a prior case available to reason from, people will find it and use it as a model for their future decision making. This process of "case-based reasoning" can be very advantageous to a decision maker who knows a large number of cases and has been able to index them so that the most relevant cases come to mind when needed. This is why case-based thinking is taught in law schools and business schools. Everyone knows how to reason from cases; they do it quite naturally.

Why do law schools and business schools teach cases? It seems obvious that both of these subjects are inherently case-based. The law depends upon judges reasoning from prior cases and lawyers trying to find prior cases that will serve as precedents in favor of their clients. The reason for this is that the law does not account for every single possibility that might ever occur in the future of mankind. There are some principles of law, to be sure, but the nuances that determine why one case is an instance of a given principle of law, while another represents a different principle are embodied in case law, that is, in the knowledge of the common set of cases that have been decided and stored away in the collective legal mind as prototypes.

It seems obvious that knowing the law in the sense of being able to practice law effectively means knowing the cases or at least knowing where to find cases when you needs them. Thus, for law at least, knowledge means knowledge of cases.

The same is true in business, but for a slightly different reason. There are some principles of business that you can learn in business school. But, to make money, which is the intent of business after all, you cannot simply follow the successful cases of the past. You have to reason from a prior case by attempting to understand what principles they teach, apart from the particulars of the given context in which that case occurred. After all, if there were simply one successful paradigmatic case to be followed, everyone would follow it and every businessman would be rich. In business, each new case changes the world sufficiently so that the methods that were specifically applied may not work again. Those methods might work, however, in a different industry, or with a different product, or in a different city. A very standard way of conducting business then, is to replicate what others have done, but not to do it identically, or if you do it identically, make sure you aren't the one who will cause there to be less business for everybody.

Thus, both law and business depend heavily upon cases. Learning in these subjects means learning the cases, and reasoning in these subjects means being able to make new decisions by abstracting the essentials from an appropriate prior case. Thus, the essence of thinking, in both law and business is the storage and retrieval of cases.

It is not law and business that are the oddballs in education or in reasoning. Rather, neither of these subjects pretend, nor ought they pretend, to be based upon systematic principles that would allow just those principles to be learned while particular cases are ignored. Other academic fields do have such pretensions, but it is my belief that the facts are otherwise in those fields as well. Mathematics, for example, may teach principles to high school students, but graduate students learn the cases. Proofs of theorems are constructed by using classic proofs as models. Take a look at a standard high school mathematics textbook and you will find that each principle is accompanied by several "example" solutions, i.e., cases using that principle, which the student is encouraged to adapt to solve the exercises.

Case-based reasoning is the essence of how human reasoning works. People reason from experience. They use their own experiences if they have a relevant one, or they make use of the experience of others to the extent that they can obtain information about such experiences. An individual's knowledge is the collection of experiences that he has had or that he has heard about.

We have so many cases available to us that finding them can be very tricky indeed. Human memory depends upon good methods of labeling cases so that they can be retrieved when needed. General principles, e.g., rules, patterns, or scripts, that we abstract from a given case or set of cases help us label cases for retrieval, determine which cases are relevant, and adapt those parts of cases that don't fit the current situation. But, it is the case that is most important, because only the case has the details needed to solve problems, carry on conversations, and so on. General principles are impoverished, compared to the original experience. Generalization is never perfect and there is always the danger of losing some quite important information. Further, when the case is told to someone else, if it is related only in terms of the generalization or principle behind the case, there aren't as many places to put the new case in memory. It is very difficult to remember an abstraction, but it is easy to remember a good coherent story. This is one of the reasons why we tell them.

If we go up to a librarian and describe our interests well enough, the librarian may do one of three things. The librarian might tell us where in the library to look for what we want want, or she might be reminded of something that she read that suits us exactly, or she might be able to find a book that she has no idea of the actual contents of, but which fits what we have described perfectly. The process by which she does these things is certainly intelligent, and in all three cases involves exactly the same issue, namely effective labeling. Now, it is natural to assume that the librarian is intelligent no matter which of the three courses of action she performs. However, if we attempted to develop a computer librarian, we can be certain that it would seem intelligent enough if it could tell us where to look for a book, even more intelligent if it could select a book for us, and maximally intelligent it it were reminded of a book that it had read and could converse with us about it.

Why does it matter which of these answers seems more intelligent? There is a tendency when talking about AI to equate intelligence with understanding. To see the difference, imagine a program that had thousands of screens of information that it could call up, each quite different. If it called up the screen you wanted when you wanted it, it would certainly have done its job, but would it be intelligent? Since such questions are very subjective, allow me to speculate that people would say that it was not intelligent if you had to call those screens by some simple label, such as their number. If you typed 2786 and got screen number 2786, you wouldn't assume that any intelligence was involved. Of course, there exist computers that can do such retrieval and no one considers them to be intelligent.

Now imagine that the correct screen was called up when you typed something more complicated, such as "who were the major league stolen base leaders in the last ten years?" Such a program would seem intelligent if it provided the right answer, but the difference between the two programs would be no more than the complexity of the labeling of the screens and the ability of the program to translate the input typed by the user of the program into labels that called up the screens.

Returning to our librarian then, if she calls up exactly the book you want, she may seem very intelligent, but her intelligence would be in translating what you said into the system of labels in terms of which she had encoded all the books she knew about. Now imagine a computer version of this librarian that responded to whatever you typed to it with just the book you had in mind and then, say, printed that book on the screen you were using. Such a program would seem quite intelligent, but it would seem obvious that the program wouldn't know what it was talking about. That is, it could retrieve the book but it wouldn't understand the book. In fact, it wouldn't even know what was in the book necessarily, apart from knowing a set of labels that described the book sufficiently to enable retrieval.

In some sense then, intelligence need not involve a great deal of understanding. Rather, what passes for intelligence may be the ability to translate descriptions into labels where those labels are sufficient to describe uniquely a piece of data in memory. Intelligence, according to the popular conception of the kind of behavior that is normally described as intelligent, need not involve understanding the data that you retrieve.

The problem that general problem solver programs have is that each and every problem presented to them has to be handled the same way. Each problem must be reduced to first principles and logical deductions made from those principles. Even mathematicians do not really behave this way. Mathematicians are often parodied by other scientists as attempting to reduce everything to known and solved problems and then to proceed from there. In fact, what mathematicians do while doing mathematics as opposed to what people seem to imagine that they do, is very much like what real people do in everyday thinking.

It is really far too difficult to attempt to be rational about every problem we face. We needn't reason logically about where the butter might be, we need merely recall where we saw it last, or if we are in a new place, where we saw it in a place that resembled the one we are in now. We don't attempt to derive the principle by which a restaurant operates, we merely recall the actions that need to be taken on our part when the time comes. Real thinking has nothing to do with logic at all. Real thinking means retrieval of the right information at the right time. It follows then, that the most difficult part of thinking is the creation of labels upon processing an input that will allow us to retrieve something we already knew that was labelled with those labels so that we can produce it as output. Thinking of the kind that GPS and other AI models that attempt to reason from first principles hardly occurs at all.

1.4 Cases versus Rules

In the last few years research into the general area of case-based reasoning has begun to flourish [Schank, 1986; Kolodner and Riesbeck, 1986; Kolodner, 1988]. Case-based reasoning has been proposed as a more psychologically plausible model of the reasoning of an expert than the more fashionable rule-based reasoning systems that are the basis of the expert systems that began to be commercially available in the 1980's. When it comes to examining the theory behind the building of a computer program that is supposed to model effectively a given person's expertise, one good question to ask is whether that expert reasons by using rules. Certainly experts are happy to tell knowledge engineers the rules that they use, but whether the experts actually use such rules when they reason is another question entirely. There is, after all, a difference between textbook knowledge and actual experience. Since most experts will tell you that their experience is what makes them experts, the real question is how that experience is encoded in their memories. It is tempting for experts to cite rules that they follow, but it is often the case that each rule has many exceptions. In fact, in very difficult cases, where the situation is not so clear cut, experts frequently cite previous cases that they have worked on that the current case reminds them of. The implication of this is clear: reminding plays a large part in expert reasoning.

One problem in discussing the modeling of expertise on a computer has to do with the notion of the problem solving paradigm in AI. Earlier we talked about the havoc that the notion of the general problem solver has caused in how AI people think about writing computer programs. In a more general way, the field of AI has been committed for some time to the notion that computer programs reason about difficult problems and provide answers to those problems. But, the concept of there being an answer available for every problem, indeed even the assumption that problems inherently have answers that the problem solver needs to discover, is open to question.

Consider a few real-world problems. Whom should the graduate admissions committee for the university's computer science department accept into graduate school this year? Which second baseman should the manager of the Mets play regularly in 1988, the rookie sensation, the steady hustler who helped win the World Series in 1986, or the guy who did the best in 1987? Should the U.S. send in troops to Nicaragua and Panama if the situations there worsen?

The above problems are only slightly less concrete than those that traditional expert systems wrestle with, but they are every bit as common in the world of the human problem solver. Furthermore, they share a common feature: there are no "right" answers. There are options and reasons for and against each option. We never really know if we have made the right choice. Rather, we only know if the choice we did make has worked out. We don't know if the alternative might have been better or worse.

Nevertheless, we can cite rules of thumb that we use. "Always take the student with the highest GRE score." "Experience is the most important factor in a pennant race." But even though we can cite rules like these, actual decision making in such cases is usually more seat of the pants in nature. We have a gut feeling about the situation *as a whole*. We can cite arguments on both sides of the issue and then make a choice that seems best at the time. Such reasoning often depends upon reminding, as I have said. If there is a prior case available, if we know some previous situation that looked a lot like the one we are now in, we rely on that prior case. That is why so many people bring up the Viet Nam war when talking about Nicaragua. It is the natural reminding. Different conclusions can be drawn from that reminding, but the reasoning process is the same. We retrieve a prior case from memory, attempt to determine its relevance, and decide what to do, based upon what happened in that case. This is what I have called case-based reasoning.

Obviously, a case-based reasoner is likely to have rules that he uses along with his cases in the reasoning process. You needn't be reminded of the last time you ate at a table in order to use a fork to get at your food. We have that rule available to us and need not rely upon a prior case. Similarly, when driving to work, we need not think of the last time we drove to work and copy that, unless the last time was also one of the only times. When an activity has been repeated often enough it becomes rule-like in nature. We do not reason from prior cases when well-established rules are available.

But, certainly, the experience of driving to work can be considered a case. It was once a case, the first time it was experienced, how did it cease to be one? The best answer to this is that, in a broad sense, everything is a case. The word case just refers to an experience. In essence then, case-based reasoning means no more than reasoning from experience. The issue of whether something is best called a case, or a rule, or a story, is one of understanding how experiences get encoded in memory.

The distinction between these three constructs is essentially a memory distinction. A rule is encoded in memory, separate from any particular instance of its use or the history of its creation. When the rule fails, the only alternative for its user is to create a case that captures that failure. A case stands alone as an exception to a rule until numerous other cases just like it are encountered. A new rule is created if those cases are sufficiently alike.

If there is sufficient uniqueness about a case, if it fails to have exact replications, or it has many replications that serve as codicils to it, that is, exceptions to the more general case, it becomes a *paradigmatic* case. A paradigmatic case tends to be a constant in memory. Thus, while other case may be coalescing into rules after multiple repetitions, the paradigmatic case stays forever, serving as the norm in terms of which other cases are judged.

These other cases, if they do not themselves replicate frequently, also remain in memory as cases, stored in terms of the paradigmatic case to which they relate. These encoding decisions are really based on little more than two basic features, the number of repetitions of an experience, and something I shall call *idiosyncratic criteriality.*

The idiosyncratic criteriality of a case determines when, and for how long, a case is paradigmatic. We all see different cases as being more central to our view of the world. The most central cases are those that have many connections to other cases. Or, to put this another way, cases that tend to stand alone, those that are not rules because they do not repeat, and those that are not paradigmatic or associated with paradigmatic cases, have a special place in memory. Those cases have significance because of the extent of their difference from other cases. They make unique predictions about special circumstances and they make themselves known to the conscious mind when those circumtances arise. Such cases we call *stories*.

Viewed in this way then, there are essentially three major types of cases: ossified cases (or rules), paradigmatic cases (and their affiliated cases), and stories.

1.4.1   Ossified Cases

Ossified cases look a lot like rules, because they have been abstracted from cases. It is quite common with ossified cases that the case from which they were originally derived is unknown and that the cases themselves are shared by large numbers of people.

A very common form of ossified case is a proverb. People use proverbs to guide decision making when no specific experience is accessible. In other words, common wisdom is accessed and adapted to a new situation as a kind of default, when there is nothing better available. Of course, not all proverbs are widely known. In a sense, we all have our own proverbs, or general rules of thumb for dealing with general situations. If such rules are free of the events from which they were originally derived, then they are considered to be ossified. But, if the original events are still accessible in memory, the rule is more easily changed. In that situation, it is the case or story from which the rule was derived that is of interest in decision making.

1.4.2   Paradigmatic Cases

Sometimes, no rule exists at all. You have only the experience to draw upon. A rule, after all, would only be derived after many experiences, allowing you to generalize the experiences, ignore the details, and abstract out the essential substance. In a world where all experiences were clearly interpretable, where every decision was black or white, such a rule generator would probably be all there was to the story.

However, the real world consists of situations which are unique and sometimes even contradictory. Sometimes you have only had one experience that was in any way relevant to what you are now experiencing, and sometimes you have had so many, with such different results, that no path is obvious. In the former case, we have a situation in which reasoning from the prototype is the best path. For these situations, there exist paradigmatic cases. The task of the reasoning system is to find where the current situation differs from the paradigmatic case, and to adapt it to help in the new situation.

1.4.3 Stories

If the basic process of thinking is the creation of new from old, the adaptation of existing cases to new situations, it follows that how smart or creative a thinking system is depends upon the cases that it has available to it, and the kind of amount of information in those cases. You can expect less new insight when drawing upon ossified cases, then when drawing upon paradigmatic cases.

Seen this way, we have a potentially paradoxical situation. If a system knows only one case, it is more likely to come up with something new than if it has had many experiences and has generalized them. In a sense, you can only be creative if you know very little. If you know a great deal and have come to conclusions that unify what you know, thus forgetting the original cases, you lose the ability to make new conclusions. While it seems clear that to a large extent people do become less creative the more they do the same thing in the same way, it also seems quite clear that there are experts in the world who have had many experiences and are still quite capable of new insights about those experiences. The claim is that those people depend upon stories.

By "stories" I mean cases that are unique and full of detail, like paradigmatic cases, but with points, like proverbs. Here's an example of a story:

> A friend of mine was describing the problems he was having with his current girlfriend. He was thinking of marrying this girl, but in fact acknowledged that he was really in love with a second girl. The problem with this second girl was that he believed her to be really crazy. He felt that he loved the first girl too, although maybe not as much, and he thought that she was a good candidate for marriage. Her one problem was that she yelled and screamed at him a lot, but he thought that he might be able to make that go away over time or minimize it.
>
> While discussing his problem I was reminded of a time when I had to choose an employee. I found a candidate who seemed perfect. As we got to know each other during the hiring and interviewing process, when the talk turned to personal issues, he frequently bragged about how he had recently won his divorce case. What this meant was that he kept all the money, the children,

and his wife was devastated. He had spent tremendous amounts of time and money in attempting to win this case, and he was very proud of himself. I wondered at the time how someone could be so vicious to someone he had loved, but did not see this as a reason for not hiring someone who otherwise seemed so perfect.

After time, we had a falling out and I watched as this man became more and more vicious towards me. Of course, I was reminded of what he had done to his wife. I told this story to my friend with the admonishment that it is important to learn to read the signs. People tell you what they will be like to deal with over the long term. You just have to learn to listen.

The basis of creativity in a cognitive system comes from the stories it knows, rather than the ossified or paradigmatic cases it has. The reason for this is that ossified cases tend to be relevant in only the arenas for which they were originally intended. That is, "a rolling stone gathers no moss" may apply to many domains of knowledge, but it still only refers, in principle, to discussions about action versus inaction. Stories, on the other hand, simply by virtue of their complexity and myriad aspects, may relate to a large variety of possible circumstances. More importantly, as we shall see later on, stories can be indexed in multiple ways, because of their numerous references, and that allows them to be more accessible, and hence more relevant than an ossified case that can only be indexed in very few ways.

To put this another way, creativity depends upon our ability to analyze incoming stories effectively. The more content, the more varied the possible analyses and the more possible it is to find germane indexes. There are very few differences in the possible analyses of an ossified case, whether that case was input in ossified form or simply ossified over time. Thus, stories can be forever re-analyzed, while ossified cases remain ossified forever.

This concept of re-analysis, then, is very important. True expertise depends upon three things in this view: on ossified cases which form the basis for making everyday decisions; paradigmatic cases which form the base of expertise that a person accumulates beyond the textbook rules that he is taught; and stories that constitute the exceptional cases, ones that are still being analyzed and understood and re-understood. It is this last group, stories, that are critical to very intelligent behavior.

We will return to this topic of creativity again, in the last chapter. Models of understanding and problem solving in everyday situations is therefore the topic of the bulk of this book.

1.5 Reminding

Human experts are not systems of rules, they are libraries of experiences. Further, these libraries are adaptable. When a new experience takes place, it isn't simply added to the data base of prior experiences. Most experiences are like others that have come before. A new experience relates to, modifies, replaces, amplifies, or otherwise perturbs many of the extant prior experiences. Learning from experience means changing what you know to accommodate the new knowledge. The idea of change in a model of expertise is critical.

The human memory system has, and hence any sensibly designed computer model of that memory system must have, the ability to cope with new information in a reasonable way. Any new input that is to be processed by a memory system is one that is altered in some way by every experience it processes. A memory system that fails to learn from its experiences is unlikely to be very useful.

In addition, any good memory system must be capable of finding what it has in it. This seems to go without saying, but the issue of what to find can be quite a problem. The first need is to find the memories or experiences that are most closely related to the input we are processing. But how do we define relatedness? A new episode can be related because it contradicts a principle derived from an old episode. It can be related cross-contextually, independent of obvious features, by some general principle that aptly describes the new episode and another one already in memory.

One phenomenon that sheds light on both the problem of retrieval and our ability to learn is the phenomenon of reminding. Reminding is a crucial aspect of human memory that has received little attention from researchers on memory. Yet reminding is an everyday occurrence, a common feature of memory. We are reminded of one person by another, of one building by another and so on. But, more significant than the reminding that a physical object can cause of another physical object, is the reminding that occurs across situations. One event can remind you of another.

Why does this happen? Far from being an irrelevant artifact of memory, reminding is at the root of how we understand. It is also at the root of how we learn. Reminding can tell us about the nature and organization of our experiences. Understanding something new means finding something in memory to relate it to. We cannot understand in a vacuum. We understand restaurants in terms of other restaurants we have visited. Finding prior restaurants seems easy enough. But, we also understand prior events where we first thought that we had won and only later found we had lost in terms of other events with similar labels. Finding the experience in memory that is most like the new experience we are currently processing is neither straightforward nor is it an all or nothing affair. There may be many possible remindings and the one that would be most helpful might be hard to come by. In the normal course of attempting to understand an event, we need to find at least some event in memory that relates to the processing of that event. The organization of memory depends upon the use of that system in understanding new situations in terms of previously processed situations .

Why one experience reminds you of another is of primary importance to any theory of human understanding and memory. If people are reminded of things during the natural course of a conversation, or while reading, or when seeing something, then this tells us something of importance about the understanding process. To be reminded of something we must have come across it while we were processing the new input. But, to have done this we either had to be looking for this reminded event or else we must have run into it accidentally. In either case, reminding reveals something significant about the nature of memory structures and the understanding process.

- If we found an episode because we were looking for it, we must ask ourselves how we knew of that episode's existence so that we were able to look for it.

- If the explanation of reminding is that we accidentally run into an episode, we must ask why that accident occurs, and whether that accident has relevance to our processing.

It is an amalgamation of these two explanations that provides us with the method by which reminding takes place. We are not consciously looking for a particular episode in memory during processing, because we do not explicitly know of that episode's existence. We do however, know where episodes like the one we are currently processing are likely to be stored. To process a new experience we must find memory structures that contain experiences that are the most closely related to that new experience. Thus, reminding occurs when we have found the most appropriate structure in memory that will help in processing a new input.

One thing that is obvious about reminding is that the more you know about a subject, the more you can be reminded of in the course of processing inputs related to that subject. Thus, experts in particular fields might be expected to have reminding experiences directly tied in with their expertise. In a case-based reasoning system then, the expertise that is carried by the library of cases might actually be of little use if the labeling of those cases is too simplistic. Part of what an expert knows is the general applicability of given cases. He knows which cases are paradigmatic and thus must be labeled such that they pop up frequently, and he knows which cases are highly idiosyncratic and thus must be labeled with complex indexes that illustrate their applicablity only in certain specialized circumstances.

Why is it that some people are reminded of a famous chess game upon viewing another game and some people are not? The answer, obviously is that not everyone has knowledge of famous chess games. Obvious as this may be, it says something very important about memory: We use what we know to help us process what we receive. We would be quite surprised if a chess expert were not reminded of a famous chess game upon seeing one that began just like it. We expect an expert to have categorized his experiences in such a way as to have them available for aid in processing new experiences.

An expert is constantly receiving new inputs and evaluating them and understanding them in terms of previously processed inputs. We understand in terms of what we already understood. But, trite as this may seem, this view of understanding has not been seriously pursued either by psychologists interested in understanding or by Artificial Intelligence (AI) researchers interested in understanding or in expert systems. To build an expert system, two possible avenues are open. One is to attempt to get at the compiled knowledge of the expert; that is, the rules he uses when he makes the decisions that reflect his expertise (see [Buchanan and Shortliffe, 1984; Hayes-Roth *et al.*, 1983] for examples of this work). This approach has the advantage of being orderly and methodical. Its disadvantage is that such a system would not be able to reorganize what it knew. It would thus have a difficult time learning.

An alternative is to attempt to model the raw memory of the expert. This would involve creating a set of categories of subdomains of the expertise in question and equipping the system with rules for the automatic modification of those categories. Such a system would attempt to process new experiences in terms of the most closely related old experiences available. Upon finding an episode that strongly related, whatever that might turn out to mean, a reminding would occur. The new episode would then be indexed in terms of the old episode. New categories would be built as needed when old categories turned out to be useless from either under-utilization or over-utilization, or because the expectations contained within them were wrong too often.

An expert then is someone who gets reminded of just the right prior experience to help him in processing his current experiences. But, in a sense, we are all experts. We are experts on our own experiences. We all must utilize some system of categories, and rules for modifying those categories to help us find what we know when we need to know it.

One important consequence of the reminding phenomenon is that it alters our view of what it means to understand. For example, when we enter Burger King, having before been to McDonald's but never having been to Burger

King, we are confronted with a new situation which we must attempt to understand. We say that a person understands such an experience (i.e., he understands Burger King in the sense of being able to operate in it) when he says "Oh I see, Burger King is just like McDonald's," and then begins to use his information about McDonald's to help him in processing what he encounters at Burger King.

To put this another way, we might expect that at some point during a trip to eat at a Burger King, a person might be reminded of McDonald's. Understanding means being reminded of the closest previously experienced phenomenon. That is, when we are reminded of some event or experience in the course of undergoing a different experience, this reminding behavior is not random. We are reminded of a particular experience because the structures we are using to process the new experience are the same structures we are using to organize memory. We cannot help but pass through the old memories while processing a new input.

Finding the right one (that is, the one that is most specific to the experience at hand) is what we mean by understanding. Does this mean that episodic memory structures and processing structures are the same thing? The answer is yes. It follows then that there is no permanent (i.e., unchangeable) data structure in memory that exists solely for processing purposes. Scripts, plans, goals, and any other structures that are of use in understanding must be useful as organizing storage devices for memories. These structures exist to help us make sense of what we have seen and will see. Thus, memory structures for storage and processing structures for analysis of inputs are exactly the same structures.

According to this view, it is hardly surprising that we are reminded of similar events. Since memory and processing structures are the same, sitting right at the very spot most relevant for processing will be the experience most like the current one. Thus, the discovery of a coherent set of principles governing what is likely to remind you of what is a crucial step in building expertise into a computer system.

According to this view there are two key questions:

1. What are the categories or classes of memory structures?

2. How are indexes formed and used in memory organization within a structure?

In addition there is a third question. Not all reminding is neatly restricted within a given memory structure that reflects one particular context (such as restaurants and airplanes). Sometimes reminding can occur across such structures. Thus we have the question:

3. How does a memory organized in one memory structure remind you of
something that would naturally be classified in a different structure?

Recall that in studying reminding we are trying to discover how an extremely relevant memory can be brought to the fore in the natural course or
processing. In the kind of reminding we just discussed, we suggested that one
way such reminding occurs is this: In attempting to make predictions about
what will happen next in a sequence of events, a relevant structure is brought
in. In the course of applying the expectations derived from that structure, we
are reminded of that structure. Thus, to get reminded in this way, there must
have been an initial match on the basis of an identity between the structure
now active and the one originally used to process the recalled episode (i.e.,
the one you were reminded of).

Now, the question is, can we ever get reminded of something that is not
from a close match in an identical structure? It is obvious that people do
get reminded across contextually bounded structures. The only way that
this could happen is if they were tracking some entity during processing that
transcended particular contexts.

There are a number of such cross-contextual entities, each of which can be
lead to remindings. We summarize them here, and refer the reader to [Schank,
1982] for a fuller discussion.

1.5.1 Goal-based Reminding

In processing an input we are not only attempting to understand each event
that happens as an event itself. We are also attempting to get a larger picture,
to see the forest for the trees so to speak. We not only want to know that
happened but why it happened. Thus we must track goals.

An example here will serve to illustrate goal-based reminding. Someone
told me about an experience of waiting on a long line at the post office and
noticing that the person ahead had been waiting all that time to buy one
stamp. This reminded me of people who buy a dollar of two of gas in a gas
station.

What could be the connection? One possibility is that I had characterized
such motorists as people who prefer to do annoying tasks over and over when
they could have done them less often if they had purchased larger quantities
in the first place. Now such a category is extremely bizarre. That is, it is
unlikely that there is such a structure in memory. The existence of so complex
a structure would imply that we are simply creating and matching categories
in our heads in order to be reminded. As this seems rather unreasonable, we
must look for some more realistic way of explaining such a reminding.

Recall that processing considerations are intimately connected with memory categorizations. If we ask what kind of processing issues might be in common between the post office experience and the gas station proposed in [Schank and Abelson, 1977], there is a very obvious similarity here. Both stories related to goal subsumption failures [Wilensky, 1978]. In processing any story we are trying to find out why the actor did what he did. Questions about the motivations of an actor are made and reached. In this story, why the person bought a stamp is easy, as is why he stood in line. But good goal-based processing should note that this story is without point if only those two goals are tracked [Schank and Wilensky, 1978]. The point of the story is that the actor's behavior was somehow unusual. This unusualness was his failure to think about the future. In particular, he could have saved himself future effort by buying more stamps either before now or at this time. But he failed to subsume this goal. Thus the story is telling us about a goal-subsumption failure of a particular kind. Understanding this story involves understanding the kind of goal failure that occurred.

One key issue in the reminding and memory storage problem, then, is the question of what higher level memory structures are used in processing a new input. We have already worked with some of these structures in [Schank and Abelson, 1977; Wilensky, 1983; Carbonell, 1979]. We have recognized such structures as Goal-Blockage, Goal-Failure, Goal-Replacement, and Goal-Competition, not to mention the various structures associated with satisfying a goal. Each time one of these goal-based structures is accessed during normal processing, that structure becomes a source of predictions that are useful for processing and learning via reminding. Structures based upon goal-tracking are thus likely to be of significance in a memory that can get reminded.

1.5.2   Plan-based Reminding

If goals are being tracked, then so are the plans that are created to satisfy these goals. If we are to learn from our remindings, and that does seem to be one of the principal uses of reminding, then we must learn at every level for which we have knowledge. It follows then, that there should be a reminding that is plan-based. Such remindings should facilitate our construction of better plans.

Consider the following example. My daughter was diving in the ocean looking for sand dollars. I pointed out where a group of them were, yet she proceeded to dive elsewhere. I asked why and she told me that the water was shallower where she was diving. This reminded me of the old joke about the drunk searching for his lost ring under the lamppost where the light was better.

People quite commonly undergo such reminding experiences, jokes or funny stories being common types of things to be reminded of. What types of processing does such a reminding imply?

The implication is that, just as script-like structures must be full of indexes to particular episodes that either justify various expectations or that codify past failed expectations, so are plans used as a memory structures as well. How would this work in this case? Here, the similarity in these two stories is that they both employed some plan that embodied the idea of looking where it is convenient. But it is not the plan itself that is the index here. You could correctly pursue that plan and not be reminded of the drunk and the lamppost. The reminding occurs because this plan has occurred in a context where that plan should have been known by the planner to be a bad plan. Hence, reminding can also be plan-based.

1.5.3 Reminding across Multiple Contexts

There is no reason why reminding must be limited to the kinds of structures and processing that we have previously worked on, and indeed it is not. Reminding can take place in terms of high level structural patterns that cut across a sequence of events, as opposed to the reminding that we have been discussing thus far, i.e., reminding that occurs at particular points in the processing of individual events. This kind of reminding occurs when a pattern of events, as analyzed in broad, goal-related terms detected and found to be similar to a previously perceived pattern from another context.

If you have seen *Romeo and Juliet* and are watching *West Side Story* for the first time, it is highly likely that at some point in the middle of *West Side Story* you will notice that it is the *Romeo and Juliet* story in a modern-day New York, with music. Such a realization is a reminding experience of a classic kind. That is, this reminding represents true understanding of the kind we mentioned earlier between McDonald's and Burger King. Here again the reminding matches the most relevant piece of memory and that brings with it a great many expectations that are both relevant and valid.

But the complexity in matching *West Side Story* to *Romeo and Juliet* is tremendous. In the Burger King example, it was only necessary to be in some sort of fast food script and proceed merrily down that script. But in this example, everything is superficially different. The city is New York, there is a gang warfare, there are songs. To see *West Side Story* as an instance of *Romeo and Juliet* one must be not only processing the normal complement of scripts and goals. One must also be, in a sense, summarizing the overall plot to oneself, because that is where the match occurs.

Thus, we have yet another level of analysis that people must be engaged in, in understanding, that of making an overall assessment of events in terms of their goals, the conditions that obtain during the pursuit of those goals, the events of their actions, the interpersonal relationships that are affected, and the eventual outcome of the entire situation.

1.5.4 Morals

When a new input is received, we draw conclusions from what we have just processed. Often these conclusions themselves can remind us of something. A moral derived from a story, the realization of the point of the story, and so on, can each serve as an index to memories that have been stored in terms of the points they illustrate or the messages they convey.

Such reminding depends, of course, on our having made the actual categorization or index for a paradigmatic story. In other words, unlike the other kinds of reminding that we have so far discussed, here we would have had to pre-analyze the paradigmatic story in terms of its moral message or point. Indeed, we probably do just that. Why else would we choose to remember a joke or story unless it had a point we were particularly fond of?

But here the problem is one of finding the adage or joke that is relevant. We found the drunk joke because the plans being used were the same. Similarly, we can find morals when physical or situational structures such as scripts are the same. But what do we do when the only similarity is the moral itself? To find memories that way implies that there are higher level structures in memory that correspond to such morals.

1.5.5 Intentional Reminding

One type of reminding worth mentioning in any discussion of case-based reasoning is intentional reminding. Sometimes you can get reminded of something by the desire to call some relevant past experience to mind. We know that if only we were to be reminded of something here, it would help us in our processing. We thus try to get reminded. If we are trying to answer a question, then reminding is a form of getting the answer. In other words, we try to remind ourselves of the answer. But, even if what we are doing is simply trying to understand a situation, intentional reminding represents our attempt to come up with a relevant experience that will help us to understand our current situation. Not all intentional reminding is consciously intended, however, Much of it comes from just thinking about what is happening to us at a given time, without any conscious feeling that we wish we were reminded of something. Our thinking of a way to solve a particular problem often causes us to be reminded.

On a walk on the beach, I was asked by the person whom I was walking with if he should take his dog along. This reminded me of the last time I went walking with someone who had taken the resident dog along. I had objected, but my host said that we had to take it, to protect us from other dogs. This reminding experience caused me to ask myself if we would need the dog on the beach in the same way. I thought not and said so.

The above is an example of intentional reminding. Had I not been reminded at all, I would have simply responded that I didn't want to take the dog, since I don't especially like dogs. Instead I posed a problem to myself. Knowing how and when to pose the problem (here, finding the possible advantages of taking the dog) is a complex problem. To solve this problem, I attempted to be reminded of a relevant experience, if there was one.

Intentional reminding is extremely common. It forms the basis of a good deal of our conversation and of our thought. It forms the basis of our expertise. We try to get reminded by narrowing the contexts that we are thinking about until a memory item is reached. This narrowing is effected by a series of indexes. Often these indexes are provided by the input, but sometimes they must be provided by the person doing the thinking in an attempt to consciously narrow the context.

In the situation above, two contexts were active: visiting a colleague at his home and taking a walk. Each of these contexts alone had too many experiences in it to come up with any actual memories. but the index of dog changes things. The dog index is what is necessary to focus the search. Taking the dog was a sufficient cue for me because I so rarely did it.

The process of searching memory depends upon having a set of structures that adequately describe the contents of memory and a set of indexes that point out the usual features of the structures. Given such entities, it is then possible to search memory for intentional reminding.

1.5.6 A Perspective on Reminding

Reminding, then, is a highly significant phenomenon that has much to say to us about the nature of memory. It tells us about how memory is organized. It also tells us about learning and generalization. If memory has within it a set of structures, it seems obvious that these structures cannot be immutable. As new information enters memory, the structures adapt. Adapting initially means storing new episodes in terms of old expectations generated by existing structures. Eventually expectations that used to work will have to be invalidated. Indices that were once useful will cease to be of use because the unique instances they indexed are no longer unique. New structures will have to be built.

The ramifications of this for a case-based reasoning system are clear. It is the job of the case-based reasoner to have a library of cases; a method of storing new cases that allows them to found again when needed; an indexing scheme that reflects processing that has gone on while a case was initially considered; a method of partial matching that allows new cases to be considered in terms of similar ones; and, a method of adaptation that allows information garnered from one case to be applied to another. Human experts have all these abilities hidden under the notion of reminding. To make computer experts, we must build computer systems that get reminded.

2

Case-based Reasoners

2.1 Introduction

The basic idea in case-based reasoning is simple:

> A case-based reasoner solves new problems by adapting solutions that were used to solve old problems.

This differs from rule-based reasoning which solves problems by chaining rules of inference together. A case-based reasoner

- finds those cases in memory that solved problems similar to the current problem, and

- adapts the previous solution or solutions to fit the current problem, taking into account any difference between the current and previous situations.

Finding relevant cases involves

- characterizing the input problem, by assigning the appropriate features to it,

- retrieving the cases from memory with those features,

- picking the case or cases that match the input best.

Case-based reasoning means reasoning from prior examples. A case-based reasoner (CBR) has a case library. In a problem-solving system, each case would describe a problem and a solution to that problem. The reasoner solves new problems by adapting relevant cases from the library.

Case-based reasoning is an alternative to rule-based reasoning. A rule-based reasoner has a large library of rules of the form, "IF A THEN B." These are chained together in various combinations to solve problems. Some of the differences between case-based and rule-based reasoning can be understood by analogy to human problem solving. Suppose we show an assembly of pulleys to both a student in a physics course and a foreman responsible for loading cargo onto ships, and then ask them questions about how the pulleys will behave when used to lift weights. The physics student most likely will solve the problem by using rule-based reasoning, applying various formulas involving forces, momentum, and so on. The foreman probably will solve the problem using case-based reasoning, relating the given assembly to ones he has seen used. The student will take several minutes, will probably make some mistakes, but eventually will produce an exact answer, and will be able to handle almost any problem. The foreman, on the other hand, will be able to give an approximate answer almost instantly, but not an exact answer, and will probably have problems with unusual pulley setups.

These tradeoffs hold in general between rule-based and case-based reasoning. A rule-based system will be flexible and produce nearly optimal answers, but it will be slow and prone to error. A case-based system will be restricted to variations on known situations and produce approximate answers, but it will be quick and its answers will be grounded in actual experience. In very limited domains, the tradeoffs favor the rule-based reasoner, but the balance changes as domains become more realistically complex. Once we leave simple domains like pulley systems, we need a lot of rules, many of them quite subtle and hard to verify, and the chains of reasoning get long and tenuous. With case-based reasoning, there is always a short connection between the input case and the retrieved solution.

Case-based reasoning offers two main advantages over rule-based reasoning. First, expertise is more like a library of past experience than a set of rules; hence cases better support knowledge transfer (communication of expertise from domain experts to system) and explanation (justification of solution from system to domain experts). Second, many real-world domains are so complex that it is either impossible or impractical to specify fully all the rules involved; on the other hand, cases, i.e., solutions for problems, can always be given.

2.2   Case Studies in Case-based Reasoning

In this book, we make frequent reference to a number of major case-based reasoning programs. In particular, we detail three case-based reasoners, developed during doctoral research, (JUDGE, CHEF, and COACH) and one case-based understander (DMAP). In addition, we sometimes refer to several other important CBR programs. The summaries below provide a quick overview of each the main programs that are either referenced or detailed in the course of this book.

2.2.1 IPP

The IPP (Integrated Partial Parser) system [Lebowitz, 1980] is a model of memory organization and memory-driven text understanding, using the MOPs model of dynamic memory [Schank, 1982] that will be described in detail later. IPP reads texts about terrorist activities, e.g., bombings, kidnappings, and hijackings, stores its interpretations in memory, makes generalizations, and uses these generalizations to guide future story understanding. Key elements of IPP which will be discussed are its model of memory, its rules for forming generalizations, and its use of memory to guide parsing.

2.2.2 CYRUS

The CYRUS program [Kolodner, 1984], developed at the same time as IPP, is also a MOP-based story understanding program, but with a focus on how memory is used to answer questions after understanding. CYRUS reads stories about Cyrus Vance's diplomatic travels, stores its interpretations, makes generalizations, and answers questions, such as "When did you meet Begin last?" and "Did you ever meet Mrs. Begin?" The latter question is important because it is not plausible that CYRUS can either (a) look at every episode in memory in order to answer a question, or (b) index every episode in advance under every possible question that could be asked about it. Therefore, to answer a question such as "Did you ever meet Mrs. Begin?" CYRUS generates subquestions such as "When would I meet a spouse of a diplomat? (at a state dinner)," "When would I go to a state dinner with Begin? (on a diplomatic visit to Israel)," and so on. Such subquestions are generated until either a memory is retrieved with an answer, or no more elaborations are possible.

2.2.3 JUDGE

The JUDGE program, described in Chapters 4 and [Bain, 1986], works in the domain of criminal sentencing. It models a judge who is determining sentences for people convicted of crimes. The input is a description of the case, including the charge, the events that occurred, and the legal statutes regarding crimes of this nature, e.g., the range of imprisonment allowed and parole conditions.

The case library contains previous crimes and the sentences determined for each. JUDGE begins with an empty case library and a handful of heuristics for determining sentences when no cases can be applied to a new situation. It then builds a case base by tracking its own past decisions.

This domain involves no feedback. A sentence within legal limits can't be said to be "wrong." This makes it a *subjective appraisal* problem, similar to risk assessment problems, real estate appraisals, and so on. In such a domain, where right and wrong are basically impossible to determine, it is important to be consistent. The JUDGE program uses the case library to maintain a consistent sentencing pattern. A new crime is first interpreted by evaluating the events for seriousness, intentionality, justification, and so on, guided by interpretations assigned to prior cases. Then, the interpreted case is used to retrieve similar cases from the library. Finally, the sentence stored in the retrieved case is adapted to the current crime by making the sentence more or less stringent, depending how the new crime compared to the old one.

2.2.4   CHEF

The CHEF program, described in Chapter 6 and [Hammond, 1989], works in the cooking domain. It generates new recipes (primarily Chinese stir-fry and soufflé recipes) by adapting old recipes. This is a *design domain*, where an object has to be constructed to satisfy several goals simultaneously. Architecture, programming, and plan generation are other examples of design domains.

CHEF begins with a library of about 20 working recipes. The input to CHEF is a list of goals, such as "give me a hot stir-fry dish, with chicken and broccoli." The output is a recipe. The user of CHEF then evaluates the results. If there are problems, the user submits a failure report to CHEF. CHEF repairs the recipe, and also modifies its case library to avoid making the same kind of error in similar situations in the future.

CHEF differs from JUDGE in that it learns from its failures and its adaptation process is more complex. On the other hand, JUDGE's interpretation of input events is more complex than CHEF's analysis of its input goals.

2.2.5   COACH

The COACH program, described in Chapter 8 and [Collins, 1987], works in the football domain. It generates new football plays by improving old plays. This is another example of a design domain.

The focus of the research in COACH has been on debugging and repairing stored plans. Thus COACH only had a few plays in its case library, but it had a number of strategies for modifying plays to form new ones. Which modification should be used depended on the nature of the bug found in the existing play.

2.2.6 MEDIATOR

The MEDIATOR program [Simpson, 1985] works in the domain of dispute resolution. Given a conflict of goals between several parties, it proposes possible compromises. If one proposal fails to satisfy all parties involved, MEDIATOR generates a new proposal. It also stores a record of the failure of the first proposal to help it predict and avoid such failures in the future.

2.2.7 HYPO

HYPO [Rissland and Ashley, 1986; Ashley, 1987] does case-based legal reasoning in the area of patent law. Given a description of a case involving some claimed violation, HYPO uses its base of precedent cases to generate plausible arguments for the prosecution or the defense. For example, given a case description, such as the release of trade secrets to a competitor, and the goal of arguing for the defense, HYPO looks for those cases in memory most similar to the given case that were decided in favor of the defense. HYPO then looks for ways in which to reduce the apparent differences, if any, between the given case and the retrieved successful cases.

2.2.8 PLEXUS

PLEXUS [Alterman, 1986] is a planner that adapts old plans to new situations. Descriptions of PLEXUS have focussed on one example involving adapting the normal plan for riding San Francisco's BART subway system into a plan for riding New York's subway system. Although PLEXUS does not appear to have a significant case base, it is of interest for the mechanisms it uses in adapting old plans.

2.2.9 PERSUADER

Like MEDIATOR ,PERSUADER [Sycara, 1987] proposes resolutions for dispute situations. Like HYPO, PERSUADER also argues for its proposals. PERSUADER's domain is labor negotiations. It creates and argues for labor contracts. The input is a description of a dispute between management and labor over some wage-benefits package. PERSUADER creates a compromise package based on the goals of the actors and the standards of the industry. It

does this by adapting contracts that were already in place in similar companies. Unlike most case-based reasoners developed so far, PERSUADER also
has a backup planner, capable of generating new contracts when no existing
ones can be found or adapted.

2.2.10   CASEY

The CASEY system [Koton, 1988], diagnoses heart failures. It takes a description of a patient's symptoms and produces a causal network of possible
internal states that could lead to those symptoms. CASEY sits on top of
a more complete model-based diagnostic system, which is the source of the
initial case library of diagnoses. When new cases comes in, CASEY looks
for cases of patients with similar, but not necessarily identical symptoms. If
it finds a good match, CASEY then tries to adapt the retrieved diagnosis,
taking into account differences in symptoms between the old and new cases.
CASEY's adapted diagnoses match those built by the complete model-based
system quite well, but are constructed much more efficiently.

2.2.11   SWALE

The SWALE system [Schank, 1986; Kass, 1986; Leake and Owens, 1986] is a
case-based creative explainer. SWALE has a library of patterns for explaining
why animals and people die, such as old age, being run over by a car, and so
on. SWALE is given an anomalous event, most notably, the death of a young,
apparently healthy, very successful race horse named Swale. This event can't
be explained by any of the normal explanation patterns. Swale therefore starts
searching memory for other explanations of death in other contexts, such as
rock stars dying of drug overdoses, or people being murdered by spouses for
their life insurance. It then tries to adapt explanation to fit the situation
surrounding the anomaly, e.g., replacing "spouse kills spouse for life insurance"
with "owner kills horse for property insurance."

2.3   Rule-based Reasoning

Rule-based systems have two basic components: a *rule base* (or rule memory)
of domain-specific knowledge, and a domain-independent *rule interpreter* that
combines the rules to construct answers to problems. Most rule-based systems
are *production systems*, with rules of the form "IF some conditions are met
THEN take some action," but a few are *deductive systems*, with rules of the
form "IF some predications are true, THEN conclude some other predications

are also true." These systems have anywhere from several dozen to several thousand rules.

A major potential advantage of rule-based systems is called *additivity*. Ideally, adding a new piece of behavior means adding a new rule or modifying an existing one. Several models of learning have been proposed based on the notion of adding rules to a production system or optimizing the ones that exist [Anderson, 1986; Laird *et al.*, 1986; Waterman, 1975].

Compared to the monolithic blocks of Lisp code that preceded them, rule-based systems are clearly more intuitive and do a better job of representing some of the kinds of knowledge that people seem to have. But rules have a number of bad properties as well. First, additivity is hard to achieve in a large production-style rule-based system. Rules capture "what to do" knowledge, but usually not "why it works" or "what it means" knowledge. A rule that says "if someone has a runny nose and and red eyes, then that person may have a cold" does not say why this is a plausible conclusion, when it might not be, e.g., in hay fever season, or how it relates to other knowledge, e.g., if a person takes an antihistamine, then that person will not have a runny nose, but they will still have a cold. This knowledge is usually called *deep domain knowledge* [Chandrasekaran and Mittal, 1982].

A second problem with purely rule-based systems is that the knowledge of the system ends up being scattered into hundreds of individual pieces. This seems fairly improbable as a way to model of the very large diverse bodies of knowledge that people have, partly because the normal effect of such an organization is to make a system run slower the more facts it knows. It seems much more plausible that knowledge is organized so that related items are "near" each other [Smith *et al.*, 1978].

A third problem is that rules are not a good way to represent experiences. That is, if I go to an Ethiopian restaurant, I will learn that a very soft bread is used to hold and pick up food, playing the roles of both silverware and plate. While rules could be used to represent my new knowledge of how to eat in an Ethiopian restaurant, it does not represent the experience I had at that restaurant. That is, rules do not represent things like sequences of events. But if we add event structures to memory, how should we transform knowledge in this form into IF-THEN rules? One answer is to not transform it at all, but to use event memory to represent "how to" knowledge directly. This is the technical essence of case-based reasoning.

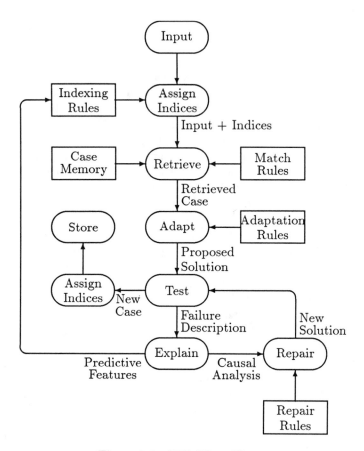

Figure 2.1: CBR Flow Chart

2.4   Case-based Reasoning

The basic cycle of a case-based reasoner is "input a problem, find a relevant old solution, adapt it." Figure 2.1 adds some detail to this basic flow of control and we discuss each part below.

The first problem for a CBR system is determining what old situations are "similar" to the current case. The relevant old solutions have to be labeled and organized so that features of input problems can be used to find them. Relevance in all but the most trivial domains is usually determined not by the obvious features of the input problem, but by abstract relationships between features, absence of features, and so on. For example, in JUDGE, the input is a description of a fight between two parties. The actual people involved and the particular events are not so important as the moral justification for each event, the degree of escalation between events, and so on. Hence, when a problem is input to a case-based reasoner, an *analysis phase* determines the features relevant to finding similar cases. These features are often called *indexes* in the CBR literature. The *indexing problem*, as it is sometimes called, is the problem of determining what extra, non-obvious, non-input features are needed for a particular domain.

Usually, the indexes will retrieve a set of potentially relevant old cases. The next step is to *match* the old cases against the input to (a) reject cases that are too different from the input situation, and (b) determine which of the remaining cases is most similar to the input. The similarity of cases depends on (a) how well they match on each dimension, and (b) how important each dimension is. JUDGE, for example, has to determine how similar two fights are. The dimension of time, i.e., when the fights occurred, is not important, but how justified the actors were, is.

After a best match has been determined, it must be adapted to fit the situation at hand. The adaptation process consists of two parts: determining what's different between the input and the retrieved case, and modifying the solution stored in the retrieved case to take those differences into account. The rules needed for this process are complex and hard to characterize in a general way. We will discuss different adaptation techniques that have been used in detail shortly.

How much adaptation needs to be done depends on the nature of the differences between the input and the retrieved case. Sometimes, what was done in a previous case will be the right thing to do again. Other times, simple alterations need to be done. Finally, there will be times when the selected case mismatches the input to such an extent that the case-based reasoner will be unable to make the needed fixes. When this happens, the CBR's best plan is to ask a human expert solve the problem and save the answer in the case library for future use.

2.5 Memory Organization

The micro CBR programs implemented in this book organize memory using MOPs (Memory Organization Packages) [Schank, 1982]. MOP-based memory techniques involve standard AI notions, such as frames, abstraction, inheritance, and so on, but applied to dynamically changing knowledge bases, i.e., systems that learning new knowledge in the process of understanding and problem solving.

2.5.1   Memory Organization Packages (MOPs)

The basic unit in dynamic memory is the MOP (Memory Organization Package). A MOP is used to represent knowledge about classes of events, especially complex events. For example, "going on a trip" would be represented with a MOP. A MOP contains a set of *norms* which represent the basic features of the MOP, e.g., what events occur, what goals are accomplished, what actors are involved, and so on. The norms of "going on a trip" would include the fact that there is a human actor who travels some place to accomplish some goal. These event MOPs basically contain the same information that scripts did in Schank and Abelson's script model of knowledge [1977]. The differences are that scripts were not organized into the interlinked networks described below, nor did they change with use, the way MOPs do, as we shall see. Scripts and plan structures were static knowledge structures, while MOPs are dynamic memory structures.

A MOP can have *specializations*, that is, MOPs that are more specific versions of the MOP. "Going on a vacation" and "going on a business trip" are two MOPs that are specializations of the "going on a trip" MOP. We say that "going on a trip" is an *abstraction* of "going on a vacation." A MOP that refers to a particular occurrence of an event is called an *instance*. Sometimes when we say "case," we'll mean an instance, i.e., a real event or problem-solving situation. Other times, we will use "case" to mean either an instance or a more general MOP.

MOPs in a dynamic memory are joined together by links. A case-based reasoner follows these links to get from one MOP to the next. Links play a critical role in case-based reasoning because they determine what information is available to a reasoner and when. There are several basic kinds of links. First, a MOP has *abstraction* links to those MOPs that are its abstractions. Thus, the "going on a business trip" MOP would have an abstraction link to the "going on a trip" MOP.

Second, a MOP representing a script event has *scene* links to various subevents. Getting a ticket, for example, would be one scene in a "going on a plane trip" MOP.

Third, a MOP may have *exemplar* links to particular instances of the MOP. In some systems, exemplar links point to those instances from which the MOP was originally derived. In other systems, they point to protoypical examples of the MOP.

Fourth, a MOP may have *index* links to specializations of that MOP. An index link is labeled with an attribute-value pair. For example, "purpose of trip" is an attribute. One possible value of this attribute is "pleasure," and another is "business." The index link labeled "purpose of trip = pleasure" would link the "going on a trip" MOP to the "going on a vacation" MOP.

One key point about index links is that an index is based on attributes and values that are not norms for the MOP. If the event "going to Hawaii to surf" was stored under the "going on a vacation" MOP, we would not index "going to Hawaii to surf" with "purpose of trip = pleasure," because that attribute is a norm of "going on a vacation," and hence, by definition, true of every specialization of the MOP. Such an index would not distinguish one vacation event from another. It is also important to note that if a MOP is indexed by some attribute-value pair, then that attribute-value pair is automatically a norm of the MOP. The only way any event could reach this MOP would be to have the given attribute-value pair; thus every event under this MOP will have this feature.

Finally, a MOP may have *failure* links to instances of the MOP that involved an expectation failure, that is, the actual events were not what the MOP predicted. For example, the "going on a vacation" MOP might have failure links to particularly disastrous vacations. It might also have failure links to unexpectedly successful vacations. Expectation failure does not mean goal failure; it only means "not what I expected."

If we look just at abstraction links between MOPs, we see a network of MOPs, going from very specific instances at the bottom up to very abstract general knowledge at the top. This is called the *abstraction hierarchy*. For example, a particular trip to the dentist is an instance, above which sits the MOP describing trips to dentists in general. Above the dentist MOP sits the MOP describing trips to professional services, e.g., to dentists, lawyers and psychiatrists. Above the professional service MOP sits the MOP describing errands in general, e.g., going to stores, going to the professional services, and so on.

The norms of each MOP are inherited by the MOPs below it. For example, paying for professional services is a norm of trips to professional services. Consequently, the system can know that trips to the dentist involve paying the dentist, even if the dentist MOP contains no explicit mention of payment.

If we look at just the scene links between MOPs, we see a network called the *packaging hierarchy*. At the top are MOPs representing very complex events. These events are broken down into subMOPs, which in turn may be broken down into even smaller MOPs, until eventually we reach some set of primitive non-decomposable actions, such as Conceptual Dependency [Schank, 1975]. For example, going on a vacation is a complex MOP, one of whose scenes may involve taking a plane, and one of the scenes of taking a plane is getting a ticket, and one of the scenes of getting a ticket is talking to a travel agent.

If we look just at the index links connecting MOPs together, we see a *discrimination net* [Charniak et al., 1987]. The MOPs are linked by sequences of predicates and predicate values that subdivide the set of subMOPs under a MOP into more manageable chunks.

For example, in the CYRUS program, which tracked events involving Cyrus Vance in his role as Secretary of State, there were hundreds of specializations of the MOP for diplomatic meetings. Therefore they were subdivided according to features (indexes) such as who the meeting was with, where the meeting was held, and so on. Thus, all the meetings with Begin were in one subset, meetings with Gromyko in another, and meetings in Israel in another. In this way, the specializations of diplomatic meetings under consideration at any one time was kept to a manageable size. Some meetings appeared in several sets, e.g., a meeting with Begin might be in Israel, so it was indexed both under "meetings with Begin" and "meetings in Israel."

2.5.2   Case-based Learning and Memory Organization

There are three major kinds of changes that can occur in a MOP-based case library. It can add

- new instances,

- new abstractions, or

- new indexes.

New instances are added during normal use of MOP memory for solving problems. For example, when IPP or CYRUS understand a story, they create a new instance of the most specific MOP that applies to the story. When CHEF creates a recipe, it creates a new instance of some recipe MOP. When MEDIATOR generates a dispute resolution, it creates a new instance of a MOP for some plan for resolving disputes. Instances record experiences in terms of MOPs. In PERSUADER, even the steps in the problem solving process are recorded in MOPs.

New abstractions are formed when a number of cases are discovered to share some common set of features. The common features are used to create the norms of the new MOPs, and the unshared features are used as indexes to the original MOPs. This is called *similarity-based generalization.*

The processes for noticing when features are shared, deciding that it is worth creating an abstraction, and choosing indexes, vary from system to system. When IPP adds a new instance to a set of instances under some index, it automatically checks to see if any generalizations are worth forming from that set of instances. A generalization is worth forming if there are enough instances with enough features in common, where "enough" was defined by thresholds, e.g., at least 3 instances sharing at least 2 features. For example, after seeing several examples of bombs in post offices in England left by IRA terrorists, IPP formed an abstraction for IRA post office bombings.

Forming new abstractions simply on the basis of shared features is not a very good technique. In realistic domains, such as IPP's terrorism domain, spurious generalizations or silly abstractions will be formed that will remain until enough further examples are found. IPP, for example, once noticed that the several cases of bombings it knew of in El Salvador resulted in exactly 2 deaths, so it formed an abstract MOP for bombings in El Salvador, and included 2 deaths in the norms for that MOP. While more examples would eventually cause it to change this MOP, it seems like an unreasonable norm to have formed in the first place. People know better; they know that the results of bombings are quite erratic, and that it would be almost impossible for some terrorist group to guarantee that 2 people would die in every explosion. On the other hand, it is causally possible that Italian terrorists could guarantee that only businessmen were kidnapped.

In CYRUS, generalizations are formed in stages. When a new event is indexed to the same place in memory, i.e., under the same MOP, as a previous event, an abstraction is formed with all the features the events shared in common that are not already in the existing MOPs above the events. The norms of this abstraction are marked as "potential" because so little evidence for them exists. As more events are added to this MOP, the actual norms can be determined. Some features that are potential will disappear, because later events do not share them, and some features that are not potential will be added, because they are shared by most of the later events. For example, after reading several stories about Vance's visits to the Middle East, CYRUS might form an abstraction for diplomatic visits related to peace talks in the Middle East. If the stories seen so far always involve a state dinner, then state dinners are a potential norm of this abstraction. Later, if CYRUS sees stories about such visits without state dinners, it will remove this norm.

One approach to avoiding some of the problems with forming norms that turn out to be accidental is a technique known as Explanation-based Generalization (EBG) [Mitchell *et al.*, 1986; DeJong and Mooney, 1986]. The idea is that an abstraction is made only when a plausible reason for its existence can be inferred, based on prior causal knowledge. An abstraction can be formed from just one example, if the system can supply enough of the causality to explain the basic features of the case. Furthermore, only features relevant to the causality are kept in the abstraction, so spurious features are less of a problem. In DeJong's work, one story about a kidnapping is enough to allow the system to generate most of the abstraction for kidnapping events, because the system can understand the causalities between kidnapping, ransoms, getting money, and avoiding capture. In Mitchell's work, one example of using a particular method for integrating some formula can generate a reasonable abstraction for using that method in general.

The problem with explanation-based generalization is that it can end up doing a lot of work to create an abstraction for a one-time only event. Consequently, it seems most reasonable for case-based learners to use a mixed approach. It would seem best to do the normal causal analysis needed to understand the event or solve the problem and place it in memory, but not create an abstraction until a similar event is seen. At that time, explanation-based generalization could carry on and generate an abstraction based on its causal understanding of the two events.

Several case-based reasoners do a form of EBG called *failure-driven learning*. CHEF, MEDIATOR [Simpson, 1985] and PERSUADER [Sycara, 1987] learn not only by saving solutions but also by forming general explanations of why some solutions don't work. In a case-based reasoner with failure-driven learning, a failure report comes back from the real world, entered either by a user or generated automatically by the CBR attempting to execute the solution. The reasoner repairs the case, stores the repair, and reorganizes the case library so that the repair will be retrieved in similar situations in the future. This last step is important and necessary. It isn't enough to remove the failed case from memory, because the CBR would then just retrieve the case that generated the failed case. We don't want to remove that original case because it is still the correct case to use in many situations. Instead, we want the CBR to know when not to use that case. We want the CBR to change how it indexes such cases, to take into account some feature that was not considered before.

Consider the situation in which CHEF adapts a chicken and green beans recipe into a recipe that stir fries beef and broccoli together. This recipe fails when executed: the broccoli comes out very limp and soggy. The explanation for this is that meat sweats, i.e., gives off water, when fried, and broccoli gets soggy when cooked in water. The original recipe did not have this problem because green beans don't get soggy that quickly when cooked in water.

First CHEF uses the explanation of the failure to guide repair of the recipe. Since the failure depends on the beef and broccoli cooking together, one repair would be to change the recipe to fry the beef and broccoli in separate steps. CHEF then uses the explanation to change how cases are indexed, so that this kind of failure would not arise again. CHEF has to make sure that new requests for a recipe like beef and broccoli do not retrieve the same chicken and green beans recipe.

The crucial parts of the explanation are (1) meats sweat when fried, (2) beef is a meat, (3) certain crisp vegetables get soggy when cooked in water, and (4) broccoli is such a vegetable. From this, CHEF concludes that the conjunction of "has meat" and "has crisp vegetable" is an important thing to look for. Beef and broccoli *per se* are not important here, since the same failure would happen with any other meat and crisp vegetable.

In our framework, CHEF can be seen as making three changes:

- creating a new feature "Includes meat and crisp vegetable?"

- giving this feature a high importance level

- indexing the repaired beef and broccoli recipe under it ingredients.

With these changes, requests for recipes with meats and crisp vegetables will retrieve the repaired beef and broccoli recipe. Adapting this recipe will not cause the soggy vegetable failure. Requests for meats and non-crisp vegetables will retrieve the original chicken and green beans recipe that has the more efficient merged stir-fry step.

Note that a great deal of important learning is essentially a matter of moving information we already know into the right places. CHEF already knew about meats and crisp vegetables and how to explain failures that might occur when cooking them together. Now CHEF has learned how to use this information to avoid failures, rather then just explain and repair them.

Both approaches to generalization will miss some potential abstractions in a MOP-based memory, because a case is checked against only those cases that are retrieved when the current case is indexed into memory. There might be other cases in memory that share many features with the current case which are not found because the features involved are not used for indexing. Whether this is a bug or a feature depends on whether the generalizations that the system misses are the same ones that people miss or not.

When an abstraction is formed, everything that is shared by the cases that the abstraction generalizes is put in the norms of the new MOP. Everything that is not shared is used to index the old MOPs under the new MOP. If CYRUS forms a "meetings with Begin" MOP, it will generate indexes by looking for features of those meetings with Begin that make them different from the abstraction. However, we must be careful not to take the search for distinguishing features to an extreme, since the primary purpose of memory organization is to make information available for future use. Hence the following heuristic:

> A good index for case-based reasoning is distinctive but not unique.

Some indexes are too distinctive. If CYRUS indexes meetings by their date and time, no future meeting will ever remind CYRUS of previous meetings, and the memory would be useless for case-based reasoning. The most useful features to use for indexing are the features shared by many instances in memory as a whole, but by only a few of the instances under the abstract MOP being formed. Thus, suppose only a few of Vance's meetings with Begin include state dinners, but many other international political meetings have accompanying state dinners. The index "State dinner?–No" would be a good index for "meetings with Begin" because it would select a small set of meetings, many of which were with Begin.

Picking indexes on the basis of how well they distinguish a set of cases is an information-theoretical approach, based on the statistics of the set of cases. The information-theoretical approach can be quite powerful [Quinlan, 1983]. It is what is known as a "weak method," that is, a method that is generally applicable, but that makes no use of specific background knowledge. CYRUS uses a knowledge-based approach to select indexes. Different attributes are marked as being normally "predictive" in certain contexts, that is, as being attributes that usually correlated with other interesting features. For example, in diplomatic meetings, the nationalities of the parties involved is normally a predictive feature. When CYRUS generates indexes for a set of cases, it uses all the features it can find in the cases involved that are predictive for the given context.

2.5.3   Thematic Organization Packets

There is an important level of abstraction in case-based reasoning systems that connects cases to problem-solving goals. The units at this level of abstraction are called Thematic Organization Packets (TOPs) [Schank, 1982]. In CHEF, TOPs were used to characterize abstractly the interactions between steps in a recipe. For example, one TOP is SIDE EFFECT: DISABLED CONDITION: CONCURRENT. CONCURRENT means that two goals are being achieved by one action. SIDE EFFECT: DISABLED CONDITION means that a side effect of achieving one of the goals prevents the achievement of the other goal. This TOP characterizes the failure that occurs when cooking broccoli with beef makes the broccoli soggy. The knowledge related to cooking broccoli and other ingredients is represented in MOPs, but the knowledge about how goals can interact in general, which is independent of the particular MOPs involved, is represented in TOPs.

TOPs are important because they capture domain-independent problem-solving knowledge. For example, in CHEF, one solution to the problem posed by the TOP above is to split the action into two steps, so that the side effect of the action used to achieve one goal won't affect the achievement of the other goal. When applied to the broccoli and beef case, the TOP suggests cooking the two ingredients separately. Another TOP-based solution is to add another action to counteract the side effect. When applied to the broccoli and beef case, this would suggest adding something to absorb the water that is making the broccoli soggy. There are other possibilities. The important thing to note is that all of these strategies are very general. They can suggest repairs in any domain where the TOP arises. In each example, of course, only some suggestions will actually be implementable.

Chapter 8 on the COACH program is primarily concerned with TOP-level knowledge and its use for organizing strategies for plan repair.

2.6   Adapting Cases

The ultimate task of a case-based reasoner is to adapt the solution stored in a retrieved case to the needs of the current input. When the retriever is handed an input situation, it finds the best match that it can in memory. Normally, however, the case found will not be an exact match. There will be differences between the problem that the retrieved case handled and the current problem which must be taken into account. The adaptation process looks for salient differences between the retrieved case and the input and then applies rules that take those differences into account.

Adaptation rules are essentially mini-problem solvers. In a planning domain, they need to be able to note preconditions to steps that need to be met and find plans to achieve them. In a diagnostic task, they need to be able to find gaps in an explanation and fill in the missing causalities. For example, in the CHEF program, the user may have asked for a stir-fry dish containing chicken and green beans, but the retrieved recipe might be for beef and broccoli. There are two salient differences: the main meat in the new recipe is chicken, not beef, and the main vegetable is green beans, not broccoli. To adapt the steps in the retrieved recipe to the new recipe, the CHEF program must respond to these differences.

First, CHEF copies the old recipe, substituting the corresponding items in every step. Every step that involved beef (chopping it, marinating it, frying it, and so on) now involves chicken, and references to broccoli become references to green beans. Then CHEF checks each step to see if it can be omitted or if that step now requires changes for its new application.

The CHEF example should make it clear just how domain and task specific the adaptation rules need to be. Not only are there very specific rules about how to substitute ingredients in a recipe, there are also fairly complex rules, not described above, about how to add various kinds of steps to a recipe. For example, normally steps of a similar kind should be grouped together (e.g., do all chopping steps before stir frying). Sometimes steps can or should be merged (e.g,. chop scallions and garlic together) and sometimes they should not (e.g., if the cooking time for the meat has to be increased, rearrange steps to assure that any item being cooked with the meat is not overcooked).

As discussed in [Hammond, 1989], the advantage of case-based reasoning is that, messy though they may still be, the adaptation rules can be much simpler than those required by a purely rule-based system, if the case library is reasonably filled out. In many real-world domains it is very difficult, if not impossible, to create a complete set of rules, and applying large numbers of rules is very inefficient. A case-based reasoner can get by with a much weaker set of rules, if the case library is broad enough. In CHEF, the adaptation rules were only powerful enough to make the kinds of local patches described above. That is, they could add and delete steps, but they did not make global changes to the whole recipe. The basic ordering of steps in the original recipe was maintained, along with any optimizations that were not explicitly changed by any ingredient critics, such as which things were fried together. Moreover, the adaptation steps in CHEF were not powerful enough to generate recipes from scratch. In fact, they were not even powerful enough to guarantee that any stir-fry recipe could be adapted to any combination of ingredients. Clearly, the adaptation rules in a case-based reasoner don't have to be weak. In some domains, it might be possible to have rules that are in fact capable of generating complete solutions from scratch, or, more accurately, of adapting any retrieved case, no matter how irrelevant, to the current situation.

Here is an analogy that may help demonstrate how a bigger case library can allow the use of significantly weaker adaptation rules and still get strong results. Consider the process by which most people learned to find logarithms (base 10) in high school (pre-calculators). First, we were taught what a logarithm was, e.g., the logarithm of 50 is 1.69897 because 10 raised to the 1.69897 power equals 50. Then, we were taught to calculate the logarithm of a number by looking that number up in a table of logarithms. If our number was in the table, we were done. If not, then we took the logarithms of the two numbers in the table that were closest to our number (above and below) and used a simple ratio formula to approximate the logarithm of our number.

The table of logarithms is analogous to the case library. Looking up the closest numbers is case retrieval (analysis and retrieval in this domain is simple). Interpolating the answer using ratios is the adaptation rule. Note that this rule is much simpler and faster than trying to calculate a logarithm from scratch (a process which in fact most of us were not taught in high school because it is too complicated). However, this rule only yields reasonable answers if the table has two numbers close to our number. If the table entries are not very close to our number, then very bad results are obtained. Thus we see how a large table (case library) can improve results and enable the use of significantly simpler adaptation rules.

2.6.1 Types of Adaptation

Two very different kinds of adaptation have been described in the CBR literature. First, there is *structural adaptation*, in which the adaptation rules apply directly to the solution stored in a case. CHEF, for example, modified particular recipes, while JUDGE modified prior criminal sentences.

Second, there is *derivational adaptation*, where the rules that generated the original solution are re-run to generate the new solution. Derivational adaptation was used in MEDIATOR [Simpson, 1985], and its theoretical advantages have been discussed in [Carbonell, 1986]. The idea here is to store not only a solution with a case, but the planning sequence that constructed that solution. When a case is retrieved, the reasoner checks to see if the differences between the old situation and the input case affect any of the decisions underlying the solution stored in the case. If so, those decisions are re-evaluated using the values extant in the input situation. In other words, the stored solution is adapted not by changing it directly, but by re-executing parts of the original solution process.

In MEDIATOR, for example, there was a plan to settle a dispute between two children over the use of an orange. This plan first tried splitting the orange, but this failed, because neither child wanted half an orange. It turned out that one child wanted the peel while the other wanted the fruit. The correct plan was to give each child the part of the orange that she wanted. MEDIATOR applied this plan (determine presence of compatible goals and satisfy each) to generate a possible resolution to the dispute between Egypt and Israel over the Sinai. The result was to give Israel military control, but to give Egypt political and economic control.

There are several advantages to derivational adaptation. First, there are fewer *ad hoc* rules needed. It isn't necessary to have rules that can remove silly steps such as "bone shrimp," with which CHEF's adaptation rules have to deal. Such steps never appear when the plans are re-run in new circumstances.

Second, derivational adaptation can be used to adapt problem solving knowledge from other domains, rather than being restricted to within-domain solutions. The MEDIATOR example above is good instance of analogical reasoning, which is really only possible with derivational adaptation.

Derivational adaptation is not a replacement for structural adaptation. In any real CBR, both kinds of mechanisms would be present, because derivational adaptation depends on the presence of the planning structures for stored solutions, and not all solutions have them. There are many methods for doing things that have been learned from experience. Even the experts can't fully explain why these methods work, or how to determine when to use them. Further, for practical purposes, a domain expert will want to be able to enter many cases into a CBR without having to specify the underlying reasoning under each one. These cases will be "primitives" as far as the CBR is concerned.

Hence, a full CBR will have both structural adaptation rules to fix the "unanalyzed" solutions, and derivational mechanisms to fix the cases that are well understood by the system. Solutions generated by the system itself would be prime candidates for derivational adaptation.

2.6.2 Adaptation Techniques

In this section we will survey the different adaptation techniques, from simple to complex, that have been used in various case-based reasoning systems. We will look at several techniques that are structural adaptation techniques, one that is derivational, and we will begin with null adapation which, correctly speaking, is neither structural nor derivational.

Null Adaptation

The first and certainly simplest technique is to do nothing and simply apply whatever solution is retrieved to the new situation. In Chapter 1, we argued that people often do very little adaptation. If the situation in El Salvador reminds someone of Viet Nam, then that person often just copies the results of that experience directly over to El Salvador.

Null adaptation also comes up in tasks where, even though the reasoning to a solution may be complex, the solution itself is very simple. For example, many factors must be considered when evaluating loan applications, but the final answer is either accept or reject. If an input case best matches loans that were rejected, then it should be rejected. If it best matches loans that were accepted, then it should be accepted. In either case, the old solution is applied directly. A program that diagnosed equipment failures by suggesting faulty components would work similarly. If a certain part had caused similar failures in the past, it should suggest that the same part is at fault again.

With such simple kinds of solutions (accept, reject, part-26, wire-13, and so on), it shouldn't be surprising that there's not much that can be adapted. There are two caveats, however. First, if all we want is a simple answer, there are other techniques, such as statistical classification methods, that can work quite well, often better than people, who are more convinced by individual cases than by numbers. Second, it's rare that we really want such simple kinds of answers. A loan application evaluator that just says accept or reject, or equipment diagnoser that just says part-26, is useless in the real world. The user wants to know how the answer was arrived at, what other answers are possible, and so on. In other words, the real solution stored in the cases that the user wants is the chain of reasoning leading to the answer. Once the user sees examples of reasoning in previous similar cases, he or she can usually see how that reasoning applies to the current situation.

Parameterized Solutions

Probably the best understood adaptation technique is a structural technique which we call *parameterized solutions*. The idea is this: when a case is retrieved for an input situation, the old and new problem descriptions are compared along the specified parameters. The differences are then used to modify the solution parameters in the appropriate directions. For example, in JUDGE, a crime has parameters such as "heinousness," "seriousness of motive," and "remorse." Likewise, there are parameters involved in the solution. In JUDGE, a criminal sentence has parameters for length of imprisonment (if any), availability of parole, fines, and so on. Each problem parameter is associated with one or more solution parameters. The more heinous the crime, the harsher the sentence. The greater the remorse, the sooner the parole. Thus, if JUDGE finds the input crime is less heinous than the crime retrieved from memory, it will make the sentence milder than the one given for the previous crime.

The HYPO [Rissland and Ashley, 1986; Ashley, 1987] system, operating in the legal domain of patent law, also uses parameterized solutions to compare cases and generate hypothetical arguments. The "solution" to a retrieved case is the answer to the question "Who won, the defense or prosecution?" Correlated with this answer, directly or inversely, are a number of problem parameters. For example, consider a case in which a company claims that a former employee went to work for a competitor and revealed trade secrets to them. One problem parameter is how many other people besides the employee were privy to the secrets in question. The more people who knew the secret, the weaker the case for the company. On the other hand, the longer that the defendant worked for the company, and the higher his position in that company, the stronger is the case for the prosecution. HYPO uses this information to build a claim lattice that relates various cases together by how similar they are along these various parameters [Ashley and Rissland, 1987].

The PERSUADER system models labor-management dispute arbitration. In particular, it generates contract resolutions by modifying stored instances of

The company's #<M-TRANSIT-COMPANY 16274557>
present wage value, 6.5 dollars
is below the wage average, 8.0 dollars,
for the industry #<M-TRANSIT-TRANSPORT 16271241>
by 18.7 percent.

This, however, could be modified by area statistics

Since the cost of living in Atlanta
differs from the national average by -2.0 percent
the 18.7 percent is modified by -2.0 percent to become 16.7
percent.

Figure 2.2: Parameterized Adaptation in PERSUADER

prior successful contract negotiations. A major element of these modifications depend on parameterized solutions. For example, pay scales from a contract for one industry are modified up or down when applied to a different industry, using a standard parameter called an industry differential. Some industries, for various reasons, inherently pay more or less than others. Likewise, pay scales are modified according the geographical setting of the companies involved, using a geographical differential. These problem parameters take on discrete values and have standard incremental effects on the solution. Their use fits the basic pattern of modifying parameters of the solution up or down according to differences in the match between the input situation and the retrieved case. Figure 2.2, from [Sycara, 1987], shows a geographical differential being applied.

Although the CHEF program does not use parameterized solutions to any great extent, they are of obvious relevance to the cooking domain in which CHEF operates. In particular, cooking times and quantities of ingredients are two solution parameters that are affected by a number of problem parameters. For example, if the recipe being generated uses larger pieces of meat or vegetable than the recipe from which it is being adapted, then the cooking times need to be proportionately longer. If the desired number of servings is larger than the original recipe produced, everything needs to be scaled up appropriately. Tougher pieces of meat need to be marinated longer, and so on.

An important point to note here is that the use of parameterized solutions does not imply that there is a simple formula for getting from some set of problem parameters to a solution. JUDGE does not have a formula to generate

a prison sentence given the heinousness of the crime, HYPO cannot tell how
a case would be adjudicated simply by looking at the parameters of the case,
PERSUADER cannot create a contract merely by considering industrial and
geographical factors, and CHEF cannot calculate a recipe by producing a set
of quantities and cooking times. In each program, the parameterized solutions
are of value in modifying an existing solution, not creating a new solution *ab
initio*. Parameterized solutions are a technique for interpolation, similar to
the method used for finding logarithms in a table using only basic arithmetic.
It is a simple but powerful way to augment a case library, but it is not a
replacement for a good set of cases.

Abstraction and Respecialization

Abstraction and respecialization is a very general structural adaptation technique that can be used in both a basic way to achieve simple adaptations, and
in a complex way to generate novel, even creative solutions. The idea is this:
if a piece of the retrieved solution does not apply to the problem at hand,
look for abstractions of that piece of the solution that do not have the same
difficulty. Then, respecialize, that is, try applying other specializations of the
abstraction to the current situation. This results in trying "siblings" of the
original concept.

The PLEXUS [Alterman, 1986] planning system uses this technique as its
primary means of adapting old plans to new situations. PLEXUS, using the
null adaptation method, first applies the old plan it finds to the new situation.
When something fails, PLEXUS replans using abstraction and respecialization. For example, PLEXUS applies its plan for riding the BART subway
system in San Francisco to the subway system in New York City. Pieces of
this plan fail. In particular, you enter the BART system by getting a card
from a ticket machine and inserting it in a turnstile. In the New York City
system, there are no ticket machines. PLEXUS abstracts from the concept
of "get ticket from machine" to "get ticket," then respecializes to "get ticket
from ticket booth," as in the plan for going to a theater. This plan works
in the New York system. Though the PLEXUS system does not use MOPs,
similar techniques are used in the MOP-based SWALE system [Kass, 1986].

Another system that uses abstraction and respecialization is the PER-
SUADER system. For example, when looking for labor contracts, PER-
SUADER first looks for contracts with direct competitors of the company
involved, i.e., companies operating in the same area. If this fails, it then looks
for contracts in companies that used to be competitors. Finally, it looks for
contracts in other companies of the same type. Figure 2.3 shows some example
output.

```
Searching memory for current competitor's contracts...
Failed to find current competitor's contracts...
Failed to find past competitor's contracts...
Having found industry contracts...

Consider contracts with the same job classification
#<M-BUS-DRIVER 16271457>

Then consider contracts that resulted from
successful negotiations.

The contract I am considering is #<M-CONTRACT 16275246>
which is the contract for #<M-BUS-COMPANY 16274150>
```

Figure 2.3: Abstraction and Respecialization in PERSUADER

Using abstraction and respecialization is a form of reasoning by analogy. PLEXUS and PERSUADER abstract only slightly from the original solutions, so the respecialized solutions are very close to the originals. But if we start abstracting farther, then the respecialized solutions will differ much more from their starting points. This is what the SWALE system does to generate creative solutions to a problem. Given the problem of explaining why a famous racehorse died in his stall while apparently at the peak of his career, SWALE abstracts to very general explanations of death, such as murder, or high living. It then respecializes to particular explanations, e.g., someone murdered for their life insurance, or a rock star dying from a drug overdose. What makes this use of abstraction and respecialization complicated is that the new solutions usually can't be applied directly, for many reasons, and they need to be "tweaked" first. Tweaking a solution involves abstracting and respecializing pieces of the new solution back toward the original domain. A horse wouldn't have life insurance or a murderous spouse, but it might have property insurance and an unscrupulous owner. A horse doesn't do drugs for pleasure, but an owner might drug a horse to make it race better. In both of these examples, SWALE creates a novel solution by first making a big leap (via abstraction and respecialization) in order to find a possible solution in another domain, and then making smaller changes (again via abstraction and respecialization) in order to bring the solution back into the domain of the original problem.

Critic-based Adaptation

The notion of solving problems by using critics to debug nearly correct solutions was first proposed in [Sussman, 1975] and developed more recently in [Simmons, 1988]. Although the ballpark solutions in these systems are created with simple combining rules, rather than retrieved from memory, the solution critics are very similar in spirit, and sometimes in content, to the critics used by case-based reasoners.

A critic looks for some combination of features that can cause a problem in a plan. Associated with different problems are strategies for repair. The combinations for which it is worth checking depends in part on how the plans are derived. In Sussman's work, a plan for achieving several goals simultaneously is derived by putting together plans that could achieve each goal independently. The critics can then check if (1) any plans interfered with each other, or (2) any plans were redundant. For example, given the two goals "paint the ladder and the ceiling," the simple combining rules might generate the plan "paint ladder; climb ladder; paint ceiling." Unfortunately, painting the ladder makes it unusable, at least until the paint dries. This would be discovered by a critic that checks for any step with a side effect that makes a later step difficult. One repair strategy associated with this problem is to reverse the order of the steps. In some cases, this will work, while in other cases some other repair will be needed.

CHEF gets a ballpark solution by taking an old recipe and substituting the desired new ingredients for the old ones. Then its ingredient critics check for unnecessary steps, such as chopping ingredients that are already small, or missing steps, such as boning meats that are going to be chopped. Later, when repairing a recipe that doesn't work, its repair critics separate steps that interfere with each other.

PERSUADER gets a ballpark solution by taking a negotiated labor contract from a prior case and adjusting it according to various industry-specific differentials, as discussed in the preceding section on parameterized solutions. PERSUADER then uses critics to see if the goals of the various actors would be satisfied by this solution. Usually problems do exist because if the obvious solution could work, a negotiator wouldn't be needed. For example, a company's management might be claiming that economic circumstances prevent it from offering pay and benefits equal to those offered by other companies in the same industry elsewhere in the country. A critic might suggest offering less of something that labor might consider less important, e.g., retirement benefits in a company with a high turnover rate.

The same point made about parameterized solutions also applies here. Critics, as defined by Sussman and used in case-based reasoning, are not capable of generating complete solutions on their own. They are quite limited in the kinds of patches they can make to solutions. They make local changes, rather than globally reorganizing everything. The basic form of the final solution will still reflect the original solution from which it was derived.

Reinstantiation

The techniques described above are what we have called "structural" adaptation methods. They operate directly on old solutions to produce new ones. Reinstantiation is a "derivational" adaptation method. It operates not on the original solution, but on the method that was used to generate that solution. Reinstantiation means replacing a step in a solution by taking the plan that generated that step and rerunning it in the context of the current situation.

The MEDIATOR system uses this technique to generate resolutions between two disputants. For example, it attempts to resolve the dispute between Egypt and Israel over control of the Sinai by using a solution applied when the USA and Panama were in conflict over control of the Panama Canal. The plan used was "divide into different parts," separating control of the Canal along political and military lines. In the current situation, a similar solution is to give military control to Israel, for its national security, and political control to Egypt, for its national integrity. Figure 2.4 shows the output.

In simple cases, reinstantiation has the same effect as some of the substitution techniques used in the structural adapters. CHEF, for example, replaces green beans with broccoli not by rerunning the plans for "chop vegetable," "cook vegetable," and so on, but by simply substituting one vegetable for the other in all the steps of the recipe. However, CHEF then has to check each step to see if it is really needed or requires any other steps. In MEDIATOR, these checks are done when reinstantiating. If chopping chicken requires the extra step of boning it, for example, it will be produced while reinstantiating the basic plan of "chop food" when applied to chicken.

The power of reinstantiation is limited by the planning power of the reasoner since (re)instantiating a plan *is* planning. MEDIATOR can reinstantiate a low-level plan such as "divide equally," but not a high-level one such as "resolve dispute." MEDIATOR has to find a case containing an instance of a dispute resolution. It can then reinstantiate pieces of that case, as needed. The planner in PERSUADER, on the other hand, can instantiate any plan in the system (generate contracts for labor-management disputes), if no case is found applicable to the current situation. PERSUADER is an example of case-based reasoning integrated with other planning techniques (see also JULIA [Kolodner, 1987]).

Considering the following problem:

Israel and Egypt both want the Sinai
which has been presented as ako M-PHYS-DISPUTE.
...
Goal relationship is CONCORDANT.

ATTEMPTING TO SELECT A MEDIATION PLAN
TO RESOLVE THE DISPUTE IDENTIFIED AS #<M-PHYS-DISPUTE 40533552>.

ATTEMPTING TO RECALL SIMILAR DISPUTES...
...
There was one previous case with the same CONCORDANT goal
relationship.
It was resolved using the plan known as "divide into different
parts"
Checking for applicability of that plan to the current case...
I suggest that the plan called "divide into different parts" be
used.

INSTANTIATING EXPECTED CONTRACT RESULTING FROM PLAN APPLICATION.
using the Panama Canal dispute to guide current contract
construction

matching ISRAEL with USA...
matching EGYPT with PANAMA...
matching SINAI with PANAMA-CANAL...
matching
(*GOAL* (*NAT-SECURITY* (ACTOR ISRAEL) (OBJECT SINAI))) with
(*GOAL* (*MIL-SECURITY* (ACTOR USA) (OBJECT PANAMA-CANAL)))
matching
(*GOAL* (*NAT-INTEGRITY* (ACTOR EGYPT) (OBJECT SINAI))) with
(*GOAL* (*POLITICAL-CONTROL* (ACTOR PANAMA) (OBJECT
PANAMA-CANAL)))

transferring other components of contract unchanged.

Figure 2.4: Reinstantiation in MEDIATOR

2.7   Explanation and Repair

When a case-based reasoner fails, it has to explain its failure and repair it. In some domains, the explanation comes first, and the repair is based on the explanation. For example, if a plan fails, the cause of the failure is explained first, and the explanation guides the repair. In other task domains, the repair has to come first. For example, suppose we have a system that diagnosis faults in electronic equipment by comparing what's going wrong in some system with things it has seen go wrong before. Suppose further that this system says that the fault is with some part and that part turns out to be in working order. Until the system generates a correct diagnosis and pinpoints what is really broken, it can't explain what's going on.

There are two kinds of failures when generating plans or other designs:

- Goals specified in the input are simply not achieved, i.e., a plan does not do what it's supposed to do, or a component blamed for a fault is in fact in working order.

- Implicit goals, not specified in the input, are violated, i.e., a plan achieves a goal but costs too much.

Implicit goals exist because there are usually so many possible things that might go wrong that it would be impractical to make avoiding them all explicit goals in every input. This is discussed further in Chapter 8. When an implicit goal is violated, the first thing to do is make it explicit for the given input situation. This is done in CHEF. Initially, for example, the input says "give me a spicy dish with beef and broccoli." When the recipe it generates produces soggy broccoli, violating the implicit goal of crisp broccoli, CHEF adds "keep broccoli crisp" as an implicit goal for the recipe. This means that when any future request retrieves this particular recipe, the goal "keep broccoli crisp" will be there for the adaptation rules to see.

The task of the explanation process is to generate a domain specific explanation of why the proposed solution failed. In a planning program, such as CHEF, the explanation is a causal chain leading from the steps in the plan to the violation of the goal. In a component fault diagnosis domain, the explanation is a causal chain leading from the failure of some component, other than the one diagnosed, to the observed fault symptoms.

The nature of the explanation process is a matter of current research. CHEF and COACH used rules to generate their explanations, but the complexity of the explanation process suggests that it is more often case-based than rule-based. The SWALE system explains by adapting explanations [Schank, 1986; Kass, 1986; Leake and Owens, 1986]. This approach is needed because there are so many possible explanations for anomalous events that we need to restrict the search to known classes of explanation.

2.7.1 Repair

Repair is similar to adaptation, in that a solution has to be modified to fit a situation. The difference is that adaptation starts with an old solution and a new case and adapts the solution to the new situation, while repair starts with a solution, a failure report, and maybe an explanation, and modifies the solution to remove the failure.

In domains where explanation precedes repair, the explanation of the failure will usually provide clues to the repairs needed. For example, in CHEF, explanations are linked via abstraction links to Thematic Organization Packages (TOPs). TOPs group failures into very general classes. The fact that cooking beef and broccoli together makes the broccoli soggy is a particular case of trying to do two goals with one action and having an unexpected interaction. Attached to TOPs are general heuristics for repairing the problem. Thus, one kind of repair associated with this TOP would be to use separate actions to achieve the two goals. Other repairs would try to prevent or counteract the bad interaction. CHEF would then turn these general suggestions into particular modifications for the problematic recipe. In the CHEF model, repair information attached to TOPs is independent of particular domains.

The CHEF model of repair does not apply to domains where explanations aren't possible until a correct solution has been found, such as in fault diagnosis. In this case, the only information available to the repair process is the diagnostic failure, e.g., "the part selected as cause of failure is not broken," or "the patient's spleen is not abnormal."

When the only information available is that a proposed solution didn't work, one repair strategy is to add whatever new information is available in the failure report, e.g., that a particular part is working or the patient's spleen is normal, and then search memory again for the best match. If the additional information causes a different case to be retrieved, then it should be adapted as the next solution. If the same case is retrieved as before, then an alternative repair strategy is to try adapting the second-best match.

Whenever solutions fail and are repaired, by whatever means, an important thing to do is to store a link between the solution that didn't work and the one that finally did. This is the failure link mentioned in the section on memory organization. It has the following purpose. Suppose the same case fails to apply again, in some other situation. That is, despite repairs and changes to the indexing and retrieval strategies after the first failure, the same case is again retrieved in inappropriate circumstances. When this happens, the system can look at any other failures associated with this case and try to generalize what is in common, if anything, between these times when this case has failed to worked. Both similarity-based and explanation-based generalization techniques would be applicable here. The goal is to find some characterization of the failing situations. With this characterization the system may be able to fix itself and avoid that class of failures in the future. At the very least, the system will be able to know when it is in situations where it has had difficulties before.

3

Implementing Micro MOPS

3.1 Introduction

This chapter contains an implementation of a miniature MOP-based memory system. The implementation is in a small subset (less than 10%) of the Common Lisp dialect of Lisp. There are a number of good introductions to Common Lisp available. We recommend in particular *Essential Lisp* [Anderson *et al.*, 1987], *Common Lispcraft* [Wilensky, 1986], and *Lisp, Second Edition*, [Winston and Horn, 1984]. For more advanced techniques, see *Artificial Intelligence Programming, Second Edition* [1987]. The ultimate authority and essential reference of course is the Common Lisp manual [Steele, 1984].

3.2 Some Basic Lisp Utilities

Before we can present our implementation of MOPs, we first have to define several utilities that will make our life as implementors a little easier. The code to implement these utilities appear in the Listings that follow. The Lisp interpreter will need all of this code before you can run any of the micro programs. Because of space considerations, and because Common Lisp is not really the topic of this book, we will not spend much time describing the various Common Lisp functions used in defining these utilites. Check your manual and the references on Common Lisp given above for more information.

3.2.1 Catching Errors

Our first utility is a simple function for nipping errors in the bud. One of the things that makes debugging a program hard is that when something goes wrong, e.g., a function gets a bad argument or returns a bad result, the

```
(DEFMACRO INSIST (FNNAME &REST EXPS)
 '(AND ,@(MAKE-INSIST-FORMS FNNAME EXPS)))

(DEFUN MAKE-INSIST-FORMS (FNNAME EXPS)
 (AND (NOT (NULL EXPS))
      (CONS '(OR ,(CAR EXPS)
                 (ERROR "~S failed in ~S"
                        ',(CAR EXPS) ',FNNAME))
            (MAKE-INSIST-FORMS FNNAME (CDR EXPS)))))
```

Listing 3.1: INSIST

evaluation process may continue for some time before something bad enough occurs for Lisp to complain with an error message. Sometimes, in fact, nothing may go wrong as far as Lisp is concerned. You run your 10,000 line Lisp program and it returns NIL instead of an in-depth analysis of *Hamlet*. Where did it start to go wrong?

The INSIST macro, defined in Listing 3.1, makes it relatively easy to put in run-time checks in your code to catch problems before they grow.

(INSIST *function-name expression*₁ *expression*₂ ...)

- INSIST evaluates the *expresssion*ᵢ from left to right. If one of them returns false, the message "*expresssion*ᵢ failed in *function-name*" is printed and the evaluation process halts. If all of the expressions return true, INSIST returns the value of the last expression.

For example, here's a definition of a function, SUM-SQUARES, that takes two numbers, squares them, and adds the results. We use INSIST to make sure that the arguments SUM-SQUARES gets really are numbers.

```
(DEFUN SUM-SQUARES (X Y)
 (INSIST SUM-SQUARES (NUMBERP X) (NUMBERP Y))
 (+ (* X X) (* Y Y)))
```

(SUM-SQUARES 5 9) will return 106. (SUM-SQUARES 5 'A) will cause the error messsage "(NUMBERP Y) failed in SUM-SQUARES" to be printed.

3.3   Tables

Our next utility makes it easy to store information in tables, indexed by symbols. One way to do this is to use *property lists*. A property list or *plist* in Common Lisp is a list (possibly NIL) of the form (key_1 $value_1$ key_2 $value_2$ ...). The key_i are usually symbols, and the $value_i$ can be anything.

```
(DEFINE-TABLE table-name (key) place)
```

DEFINE-TABLE is a macro. It does not evaluate its arguments. It defines *table-name* so that:

- (*table-name key*) returns the expression attached to *key* in the plist stored in *place*, if any.

- (SETF (*table-name key*) *value*) attaches *value* to *key* in the plist stored in *place*.

A *place* in Common Lisp is anything that can be assigned a value with SETF. For our purposes, *place* will be either a variable or another table.

We'll also define two auxilliary functions for manipulating the plists.

- (DELETE-KEY *plist key*) removes *key* and its value, if any, from *plist*.

- (TABLE-KEYS *plist*) returns a list of the keys in *plist*.

Here's an example that uses a table of employees and their ages:

```
(SETF *EMPLOYEE-AGES* NIL)
(DEFINE-TABLE EMPLOYEE-AGE (NAME) *EMPLOYEE-AGES*)
(SETF (EMPLOYEE-AGE 'JOHN) 30)
(EMPLOYEE-AGE 'JOHN)              ;returns 30
(SETF (EMPLOYEE-AGE 'MARY) 38)
(EMPLOYEE-AGE 'MARY)             ;returns 38
(TABLE-KEYS *EMPLOYEE-AGES*)     ;returns (MARY JOHN)
                                 ; or (JOHN MARY)
(DELETE-KEY *EMPLOYEE-AGES* 'JOHN)
(TABLE-KEYS *EMPLOYEE-AGES*)     ;returns (MARY)
```

With (TABLE-KEYS *plist*), we can tell whether a (*table-name key*) is returning NIL because *key* is not in the table or because NIL is the value assigned to *key*.

Listing 3.2 defines DEFINE-TABLE, DELETE-KEY and TABLE-KEYS. Figure 3.1 shows what DEFINE-TABLE expands into.

```
(DEFMACRO DEFINE-TABLE (FN VARS PLACE)
 (LET ((KEY (CAR VARS))
       (SET-FN (GENTEMP "SET-FN."))
       (VAL (GENTEMP "VAL.")))
  `(PROGN (DEFUN ,FN (,KEY) (GETF ,PLACE ,KEY))
          (DEFUN ,SET-FN (,KEY ,VAL)
           (SETF (GETF ,PLACE ,KEY) ,VAL))
          (DEFSETF ,FN ,SET-FN)
          ',FN)))

(DEFUN DELETE-KEY (TABLE KEY)
 (REMF TABLE KEY) TABLE)

(DEFUN TABLE-KEYS (TABLE)
 (AND TABLE
      (CONS (CAR TABLE)
            (TABLE-KEYS (CDR (CDR TABLE))))))
```

Listing 3.2: Definition of DEFINE-TABLE

```
(DEFINE-TABLE EMPLOYEE-AGE (NAME) *EMPLOYEE-AGES*)

;expands into

(PROGN (DEFUN EMPLOYEE-AGE (NAME)
        (GET *EMPLOYEE-AGE* NAME))
       (DEFUN SET-FN.1 (NAME VAL.2)
        (SETF (GETF *EMPLOYEE-AGES* NAME) VAL.2))
       (DEFSETF EMPLOYEE-AGE SET-FN.1)
       'EMPLOYEE-AGE)
```

Figure 3.1: Example Expansion of DEFINE-TABLE

3.4 Iteration with the FOR Macro

Standard Common Lisp has a set of *mapping functions* that apply a function to every element in a list: MAPC, MAPCAR, MAPCAN, EVERY, and so on. Which mapping function should be used depends on what needs to be done with those elements. Often, a minor change, such as skipping every element that is negative, can change the mapping function needed and the function applied by of the mapping function. The names of these mapping functions are not very perspicuous either.

The macro FOR is designed to make it easier to write iterations over lists. The macro expands into the appropriate call to a mapping function. For example, the following expression takes a list of numbers and adds them up.

```
(LET ((SUM 0))
  (FOR (X :IN '(9 2 -3 4 0 -1))
     :DO (SETF SUM (+ SUM X)))
  SUM)
```

The FOR sets X to 9, the first element of L, evaluates (SETF SUM (+ SUM X)), sets X to 2, reevaluates (SETF SUM (+ SUM X)), and so on, until all elements of L have been used. When the iteration is done, SUM will contain the final sum of 11.

If we wanted to return a list of each successive value of SUM, all we need to do is change the :DO in the FOR to :SAVE.

```
(LET ((SUM 0))
  (FOR (X :IN '(9 2 -3 4 0 -1))
     :SAVE (SETF SUM (+ SUM X)))
  SUM)
```

This returns the list (9 11 8 12 12 11). If we wanted to skip the negative numbers, we just add a :WHEN *expression* before the :SAVE or :DO. On each iteration, FOR will do the :SAVE or :DO only if the :WHEN expression is true.

```
(LET ((SUM 0))
  (FOR (X :IN '(9 2 -3 4 0 -1))
     :WHEN (NOT (< X 0))
     :SAVE (SETF SUM (+ SUM X)))
  SUM)
```

This returns the list (9 11 15 15).

FOR is called with the following format:

FOR-keyword	value of FOR
:ALWAYS	true if all the values of body are true
:DO	depends on Lisp implementation
:FILTER	a list of the non-NIL values of body
:FIRST	the first non-NIL value of body
:SAVE	a list of all the values of body
:SPLICE	a list of all the values of body, APPENDed together

Table 3.1: Rules for Final Value of FOR Forms

```
(FOR ((variable₁ :IN list₁)
      (variable₂ :IN list₂)
      ⋮)
     :WHEN when-expression
     FOR-keyword expression₁ expression₂ ...)
```

The $expression_i$ following *FOR-keyword* are called the *body* of the FOR. The evaluation rule for FOR is:

- Evaluate each $list_i$ form.

- Assign the first element of each list to the corresponding $variable_i$, and evaluate the body of the FOR.

- Assign the second element of each list to the corresponding $variable_i$ and evaluate the body again.

- Repeat until some list runs out of elements or the final value of the FOR is determined. Use Table 3.1 to determine the final value.

- If there is a :WHEN, then, on each iteration, evaluate the expression after the :WHEN and before the *FOR-keyword*. If the value of the :WHEN expression is true, evaluate the body of the FOR, otherwise skip to the next iteration.

If *FOR-keyword* is :ALWAYS or :FIRST, then the final value of the FOR form is determined as soon as a NIL or non-NIL is seen, respectively, in which case the iteration will stop before all list elements are examined.

Listing 3.3 gives the macro definition for FOR. Note that this code does not determine which mapping function to use, and what function should be mapped. That's done by procedures stored in tables, indexed by the different FOR-keywords. The code in Listing 3.3 puts the pieces together.

(FOR ...) is the FOR macro. Its syntax and semantics have already been discussed.

(FOR-VAR-FORMS *FOR-args*) is called with the arguments passed to FOR and returns a list of the (*variable* :IN *list*) forms. For simplicity, this definition assumes that everything up to the first atomic keyword is a variable specifier.

(FOR-BODY *FOR-args*) is called with the arguments passed to FOR and returns a list of the FOR-keyword and the expressions that follow it. Note that :WHEN is not a FOR-keyword. :WHEN is handled specially by FOR and should not be put in the FOR-keyword table.

(FOR-EXPANDER *var-form-list when-form body-form-list*) expands calls to the macro FOR. It calls the procedure attached to the FOR-keyword that begins *body-form-list* to get the mapping function and the body of the LAMBDA and it extracts the variables and values from *var-form-list*.

(DEFINE-FOR-KEY ...) is a macro for defining FOR keywords. The format for calling it is:

> (DEFINE-FOR-KEY *FOR-keyword* (*test-variable body-variable*)
> *mapping-function* LAMBDA-*body*)

DEFINE-FOR-KEY does not evaluate its arguments. When a FOR keyword is seen, the body, *test-variable* is set to the *expression* following the :WHEN and *body-variable* is set to the expression following the FOR keyword. (If more than one expression comes after the keyword, (PROGN *expression expression* ...) is created and passed.) The *mapping-function* and LAMBDA-*body* expressions are evaluated and a list of the two results is returned.

Definitions for FOR-keywords are stored in the table *FOR-KEYS* and accessed with the function FOR-KEY.

Listing 3.4 defines the standard set of FOR-keywords, using the macro DEFINE-FOR-KEY. Most of these definitions are straightforward. The definition for :SAVE checks for a :WHEN test in the FOR. A FOR with :SAVE and no :WHEN turns into a MAPCAR. Otherwise, a MAPCAN is needed, to splice out the NIL cases. The definition for :SPLICE uses COPY-LIST to copy the results of the FOR body before MAPCAN splices them together, to avoid unexpected side effects.

3.5 MOP-based Memory

The job of the memory system is to store and retrieve knowledge. This knowledge is represented in the form of Memory Organization Packagess (MOPs) [Schank, 1982], which are a kind of *frame* [Minsky, 1975]. There are basically two kind of MOPs: instances and abstractions. By convention, we will use

```
(SETF *FOR-KEYS* NIL)
(DEFINE-TABLE FOR-KEY (KEY) *FOR-KEYS*)

(DEFMACRO FOR (&REST FOR-CLAUSES)
 (LET ((WHEN-PART (MEMBER ':WHEN FOR-CLAUSES)))
  (FOR-EXPANDER (FOR-VAR-FORMS FOR-CLAUSES)
                (AND WHEN-PART (CAR (CDR WHEN-PART)))
                (FOR-BODY FOR-CLAUSES))))

(DEFUN FOR-VAR-FORMS (L)
 (AND L (LISTP (CAR L))
      (CONS (CAR L) (FOR-VAR-FORMS (CDR L)))))

(DEFUN FOR-BODY (L)
 (AND L (OR (AND (FOR-KEY (CAR L)) L)
            (FOR-BODY (CDR L)))))

(DEFUN FOR-EXPANDER (VAR-FORMS WHEN-FORM BODY-FORMS)
 (INSIST FOR
         (NOT (NULL VAR-FORMS))
         (NOT (NULL BODY-FORMS)))
 (LET ((VARS (MAPCAR #'CAR VAR-FORMS))
       (LISTS (MAPCAR #'(LAMBDA (VAR-FORM)
                          (CAR (CDR (CDR VAR-FORM))))
                      VAR-FORMS))
       (MAPFN-BODY (FUNCALL (FOR-KEY (CAR BODY-FORMS))
                            WHEN-FORM
                            '(PROGN ,@(CDR BODY-FORMS)))))
  '(,(CAR MAPFN-BODY)
    #'(LAMBDA ,VARS ,(CAR (CDR MAPFN-BODY)))
    ,@LISTS)))

(DEFMACRO DEFINE-FOR-KEY (KEY VARS MAPFN BODY)
 '(PROGN (SETF (FOR-KEY ',KEY)
               #'(LAMBDA ,VARS (LIST ,MAPFN ,BODY)))
         ',KEY))
```

Listing 3.3: Definition of FOR

```
(DEFINE-FOR-KEY :ALWAYS (TEST BODY)
 'EVERY
 (COND (TEST '(OR (NOT ,TEST) ,BODY)) (T BODY)))

(DEFINE-FOR-KEY :DO (TEST BODY)
 'MAPC (COND (TEST '(AND ,TEST ,BODY)) (T BODY)))

(DEFINE-FOR-KEY :FILTER (TEST BODY)
 'MAPCAN
 (LET ((FBODY '(LET ((X ,BODY)) (AND X (LIST X)))))
  (COND (TEST '(AND ,TEST ,FBODY)) (T FBODY))))

(DEFINE-FOR-KEY :FIRST (TEST BODY)
 'SOME (COND (TEST '(AND ,TEST ,BODY)) (T BODY)))

(DEFINE-FOR-KEY :SAVE (TEST BODY)
 (COND (TEST 'MAPCAN) (T 'MAPCAR))
 (COND (TEST '(AND ,TEST (LIST ,BODY)))
       (T BODY)))

(DEFINE-FOR-KEY :SPLICE (TEST BODY)
 'MAPCAN
 '(COPY-LIST
    ,(COND (TEST '(AND ,TEST ,BODY)) (T BODY))))
```

Listing 3.4: Definition of FOR Keywords

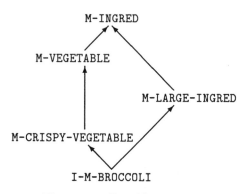

Figure 3.2: Toy Abstraction Hierarchy

names starting with M- for abstractions and names starting with I-M- for instances.

Instances sit at the bottom of the abstraction hierarchy. They have abstractions but no specializations. Instances represent cases, individual events, or objects. Abstractions are generalized versions of instances or other abstractions. One MOP is an *immediate abstraction* of another if there is a direct link from the more specific MOP to the more abstract MOP. Normally we will be interested in all the abstractions of a MOP. These include the MOP itself, its immediate abstractions, the immediate abstractions of the immediate abstractions, and so on.

One particular MOP, called M-ROOT, is the most abstract MOP of all, and sits at the top of the abstraction hierarchy. It has no immediate abstractions. Every other MOP has one or more immediate abstractions.

One important subclass of abstractions are *slotless abstractions*, that is, abstractions with no slots. These are necessary for concepts like M-INGRED (from Chapter 7), shown in Figure 3.2, which are defined solely by the MOPs or instances stored below them. Note that the instance I-M-BROCCOLI has two immediate abstractions, because it is both a large ingredient and a crisp vegetable.

The central process in MOP-based memory is the one that searches memory. The basic idea is simple. We start with a MOP and a set of slots describing an instance of that MOP. Each slot has a packaging link, called a *role*, and the MOP, called the *filler*, that the link points to. We search for the most specific specializations of the MOP that have slots compatible with the input slots. We might find an instance already in memory with exactly those slots, or we might have to add one.

For example, the abstraction hierarchy in Figure 3.3 is part of the one

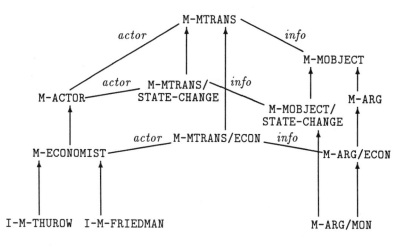

Figure 3.3: The Abstraction Hierarchy under M-MTRANS

used in micro DMAP (Chapter 11). M-MTRANS is the MOP that abstracts communication events. It has two specializations. M-MTRANS/ECON represents economists giving economic causal arguments. M-MTRANS/STATE-CHANGE represents someone predicting a state change.[1] There is also the MOP M-MOBJECT, which represents MOPs that can be the "mental" object of an M-MTRANS. A mental object has a CONTENT slot. If that slot is filled with an economic causal, then we have an M-ECON/ARG. If it is filled with a state change, then we have an M-MOBJECT/STATE-CHANGE. Figure 3.3 also shows two economists that can be actors of an M-MTRANS.

Suppose our input MOP M-MTRANS has the slots ((ACTOR M-ECONOMIST) (INFO M-ARG/ECON)). These slots match those of the MOP M-MTRANS/ECON under M-MTRANS, but not of M-MTRANS/STATE-CHANGE, so we refine the slots to M-MTRANS/ECON. This MOP has the same slots we gave as input, so all we need to do is return M-MTRANS/ECON.

Now suppose our input is M-MTRANS and the slots ((ACTOR I-M-FRIEDMAN) (INFO I-M-ARG.23)), where I-M-ARG.23 is an instance of M-ARG/MON. Once again, our input can be refined to the MOP M-MTRANS/ECON. In this case, however, our input slots are more specific than those of the MOP we have refined to. Therefore, we add a new instance under M-MTRANS/ECON. Our hierarchy will now look like that in Figure 3.4. Note that M-ARG/MON also has

---

[1]Since none of our micro programs have representations of time, the notion of "prediction" is not fully captured here.

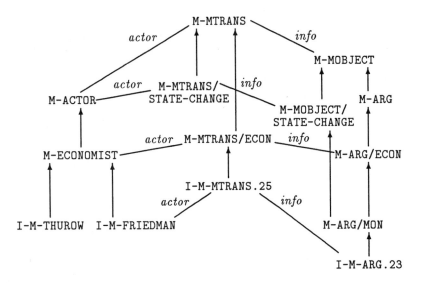

Figure 3.4: The New Abstraction Hierarchy under M-MTRANS

a new instance.

Now suppose we give the same input again, i.e., M-MTRANS and the slots ((ACTOR I-M-FRIEDMAN) (INFO I-M-ARG.23)). As before, our input can be refined to the MOP M-MTRANS/ECON. Now, however, it can be further refined to I-M-MTRANS.25.

This basic refinement process is pretty simple. It is a kind of pattern matching, where a set of slots matches another if every slot in the second set is filled with an abstraction of the corresponding filler in the first set. Thus, every filler in M-MTRANS/ECON is an abstraction of the corresponding filler in I-M-MTRANS.25.

This definition of matching is not complete. There are several situations we have to take care of. First, what should it do if our input has extra slots that are not in the MOP we are matching against? For example, suppose our input was the set of slots used above, plus the slot (TO I-M-REAGAN)? Should this still match M-MTRANS/ECON? How about I-M-MTRANS.25?

When matching slots against a MOP, our algorithm only looks at the slots mentioned by the MOP in memory. Extra slots in the input do not make any difference. This is compatible with the notion that if an abstraction does not mention a slot, then it doesn't care what value fills that slot.

However, once it reaches the bottom of the hierarchy, our algorithm checks to see if any instance in memory has all the slots in the input. Thus, if an input has slots not in any instance, a new instance will be built.

What should the algorithm do if there are slots in the MOP in memory that are not in the input? That is, should (ACTOR I-M-FRIEDMAN) match M-MTRANS/ECON, even though there is no INFO slot in the input? On the one hand, we could say "yes," because if the input doesn't say anything about a slot, then that slot might be what the MOP wants. On the other hand, very unintuitive matches result when this rule is combined with the previous one. For example, the input slots ((ANTE M-STATE-CHANGE) (CNSQ M-STATE-CHANGE)), which usually appear with M-CAUSAL, would match the slots of M-MTRANS/ECON because (1) the extra input slots ANTE and CNSQ would be ignored, and (2) the MOP slots ACTOR and INFO would match by default, because they don't appear in the input. When a causal form matches a communication event, something's amiss!

Our algorithm takes a compromise solution. If a MOP has a filler that is either an abstraction or a pattern (patterns will be described later), then the input must have the corresponding slot with a matching filler. However, if the MOP has a filler that is an instance and the input has no corresponding filler, the input matches the MOP.

Finally, what about slotless abstractions? Since they have no slots, any set of input slots would match them. Clearly we don't want a set of input slots describing an M-MTRANS to end up creating an instance under M-INGRED or M-ACTOR. Therefore, our algorithm says that input slots never match a slotless abstraction.

3.6 Implementation

We are going to represent MOPs with symbols; e.g., the symbol M-MTRANS is a MOP used in micro DMAP. This representation makes it very simple for the user to type MOPs into the system and for the system to print MOPs to the user. MOPs are linked to other MOPs via abstraction and packaging links.

Listing 3.5 defines a set of tables to hold these links. *MOP-TABLES* is a table of tables, indexed by table names. Each subtable is a table of MOP information, indexed by MOP name. Thus, (MOP-TABLE 'ABSTS) returns the table of immediate abstractions, and (MOP-ABSTS mop) looks in that table to find the immediate abstractions of mop. We put all the tables together into one master table to make it easier to do things like removing all traces of a MOP from memory.

MOP-ABSTS gives the *immediate* abstractions of a MOP. An immediate abstraction of a MOP is any other MOP that is exactly one abstraction link

```
(SETF *MOP-TABLES* NIL)

(DEFINE-TABLE MOP-TABLE (TABLE-NAME) *MOP-TABLES*)

(DEFINE-TABLE MOP-ABSTS (MOP) (MOP-TABLE 'ABSTS))
(DEFINE-TABLE MOP-ALL-ABSTS (MOP)
 (MOP-TABLE 'ALL-ABSTS))
(DEFINE-TABLE MOP-SPECS (MOP) (MOP-TABLE 'SPECS))
(DEFINE-TABLE MOP-SLOTS (MOP) (MOP-TABLE 'SLOTS))
(DEFINE-TABLE MOP-TYPE (MOP) (MOP-TABLE 'TYPE))
```

─────────────────────────── Listing 3.5: MOP Access Functions

above the first MOP. A MOP can not have an immediate abstraction link to itself.

MOP-ALL-ABSTS is a table of all the abstractions of MOPs. Listing 3.8 defines functions to calculate all the abstractions of a MOP.

MOP-SPECS is the opposite of MOP-ABSTS. It is a table of the immediate specializations of MOPs.

MOP-SLOTS is a table of the packaging links of MOPs. An entry in this table is a list of *slots*, where a slot is a list of a *role*, such as ACTOR or OBJECT, and a *filler*, which is any MOP.

MOP-TYPE holds the types of MOPs. Type can be either INSTANCE or MOP.

Listing 3.6 defines several basic MOP predicates.

(MOPP *exp*) returns true if *exp* is a MOP. A MOP is either a number or a symbol that has been stored in the table of MOP types. Every MOP has a type, so this is a good test of whether a symbol is really a MOP.

(INSTANCE-MOPP *exp*) returns true if *exp* is an instance.

(ABST-MOPP *exp*) returns true if *exp* is a abstraction MOP.

(ABSTP mop_1 mop_2) returns true if mop_1 is an abstraction, not necessarily immediate, of mop_2. The explicit EQL is needed for numbers, which aren't stored in MOP-ALL-ABSTS.

(PATTERNP *mop*) returns true if *mop* is a specialization of the M-PATTERN. Pattern MOPs are used to hold pattern matching and role filling information, and will be described later.

(GROUPP *mop*) returns true if *mop* is a specialization of the MOP M-GROUP. Group MOPs are used to hold groups of MOPs, e.g., the group of steps in a recipe or the group of events in a fight. Functions for manipulating group MOPs will be defined later.

```
(DEFUN MOPP (X)
 (OR (NUMBERP X) (AND (SYMBOLP X) (MOP-TYPE X))))

(DEFUN INSTANCE-MOPP (X)
 (AND (MOPP X)
      (OR (NUMBERP X)
          (EQL (MOP-TYPE X) 'INSTANCE))))

(DEFUN ABST-MOPP (X)
 (AND (MOPP X)
      (EQL (MOP-TYPE X) 'MOP)))

(DEFUN ABSTP (ABST SPEC)
 (OR (EQL ABST SPEC)
     (MEMBER ABST (MOP-ALL-ABSTS SPEC))))

(DEFUN PATTERNP (X) (ABSTP 'M-PATTERN X))

(DEFUN GROUPP (X) (ABSTP 'M-GROUP X))
```

Listing 3.6: MOP Predicates

Listing 3.7 defines the functions for getting at the slots of a MOP. A slot has the form (*role filler*) where *role* is a symbol or number representing role name, and *filler* is either a MOP or NIL.

(SLOT-ROLE *slot*) returns the role of *slot*.

(SLOT-FILLER *slot*) returns the filler of *slot*.

(MAKE-SLOT *role mop*) makes a slot containing *role* and *mop*.

(ROLE-SLOT *role slot-source*) returns the slot in *slot-source* whose role is *role*. *slot-source* can either be a list of slots or a MOP, in which case the slots of the MOP are searched.

(ROLE-FILLER *role slot-source*) returns the filler associated with *role* in the slots in *slot-source*.

(ADD-ROLE-FILLER *role mop filler*) adds the slot (*role filler*) to the slots of *mop*. *filler* is returned. ADD-ROLE-FILLER prints a message to help you keep track of what's going on. It is an error if *mop* already has a slot with the given role.

Listing 3.8 defines the functions that link MOPs to their abstractions and specializations.

(LINK-ABST *mop₁ mop₂*) makes *mop₂* an immediate abstraction of *mop₁*. It prevents linking a MOP to an instance, itself or an abstraction of itself. If the MOPs are already linked, nothing happens. Otherwise *mop₂* is put in the immediate abstraction table for *mop₁* and *mop₁* is put in the immediate specialization table for *mop₂*. The abstraction hierarchy is updated and *mop₁* is returned.

(UNLINK-ABST *mop₁ mop₂*) removes the abstraction link between the two mops, if any, updates the abstraction hierarchy, and returns *mop₁*.

(REDO-ALL-ABSTS *mop*) recalculates all the abstractions for *mop*. It then recursively calls itself to recalculate all the abstractions for the specializations of *mop*.

(CALC-ALL-ABSTS *mop*) calculates a list of all the abstractions for *mop*. We assume that all the abstractions are correct for the immediate abstractions of *mop*, so all we have to do is get those abstractions, with MOP-ALL-ABSTS, add *mop* itself to the front of the list, and remove duplicates. An important property of this list of all abstractions is that no MOP appears before any of its specializations. For example, in the list of all abstractions of I-M-BROCCOLI in Figure 3.2, M-INGRED must appear last, and M-VEGETABLE must appear after M-CRISP-VEGETABLE. The Common Lisp function REMOVE-DUPLICATES, which removes the earlier occurrences of duplicates from a list, does just the right thing.

Listing 3.9 defines the functions to make a MOP.

(NEW-MOP *name mop-list type slot-list*) makes a MOP named *name*, of

```
(DEFUN SLOT-ROLE (SLOT) (CAR SLOT))
(DEFUN SLOT-FILLER (SLOT) (CAR (CDR SLOT)))
(DEFUN MAKE-SLOT (ROLE MOP) (LIST ROLE MOP))

(DEFUN ROLE-SLOT (ROLE X)
 (INSIST ROLE-SLOT
         (OR (MOPP X) (LISTP X)))
 (ASSOC ROLE
        (COND ((MOPP X) (MOP-SLOTS X))
              (T X))))

(DEFUN ROLE-FILLER (ROLE X)
 (SLOT-FILLER (ROLE-SLOT ROLE X)))

(DEFUN ADD-ROLE-FILLER (ROLE MOP FILLER)
 (INSIST ADD-ROLE-FILLER
         (MOPP MOP) (NULL (ROLE-FILLER ROLE MOP)))
 (FORMAT T "~&~S:~S <= ~S" MOP ROLE FILLER)
 (SETF (MOP-SLOTS MOP)
       (CONS (MAKE-SLOT ROLE FILLER)
             (MOP-SLOTS MOP)))
 FILLER)
```

Listing 3.7: Basic Role Access Functions

```
(DEFUN LINK-ABST (SPEC ABST)
 (INSIST LINK-ABST (ABST-MOPP ABST) (MOPP SPEC)
                   (NOT (ABSTP SPEC ABST)))
 (COND ((NOT (ABSTP ABST SPEC))
        (SETF (MOP-ABSTS SPEC)
              (CONS ABST (MOP-ABSTS SPEC)))
        (SETF (MOP-SPECS ABST)
              (CONS SPEC (MOP-SPECS ABST)))
        (REDO-ALL-ABSTS SPEC)))
 SPEC)

(DEFUN UNLINK-ABST (SPEC ABST)
 (COND ((ABSTP ABST SPEC)
        (SETF (MOP-ABSTS SPEC)
              (REMOVE ABST (MOP-ABSTS SPEC)))
        (SETF (MOP-SPECS ABST)
              (REMOVE SPEC (MOP-SPECS ABST)))
        (REDO-ALL-ABSTS SPEC)))
 SPEC)

(DEFUN REDO-ALL-ABSTS (MOP)
 (SETF (MOP-ALL-ABSTS MOP) (CALC-ALL-ABSTS MOP))
 (FOR (SPEC :IN (MOP-SPECS MOP))
    :DO (REDO-ALL-ABSTS SPEC)))

(DEFUN CALC-ALL-ABSTS (MOP)
 (REMOVE-DUPLICATES
  (CONS MOP (FOR (ABST :IN (MOP-ABSTS MOP))
               :SPLICE (MOP-ALL-ABSTS ABST)))))
```

Listing 3.8: Basic MOP Abstraction Functions

```
(DEFUN NEW-MOP (NAME ABSTS TYPE SLOTS)
 (INSIST NEW-MOP
         (SYMBOLP NAME)
         (FOR (ABST :IN ABSTS) :ALWAYS (MOPP ABST)))
 (OR TYPE (SETF TYPE (CALC-TYPE ABSTS SLOTS)))
 (OR NAME (SETF NAME (SPEC-NAME ABSTS TYPE)))
 (SETF (MOP-TYPE NAME) TYPE)
 (AND SLOTS (SETF (MOP-SLOTS NAME) SLOTS))
 (FOR (ABST :IN ABSTS) :DO (LINK-ABST NAME ABST))
 NAME)

(DEFUN CALC-TYPE (ABSTS SLOTS)
 (OR (FOR (ABST :IN ABSTS)
         :WHEN (PATTERNP ABST)
         :FIRST 'MOP)
     (AND (NULL SLOTS) 'MOP)
     (FOR (SLOT :IN SLOTS)
         :WHEN (NOT (INSTANCE-MOPP (SLOT-FILLER SLOT)))
         :FIRST 'MOP)
     'INSTANCE))

(DEFUN SPEC-NAME (ABSTS TYPE)
 (GENTEMP (FORMAT NIL (COND ((EQL TYPE 'MOP) "~S.")
                           (T "I-~S."))
                 (CAR ABSTS))))
```

Listing 3.9: MOP Construction Functions

type *type*, immediate abstractions *mop-list*, and slots *slot-list*. *type* can be either MOP, INSTANCE or NIL. If it's NIL, a default type is calculated. *name* must be a symbol or NIL. If it is NIL, a default name is calculated.

(CALC-TYPE *mop-list slot-list*) calculates the default type for a MOP with the given abstractions and slots. The result is INSTANCE if the MOP is not a specialization of a pattern MOP, has slots, and all the slot fillers are instances. Otherwise the result is MOP.

(SPEC-NAME *mop-list type*) constructs a name of the form *mop.integer* (or I-*mop.integer* for instances), where *mop* is the first MOP in *mop-list*. GENTEMP guarantees always to return a new name.

Listing 3.10 gives some bookkeeping functions for managing memory.

```
(DEFUN CLEAR-MEMORY ()
 (SETF *MOP-TABLES* NIL)
 (NEW-MOP 'M-ROOT NIL 'MOP NIL)
 (SETF (MOP-ALL-ABSTS 'M-ROOT)
       (CALC-ALL-ABSTS 'M-ROOT))
 'M-ROOT)

(DEFUN ALL-MOPS () (TABLE-KEYS (MOP-TABLE 'TYPE)))

(DEFUN REMOVE-MOP (NAME)
 (FOR (ABST :IN (MOP-ABSTS NAME))
   :DO (UNLINK-ABST NAME ABST))
 (FOR (TABLE-NAME :IN (TABLE-KEYS *MOP-TABLES*))
   :DO (SETF (MOP-TABLE TABLE-NAME)
             (DELETE-KEY (MOP-TABLE TABLE-NAME)
                         NAME)))))
```

Listing 3.10: Memory Management Functions

(CLEAR-MEMORY) removes all MOPs from memory and re-installs the root MOP M-ROOT. All MOPs in memory are attached somewhere under M-ROOT.

(ALL-MOPS) returns a list of all the MOPs in memory. It does this by getting all the keys in the MOP type table.

(REMOVE-MOP *mop*) removes *mop* from memory, by unlinking it from all its abstractions and then deleting it as a key from all the tables. Note that the table deletion has to come second, because we need to use the tables to get the abstractions of *mop*.

Listing 3.11 defines extensions of ROLE-FILLER that can find the fillers that a MOP inherits from its abstractions.

(INHERIT-FILLER *role mop*) returns the first filler of *role* found in either *mop* or one of its abstractions. The filler might be an instance, abstraction, or pattern MOP.

(GET-FILLER *role mop*) returns the filler for *role* in *mop*. The filler can either be an inherited instance or a calculated value. If a filler has to be calculated, a slot for that role and filler is added to *mop*. A filler is calculated when *role* inherits a pattern MOP with a *calculation function*. That function is called and the result is the new filler.

A calculation function is the name of a Lisp function, stored in the CALC-FN role of the pattern MOP. A calculation function should be defined with two

```
(DEFUN INHERIT-FILLER (ROLE MOP)
  (FOR (ABST :IN (MOP-ALL-ABSTS MOP))
     :FIRST (ROLE-FILLER ROLE ABST)))

(DEFUN GET-FILLER (ROLE MOP)
  (OR (ROLE-FILLER ROLE MOP)
    (LET ((FILLER (INHERIT-FILLER ROLE MOP)))
      (AND FILLER
        (OR (AND (INSTANCE-MOPP FILLER) FILLER)
          (AND (ABSTP 'M-FUNCTION FILLER) FILLER)
          (LET ((FN (GET-FILLER 'CALC-FN FILLER)))
            (AND FN
              (LET ((NEW-FILLER (FUNCALL FN FILLER MOP)))
                (AND NEW-FILLER
                  (ADD-ROLE-FILLER ROLE MOP
                                   NEW-FILLER)))))))))))

(DEFUN PATH-FILLER (PATH MOP)
  (AND (FOR (ROLE :IN PATH)
           :ALWAYS (SETF MOP (GET-FILLER ROLE MOP)))
       MOP))
```

Listing 3.11: Extended Role Access Functions

parameters, to hold the inherited pattern MOP filler and *mop*. One important type of calculation function is the *adaptation function*. An adaptation function calculates the filler of a role by adapting the filler of that same role in some sibling instance.

(PATH-FILLER *path mop*) returns the filler for *path* in *mop*. A path is a list of roles, and PATH-FILLER follows that list in order, using GET-FILLER. For example, (PATH-FILLER '(EXPLANATION CAUSE) 'I-M-REPAIR.12) first gets the EXPLANATION filler of I-M-REPAIR.12, and, if that succeeds, gets the CAUSE filler of the result.

Listing 3.12 defines functions for comparing MOPs. These functions are used when a new MOP is stored to determine where it can fit in memory.

(SLOTS-ABSTP *mop slot-source*) returns true if every slot in *mop* is "satisfied" by the corresponding slot in *slot-source*. *slot-source* is usually an instance, though it can be a list of slots. The slot fillers in *mop* are treated as *constraints* on the slot fillers in *slot-source*. *mop* must be an abstraction and have at least one slot to be satisfied.

(SATISFIEDP *constraint filler slot-source*) returns true if *filler* satisfies the conditions specified by *constraint*. A constraint is satisfied if

- The constraint is NIL.

- The constraint is a pattern MOP whose *abstraction function* returns true when called with *constraint, filler* and *slot-source*. An abstraction function is the name of a Lisp function stored in the ABST-FN role of the pattern MOP.

- The constraint is an abstraction of the filler.

- The constraint is an instance MOP and the filler is empty. The slot source can inherit the instance when needed.

- The constraint has at least one slot, the filler is not empty, and all of its slots are satisfied by the slots of the filler.

Slotless abstractions are treated specially, because they have no slots to constrain what can go under them. Strictly speaking, anything could go under any slotless abstraction. To reduce things going where they don't belong, MOPs can only be put under slotless abstractions with explicit calls to NEW-MOP or DEFMOP.

Listing 3.13 defines functions for determining if one MOP is the same as another.

(MOP-INCLUDESP mop_1 mop_2) returns mop_1 if it includes mop_2. This is true if the two MOPs have the same type and every slot in mop_2 is also in mop_1. mop_1 might have slots that are not in mop_2.

(MOP-EQUALP mop_1 mop_2) returns mop_1 if mop_1 and mop_2 are the same.

(GET-TWIN *mop*) returns the first MOP in memory it can find that is equal to *mop*, if any.

Listing 3.14 defines a function that *refines* instances. Refining an instance means pushing the instance farther down the abstraction hierarchy, by replacing some abstraction of the instance with specializations of that abstraction.

(REFINE-INSTANCE *instance*) takes each abstraction of *instance* and tries to replace it with one or more specializations of the abstraction. It repeats this process until all abstractions of *instance* are as specialized as possible.

(MOPS-ABSTP *mop-list instance*) looks at each MOP in *mop-list*. If the MOP can abstract *instance*, a link from *instance* to the MOP is made. True is returned if at least one such MOP is found.

Listing 3.15 defines the functions that store an instance in memory. This involves first moving the instance as low in memory as possible, by refining

```
(DEFUN SLOTS-ABSTP (MOP SLOTS)
  (AND (ABST-MOPP MOP)
       (NOT (NULL (MOP-SLOTS MOP)))
       (FOR (SLOT :IN (MOP-SLOTS MOP))
          :ALWAYS (SATISFIEDP (SLOT-FILLER SLOT)
                      (GET-FILLER (SLOT-ROLE SLOT)
                                  SLOTS)
                      SLOTS)))))

(DEFUN SATISFIEDP (CONSTRAINT FILLER SLOTS)
  (COND ((NULL CONSTRAINT))
        ((PATTERNP CONSTRAINT)
         (FUNCALL (INHERIT-FILLER 'ABST-FN CONSTRAINT)
                  CONSTRAINT FILLER SLOTS))
        ((ABSTP CONSTRAINT FILLER))
        ((INSTANCE-MOPP CONSTRAINT) (NULL FILLER))
        (FILLER (SLOTS-ABSTP CONSTRAINT FILLER))
        (T NIL)))
```

Listing 3.12: Extended MOP Abstraction Predicates

```
(DEFUN MOP-INCLUDESP (MOP1 MOP2)
 (AND (EQL (MOP-TYPE MOP1) (MOP-TYPE MOP2))
      (FOR (SLOT :IN (MOP-SLOTS MOP2))
         :ALWAYS (EQL (SLOT-FILLER SLOT)
                      (GET-FILLER (SLOT-ROLE SLOT)
                                  MOP1)))
      MOP1))

(DEFUN MOP-EQUALP (MOP1 MOP2)
 (AND (MOP-INCLUDESP MOP2 MOP1)
      (MOP-INCLUDESP MOP1 MOP2)))

(DEFUN GET-TWIN (MOP)
 (FOR (ABST :IN (MOP-ABSTS MOP))
    :FIRST (FOR (SPEC :IN (MOP-SPECS ABST))
             :WHEN (NOT (EQL SPEC MOP))
             :FIRST (MOP-EQUALP SPEC MOP))))
```

Listing 3.13: MOP Equality Functions

```
(DEFUN REFINE-INSTANCE (INSTANCE)
 (FOR (ABST :IN (MOP-ABSTS INSTANCE))
    :WHEN (MOPS-ABSTP (MOP-SPECS ABST) INSTANCE)
    :FIRST (UNLINK-ABST INSTANCE ABST)
           (REFINE-INSTANCE INSTANCE)))

(DEFUN MOPS-ABSTP (MOPS INSTANCE)
 (NOT (NULL (FOR (MOP :IN MOPS)
               :WHEN (SLOTS-ABSTP MOP INSTANCE)
               :SAVE (LINK-ABST INSTANCE MOP)))))
```

Listing 3.14: Refining Functions

```
(DEFUN INSTALL-INSTANCE (INSTANCE)
 (REFINE-INSTANCE INSTANCE)
 (LET ((TWIN (GET-TWIN INSTANCE)))
  (COND (TWIN (REMOVE-MOP INSTANCE) TWIN)
        ((HAS-LEGAL-ABSTS-P INSTANCE) INSTANCE)
        (T (REMOVE-MOP INSTANCE) NIL))))

(DEFUN HAS-LEGAL-ABSTS-P (INSTANCE)
 (FOR (ABST :IN (MOP-ABSTS INSTANCE))
   :WHEN (NOT (LEGAL-ABSTP ABST INSTANCE))
   :DO (UNLINK-ABST INSTANCE ABST))
 (MOP-ABSTS INSTANCE))

(DEFUN LEGAL-ABSTP (ABST INSTANCE)
 (AND (MOP-SLOTS ABST)
      (FOR (SPEC :IN (MOP-SPECS ABST))
        :ALWAYS (INSTANCE-MOPP SPEC))))
```

Listing 3.15: Instance Installation Functions

its abstractions, then checking to see if the instance is already in memory under another name. We also impose the additional constraints that instances can not go under instances, slotless abstractions, or abstractions of abstractions. It is an enlightening experiment to relax these rules by redefining HAS-LEGAL-ABSTS-P to return true always. You'll find instances ending up in places you never expected.

(INSTALL-INSTANCE *instance*) puts an instance in memory. First it refines the instance's abstractions, then it checks if any instance in memory includes this one. If so, *instance* is removed and the old instance is returned. If not, illegal abstractions are unlinked. If any abstractions are left, *instance* is returned, otherwise *instance* is removed and NIL is returned.

(HAS-LEGAL-ABSTS-P *instance*) unlinks every immediate abstraction of *instance* that is not a legal place to put *instance*, and returns whatever immediate abstractions are left.

(LEGAL-ABSTP *mop instance*) returns true if *mop* is a legal place to put *instance*, i.e., *mop* is not slotless and does not have abtractions below it.

Listing 3.16 defines the functions for adding an abstraction to memory. Abstraction MOPs are not "pushed down" in memory, but are attached directly to whatever abstractions are explicitly specified, unless an identical

```
(DEFUN INSTALL-ABSTRACTION (MOP)
 (LET ((TWIN (GET-TWIN MOP)))
  (COND (TWIN (REMOVE-MOP MOP) TWIN)
        (T (REINDEX-SIBLINGS MOP)))))

(DEFUN REINDEX-SIBLINGS (MOP)
 (FOR (ABST :IN (MOP-ABSTS MOP))
    :DO (FOR (SPEC :IN (MOP-SPECS ABST))
          :WHEN (AND (INSTANCE-MOPP SPEC)
                     (SLOTS-ABSTP MOP SPEC))
          :DO (UNLINK-ABST SPEC ABST)
              (LINK-ABST SPEC MOP)))
  MOP)
```

Listing 3.16: Abstraction Installation Functions

MOP already exists.

(INSTALL-ABSTRACTION *mop*) installs a new abstraction. If an identical MOP is already in memory, it is returned. Otherwise, any instances of *mop*'s abstractions that can go under *mop* are put there, and *mop* is returned.

(REINDEX-SIBLINGS *mop*) finds all instances that are immediate specializations of immediate abstractions of *mop*. The instances are unlinked from their abstractions and relinked to *mop*. *mop* is returned.

Listing 3.17 defines the function that adds a new MOP to memory.

(SLOTS->MOP *slot-list mop-list must-work*) returns a MOP with the slots in *slot-list* and the abstractions in *mop-list*. If the first element of *slot-list* is an atom, it is the type of MOP desired, i.e., MOP or INSTANCE. If *slot-list* is empty and *mop-list* contains just one MOP, that MOP is returned immediately. Otherwise a MOP is constructed and installed as an instance or abstraction, as appropriate. Installation may return an existing MOP in memory or the MOP just constructed. If *must-work* is true, an error is signaled if a MOP can't be installed for some reason. If *must-work* is false, then NIL is returned when installation fails.

Listing 3.18 defines functions that convert lists into MOPs. DEFMOP is the basic macro for defining new MOPs. The calling format is:

(DEFMOP *name mop-list type slot-form$_1$ slot-form$_2$* ...)

where *type* is an optional argument specifying the type of the MOP being defined. If present, it should be either MOP or INSTANCE. If omitted, the type will be calculated by CALC-TYPES (Listing 3.9).

```
(DEFUN SLOTS->MOP (SLOTS ABSTS MUST-WORK)
 (INSIST SLOTS->MOP
         (NOT (NULL ABSTS))
         (FOR (ABST :IN ABSTS) :ALWAYS (MOPP ABST)))
 (OR (AND (NULL SLOTS) (NULL (CDR ABSTS)) (CAR ABSTS))
     (LET ((TYPE (AND SLOTS (ATOM (CAR SLOTS))
                       (CAR SLOTS))))
      (AND TYPE (SETF SLOTS (CDR SLOTS)))
      (LET ((MOP (NEW-MOP NIL ABSTS TYPE SLOTS)))
       (LET ((RESULT
              (COND ((INSTANCE-MOPP MOP)
                     (INSTALL-INSTANCE MOP))
                    (T (INSTALL-ABSTRACTION MOP)))))
        (INSIST SLOTS->MOP
                (OR RESULT (NULL MUST-WORK)))
        RESULT)))))
```

Listing 3.17: Top-Level Memory Update Functions

DEFMOP defines a MOP named *name* with the immediate abtractions *mop-list*, type *type*, and slots as specified by the slot-forms *slot-form$_i$*. A slot form is a list containing a role name, a MOP, an optional MOP type (MOP or INSTANCE), and zero or more slot forms.

DEFMOP expands into the appropriate call to NEW-MOP and FORMS->SLOTS. Because LINK-ABST (Listing 3.8) and NEW-MOP (Listing 3.9) insist that the abstraction be an already defined MOP, the abstractions of a MOP should always be defined first. It's not hard to remove this constraint, but it's easier to catch spelling errors this way.

(FORMS->SLOTS *slot-form-list mop*) converts a list of slot forms into a list of slots. A slot is a list of the form (*role filler-mop*). A slot form may either have this form, in which case it is already a slot, or it may have one or more slot forms following *filler-mop*. In this case, the slot forms are converted to slots recursively and the result is turned into a specialization of *filler-mop*, using SLOTS->MOP. If the first element of *slot-form-list* is an atom, it is kept for later use as a MOP type by SLOTS->MOP.

For example,

```
(DEFMOP M-MTRANS/ECON (M-MTRANS)
    (ACTOR M-ECONOMIST)
    (INFO M-ARG (CONTENT M-CAUSAL/ECON)))
```

```
(DEFMACRO DEFMOP (NAME ABSTS &REST ARGS)
 (LET ((TYPE (AND ARGS (ATOM (CAR ARGS)) (CAR ARGS))))
  (LET ((SLOT-FORMS (COND (TYPE (CDR ARGS))
                          (T ARGS))))
   '(NEW-MOP ',NAME ',ABSTS ',TYPE
             (FORMS->SLOTS ',SLOT-FORMS)))))

(DEFUN FORMS->SLOTS (SLOT-FORMS)
 (FOR (SLOT-FORM :IN SLOT-FORMS)
    :SAVE
      (COND ((ATOM SLOT-FORM) SLOT-FORM)
        (T (MAKE-SLOT (SLOT-ROLE SLOT-FORM)
              (LET ((ABST (CAR (CDR SLOT-FORM))))
               (INSIST FORMS->SLOTS (ATOM ABST))
               (AND ABST
                 (SLOTS->MOP
                  (FORMS->SLOTS (CDR (CDR SLOT-FORM)))
                  (LIST ABST)
                  T)))))))))
```

Listing 3.18: Form to MOP Functions

defines a MOP called M-MTRANS/ECON which is a specialization of M-MTRANS. There are two slot forms. (ACTOR M-ECONOMIST) is already a slot, but (INFO M-ARG (CONTENT M-CAUSAL/ECON)) has to be converted, by finding (or creating) a MOP under M-ARG with the slot (CONTENT M-CAUSAL/ECON).

Listing 3.19 defines functions for manipulating groups, which are particular kind of MOP. A group MOP represents a set of MOPs, such as the steps in a recipe. If n is the size of a group, then the slots of the group are (1 mop_1), (2 mop_2), ... (n mop_n). The empty group is represented by the instance I-M-EMPTY-GROUP, which is not the same as the MOP M-GROUP, even though both are slotless MOPs. The former is the (unique) instance of the empty group, while the latter is the slotless abstraction of all groups, empty and filled.

The implementation below does not check to see if the roles are correctly numbered and ordered. There are two functions for converting between lists and groups.

(GROUP-SIZE *group*) returns the size of the group.

(GROUP->LIST *group*) returns a list of the members of the group. The

```
(DEFUN GROUP-SIZE (X)
  (AND (GROUPP X) (LENGTH (MOP-SLOTS X))))

(DEFUN GROUP->LIST (GROUP)
  (AND GROUP
       (INSIST GROUP->LIST (GROUPP GROUP))
       (FOR (INDEX :IN (MAKE-M-N 1 (GROUP-SIZE GROUP)))
         :FILTER (ROLE-FILLER INDEX GROUP))))

(DEFUN LIST->GROUP (L)
  (COND ((NULL L) 'I-M-EMPTY-GROUP)
        (T (SLOTS->MOP
             (FOR (X :IN L)
                  (I :IN (MAKE-M-N 1 (LENGTH L)))
               :SAVE (MAKE-SLOT I X))
             '(M-GROUP)
             T))))

(DEFUN MAKE-M-N (M N)
  (INSIST MAKE-M-N (INTEGERP M) (INTEGERP N))
  (COND ((EQL M N) (LIST N))
        ((< M N) (CONS M (MAKE-M-N (+ M 1) N)))
        (T (CONS M (MAKE-M-N (- M 1) N)))))
```

Listing 3.19: Group MOP Functions

filler of role 1 is first, role 2 is second, and so on.

(LIST->GROUP *list*) returns a group MOP with members from *list*. The first element of *list* fills role 1, the second fills role 2, and so on. If the list is empty, the special empty group is returned.

(MAKE-M-N *integer$_1$ integer$_2$*) generates a list of integers from *integer$_1$* to *integer$_2$*, inclusive. The first integer can be greater than, equal to, or smaller than the second.

Listing 3.20 defines some functions for printing the contents of memory in a readable format. The functions DAH and DPH have short but cryptic names to make them easier to type interactively. They call a set of internal functions that search memory and return a list representation of the tree of connections between MOPs. These internal functions all take a list of MOPs as their second argument, which is used to avoid visiting the same MOP twice.

(DAH *mop*) prints all the specializations under *mop*. The name is short for "display abstraction hierarchy."

(DPH *mop*) prints the slots of *mop*, the slots of the fillers of the slots of *mop*, and so on. The name is short for "display packaging hierarchy."

(SPECS->LIST *mop mop-list*) returns a list starting with *mop*, followed by the specialization tree under each specializations of *mop*.

(SLOTS->FORMS *mop mop-list*) converts the slots in *mop* into a list of slot forms, by expanding out the slots in each slot filler.

(MOP->FORM *mop mop-list*) returns a list starting with *mop*, followed by slots of MOP converted into slot forms.

(TREE->LIST *mop function mop-list*) returns a list starting with *mop*, followed by the elements of the list returned by calling *function* with *mop* and *mop-list* updated to include *mop*. If *mop* is already in *mop-list*, just a list with *mop* is returned.

Listing 3.21 defines a few basic MOPs used by all of the micro programs. The first few are obvious. Note that we use the convention of beginning abstraction names with M- and instance names with I-M-, except for certain special cases, such as the names of roles and Lisp functions.

Under M-GROUP we define both the MOP M-EMPTY-GROUP and the instance I-M-EMPTY-GROUP. This is because we want M-GROUP to organize abstractions such as the MOP for all groups of events and the MOP for all groups of objects. If M-GROUP is to hold MOPs, however, then it shouldn't also hold instances, according to LEGAL-ABSTP in Listing 3.15. So we create a dummy abstraction MOP under which we can put the instance I-M-EMPTY-GROUP.

M-FUNCTION is the MOP under which we put the names of all Lisp functions referred to in pattern MOPs. The specializations of M-FUNCTION referred to in this Listing are defined in Lisp in Listing 3.22.

M-PATTERN is for pattern MOPs. It's abstraction function, CONSTRAINT-FN, always returns true. Any specialization of M-PATTERN that does not define its own abstraction function will call this one.

M-CASE is the MOP that supports case-based adaptation. Every specialization of M-CASE inherits the OLD slot into which a case for adaptation will be put, on demand, by the GET-SIBLING calculation function.

M-ROLE is the MOP for roles, e.g., ACTOR or OBJECT. Many pattern MOPs use roles to refer to parts of a MOP. Strictly speaking, we should define all roles that we use as M-ROLE's, but, for brevity, we'll only define those actually used as fillers in pattern MOPs. Micro MOPS will complain if you try to use an undefined role.

M-NOT is a pattern MOP for negative constraints. NOT-CONSTRAINT is its abstraction function.

```
(DEFUN DAH (MOP)
 (PPRINT (TREE->LIST MOP #'SPECS->LIST NIL)))

(DEFUN DPH (MOP)
 (PPRINT (TREE->LIST MOP #'SLOTS->FORMS NIL)))

(DEFUN SPECS->LIST (MOP VISITED)
 (FOR (SPEC :IN (MOP-SPECS MOP))
    :SAVE (TREE->LIST SPEC #'SPECS->LIST VISITED)))

(DEFUN SLOTS->FORMS (MOP VISITED)
 (FOR (SLOT :IN (MOP-SLOTS MOP))
    :SAVE (CONS (SLOT-ROLE SLOT)
               (MOP->FORM (SLOT-FILLER SLOT)
                          VISITED))))

(DEFUN MOP->FORM (MOP VISITED)
 (TREE->LIST MOP #'SLOTS->FORMS VISITED))

(DEFUN TREE->LIST (MOP FN VISITED)
 (COND ((MEMBER MOP VISITED) (LIST MOP))
       (T (SETF VISITED (CONS MOP VISITED))
          '(,MOP ,@(FUNCALL FN MOP VISITED)))))
```

Listing 3.20: MOP Display Functions

```
(DEFMOP M-EVENT (M-ROOT))
(DEFMOP M-STATE (M-ROOT))
(DEFMOP M-ACT (M-ROOT))
(DEFMOP M-ACTOR (M-ROOT))

(DEFMOP M-GROUP (M-ROOT))
(DEFMOP M-EMPTY-GROUP (M-GROUP))
(DEFMOP I-M-EMPTY-GROUP (M-EMPTY-GROUP) INSTANCE)

(DEFMOP M-FUNCTION (M-ROOT))
(DEFMOP CONSTRAINT-FN (M-FUNCTION))

(DEFMOP M-PATTERN (M-ROOT) (ABST-FN CONSTRAINT-FN))

(DEFMOP GET-SIBLING (M-FUNCTION))

(DEFMOP M-CASE (M-ROOT)
    (OLD M-PATTERN (CALC-FN GET-SIBLING)))

(DEFMOP M-ROLE (M-ROOT))

(DEFMOP NOT-CONSTRAINT (CONSTRAINT-FN))
(DEFMOP M-NOT (M-PATTERN) (ABST-FN NOT-CONSTRAINT))

(DEFMOP M-FAILED-SOLUTION (M-ROOT))
```

Listing 3.21: Basic MOPS

M-FAILED-SOLUTION is the MOP under which all solutions that fail are placed. Such solutions are not selected for adaptation.

Listing 3.22 defines the abstraction and calculation functions referred to in Listing 3.21. All abstraction functions take three arguments: a constraint, a filler, and the source of slots the filler came from (see Listing 3.12). They should return true only if the filler satisfies the constraint.

(CONSTRAINT-FN *constraint filler slot-source*) always returns true, that is, there is no constraint on *filler*.

(NOT-CONSTRAINT *constraint filler slot-source*) is true if *filler* does not satisfy the constraint found in the OBJECT slot of *constraint*. For example, M-NOT (OBJECT M-INGRED) would be satisfied by any MOP that is not an

```
(DEFUN CONSTRAINT-FN (CONSTRAINT FILLER SLOTS) T)

(DEFUN NOT-CONSTRAINT (CONSTRAINT FILLER SLOTS)
 (INSIST NOT-CONSTRAINT (NOT (NULL FILLER)))
 (NOT (SATISFIEDP (GET-FILLER 'OBJECT CONSTRAINT)
                  FILLER SLOTS)))

(DEFUN GET-SIBLING (PATTERN MOP)
 (FOR (ABST :IN (MOP-ABSTS MOP))
   :FIRST (FOR (SPEC :IN (MOP-SPECS ABST))
              :WHEN (AND (INSTANCE-MOPP SPEC)
                         (NOT (EQL SPEC MOP))
                         (NOT (ABSTP
                                 'M-FAILED-SOLUTION
                                 SPEC)))
              :FIRST SPEC)))
```

Listing 3.22: Basic Abstraction and Calculation Functions

M-INGRED.

All calculation functions take two arguments: a pattern and a MOP (see Listing 3.11). They should return a MOP.

(GET-SIBLING *pattern mop*) finds a sibling of *mop*. It is only defined for instance MOPs.

3.7 Extensions

The model of MOP-based memory presented in this chapter is in many ways much simpler than those to be found in systems such as IPP [Lebowitz, 1980] or CYRUS [Kolodner, 1984]. On the other hand, the use of pattern MOPs to link in procedural information is an extension to the standard MOP systems.

It's hard to discuss extensions to micro MOPS until we have some applications to motivate them. Thus, most extensions to micro MOPS will arise in the extensions proposed in the later chapters describing the micro case-based reasoners.

3.7.1   Structures versus Tables

To keep things simple, and to allow for easy transfer to Lisp subsets, we stored all MOP information in tables. The more common technique in Common Lisp would be to store most of this information with *structures*. Structures are convenient and, depending on your implementation, can be very efficient. They are defined with the function DEFSTRUCT. For example,

```
(DEFSTRUCT MOP NAME ABSTS ALL-ABSTS SPECS SLOTS TYPE)
```

would define the functions MOP-NAME, MOP-ABSTS, MOP-ALL-ABSTS, and so on, for accessing and setting the attributes of a MOP, e.g., (SETF (MOP-TYPE *mop*) *type*) would set the type of *mop*. Furthermore, this DEFSTRUCT would define a function called MAKE-MOP for constructing MOPs. NEW-MOP in Listing 3.9 would call MAKE-MOP to put all the attributes together.

If we use structures, most of our changes in micro MOPS will occur in Listing 3.9. A MOP would no longer be identical with its name, so we would need functions to go from names to MOP structures and back. The DEFSTRUCT above defines a field MOP-NAME where we can store a MOP's name, so (MOP-NAME *mop*) would map MOPs to names. We should define NAME->MOP to be a table of MOPs indexed by MOP names, so that (NAME->MOP *name*) would map names to MOPs. We would also probably want to define a *print-function* for MOPs, so that MOP structures would be automatically printed in a readable fashion, e.g., #<MOP *name*>. See [Steele, 1984] for details on using structures. If you are using a dialect of Lisp, see if it has something equivalent to DEFSTRUCT. If not, see [Charniak *et al.*, 1980] for details on how to define your own structure package.

3.7.2   Debugging Tools

As you play with the micro programs in the later chapters, you'll certainly run into bugs. The most common problem is misplaced MOPs. SLOTS->MOP puts a set of input slots where you didn't want it, and/or doesn't put it where you did want it. The source of the bug might be a simple typographical error, or a subtle mistake in the definition of a pattern constraint. If you start playing with the basic refinement functions, e.g., those in Listing 3.12, MOPs may end up in all sorts of unexpected places.

Experiment with creating different tools for finding these bugs and tracking down their causes. For example, most Lisp's have a facility for *tracing* a function, which means that whenever that function is called, a message is printed, indicating what arguments the function was called with and what value it returned. Some Lisps also have a facility for *breaking* a function, which means that whenever that function is called, a message is printed, and Lisp stops to let you type commands and see what is going on.

Try defining functions for tracing or breaking a MOP. The trace or break would be triggered when that MOP is matched against, or perhaps when it gets a new immediate specialization. Defining these functions will also require changing some of the functions in Listing 3.12 so that they look for traced or broken MOPs.

Try defining a function for testing slots that will tell you where a set of slots would go under a MOP, without actually installing anything in memory.

3.7.3 Memory Statistics

After running one of the micro programs, you can use DAH to look at the memory hierarchy. However, it can be easy to miss certain problems, such as instances being installed in unexpected places. It helps to create some tools for analyzing the state of memory.

Define a function, EMPTY-MOPS, that returns all the abstraction MOPs in memory that have no specializations. A few MOPs defined in Listing 3.21, such as M-ACTOR are not used in every micro program, but others may be empty because the instances that were supposed to go under them went astray.

Define another function, NON-EMPTY-INSTANCES, that returns all instances with specializations. There shouldn't be any, unless you made changes (intentionally or not) to the code for installing MOPs and instances.

Define another function, MIXED-MOPS, that returns all abstractions that have both instances and abstractions as immediate specializations. It is not necessarily wrong for this to happen, but we've avoided it in our definitions and code, and you should at least know if it's happening.

3.7.4 Improving Efficiency

Though it may not appear so, we tried very hard to keep the code for micro MOPS as short and simple as possible, given the applications we wanted to implement in it. There are many places where things could be made more efficient.

One of the simplest things you can do is compile your code, if your Lisp has a compiler. Some Lisps have no compiler, and some Lisps automatically compile everything, but most Lisps make compilation an optional extra step. One of the most important benefits of Common Lisp over earlier Lisp dialects is that compiling a program should only make the program run faster, but not change what the program does. At the very least, the utilities such as INSIST and FOR should be compiled.

The next thing to do is to analyze your code to see where the bottlenecks are. Do this after you've implemented at least two of the micro programs in the later chapters. Look in particular for code that creates lists, using CONS, APPEND, backquote, and so on. Every time a list is created, the Lisp system has to find memory space for it. Eventually Lisp runs out of space and has to execute a process called *garbage collection*. This involves looking through memory for all lists that are no longer being used, and marking the memory that those lists take up as available for recycling into future lists. Garbage collection is an expensive process, compared to most other operations, so it pays to avoid it as much as possible. The way to do that is to avoid making new lists as much as possible.

Look to see which code is being executed the most often. Some Lisps have *profiling* functions available, that allow you to find out which functions are called most often. You may be quite surprised at the results. Often the functions called most frequently are not the big complicated routines that stand out in your mind, but the low-level ones, such as type checkers. Commonly called functions in micro MOPS are abstraction checkers such as ABSTP and slot filler extracters such as INHERIT-FILLER. If you trace these functions, you'll see them being called over and over again, often with the same arguments. It makes sense then to consider ways in which these functions can be made cheaper to run, or can be called less often.

3.7.5   Indexing MOPs

One major difference between micro MOPs and the other systems is that micro MOPs does not have the index links with attribute-value pairs, as described in Chapter 2. Part of the functionality of index links can be captured using abstractions. For example, if we wanted to index recipes by the cooking style, we could create a set of abstractions under the recipe MOP, where each abstraction had only one slot, namely the slot for cooking style. We would then put each instance of a recipe under the appropriate abstraction. While this will subdivide memory in the same way, it still doesn't represent the knowledge that cooking style is an index. If a recipe comes in with a new kind of cooking style, the system will have no clue that it should build a new abstraction with the appropriate cooking style slot.

So, one possible extension to add true index structures. MOP-SPECS, the table that contains the specializations of MOPs, would be replaced by a table MOP-INDEXES containing indexes. Each index would have attribute name, plus a list of lists of attribute values followed by those specializations that have that value for that attribute. Attribute here is not exactly the same as role, because some attributes are relationships between role fillers. Micro CHEF is a good test bed for this extension. It builds a new index for recipes that have a meat and crisp vegetable in them. The attribute might look something like (AND (= MEAT M-MEAT) (= VEGE CRISP-VEGETABLE)) and there would be two possible attribute values, T and NIL.

3.7.6 Generalization

Both IPP and CYRUS automatically created abstraction MOPs when new instances were added to memory. The basic idea is simple: if several instances under a MOP all share some slots, create an abstraction with the shared slots. This approach is too simple to really be useful, but it is worth implementing as a basis for experimentation. You'll need to find a set of instances from which to generalize. You should have at least several dozen instances. It's best to have real data with semantic content, rather than artificial data, generated by some simple set of rules, because the point of this exercise is to see where simple rules break down. A generalization procedure that seems to work fine for data like "small green circles are good," "large red squares are bad," "small red triangles are good," and so on, will almost certainly produce silly results when applied to something real. Almanacs are a good source of ideas for data. [Lebowitz, 1986a], for example, studied the task of generalizing Congressional voting records, taken from the *Almanac of American Politics*, while [Lebowitz, 1986b] looked at information about American colleges.

Once you've implemented the basic generalization scheme, you can start exploring the many possible variations. For example, you can have a threshold saying how many instances have to share a feature before forming an abstraction based on that feature. This helps avoid premature generalization. In CYRUS, if most of an abstraction's instances fell under one of its specializations, then the two were merged together. This helps to remove useless abstractions. As you see your system forming silly abstractions based on simple coincidences, you can also start exploring the topic of explanation-based generalization. What do you know that tells you when something is a coincidence and when it is a potential abstraction? How might you represent this knowledge? How might your system apply it? One possible way to capture knowledge about abstractions in MOPs is to implement a rule that forms abstractions only when there are "similar" abstractions already in memory. Can you make this idea work?

4

Judge

William M. Bain[1]

4.1 Protocol Data: What A Judge Does

When people run out of rules to guide them, they reason about problems subjectively, offering anecdotes from their own experiences to illustrate the sense of their points of view. Domains where expert reasoning of this type occurs usually come packaged with a starter kit of traditions, prototypes, and precedents; such is the case, for example, with legal reasoning, various methods of scientific discovery, and art. Beyond such initial guidelines, however, a person often finds himself in uncharted territory. The judicial task of sentencing criminals entails that judges form dispositions for cases with a minimum of guidance from codified law, and thus they are frequently left to their own consciences to decide the fate of men's lives. How do judges form sentences? What knowledge do they bring to bear on the task? What processes do they use?

This research has been directed at modeling by computer the behavior of judges who sentence criminals. Our effort has not been to examine sentencing as a representative example of legal reasoning. Instead, we have viewed it as a more generic reasoning task in which people learn empirically from having to produce relative assessments of input situations with respect to several different concerns. This domain thus offers the opportunity to study the content of assessment criteria—metrics for comparing and ranking situations—and the manner in which people allow them to function. In addition, because judges receive little external feedback from sentencing that they can directly apply to future cases, studying this task can help us to understand better the nature

---

[1]The material in this chapter has been edited from [Bain, 1986]

of subjectivity, and how to get computer programs to reason subjectively.

To facilitate building a sentencing model, we considered how judges face the task of fashioning sentences by talking with two judges who were sitting on the bench in Connecticut at the Superior Court level. Our protocols initially consisted of discussions about cases which they had heard or adjudicated, and for which they were expected to fashion sentences. We were also able to observe them as they sentenced offenders in court. In addition, we presented them with a number of fictionally augmented examples of real cases in order to reveal the kinds of knowledge which they found necessary and sufficient to bring to bear on the task.

The usual scenario for discussing augmented real cases involved presenting a judge with only rudimentary facts about a case. The judge was asked to prompt us with questions to ascertain additional knowledge. In normal circumstances, judges learn about the relevant details of cases by reading documents prepared by the police, the state's attorney's office, and the defense attorney, and also by listening to arguments presented by attorneys, both privately in chambers and publicly in court. However, many of the documents which the judges saw prior to sentencing were restricted from the public domain, and thus we were usually unable to monitor closely the information that the judges used as input. To get around this restriction and collect data in a manner that gave us access to the same knowledge that the judges got, we presented the judges sets of facts from real cases and invented as augmentation answers that the judges needed as additional information. In one case that we discussed with a judge we were allowed to review extensive court information about the offender, thus circumventing any need to augment the facts; that case is discussed later on below.

4.2   Case of the 16-year-old offender

An example discussion which I had with a judge follows. I described to him briefly my version of a real case which was new to him. This crime was unusual in that it involved a child molestation where the offender was himself only sixteen years old.

> [1] Interviewer: This is a Risk of Injury to a Minor case, against a boy named Tom who is sixteen-years old.
> [2] Judge: OK.
> [3] Interviewer: That's what I'll tell you; now you can ask questions.
> [4] Judge: A first offender?
> [5] Interviewer: Yes.

[6] Judge: No juvenile record?

[7] Interviewer: No juvenile record, no.

[8] Judge: Being treated as an adult?

[9] Interviewer: Yes.

[10] Judge: How old was the victim, male or female?

[11] Interviewer: Two victims, one a female, one a male. The girl was about six or seven and the boy was about four.

[12] Judge: What kind of Risk of Injury?

[13] Interviewer: It's a sexual assault.

[14] Judge: That's why I asked you because there's a difference. Risk of Injury could be acts short of a sexual assault, or depending on the prosecutor, what kind of case he had, it could be a sexual assault subsumed under the title of Risk of Injury.

[15] Interviewer: It was of the nature of a sexual assault, although there were no Sexual Assault charges brought.

[16] Judge: OK. So? He pleads guilty?

[17] Interviewer: He pleaded guilty.

[18] Judge: Do you have the statute? Number?

[19] Interviewer: No, I don't have the number right here, but I know what the maximum sentence is.

[20] Judge: What's the maximum?

[21] Interviewer: It's an unclassified felony carrying a maximum penalty of ten years incarceration and/or a fine not to exceed $500.

[22] Judge: I'll be right back. *[He looks up the relevant sentencing statutes.]*

[23] Interviewer: Ten years and/or a $500 fine.

[24] Judge: Two counts?

[25] Interviewer: Two counts.

[26] Judge: Was there any kind of psychiatric evaluation?

[27] Interviewer: Well, he has had some problems in school before...

[28] Judge: That has nothing to do with it.

[29] Interviewer: ...which caused him to be kept from school for a week before, but he didn't have any counseling because of that. There was some counseling as a result of this crime, which has shown that, well, up until now, he hasn't shown anything about... he hasn't externalized his sexual desires at all, he doesn't seem to know why he did what he did. The psychiatric report states very strongly that this boy is in need of psychiatric help, and that that would almost assuredly help him save him.

[30] Judge: *[laughs wryly]* I don't know what that means.

[31] Interviewer: The psychiatric therapist stated very strongly that this boy needs treatment.

[32] Judge: And he is being treated by the system as an adult offender?

[33] Interviewer: Yeah, that's right. I'm not sure exactly what that means.

[34] Judge: It means that he will not be treated as a juvenile. If it's a first offense, he may or may not be given youthful offender status, which would limit his maximum exposure to three years, if he's a youthful offender. That's why I asked you the nature of the trauma to the victims.

[35] Interviewer: Oh, the nature of the trauma to the victims was not substantial. The details of the crime were that this boy was babysitting for the two kids, and the girl went into the bathroom and called him from the toilet, and as he entered the bathroom, she got off the toilet and he fondled her. Later on she went to bed, and he went into her room and he masturbated on top of her. Her brother was in the next room. He went in there and made the boy perform fellatio on him. A few days later, the kids told their mother and she called the police. The girl was able to describe what happened to her. The little boy was upset by the event, but not severely traumatized. Neither of them needed any psychiatric treatment or care for their trauma other than some talking to by their mother–some reassurance.

[36] Judge: If he were treated as a youthful offender, then I would probably... if he were presented for determination (of youthful offender status), I would feel very strongly against it, because basically, I'd have to... it's very hard to judge, I mean, some people just goof up sexually as they're that age or so, and it's hard to tell with no prior record, I would tend to want to give someone the benefit of the doubt, especially since there is no severe trauma to the victims. I might ag... I do an awful lot of agonizing, but I might give him youthful offender status, and give him three years suspended, a maximum probation with conditions of psychiatric treatment throughout the probation. If he were not treated as a youthful offender, then I might well place him on five years, give him a suspended sentence, five years probation with the conditions of psychiatric treatment.

[37] Interviewer: OK. Who determines whether or not he goes on to the youthful offender status?

[38] Judge: He can apply. A judge ultimately has to determine whether to grant that eligibility, I mean grant that status, if he's eligible. From what you told me, he would be eligible because he has no prior... eligible in the sense that he's never used it before. It's only a one shot deal.

[39] Interviewer: As a judge who is determining a sentence in this case, would you be the one to decide, to determine that status?

[40] Judge: I could determine that status and he might decide to plead guilty or go to trial. Once you have been granted youthful offender status, you then have a right to go to trial or plead guilty. You do not have a jury trial–it's a trial to the court, i.e., to the judge, and you can be sentenced for up to three years. He also has the option of applying for accelerated rehabilitation, being treated as an adult and being denied youthful offender. Or, if treated as an adult and electing to go for accelerated instead of youthful offender.

[41] Interviewer: OK, so there are a lot of options for him.

[42] Judge: I would not be inclined to give him accelerated rehabilitation, even though that's a very harsh kind of thing to do with no prior record, but one of the reasons I would not be inclined to give him accelerated rehabilitation is because the maximum period of probation is two years. I could grant accelerated rehabilitation, continue the matter for two years with conditions of psychiatric treatment. Of course, the problem with accelerated is should he slip during those two years, he comes back and faces the original charges–that's bingo for him. He's just on a lease.

[43] Interviewer: How is it that you feel about this particular instance?

[44] Judge: I don't understand child molestation. Never have and never will. But also we are essentially talking about a child himself, the accused, and there was no severe trauma and there is no prior history... of that or anything else from what you've told me...

[45] Interviewer: That's right...

[46] Judge: So I'm trying to balance all these things.

[47] Interviewer: Is there more that you'd like to know? Is there anything else which would influence your decision at this point?

[48] Judge: I don't know, there could be a lot of things. I'm not trying the case, I'm not defending it. The state might vigorously object to either youthful offender status being granted or accelerated rehabilitation. They might feel that he should go to

prison. As I told you before, it's my understanding that sexual... crimes, or the people who commit them, generally have a high rate of recidivism, and that there is really no cure. But I don't know that this is a guy who is going to go off and commit rape because of his age, because of a lack of history. It could just be a fouled-up teenager acting out inappropriately his own sexual frustrations as he starts to blossom. Those are the sorts of things that run through my mind.

At the outset of the discussion the judge asked questions which would identify features of the case which he found to be relevant. In particular, he established that Tom had no prior record ([4] - [7]); that he could treat him as an adult for purposes of sentencing ([8], [9]); that the victims were very young ([10], [11]); the extent of the charges brought by the state against the offender ([12] - [15]); and that he had pleaded guilty ([16], [17]). These features comprise a substantial body of information which relates to the goals of the judge. We will consider the importance of these types of facts individually.

4.2.1   Prior Record

The information which judges usually requested first in our discussions of cases concerned the offender's prior record. An offender with a prior felony record represents perhaps the largest threat to a judge's authority, and is thus not likely to receive any leniency from the court. Leniency hinges on the judge's ability to predict plausibly that the offender will not repeat his crime. In the absence of information which suggests either prior misdeeds or likely recidivism, a judge may give the benefit of the doubt, as the judge did above; however, a prior record indicates that the offender did not learn his lesson, and supplies ample support for the expectation that the offender will transgress again. The fact that Tom was young added strength to this judge's view both that his past was clean and that there was reason to expect that he would not repeat his behavior. Therefore, we can conclude several things. First,

> Judges try to predict the likelihood that an offender will repeat.

Their predictions are made in service of a higher-level goal to develop some disposition for sentencing. In particular, they want to prevent the offender from repeating the crime. As a result,

> A judge will treat an offender more harshly if he believes that there is reason to predict recidivism.

Finally, the offender's prior record is a feature which judges use in the prediction task:

> Judges base their predictions about an offender's future behavior in part on the presence and severity of a prior record.

4.2.2 Forming Explanations

It is interesting to note in [36] the sudden change in the judge's attitude about granting youthful offender status in this case. He began by saying that he was very strongly against it; however, he changed his mind immediately in mid-sentence and he began to defend the use of the status. What is strange is that he believed his initial feelings to be so strong, and yet he then realized that his doubts were just as reasonable. What might account for this is that he suddenly came upon a partial explanation for why Tom acted as he did, which was that "some people just goof up sexually when they're that age" and that Tom "could just be a fouled-up teenager acting out inappropriately his own sexual frustrations as he starts to blossom." That explanation, if argued effectively by a defense attorney in court, could apparently convince this judge to treat Tom as a youthful offender, if the determination were left to him. We can conclude a couple of things from this account.

> Judges seek reasonable explanations for criminal behavior.

[Pennington and Hastie, 1981] concludes that members of criminal *juries* construct causally based stories as part of the decision process for determining guilt. Explanations are used to predict recidivism, and thereby help assess the risk involved in giving an offender a suspended sentence. For instance, the "fouled-up teenager" explanation in this example suggests that the crime was not only anomalous for this offender, but that therapy could help him deal with his sexual feelings appropriately in the future. In addition, explanations of criminal behavior help judges to determine the extent to which offenders ought to be punished. This extent often correlates with the degree to which the offender's intentionality is considered heinous, according to studies made of parole boards [Carroll and Payne, 1976].

A related conclusion is that

> Judges base their expectations about the arguments of the attorneys in a case on their own explanations of the offender's behavior.

If this were a real case, the judge would probably look for signs from the defense attorney, and from the offender himself, that Tom was indeed a fouled-up teenager. It is difficult to ascertain from the discussion in this protocol alone what other defenses, if any, that this judge might consider reasonable.

4.2.3   The Victims

In [10] - [15], we discussed the victims, in particular their ages and the offenses against them. Further information about these victims was provided to the judge in [35]. The judge's interest in the victims stemmed from his need to assess the nature and extent of harm and trauma which they suffered. The degree to which victims were hurt tends to have a direct bearing on the extent of the punishment which a judge, who is acting on behalf of the victims, will mete out. ("The punishment should fit the crime," as they say.) Furthermore, although the crimes of offenders are classified by the statutory charges brought against them, the result in every case is unique; different people are affected differently by similar crimes. It is reasonable to conclude that

> A judge tries to punish an offender to an extent which is consistent in part with the amount of harm caused to the victims.

The hedging "in part" in this generalization results from the fact that the judges we spoke with did not always tell us that they accounted in their sentences for the degree to which victims were hurt. Sometimes this concern was a major factor, while at others it was hardly apparent, although not necessarily ignored.

4.2.4   Legal Constraints and the Plea

The judge does not decide what specific charges to bring against an offender. That is done either by the state's attorney (the prosecutor); by a jury, which can, in some instances find an offender guilty of crimes other than those for which he was charged; or by a plea bargaining agreement between the prosecuting and defense attorneys. The role of the judge in sentencing depends on the manner in which the charges are made. In a plea bargain, for example, the attorneys can agree not only on the charges to which the offender will plead guilty, but also on the sentence that the state will recommend to the judge. In this type of sentencing, which is very common, the judge would merely approve or disapprove the sentence; the charges themselves are the business of the state's attorney. Should the judge disapprove of the plea bargain, the offender can withdraw his guilty plea and face trial on the original charges.

A judge who sentences without a plea arrangement that specifies a sentence may level any sentence which conforms to the minimum and maximum punishments associated in the statutes with each charge made.

A good demonstration of remorse by an offender can go a long way to indicate that it is unlikely that he will repeat his crime. The fact that an offender pleads guilty without a plea bargain can suggest that he feels some remorse, that he is willing to accept the consequences of his behavior, and that he is not wasting the court's time. However, the guilty plea alone does not strongly support the view that the offender feels remorse. The converse indicates the stronger position, given by the judge in the case discussed next: when an offender pleads innocent and is found guilty at trial, he has blown a good chance to show remorse.

4.3 The Case of the 16-year-old Molester Revisited

A month and a half later, I met with the judge interviewed above to discuss, among other things, the case dealing with the 16-year-old child molester, Tom. This time his reaction to the issue of youthful offender status was markedly different, even after such a short period of time.

> [1] Interviewer: When I talked to you before, in December, we talked about a couple of cases. I don't know if you remember those cases.
>
> [2] Judge: No.
>
> [3] Interviewer: One of them dealt with Tom, a sixteen-year-old boy, who was charged with two counts of Risk of Injury. [Repetition of case description]
>
> [4] Judge: What did I say about that? I don't remember what I said. As you talked, the fact situation sounds very familiar.
>
> [5] Interviewer: OK. One of the... the boy was sixteen, so one of the things you wanted to know was whether he should, whether he was being treated as a juvenile or an adult.
>
> [6] Judge: Was he? Or, which was he?
>
> . . .
>
> [9] Interviewer: I told you as an adult. I want to see what your reaction is to this case at this point. This will help me.
>
> [10] Judge: In what respect? As, should he be treated as an adult?
>
> [11] Interviewer: Yeah.

[12] Judge: Yeah, he should be treated as an adult. He's not a kid.

[13] Interviewer: OK. He has no prior record of any kind, and he entered a plea of guilty.

[14] Judge: ...And he's got two counts, right?

[15] Interviewer: Two counts, Risk of Injury this time, yeah.

[16] Judge: ...That's a place, a situation where I would find it hard not to consider a suspended sentence and a long, perhaps maximum period of probation with psychiatric treatment, if that's possible. Notwithstanding my feeling that it's going to simply be a waste of time. But who knows, you know? You're giving someone the benefit of the doubt at that age.

[17] Interviewer: How long a period of probation?

[18] Judge: At least five years.

[19] Interviewer: Would you treat him as a juvenile? If you did...

[20] Judge: If he's not being presented as a juvenile, I can't...

[21] Interviewer: If he were presented to you for determination as a juvenile.

[22] Judge: No I would not. Not at sixteen.

[23] Interviewer: Why not?

[24] Judge: Because I don't think he should be treated as a juvenile at sixteen.

[25] Interviewer: OK.

[26] Judge: OK? I just, if that means I don't think we should be saying, "Oh, he's nothing but a little kid." And besides that, nothing happens in juvenile court. Absolutely nothing. I mean you go through a charade and kids walk out of there laughing. I don't think that's a laughing matter. I mean you can commit murder in our society if you're a juvenile, and get tapped on the wrists; where you gonna send 'em? What are you going to do with them?

[27] Interviewer: Again, he's got a completely clean record, and there's a psychological report that says that he is in dire need of psychiatric treatment at this point.

[28] Judge: Probably for a lot of things. That wouldn't change the situation.

4.3.1 Experience-based Generalizations

The judge's staunch attitude against the offender on this second occasion differed dramatically from his previous position of feeling uncertain yet beneficent toward him. When we discussed this case a month and a half earlier, the judge stated that "some people just goof up sexually as they're that age or so, and it's hard to tell with no prior record, I would tend to want to give someone the benefit of the doubt, especially since there is no severe trauma to the victims." He then went on to formulate a sentence that he might impose if he were indeed to grant youthful offender status. He summarized his doubt at the end of that discussion by saying, "But I don't know that this is a guy who is going to go off and commit rape because of his age, because of a lack of history. It could just be a fouled-up teenager acting out inappropriately his own sexual frustrations as he starts to blossom." These statements made his doubt very clear.

Part of the judge's earlier uncertainty was also apparent when he proposed two possible sentences for Tom: one for the condition in which he would grant youthful offender status, and one if he were to treat him as an adult. In the second discussion above, however, he made no such provisions for doubt. In [12], he made the strong statement that this offender was an adult and not a child. He did soften this position a bit in [16] by suggesting, as before, that Tom should be given the benefit of the doubt; however, his sentence proposal in [18] of "at least five years" was substantially harsher than the tentative sentences which he had mentioned earlier (3 years with youthful offender status or 5 years as an adult—see [36] in the first discussion). Moreover, his attitude in denying youthful offender status this time could only be described as hostile. His justification in [26] indicated a great deal of anger toward juvenile offenders, and suggested that he felt powerless to deal with them adequately.

The only explanations which the judge gave for his changed attitude were insubstantial. After the tape recorder was turned off during the session above, he told me that he had been in a better mood before Christmas than he was now. About six months later, as we began a new discussion, he brought up this case himself. This was the only time that either one of the judges recalled on his own any of the augmented real cases which I presented to them (as opposed to cases which they had themselves adjudicated in court). He said that he had presided in a juvenile case just after Christmas which had been particularly agonizing for him; unfortunately, he gave me no details of the case. However, it is noteworthy that the case he heard during that month and a half contributed to his using a different perspective for dealing with juveniles than he had used before, to the point that he reacted to the same set of facts quite differently the second time. From this we observe that

> The extent to which a judge considers certain features of cases
> and of offenders to be significant is a function of recent expe-
> riences he has in dealing with those features.

In this particular instance, the judge changed his attitude about juvenile
offenders on the basis of having one or more experiences in "kiddie court"
which led him to feel that *not* giving the benefit of the doubt to juvenile
offenders was more appropriate than giving it to them. He learned through
experience that juvenile offender status did not give him the control over
the offender that he wished to exercise. As a result, he reacted strongly to
that feature even though he was discussing the case for the second time. His
behavior showed that recency can have a strong effect on the extent to which
a feature is considered critical.

Had the judge not had this particular intervening experience with juvenile
court, he may very well have reacted to the case the second time the same
way that he did the first time. In that event we would have observed that

> The extent to which a judge considers certain features of cases
> and of offenders to be significant is a function of *prototypical*
> experiences he has in dealing with those features.

Besides the occasional changes that I found in the attitudes of judges
toward particular features in cases, I often noted a certain degree of continuity
and consistency between each of their attitudes from one discussion to the
next. The two observations above partly account for a person's capacities
both for maintaining standard attitudes and beliefs as well as for amending
his attitudes and beliefs in the face of experiences which challenge the norm.
If this judge's attitude toward youthful offenders was previously normally
beneficent, it was challenged by his time in juvenile court when he felt the
whole scenario was a "charade" and he saw "kids walk out of there laughing."
On the other hand, had the judge encountered cases where otherwise model
juveniles were accused of committing serious crimes which were totally out
of character for them, and which could be reasonably punished with short
periods of probation, there would have been no reason for him to challenge
his charitable attitude.

4.3.2   Choosing a Structure for Sentencing

In general, judges must themselves decide on the structure of every sentence
that they give. Few laws impose that structure without judicial decision-
making; in fact, each of the statutory charges made against most criminal

offenders carries several sentencing options. For example, the charges brought in one case were two counts of Risk of Injury to a Minor. This unclassified felony carries a maximum sentence on the books of a fine not to exceed $500 on each count and/or a term of imprisonment not to exceed ten years. So the judge could in fact level a maximum fine of $1,000 against this offender and send him on his way. Although such a sentence would be most unusual, it would be perfectly legal. Many recent laws do impose mandatory sentences, such as those involving either drunken driving or the use of handguns.

In any situation where a judge can impose a prison sentence, he also has the option of suspending execution of all or part of the sentence, and imposing a period of probation, unless he is otherwise restricted by the statutes. The combined periods of prison and probation may not exceed the maximum sentence that he can legally give.

In general,

> Judges enumerate the set of choices which they believe they could impose as sentences.

Previously, in the very first child molestation case of Section 4.2, with the sixteen-year-old offender, we observed Judge 1 state in [36] that he would give either a three-year suspended sentence or a five-year suspended sentence based on whether the offender was treated as a juvenile or an adult.

> The more a judge believes that an offender is likely to repeat a crime which involves victims, the more he will prefer to remove the offender from society by giving him a prison term.

This notion can explain the disparity between adult and juvenile sentences, and it also accounts for the fact that judges don't typically levy fines in sex crime cases. In fact, there is no principled reason that judges should impose prison sentences instead of fines for sex crimes.[2] After all, both are forms of punishment, and nobody really expects either one to curb deviant sexual desires. However, prison does satisfy a judge's goal to remove an offender from society, at least to keep him from harming other people for a time. Even so, this goal was not apparent in the suspended sentence options proposed in the case of the sixteen-year-old molester, even if he were to have been sentenced as an adult. This is probably because the judge was more concerned with deterring the offender than with protecting society. It seems that when judges decide on possible sentences they draw heavily on their experiences to indicate what would be "normal" for the given circumstances.

---

[2]It should be pointed out that the fine for Risk of Injury to a Minor is exceptionally low at $500. Most other sex crimes carry a maximum fine of at least $5,000 for each count.

4.3.3   Conditions on Choices

Another judge during an interview indicated that there were certain conditions
under which he would choose a sentence incorporating a prison term over one
that did not. In general,

> Judges attach conditions to the sentencing choices which they
> enumerate.

The judge specified exactly what his concern was about suspending the
sentence and giving the offender probation. He was afraid that this molester
might be too unpredictable to put on probation, that he might be an extreme
recidivist, and that he might become violent. Even though he had no evidence
upon which to base his prediction of violence, the judge did specify the kind of
knowledge which he felt would help him to determine that this offender should
stay out of prison. He said, later in the interview, that he would consult a
psychiatrist to ask about the tendencies of child molesters in general. It is not
at all clear from the discussion how the judge would sentence this crime if he
gained no substantial information regarding this condition. We'll see how his
reasoning developed in a moment by looking at a later discussion of the same
case.

4.3.4   Motivations of the Offender

Although judges do try to find some explanation to account for the offender's
behavior, it is usually very difficult for them to explain the motivations which
lead to child molestation. Furthermore, the crime simply cannot be justified;
as a result, child molesters are always viewed negatively on strictly moral
grounds.

> The process of explaining an offender's behavior involves in-
> ferring his motivations.

Although judges find these inferences difficult to make in child molestation
cases, it is much easier for them in many other situations, from white collar
crimes to assault. I shall further discuss explanations about motivation later.

4.4   Case-based Reasoning

In one of the interviews I had with the second judge about one case, he stated
that he was uncertain about whether he should sentence a child molester, who

was a salesman, to prison, but he could give the conditions under which he would decide that prison was appropriate for that offender. A month and a half later, just a week and a half before the sentencing was scheduled, he still had not firmly decided on prison, but he was seriously considering it. This new decision was apparently entirely based on an intervening case where a man molested the children of his common-law wife; however, there is no evidence to indicate that the intervening case provided him with explicit information concerning the choice conditions he articulated earlier. He didn't learn from the case, for example, that child molesters murder their victims if they resist. When asked why he was seriously considering prison, he referred *immediately* to the common-law father case, describing it as being a rather similar crime. In this new case, the lawyers had already formulated and agreed on the sentence and presented it to the judge.

Why would the judge apparent abandon directly resolving the choice conditions he had previously specified in favor of using a "prefabricated" type of sentence structure? One explanation for this comes from the following generalization:

> Judges sometimes formulate sentences by using case-based reasoning.

In other words, to deal with a given situation a judge will use a strategy which was used in another, similar situation. Case-based reasoning (see, for example, [Simpson, 1984]) involves the following steps. First, a reasoner encounters a situation which has features that remind him of a similar situation that he had dealt with previously. The reasoner is reminded also of the strategies used to deal with the earlier experience. He then adapts those strategies to the fit the current situation. The new situation, along with the adapted strategies, are stored in memory, indexed by those features that distinguish the new feature from the old, thus effecting incremental learning. New and old strategies can in turn be used later on to help deal with still new input situations.

The current example of the judge's behavior can be interpreted as a variant form of case-based reasoning. While trying to deal with one case, he encounters another similar case whose solution has been already worked out by the attorneys. Because the defense lawyer agreed to a prison sentence, the judge was persuaded that prison was indeed a reasonable strategy for dealing with child molesters in general and the salesman in his current case in particular.

When the judge returned to discussing the salesman case, he indicated crucial differences between it and the new one. He pointed out that the common-law father had behaved more violently than the salesman had, but that the mother asked for no prison, while the parents in the salesman case were vehement about wanting as harsh a sentence as possible for the molester. The judge adapted the sentencing strategy to the salesman case by giving a harsher sentence. We'll look at how the judge actually did sentence the salesman ten days later in a moment, but for now we conclude that

> When a judge applies a sentencing strategy from one case to another, he'll modify the sentence to accommodate feature differences between the cases.

This form of case-based reasoning, where a new situation, rather than a prior experience, is used to help resolve an on-going problem, is known as opportunistic problem-solving [Hayes-Roth and Hayes-Roth, 1979; Birnbaum, 1986].

4.4.1   Rationalization

Much of the strength of strategy modification in this domain seems to rely on reasoning which is prone to rationalization. The tendency I've observed is that

> Judges stress the relative importance of specific features of cases to support the rationality of their sentences.

In the common-law father molestation case, for example, the judge felt that the mother's reaction that the offender not be imprisoned was critical; he focused on that feature to support his position that the agreed-on sentence, though otherwise perhaps too lenient, was reasonable if all things were considered. However, in light of other details of this case, the judge's stress on that feature can be considered odd indeed. The information from the court documents show that the common-law father was much more brutal to his victims than the salesman had been to his. His crime was an enormous violation of the trust that children are expected to have in their parents. According to the mother, he had a history of violent behavior. Finally, he had a criminal record which, although mostly dated, indicated that he had spent time in jail. In contrast, the salesman had what the judge himself termed "an affectionate relationship" with his victims, but was otherwise a relative stranger to the children who meant relatively little to them. He had no prior record at all. These facts would seem to be much more significant than what the mothers had to say; nevertheless, the judge placed a greater emphasis on what the parents of the victims wanted in each case. He stated that he felt that the woman's desire to have her common-law husband not sent to prison supported a shorter sentence for him than for the salesman, where the parents "want his head."

The way the judge appeared to rationalize his decision lends support to the claim that he was trying to formulate a sentence with a case-based reasoning technique. Originally the judge was uncertain about sending the salesman to prison. Then the common-law father case came along with a sentence already prepared and agreed on by the attorneys from both sides. The judge had to decide whether this sentence was reasonable. The judge stated that the presentence report for the common-law father "brought this [salesman case] very realistically to my mind." Next, he stated that he had tentatively decided to give the salesman a jail term, to suspend part of it and give him a long period of probation with psychotherapy. Not coincidentally, this was precisely the structure of the agreed sentence provided to the judge for the common-law father: three years in prison suspended after 18 months, followed by five years of probation with psychotherapy.

In order to justify using the sentencing strategy from the common-law father case in the salesman case, the judge found a feature difference that supported it, namely the attitudes of the victims' parents. This feature indicated that one could view the salesman's crime as being at least as bad as the common-law father's crime. Thus, prison would be appropriate for the salesman as well. Had the judge not been able to make some argument that the salesman's crime was at least as bad as the common-law father's, then he would not have been able to justify applying the prison sentence strategy to the salesman case. The feature chosen, i.e., the parents' wishes, not only supported the prison sentence, but, contrary to several other features, led to an adapted sentence that was harsher.

To summarize, rationalization plays the important role in case-based reasoning of supporting the transfer and/or modification of strategies from one situation for use in another. Given the goal of using a particular case-based strategy, rationalization is used to find those features that justify that strategy.

4.5 Indexing and Retrieval

At one point, I discussed with a judge a case involving arson and murder. Afterwards, when I told the judge that the case was real and recent, he immediately recalled it. He remembered that the adult victim was the mother of the children and the wife of the killer. In addition to recalling the arson-murder, he also remembered the three murder cases with which he had previously been involved. From this we can see that

> Judges retrieve cases from memory—their own cases as well as others—to compare to new cases.

The importance of this conclusion bears heavily on case-based reasoning, and in fact follows as a consequence of using the process. A reasoner who uses previous experiences either to find strategies for dealing with new situations or to verify the utility of a chosen strategy, must have access to those previous experiences. Furthermore, the knowledge of the experiences must be organized in a way that facilitates access, for example, with the use of index keys derived from the features of an input description which are found to be similar to features of the stored knowledge.

The judge used the cases that he recalled in two ways. First, his recollection of the arson-murder gave him at least a rudimentary strategy for assessing the heinousness of the crime. Although he said that his recollection of people's feelings about the case was "neither here nor there," he did point out that it had been considered "the most gruesome, brutal, grisly kind of thing ever to happen in the state of Connecticut." Such an extreme description is not easy to overlook. In fact, the judge found a way to use this recollection with the facts that I presented by claiming that he could not find any mitigating factors to take into account. It is indeed unlikely that the most gruesome, brutal, grisly kind of thing ever to happen in Connecticut would have any mitigating factors. He therefore didn't bother to inquire further about the motivations of this offender.

The second purpose for which this judge used recollection was to compare the old cases and their sentences to the new case and its sentence. First, he described the three other murder/manslaughter cases. For each of them, he outlined causally what happened to contribute to the death of the victim, the motivations and moral justification of each death-causer, and the disposition that was reached by the judicial system. He then compared them to the arson-murder, both by saying that the situations were very different (implying that the arson-murder was much worse), and that the arson-murderer deserved a harsher sentence. This shows that

> Judges relate causal differences in cases to differences in the sentences which they give.

The mapping of comparative heinousness of a crime to severity in sentencing underlies a judge's goal to be fair. The judge felt that a 105-year sentence would be fair, though he noted that this was his assessment of relative fairness and not absolute fairness.

4.6 Summary of Protocol Data

What judges do when they sentence sounds very much like the way that anyone else acts in a position of authority: they listen to input facts; they react to them; they try to construct some scenario which can explain them and account for them, or they'll accept someone else's account; they make predictions based their explanations; they outline their alternatives for dealing with the situation; and finally, they announce a decision formed from among their choices. Along the way, they use their own experiences to guide them, and they use strategies from other similar situations. What makes this particular task unique is that the ultimate decisions can have grave and far-reaching consequences on the lives of other people; judges are not immune from recognizing this dimension of what they do.

The following is a summary of the conclusions which I drew from the protocol data, organized more or less according to the above higher-level description of the task. Those items that I have attempted to model in the JUDGE program are marked in bold:

- Feature Significance

  - Judges consider a guilty plea to be somewhat favorable to the offender.

  - A judge tries to punish an offender to an extent which is consistent in part with the amount of harm caused to the victims.

  - The extent to which a judge considers certain features of cases and of offenders to be significant is a function of both recent and prototypical experiences he has in dealing with those features.

  - **Judges stress the relative importance of specific features of cases to support the rationality of their sentences.**

  - Judges look for features that will mitigate the responsibility of the offender.

- Explanation and Interpretation

  - Judges seek reasonable explanations for criminal behavior.

  - **The process of explaining an offender's behavior involves inferring his motivations.**

  - Judges listen to the arguments of attorneys and select the ones which they believe to be reasonable and fair.

- **Judges seek moral justification for crimes, and for the actions which lead to harm.**

- Prediction

    - Judges try to predict the likelihood that an offender will repeat.

    - A judge will treat an offender more harshly if he believes that there is reason to predict recidivism.

    - Judges base their predictions about an offender's future behavior in part on the presence and severity of a prior record.

    - Judges use standard knowledge to account for an offender's actions and motivations, and to predict the chance he will repeat.

    - The more a judge believes that an offender is likely to repeat a crime which involves victims, the more he will prefer to remove the offender from society by giving him a prison term.

- Memory, Experience, and Learning

    - Judges base the structure and severity of the sentences that they choose on experience and custom.

    - **Judges retrieve cases from memory—their own cases as well as others—to compare to new cases.**

    - **Judges sometimes formulate sentences by using case-based reasoning.**

- Choice

    - Judges enumerate the set of choices which they believe they could impose as sentences.

    - Judges attach conditions to the sentencing choices which they enumerate.

    - The more a judge believes that an offender is likely to repeat a crime which involves victims, the more he will prefer to remove the offender from society by giving him a prison term.

    - Judges take into account last-minute factors, arguments, and observations when they sentence.

- Strategy Modification

- When a judge applies a sentencing strategy from one case to another, he'll modify the sentence to accommodate feature differences between the cases.

- Judges relate causal differences in cases to differences in the sentences which they give.

4.7 The JUDGE Program

The JUDGE program is a case-based model of sentencing. The program starts off with a simple set of strategies for forming sentences. After only a few cases, however, it begins to retrieve remindings of its own cases from memory and to modify the strategies associated with those cases to form new sentences.

Writing this program required reducing the normally large amount of knowledge available both in legal reasoning tasks in general and for sentencing criminal cases in particular. The processes required for reasoning in these domains were simplified as well. JUDGE does not handle child molestation cases, for example. It seemed from our protocols that any causal models which the judges used to assess child molestation cases were too idiosyncratic to pin down, and varied tremendously from one judge to the next. For example, one of the judges saw that he could view one child molester's treatment of his victims as being "tender," while the other stated that he had absolutely no basis for understanding the motivations of adults who molest children.

Instead, JUDGE reasons about murder, manslaughter, and assault cases, cases in which the actions can sometimes be found justified, and for which various interpretations can be effectively argued. The 55 cases we gave JUDGE all concerned fights, with various actions such as hitting, pushing, knifing, and shooting, and a number of common results, such as killing, maiming, cutting, and bruising. The system knows about 16 kinds of actions and 21 types of results. This set is by no means exhaustive. Some of the cases presented to the system were based on real cases of manslaughter and assault, but the majority of the cases were constructed to include a variety of actions, results, and degrees of justification.

JUDGE does not use all of the information available for real cases to determine its sentences. For example, it isn't concerned with whether the offender pleaded guilty, the likelihood that he'll repeat, or the gravity of his prior record. Instead, JUDGE only considers the relative heinousness of crimes, as is indicated by how badly victims were hurt and the degree to which the offenders lacked moral justification for acting as they did. As a result, the system sentences by essentially mapping a partial ordering of crime heinousness onto a partial ordering of sentence types and durations. No explicit representation of crime heinousness is ever used; sentences, on the other hand, are given either in numbers of months or years, or in ranges of time. The sentence is simplified to apply to only one count of one statutory violation.

The JUDGE system has five stages of operation:

1. An interpretation phase infers the motives of the actors in the input case and determines the extent to which each person was justified in acting violently;

2. A retrieval phase finds previous cases;

3. A differential analysis phase compares retrieved cases with the input.

4. An application and modification phase adapts sentences from old cases onto new cases, ensuring that differences in sentence severity between crimes corresponds to differences in heinousness of the crimes;

5. A generalization phase forms sentencing rules to when it finds it has several similar cases with similar sentences.

In addition to being able to generalize rules from processing its input cases, JUDGE can also modify its rules to account for feature differences between input cases and the left-hand sides of rules. When the system modifies a rule, it stores the resulting left-hand side and modified sentence as a further differentiated version of the rule. This chapter contains examples of output from the system which demonstrate each of these functional abilities.

The stages of the program correspond with certain aspects of the behavior of judges that we observed, and require information similar to that which they use. For example, we noted previously that:

- The process of explaining an offender's behavior involves inferring his motivations;

- Judges seek moral justification for crimes, and for the actions which lead to harm.

The interpretive phase in JUDGE allows the system to infer the motivations of the actors in a crime and to decide on the degree to which each was justified in acting. In fact, interpretations have an eventual effect on sentences precisely because of the inferences about justification of actions and motives which they provide.

4.8 Interpreting Motivations

The interpretation phase of the JUDGE system infers the motivations of the actors that are involved in the cases it sees. The input to the program is a piece of representation indicating only the actions that occurred, e.g., one person hit another person, the results of each action, e.g., the other person was knocked down, and the indirect results of each action, e.g., the person who was knocked down hit his head and lost consciousness.

JUDGE uses three primary types of interpretational structures:

- *Initial interpretations* explain why the actor who started a fight did so.

- *Intentional interpretations*, applied to subsequent actions, have two parts:

  - the relative force of the actor's response to the opponent: more (escalated), similar (parity), or less (weak) force.
  - the reason for the action: self-defense or retaliation.

  Figure 4.1 lists several intentional interpretation rules that JUDGE uses.

- *Result interpretations*, applied to subsequent actions, say whether the outcome of an action was as intended, bungled (not as severe as intended), or accidental (more severe than intended).

Because interpretations provide the actors' justifications for acting, they can be applied with prejudice to one side or the other. In JUDGE, the assignments ought to be as neutral as is plausibly possible. When the system interprets the first action in a case, it starts out siding with the victim and against the offender, thus making interpretations which are not entirely neutral. However, if the victim should later act in a manner which is clearly inconsistent with interpretations that indicate justification, or the offender should behave in a way that can be justified, the system can change its alliances, choosing favorable interpretations for the offender, and/or unfavorable ones for the victim.

Once the system has selected an interpretation, it customizes it to fit the input facts by forming inferences about the actor's motives that are supported by the interpretation and consistent with the facts. If these inferences don't meet plausibility constraints and the interpretation can suggest no alternative motives, it is abandoned for the next best interpretation.

- **Unprovoked Violation:** A person who intends to threaten or violate another person's personal/social Preservation goals with an antecedent event is not justified and becomes the *aggressor*. His victim becomes the *defender*.

- **Parity Retaliation 1:** If no threat is currently active against him, the *defender* in a crime or conflict situation is not justified in threatening or violating any P-goal of the *aggressor* at the current level of violation.

- **Parity Retaliation 2:** The current *aggressor* in a crime or conflict situation is not justified in threatening or violating any P-goal of the *defender* at the current level of violation.

- **Self Defense 1:** If a threat is currently active against him, the *defender* in a crime or conflict situation is justified in intending to threaten or violate the *aggressor* at the same (or a lower) level of P-goal threats or violations made by the *aggressor* against the *defender*.

- **Self Defense 2:** The current *aggressor* in a crime or conflict situation is not justified in retaliating against the *defender* at the parity level.

- **Escalation Rule 1:** In a crime or conflict situation, such as a fight, neither the *defender* nor the *aggressor* is justified to threaten or violate a higher-level goal than the current violation level.

- **Escalation Rule 1:** If a real-world limitation allows no other choices for preventing a violation, the *defender* is justified in threatening or violating a higher-level goal of the *aggressor* than the current violation level. The appropriate level at which to attack is the lowest possible P-goal which is higher than the current violation level.

Figure 4.1: Intention Interpretation Rules

4.8.1 Interpretation in JUDGE

This section contains output from the JUDGE program which shows the system choosing and instantiating interpretations for each action in a crime. At the time the program ran the case below, CRIME1, it had previously only seen one other case, CRIME0. During the interpretation phase, JUDGE instantiates interpretation structures to describe each "event" given in the input. An event consists of a description of an action and its direct and indirect effects. CRIME1 contains five events. Output that describes actions, results, motivations, and interpretations was generated from a template generator in JUDGE, which is capable of varying its point of view to reflect a position for either side in a case, or neutrality. The remaining generation is canned.[3]

The events in CRIME1 were:

> First, Randy struck Chuck with his fists several times. Chuck was only slightly hurt. Next, Chuck struck Randy with his fists several times. Randy was only slightly hurt. Then, Randy slashed at Chuck with a knife one time. Chuck's skin was cut. Next, Chuck slashed at Randy with a knife one time. Randy's skin was cut. Finally, Randy stabbed Chuck with a knife several times. Chuck died.

The actual input to the system is a piece of representation, and not natural language. The program looks at each such event individually.

```
EXTRACTING INDICES FOR FIRST ACTION, EVENT3:

THINGS STARTED WHEN RANDY STRUCK CHUCK WITH HIS FISTS
SEVERAL TIMES.  THE RESULT OF THIS ACTION WAS THAT CHUCK WAS
ONLY SLIGHTLY HURT.
```

The program analyzes each action in input temporal order. The analysis finds one interpretation for the action, and one for the result. Here, the action is that Randy struck Chuck and the result is that Chuck was hurt slightly. Interpretations are indexed in the system in terms of action-result pairs called EPISODEs. Initially, the system is given a set of about 30 "raw episodes." As cases are analyzed, the system saves new assignments of interpretations to action-result pair, called "new episodes." These new episodes gradually replace the original raw episodes.

---

[3]See [Hovy, 1987] for further information on the generator for JUDGE.

```
SEARCHING MEMORY FOR EPISODE-UNITS WHICH HAVE AN ACTION
SIMILAR TO THAT IN EVENT3. . .

EXACT MATCH FOUND WITH INITIAL ACTION OF PREVIOUS EPISODES
IN MEMORY: (RAW-EPISODE-21 RAW-EPISODE-20 RAW-EPISODE-18
RAW-EPISODE-15 RAW-EPISODE-14 RAW-EPISODE-13 RAW-EPISODE-11
RAW-EPISODE-10 RAW-EPISODE-7)

FOUND RAW-EPISODE-21 IN MEMORY, AN EPISODE WHICH MATCHES
EVENT3 EXACTLY. EVENT3 WILL THEREFORE INITIALLY BE
CONSIDERED AN UNPROVOKED-VIOLATION.
```

RAW-EPISODE-21 matches the initial action of EVENT3, giving EVENT3 the unfavorable interpretation, UNPROVOKED-VIOLATION because the offender acted first. A test stored with the UNPROVOKED-VIOLATION interpretation checks the applicability of this interpretation to this instance. The test simply checks to be sure that no violative incident preceded the current action. Applicability checks for other interpretations are typically more complex.

```
MAKING INTENTION INFERENCE FOR UNPROVOKED-VIOLATION
INTERPRETATION OF EVENT3:  RANDY'S INTENTION WAS TO HIT
CHUCK.

END OF ANALYSIS OF EVENT3.
```

UNPROVOKED-VIOLATION supplies an inference about the intention of actor. Other inferences, such as the fact that the actor here was not justified, are also made by the system, and are reported later.

4.9   Retrieving Previous Instances from Memory

The interpretation phase in JUDGE assigns an interpretation to each set of input actions and results. The interpretations provide the system with inferences about the motivations of actors; they also serve as indexes to cases in memory. In this section, we'll look at how indexes are used to find similar episodes and accompanying strategies in memory for sentencing cases.

In general, it is difficult to decide which of the many features of a situation are the most salient and crucial ones to focus on. JUDGE must sift through a large set of actions, results, and interpretations relating to each input crime; however, the system is provided with a set of criteria for determining feature salience. These criteria are derived from the causal structure assigned by the interpretation phase.

The first feature used is the statute which the offender violated. JUDGE tries to find in memory other instances of violations of the same statute. The next feature used is who started the fight: the defendant in the case, or the victim of the fight.[4] The relative salience of these first two features is fixed in JUDGE

The next feature is the final (violent) result that accounts for the statutory violation. Then, the elements of the interpretation are used, in reverse order. That is, the system first indexes with the final result in the crime, then with the actions which led to that result, then with the motive assigned by the interpretation phase, and so on.

Program output presented below continues with the same sample case examined in the interpretation phase, CRIME1. The facts of CRIME0, which is already in JUDGE's memory, are:

> First, Ted slashed at Al with a knife one time. Al's skin was slightly cut. Next, Al slashed at Ted with a knife one time. Ted's skin was slightly cut. Finally, Ted stabbed Al with a knife several times. Al died.

This is the only case in memory for this example. A discussion of how the system chooses between competing remindings is presented below. At this point in the processing, the system describes the reminding it has retrieved and how it compares superficially with the input case.

```
> (RETRIEVE-MEM CRIME1)

Now processing CRIME1:

STATUTORY SIMILARITY OF MURDER FOUND WITH INDEXED CRIME:
CRIME0.

FOUND PREVIOUS CRIMES IN WHICH THE SAME FINAL ACTION AND
RESULT WAS ALSO PERPETRATED AGAINST AN INITIAL-DEFENDER:
(CRIME0)
```

---

[4]The lawyers and judges whom we spoke with considered crucial the fact of who started a fight; in JUDGE it is pivotal in determining how to interpret the beginning of a fight, which has ramifications on the interpretations for the end of a fight as well.

CRIME0 was also a murder and the victim did not start the fight either (the victim was the "INITIAL-DEFENDER"). JUDGE starts working back through the interpretation structure for CRIME1.

```
COLLECTING INDICES FOR CRIME1 IN REVERSE ORDER...

COLLECTING INDICES FOR FINAL EVENT:

FINALLY, RANDY CAUSED CHUCK TO BE KILLED.

RECENT PREVIOUS INSTANCE FOUND WITH SAME FINAL RESULT AS
FINAL RESULT IN CURRENT CASE --- KILL:  CRIME0

RECENT PREVIOUS INSTANCE FOUND WITH SAME FINAL ACTION AS
FINAL ACTION IN CURRENT CASE --- STAB-KNIFE:  CRIME0

RECENT PREVIOUS INSTANCE FOUND WITH SAME FINAL RESULT
INTERPRETATION AS FINAL INTERPRETATION IN CURRENT CASE ---
ACHIEVED-RESULT:  CRIME0

RECENT PREVIOUS INSTANCE FOUND WITH SAME FINAL INTENT
INTERPRETATION LEVEL AS FINAL INTERPRETATION IN CURRENT CASE
--- ESCALATED-RETALIATION:  CRIME0
```

CRIME0 matched on each one of the indexes. The program proceeds by searching for features related to the event that preceded CRIME1's final event, then the next earlier event, and so on until it reaches the first event in the crime. The search for old situations that matched the features of the initial event in CRIME1 comes up empty. None of the features of CRIME0 match it and CRIME0 is the only other crime in memory.

```
COLLECTING INDICES FOR PRECEDING EVENT:

. . .

COLLECTING INDICES FOR INITIAL EVENT IN CRIME:

THE FIRST VIOLATIVE ACTION OCCURRED WHEN RANDY HIT CHUCK
SEVERAL TIMES; CHUCK WAS ONLY SLIGHTLY HURT.

NO PREVIOUS INSTANCES FOUND WITH SAME RESULT AS INTERMEDIATE
HARM IN CURRENT CASE --- VIOLATED-BRUISE.
```

```
NO PREVIOUS INSTANCES FOUND WITH SAME ACTION AS INTERMEDIATE
HARM IN CURRENT CASE --- HIT-BODY.
```

```
NO PREVIOUS INSTANCES FOUND WITH SAME INTENT INTERPRETATION
LEVEL AS THAT IN CURRENT EVENT --- UNPROVOKED-VIOLATION.
```

CRIME0 involved an UNPROVOKED-VIOLATION too, but it was an unprovoked stabbing, not an unprovoked hitting. This system distinguishes between such interactions in its storage and retrieval.

```
A PREVIOUS SITUATION INVOLVING SIMILAR ACTIONS AND A KILL
RESULT, CRIME0, WAS QUITE SIMILAR TO THE CURRENT CASE.
```

```
CRIME1 CONTAINED THE SAME SEQUENCE OF ACTIONS AND RESULTS AS
CRIME0, EXCEPT THAT IT WAS PRECEDED BY HITTING.
```

CRIME0 contained many of the same features as CRIME1 and was an obvious candidate for recall. However, it isn't always the case that just because there are items in JUDGE's memory that something will be recalled. The system must find at least a threshold level of feature matches before it considers an old case to be similar, and thus retrievable.[5] If nothing is found in memory, the system must form a sentence on the basis of analyzing a fixed set of features of the input crime.

When many different cases match the features of a case, as is more typical, selecting a previous instance for recall is more problematic. Three strategies guide the program's ability to choose a previous case from among those in the lists of feature matches. First, the system prefers cases containing NEW-EPISODES which were used when the interpretation phase processed the current input. Second, the system prefers more recent cases to older ones. Third, the system assigns different weights to different features, and prefers those cases with the best total score. The features of statute, final-victim, result, action, etc., are weighted from heaviest to lightest, in that order. Thus, for instance, crimes with similar statutes and results are preferred over crimes with similar statutes and actions. This notion of salience corresponds to the order of causal traversal of crime representations and the order is used later on to compare cases causally. Hence, this notion of feature salience is implicit in the processing algorithms of the system.

---

[5]The system considers a match on the statutory violation to be minimal; the only other established minimum is in situations where an old case contained similar intentional and result interpretations and was started by the same person (either the victim or the offender).

4.10   Differentiating Cases

After JUDGE has found a case in memory that shares features with the input case, it begins to look how the cases differ. If no differences are found, the new case can simply inherit the sentence of the old case. Usually, however, there are a number of differences between cases and modification strategies are needed to tailor the old sentence to fit the new case. One of the ways in which the system differentiates cases is by comparing causal features. Below, for example, is output from an in-depth comparison between the input case CRIME1, involving Randy and Chuck, and the retrieved case CRIME0, involving Ted and Al.

The system first compares how much harm was caused by the last actions of each case. Then it compares the intentions which led to each action.

```
IN BOTH CRIMES, THE VICTIM WAS KILLED.  NOT ONLY WERE BOTH
OF THESE OUTCOMES THE RESULT OF DIRECT INTENTIONS, BUT THE
ACTORS INTENDED AND CAUSED THE SAME AMOUNT OF HARM.

TED DEMONSTRATED AN EXTREME USE OF FORCE AGAINST AL WHEN HE
ACTED TO STAB AL TO DEATH IN RESPONSE TO HAVING HIS SKIN
CUT.

RANDY DEMONSTRATED AN EXTREME USE OF FORCE AGAINST CHUCK
WHEN HE ACTED TO STAB CHUCK TO DEATH IN RESPONSE TO HAVING
HIS SKIN CUT.

UNABLE TO DISTINGUISH WHETHER THE EXTREME FORCE USED IN
EITHER CRIME WAS WORSE.

THE INTENT OF BOTH OFFENDERS WAS TO ACT REPEATEDLY TO STAB
THE VICTIM TO DEATH.  IN ADDITION, NEITHER ACTOR'S
INTENTIONS WERE JUSTIFIED, AND BOTH ESCALATED THE LEVEL OF
VIOLENCE ABOUT THE SAME DEGREE.
```

At this point, JUDGE cannot find a substantial difference between the two cases. As a result, it backs up to compare the events that led to these intentions, actions, and results.

```
IN BOTH CRIMES, THE OFFENDER'S SKIN WAS CUT.  NOT ONLY WERE
BOTH OF THESE OUTCOMES THE RESULT OF DIRECT INTENTIONS, BUT
THE ACTORS INTENDED AND CAUSED THE SAME AMOUNT OF HARM.

THE INTENT OF BOTH VICTIMS WAS TO ACT ONLY ONE TIME   TO
```

SLASH AT THE OFFENDER WITH A KNIFE. IN ADDITION, THE
INTENTIONS OF BOTH ACTORS WERE JUSTIFIED, AND NEITHER
INTENDED TO ESCALATE THE LEVEL OF VIOLENCE.

Again, JUDGE has failed to find one of the crimes more heinous than the
other, and so it backs up again to consider the actions which led to those just
compared.

IN BOTH CRIMES, THE VICTIM'S SKIN WAS CUT. NOT ONLY WERE
BOTH OF THESE OUTCOMES THE RESULT OF DIRECT INTENTIONS, BUT
THE ACTORS INTENDED AND CAUSED THE SAME AMOUNT OF HARM.

TED DEMONSTRATED AN EXTREME USE OF FORCE AGAINST AL WHEN HE
ACTED TO SLASH AT AL WITH A KNIFE. THIS ACTION WAS
UNPROVOKED.

RANDY DEMONSTRATED AN EXTREME USE OF FORCE AGAINST CHUCK
WHEN HE ACTED TO SLASH AT CHUCK WITH A KNIFE IN RESPONSE TO
BEING HIT HARD.

The program has at this point detected a difference in the extent of force
that the offenders used against their victims.

THE MAGNITUDE OF THE EXTREME FORCE USED IN THE FIRST CRIME
WAS GREATER THAN THAT IN THE SECOND, AND SO THE FIRST CRIME
WILL BE CONSIDERED WORSE.

THE INTENT OF BOTH OFFENDERS WAS TO ACT ONLY ONE TIME TO
SLASH AT THE VICTIM WITH A KNIFE. HOWEVER, ALTHOUGH NEITHER
ACTOR'S INTENTION WAS JUSTIFIED AND BOTH OF THEM ESCALATED
THE LEVEL OF FORCE, TED ESCALATED MORE.

COMPARISON FINISHED WITH RESULT THAT THE OLD CRIME, CRIME0,
IS SOMEWHAT WORSE.

It took the program several iterations to determine that CRIME0 was worse
than CRIME1. What it found was a difference between the extent to which
the offenders escalated the violence in their respective crimes. The offender in
the old case, CRIME0, had started the fight by slashing at his eventual victim
with a knife. The offender in CRIME1, on the other hand, had not slashed his
victim until after they had hit each other. Because this latter escalation to a
knife fight was not as extreme as just starting up a knife fight, the program

didn't find CRIME1 to be as bad as CRIME0. However, since the difference was found several events before the ends of the crimes, the program considers the two crimes to be substantially similar for the purpose of sentencing.

In general, the system continues to compare the events of two crimes until some notable difference is found or until one or both crimes has been fully scrutinized one event at a time. Notable differences include such disparities as greater intended harm in one crime, greater caused harm, more justification to respond, extreme force used in one crime, greater relative force, and greater relative escalated force.

4.11   Generalization

When certain conditions regarding the input and retrieved cases are met, JUDGE creates its own rules to generalize certain knowledge about sentencing. The first condition is that the two cases must have shared a substantial number of features. This condition is necessary because the system was not developed to make purely inductive generalizations. For example, JUDGE does not produce observations such as that murders tend to result from situations where the offender escalated the violence and was retaliating as well, if it were indeed possible to observe that coincidence.

The second condition is that the input crime must be causally similar to the retrieved crime. The system determines the extent of this similarity from the depth which the program must reach to distinguish two crimes when it compares them. For example, in the comparison made between CRIME0 and CRIME1 above, it took three iterations to find that CRIME0 was worse. During most comparisons that the program made, it tended to distinguish crime heinousness after one level of comparison. As a result, we set the threshold depth for allowing generalizations to two. The only principled reason for selecting this number stems from the fact that the features which help build generalizations come primarily from the last two events in the crimes considered in building the rules.

When a generalization is first made, the input crime simply inherits the sentence of the crime retrieved from memory. The features common to both cases are used as indexes to store the rule in memory, as shown in the output below for CRIME0 and CRIME1.

```
THE SENTENCE ORIGINALLY GIVEN FOR CRIME0, FOR VIOLATION OF
MURDER AS DEFINED IN SECTION 53A-45 IN THE CONNECTICUT PENAL
CODE, WAS A TERM OF IMPRISONMENT OF NOT LESS THAN 40 YEARS
NOR MORE THAN 50 YEARS TO BE SERVED IN THE STATE'S PRISON.
ACCORDING TO STATE LAW, 25 YEARS OF THE SENTENCE COULD NOT
```

BE REDUCED OR SUSPENDED. BECAUSE CRIME1 IS VERY SIMILAR TO
CRIME0, THE OFFENDER IN CRIME1 WILL GET A SENTENCE WHICH IS
JUST THE SAME AS THE SENTENCE FOR CRIME0.

THE SENTENCE TO BE GIVEN FOR CRIME1, FOR VIOLATION OF MURDER
AS DEFINED IN SECTION 53A-45 IN THE CONNECTICUT PENAL CODE,
WILL BE A TERM OF IMPRISONMENT OF NOT LESS THAN 40 YEARS NOR
MORE THAN 50 YEARS TO BE SERVED IN THE STATE'S PRISON. OF
THIS SENTENCE, 25 YEARS MAY NOT BE REDUCED OR SUSPENDED,
ACCORDING TO STATE LAW.

FORMING GENERAL SENTENCING RULE:

    ---   FOR VIOLATION OF MURDER,
    ---   FOR CAUSING RESULT OF KILL,
    ---   FOR USING ACTION OF STAB-KNIFE,
    ---   FOR HARMING INITIAL-DEFENDER,
    ---   FOR RESPONDING TO A SLASH-KNIFE LEVEL OF HARM,
    ---   FOR USING ESCALATED FORCE AND ACTING OUT OF RETALIATION,
    ---   FOR INTENDING TO CAUSE THE RESULT.

THE SENTENCE FOR THIS VIOLATION WILL BE THE SAME AS GIVEN
FOR CRIME1 ABOVE.

Any rules which the program develops are stored with the crimes that were
used to form them. Once the program has a rule stored in memory, it can
be used to create a sentence quickly for any situation where the rule applies.
In most circumstances, this allows the system to avoid making an in-depth
comparison of the input and retrieved cases. We'll consider next how the
program uses its rules, and then look at what it does when it discovers that
it cannot apply a rule.

4.12 Rule Differentiation

If the key features of statute or violative levels of actions and results do not
match, then the rule is not applied at all. Even when they do match, rule
features tend to differ in minor details from input features. As a result, modifications of the sentences given with rules are typically made. Once a rule has
been modified and used to form a sentence, the modified version is stored with
the input case to which it applied. The new version of a rule retains pointers
to the old version which indicate the feature differences that led to the old

rule's modification. An example of this process, which indicates what indexes are used to store a modified rule, is shown below.

To show this, we input a new crime, CRIME2, which will retrieve the rule formed above for CRIME1. The events in CRIME2 are:

> First, David slapped at Tim with his hands several times. Tim was pushed. Next, Tim struck David with his fists several times. David was only slightly hurt. Then, David hit Tim very hard one time. Tim fell down. Finally, Tim stabbed David with a knife several times. David died.

The charges for CRIME2 are:

> The offender, Tim, is charged with one count of Murder, defined in Section 53A-45 of the Connecticut Penal Code. Tim was involved in a fight with David, which David started. They traded blows, and after David knocked Tim to the ground, Tim stabbed David several times and killed him.

```
A PREVIOUS SITUATION INVOLVING SIMILAR ACTIONS AND A KILL
RESULT BUT INITIATED BY THE OFFENDER, CRIME1, WAS QUITE
SIMILAR TO THE CURRENT CASE.

CRIME1 CONTAINED SOME OF THE SAME ACTIONS AND RESULTS AS
CRIME2, EXCEPT THAT IT WAS PRECEDED BY SLASHING AND CUTTING,
WHILE CRIME2 WAS PRECEDED BY SLAPPING AND KNOCKING-ABOUT.
```

JUDGE now finds and tries to use the general rule indexed under CRIME1 that we saw created in Section 4.11.

```
ATTEMPTING TO USE SENTENCE FROM GENERAL RULE IN CRIME1

CHECKING FOR FEATURE SIMILARITY:

        ---     FOR VIOLATION OF MURDER -- CONFIRMED.
        ---     FOR CAUSING RESULT OF KILL -- CONFIRMED.
        ---     FOR USING ACTION OF STAB-KNIFE -- CONFIRMED.
        ---     FOR HARMING INITIAL-AGGRESSOR -- FAILURE.
                GENERAL RULE IN CRIME1 APPLIES TO HARM
                AGAINST INITIAL-DEFENDER.
        ---     FOR RESPONDING TO HARM AT KNOCK-DOWN LEVEL
                -- FAILURE.
```

```
                  GENERAL RULE IN CRIME1 APPLIES TO
                  RESPONSE TO SLASH-KNIFE LEVEL.
         ---      FOR USING ESCALATED FORCE AND ACTING OUT OF
                  RETALIATION -- CONFIRMED.
         ---      FOR INTENDING TO CAUSE THE RESULT -- CONFIRMED.
```

Two mismatches occurred, but they are not too big for the system to handle. The system must modify the sentence in the right-hand side of the rule to account for the differences found on the left-hand side.

```
HANDLING FAILURE TO MATCH ON FEATURES --- FEATURES WILL BE
ADDED AS NEW INDICES TO RULE.
```

```
--- REDUCING THE SENTENCE SLIGHTLY BECAUSE THE EVENTUAL
VICTIM STARTED THE VIOLENCE IN THE CURRENT SITUATION, WHILE
THE GENERAL RULE APPLIES TO SITUATIONS WHERE THE OFFENDER
INITIATED THE VIOLENCE.
```

```
--- INCREASING THE SENTENCE MODERATELY BECAUSE THE OFFENDER
RESPONDED TO A LESSER DEGREE OF VIOLENCE IN THE CURRENT ACT
THAN THE RULE ACCOUNTS FOR.
```

These modifications indicate the relative strengths of the system's strategies for dealing with feature differences. That is, who started the fight has less effect than the difference in escalation in violence at the end.

Now the system does a consistency check. It knows that the sentence for CRIME2 will be more severe than the sentence for CRIME1 because of the modifications detailed above. It also knows from information that it stored when it formed the general sentencing rule that CRIME1 was also not quite as bad as CRIME0. In order to maintain a local level of consistency in the sentence it will give to CRIME2, the system resorts to an in-depth comparison of CRIME2 and CRIME0. The result of this particular comparison is used only to ensure some degree of consistency between sentences. The actual sentence for CRIME2 will come from modifying the general rule on CRIME1.

```
***** CONSISTENCY CHECK SHOWS THAT A RELATED OLD CRIME,
CRIME0 IS ALSO KNOWN TO BE WORSE THAN CRIME1.  PROCEEDING TO
USE CRIME0 TO DEVELOP A SENTENCE FOR CRIME2...
```

```
IN BOTH CRIMES, THE VICTIM WAS KILLED.  NOT ONLY WERE BOTH
OF THESE OUTCOMES THE RESULT OF DIRECT INTENTIONS, BUT THE
ACTORS INTENDED AND CAUSED THE SAME AMOUNT OF HARM.
```

TIM DEMONSTRATED AN EXTREME USE OF FORCE AGAINST DAVID WHEN
HE ACTED TO STAB DAVID TO DEATH IN RESPONSE TO BEING KNOCKED
TO THE GROUND.

THE CORRESPONDING ACTION IN THE FIRST CASE [CRIME0] DID NOT
DEMONSTRATE SUCH EXTREME FORCE. THE SECOND CRIME WILL
THEREFORE BE CONSIDERED WORSE.

THE INTENT OF BOTH OFFENDERS WAS TO ACT REPEATEDLY TO STAB
THE VICTIM TO DEATH. HOWEVER, ALTHOUGH NEITHER ACTOR'S
INTENTIONS WERE JUSTIFIED, THOSE OF TIM [in CRIME2]
REPRESENTED A LARGER ESCALATION THAN THOSE OF TED.

COMPARISON FINISHED WITH RESULT THAT THE NEW CRIME, CRIME2,
IS SUBSTANTIALLY WORSE.

Given this comparison outcome, the system now knows that the sentence
which it gives to CRIME2 ought to be not only more severe than that of
CRIME1, but also more severe than the CRIME0 sentence as well. In this
instance, CRIME0 and CRIME1 were previously given the same sentence, so
the consistency-preserving modification is trivial. (It is not always true that
two cases compared to an input in this manner will have received the same
sentence.)

THE SENTENCE ORIGINALLY GIVEN FOR CRIME0, FOR VIOLATION OF
MURDER AS DEFINED IN SECTION 53A-45 IN THE CONNECTICUT PENAL
CODE, WAS A TERM OF IMPRISONMENT OF NOT LESS THAN 40 YEARS
NOR MORE THAN 50 YEARS TO BE SERVED IN THE STATE'S PRISON.
ACCORDING TO STATE LAW, 25 YEARS OF THE SENTENCE COULD NOT
BE REDUCED OR SUSPENDED. BECAUSE CRIME2 CONTAINS SOME
INTERPRETATIONAL DIFFERENCES FROM CRIME0, ITS SENTENCE WILL
BE MODIFIED.

THE SENTENCE TO BE GIVEN FOR CRIME2, FOR VIOLATION OF MURDER
AS DEFINED IN SECTION 53A-45 IN THE CONNECTICUT PENAL CODE,
WILL BE A TERM OF IMPRISONMENT OF NOT LESS THAN 45 YEARS NOR
MORE THAN 50 YEARS TO BE SERVED IN THE STATE'S PRISON. OF
THIS SENTENCE, 25 YEARS MAY NOT BE REDUCED OR SUSPENDED,
ACCORDING TO STATE LAW.

Because the new sentence arose from a sentencing rule, it is stored as a
differentiated version of the rule with its differences from the rule noted.

```
STORING NEW VERSION OF GENERAL SENTENCING RULE:

    ---      FOR HARMING INITIAL-AGGRESSOR,
    ---      FOR RESPONDING TO A KNOCK-DOWN LEVEL OF HARM.

THE SENTENCE FOR THIS DIFFERENTIATED VERSION OF THE CRIME0
RULE WILL BE THE SAME AS GIVEN FOR CRIME2 ABOVE.

LINKING CRIME2 INTO MEMORY.

DONE with storage of CRIME2
```

The processing of CRIME2 above contained an unusual instance of rule modification because the sentence consistency checker detected that the system might give a potentially inconsistent sentence. In the 55 cases which we have given to the system, 16 attempts are made to apply rules which the system itself forms. In only four of these cases does the consistency checker require that an in-depth comparison be made. In the remaining cases, the system is usually able to determine a sentence directly from the general rules which it retrieves. In some instances, the program is unable to give consistent sentences across cases; the most prevalent example of this is discussed in Section 4.15.

4.13   Applying Previous Strategies

The more common method that JUDGE uses to sentence an input crime is to modify the sentence from an older case directly on the basis of the outcome of the in-depth comparison made between the crimes.[6] This kind of modification is based on the extent to which the new crime is more or less heinous than the old crime, and takes into account the depth to which the crimes were found to be causally similar.

For example, if the program detects a difference in the degree to which the offender in one case escalated the level of violence, and notices that his behavior was unjustified, then that offender would be considered by the program to have behaved more heinously than the other offender, and would therefore receive a harsher sentence. The difference in heinousness would be even more

---

[6]In the example just shown, the result of comparing CRIME2 with CRIME0 was simply to make sure that CRIME2 would receive a sentence consistent with those given to CRIME0 and CRIME1; the system's sentence for CRIME2 did *not* follow directly from the output of that comparison.

pronounced if the escalation occurred near the end of the crime, rather than at the beginning.

In the example below, the system tries initially to apply a generalized sentencing rule to help determine a sentence for the input case, but finds that the differences between the features describing the rule and the features of the input are too great to reconcile easily. To deal with this conflict, the system ignores the rule completely and instead retreats to its usual style of comparing in-depth the retrieved case (under which the rule was stored) and the input case. It then forms a sentence based on the outcome of that comparison.

The input case is CRIME27, which has these events:

> First, Bob shoved Mike several times. Mike was pushed. Next, Mike struck Bob with his fists several times. Bob was only slightly hurt. Then, Bob struck Mike with his fists several times. Mike was only slightly hurt. Finally, Mike stabbed Bob with a knife several times. Bob died.

The retrieved case is CRIME21, which has:

> First, Ron shoved Biff several times. Biff was pushed. Next, Biff struck Ron with his fists several times. Ron was only slightly hurt. Finally, Ron stabbed Biff with a knife several times. Biff died.

The charges for the input CRIME27 are:

> The offender, Mike, is charged with one count of Murder, defined in Section 53A-45 of the Connecticut Penal Code. Mike allegedly killed Bob, who started a fight with him by pushing him several times. They traded several blows and then Mike pulled a knife and stabbed Bob several times, killing him.

A PREVIOUS SITUATION INVOLVING SIMILAR ACTIONS AND A KILL
RESULT BUT INITIATED BY THE OFFENDER, CRIME21, WAS QUITE
SIMILAR TO THE CURRENT CASE.

CRIME21 CONTAINED SOME OF THE SAME ACTIONS AND RESULTS AS
CRIME27, EXCEPT THAT CRIME27 WAS PRECEDED BY PUSHING.

The program considered CRIME21 to be "quite similar" due to the fact that the crime in both cases was murder, both victims were stabbed to death, and both stabbings resulted from a fistfight. Because of these similarities, the program will attempt to use the rule stored with CRIME21 to form a sentence for the input case.

```
ATTEMPTING TO USE SENTENCE FROM GENERAL RULE IN CRIME21

CHECKING FOR FEATURE SIMILARITY:

    ---     FOR VIOLATION OF MURDER -- CONFIRMED.
    ---     FOR CAUSING RESULT OF KILL -- CONFIRMED.
    ---     FOR USING ACTION OF STAB-KNIFE -- CONFIRMED.
    ---     FOR HARMING INITIAL-AGGRESSOR -- FAILURE.
    ---         GENERAL RULE IN CRIME21 APPLIES TO
                HARM AGAINST INITIAL-DEFENDER.
    ---     FOR RESPONDING TO HARM AT VIOLATED-BRUISE
                LEVEL -- CONFIRMED.
    ---     FOR USING ESCALATED FORCE -- CONFIRMED.
    ---     FOR ACTING OUT OF SELF-DEFENSE -- FAILURE.
    ---         GENERAL RULE IN CRIME21 APPLIES TO
                RETALIATION ACTIONS.
    ---     FOR INTENDING TO CAUSE THE RESULT -- CONFIRMED.
```

The mismatch in this example is one of a few that the system cannot reckon with. Not only does the rule apply to situations where the offender started the fight, but it was also previously useful in a situation where the offender's final action was retaliatory, and thus unjustified. Both of these features differ from the input, and comprise an interaction that the system is unable to recover from.

```
FAILURE TO MATCH ON WHETHER VICTIM STARTED THINGS COMBINED
WITH FAILED ACT INTERPRETATION IS TOO LARGE TO MODIFY.  WILL
RECOVER BY SENDING INPUT CRIME TO COMPARATOR.
```

Instead of attempting a rule modification, the system retreats to comparing the two cases, as we have seen it do before.

```
IN BOTH CRIMES, THE VICTIM WAS KILLED.  NOT ONLY WERE BOTH
OF THESE OUTCOMES THE RESULT OF DIRECT INTENTIONS, BUT THE
ACTORS INTENDED AND CAUSED THE SAME AMOUNT OF HARM.

RON DEMONSTRATED AN EXTREME USE OF FORCE AGAINST BIFF WHEN
HE ACTED TO STAB BIFF TO DEATH IN RESPONSE TO BEING HIT
HARD.

MIKE DEMONSTRATED AN EXTREME USE OF FORCE AGAINST BOB WHEN
HE ACTED TO STAB BOB TO DEATH IN RESPONSE TO BEING HIT HARD.
```

UNABLE TO DISTINGUISH WHETHER THE EXTREME FORCE USED IN
EITHER CRIME WAS WORSE.

Although the comparator cannot distinguish between the extent of force
each offender used, it determines that one of them had some justification for
acting violatively.

THE INTENT OF BOTH OFFENDERS WAS TO ACT REPEATEDLY TO STAB
THE VICTIM TO DEATH. HOWEVER, MIKE WAS JUSTIFIED FOR
PREVENTING FURTHER HARM BY CAUSING BOB TO BE STABBED WHILE
RON WAS NOT JUSTIFIED IN HIS INTENTION TO STAB BIFF TO
DEATH.

Once the program finds a difference in the justification behind the offenders' intentions, it attempts to account for the disparity.

RON'S LACK OF JUSTIFICATION STEMMED FROM EARLIER IN THE CASE
WHEN HE BUMPED BIFF SEVERAL TIMES. THIS WAS THE FIRST USE
OF FORCE IN THE CASE. RON'S ACTION CONSTITUTED AN
UNJUSTIFIED USE OF FORCE BECAUSE RON WAS THE INITIAL
AGGRESSOR.

COMPARISON FINISHED WITH RESULT THAT THE OLD CRIME, CRIME21,
IS SUBSTANTIALLY WORSE.

The system now has two important pieces of information at hand. First,
it knows that one offender was more justified in intending to stab his victim
than the other actor. Second, it knows that this difference occurred between
intentions which had a direct causal bearing on the end of the crimes, and
thus that it is a rather salient difference. The sentence which the program
gives to the input case is now based on what it gave to the old case and on
this new information.

THE SENTENCE ORIGINALLY GIVEN FOR CRIME21, FOR VIOLATION OF
MURDER AS DEFINED IN SECTION 53A-45 IN THE CONNECTICUT PENAL
CODE, WAS A TERM OF IMPRISONMENT OF NOT LESS THAN 50 YEARS
TO BE SERVED IN THE STATE'S PRISON. ACCORDING TO STATE LAW,
25 YEARS OF THE SENTENCE COULD NOT BE REDUCED OR SUSPENDED.
SINCE THE CIRCUMSTANCES OF CRIME21 ARE FOUND TO BE WORSE
THAN CRIME27, DUE TO MORE SEVERE ACTIONS AT THE END OF THE
CRIME, THE OFFENDER WILL GET A SENTENCE WHICH IS MORE

```
LENIENT THAN THE SENTENCE FOR CRIME21.

THE SENTENCE TO BE GIVEN FOR CRIME27, FOR VIOLATION OF
MURDER AS DEFINED IN SECTION 53A-45 IN THE CONNECTICUT PENAL
CODE, WILL BE A TERM OF IMPRISONMENT OF NOT LESS THAN 25
YEARS TO BE SERVED IN THE STATE'S PRISON.  OF THIS SENTENCE,
25 YEARS MAY NOT BE REDUCED OR SUSPENDED, ACCORDING TO STATE
LAW.  THE MAXIMUM PERIOD OF INCARCERATION ALLOWED FOR
VIOLATION OF THIS STATUTE IS 50 YEARS.
```

The actual maximum sentence allowed by the statutes in Connecticut for murder is a term of life imprisonment; 50 years is used by the program as an arbitrary number on which numerical calculations may be made. JUDGE gave the input case a sentence which was much more lenient than the sentence for CRIME21; nevertheless, the 25-year sentence, which is the minimum allowed by law for murder in Connecticut, is still a stiff penalty. Generally, when the system reduces or increases an old sentence, assigning the result to an input case, it does not automatically give the statutory minimum or maximum, respectively. In this case, the modification made to the old sentence called for a moderate reduction; the system settled on the minimum only coincidentally.

4.14   Assessing Differences between Crimes

JUDGE compares the following features of crimes:

- how violent the actions were

- how violent the outcomes were

- how the intended and actual outcomes compared

- how justified the intended outcomes were

- how escalated the actions were

JUDGE compares cases by working backwards from the last events in each case and considering the results, actions, and motives. Remember that features such as escalation and motive were attached in the original analysis phase, working forward from the first event in each case. The comparison process stops as soon as a significant difference between the cases has been detected, e.g., that one of the actors in one case was justified, but the the corresponding actor in the other case was not.

The actor in the last event is always the defendant, since it is the event in which he committed the final crime. Comparisons on this event therefore directly affect JUDGE's attitude toward the defendant. If the comparison goes to the second last event, then the actions of the victims are compared. Sometimes this has the effect of crediting the offender with justification for later actions, for example, when the victim escalated the level of violence unjustifiably.

Suppose there was a case which began with a act of great violence, but was followed by simple trading of blows. The comparison algorithm just given might not distinguish this from a case that began more casually. Two things help JUDGE notice these kinds of situations. First, the justification structures constructed in the forward pass of the analysis carry some cumulative information. Second, the analysis phase also keeps track of the MAXIMUM-OPPONENT-FORCE each actor has encountered so far. That is, if John stabs Ted in the second event, then from that point on, every event with Ted as the actor is marked with STAB as the MAXIMUM-OPPONENT-FORCE, until John does something worse. The comparison process takes this into account when comparing escalations. Suppose John stabs Ted, they trade a few blows, then Ted stabs John. Ted's action is an escalation, but not as bad as if he'd stabbed John when John had not previously stabbed him.

The comparison phase then hands the sentence modifier one of the following descriptors:

- CONFLICT — one crime had a worse outcome, but a justified intent

- AGREEMENT — both outcome and intent were worse in one of the crimes

- SIMILAR-RESULT — one crime had a worse intent, but otherwise the crimes were similar

- EXTREME FORCE — extreme force appeared in one crime, without offsetting justification

The comparison phase also says which crime was worse, and whether the difference was found immediately, i.e., by stepping back no more than two events in the chain of events.

4.15 Modifying a Stored Sentence

JUDGE applies a set of static rules to the output of the comparison phase in order to modify the old sentence to fit the new case.

If the comparison says that the cases are about the same, then the old sentence is given to the new case. If the statutes are different and have different minimum or maximum sentences, the sentence is scaled proportionately. For example, suppose the retrieved crime is a instance of assault in the second-degree, with a 1 to 5 year range of imprisonment, but the input case is an instance of assault in the third degree, with a range of 0 to 1 years. If the retrieved sentence was 2 years, the scaled new sentence would be 5 months.

If the comparison says that the two cases are different, then the following rules are used to modify the old sentence for the new case:

- IF comparison = CONFLICTING and the crimes are not immediately different THEN use the old sentence

- IF comparison = CONFLICTING and the crimes are immediately different THEN increase or decrease the old sentence by 25% as appropriate

- IF comparison = AGREED or SIMILAR-RESULT and the crimes are not immediately different THEN increase or decrease the old sentence by 25% as appropriate

- IF comparison = AGREED or SIMILAR-RESULT and the crimes are immediately different THEN increase or decrease the old sentence by 50% as appropriate

- IF comparison = EXTREME-FORCE and the crimes are not immediately different THEN increase or decrease the old sentence by 50% as appropriate

- IF comparison = EXTREME-FORCE and the crimes are immediately different THEN increase or decrease the old sentence by 75% as appropriate

In some circumstances, the system discovers that in addition to having given a minimal sentence to a case retrieved from memory, an offender in a new case deserves even less punishment; it discovers the converse situation with maximum sentences as well. This is called *bottoming-out* and *topping-out*, respectively. The strategy employed in JUDGE for dealing with these similar states of affairs has been to modify the sentence for the old case and to store it in memory with the old case as if the modified sentence had been given for that case originally. In addition, a note is made in the old case in memory that its original sentence has been tampered with, and to what degree. The newer case can then be assigned a sentence which is consistent in severity with the degree to which it differs in heinousness from the old case.

An example of output of JUDGE noticing this kind of situation is shown below, where the system compared the input CRIME4 with the stored CRIME3.

```
COMPARISON FINISHED WITH RESULT THAT THE OLD CRIME, CRIME3,
IS SUBSTANTIALLY WORSE

THE SENTENCE ORIGINALLY GIVEN FOR CRIME3, FOR VIOLATION OF
MURDER AS DEFINED IN SECTION 53A-45 IN THE CONNECTICUT PENAL
CODE, WAS A TERM OF IMPRISONMENT OF NOT LESS THAN 25 YEARS
TO BE SERVED IN THE STATE'S PRISON.  ACCORDING TO STATE LAW,
25 YEARS OF THE SENTENCE COULD NOT BE REDUCED OR SUSPENDED.
SINCE THE CIRCUMSTANCES OF CRIME3 ARE FOUND TO BE WORSE THAN
CRIME4, DUE TO AN EXTREME USE OF FORCE AT THE END OF THE
CRIME, CRIME4 WILL GET A SENTENCE WHICH IS QUITE A BIT MORE
LENIENT THAN THE SENTENCE FOR CRIME3.

FAILURE:  THE SENTENCE HAS ALREADY BOTTOMED OUT FOR CRIME3.
THE MINIMUM PERIOD OF INCARCERATION GIVEN FOR VIOLATION OF
THIS STATUTE IS 25 YEARS.  FOR FUTURE USE, THE SENTENCE FOR
CRIME3 WILL BE INCREASED TO A MINIMUM OF 35 YEARS.

THE SENTENCE TO BE GIVEN FOR CRIME4, FOR VIOLATION OF MURDER
AS DEFINED IN SECTION 53A-45 IN THE CONNECTICUT PENAL CODE,
WILL BE A TERM OF IMPRISONMENT OF NOT LESS THAN 25 YEARS TO
BE SERVED IN THE STATE'S PRISON.  OF THIS SENTENCE, 25 YEARS
MAY NOT BE REDUCED OR SUSPENDED, ACCORDING TO STATE LAW.
THE MAXIMUM PERIOD OF INCARCERATION ALLOWED FOR VIOLATION OF
THIS STATUTE IS 50 YEARS.
```

After this processing occurs, the sentence that will be discovered whenever CRIME3 is retrieved in the future is 35 years instead of 25 years. The input case above, CRIME4, was able to receive a sentence which was more lenient than the one which cases similar to CRIME3 will receive from this point on.

The extent to which the program ought to propagate its new value assignments is not at all clear. For example, the sentence originally given to CRIME3 above was probably based on a sentence given to some previous crime; is the correspondence between the heinousness of that old crime and the heinousness of CRIME3 still reflected in their respective sentences? The system could not find this out unless it were to investigate the effects of its repairs for bottoming- and topping-out. These inconsistencies could proliferate in the system without being discovered. Although the program does not currently propagate its repairs, it certainly has the facility for doing so, because it doesn't at present lose pointers from new sentences to old. The system could thus use dependency-directed backtracking [Charniak *et al.*, 1987] to weed out inconsistencies. However, an appropriate limit for stopping this propagation is not clear; as the system get more cases in memory, it becomes more unlikely to retrieve older ones. Our protocol data don't help much with this issue either: the judges didn't appear to do any backward propagation of sentencing revisions at all.

4.16   Explaining Rules

Because it links certain details about individual cases to its rules, JUDGE can provide simple explanations for the rules that it develops and uses. For example, below is the rationale that the system gives for having developed a differentiated rule when it processed CRIME2 (see Section 4.12). The system describes the facts of the cases which were involved in forming its rules, and indicates which features caused it to make modifications. This example is presented to show what the system must store in memory in order to remain functional.

```
> (EXPLAIN-RULE CRIME2)

The rule used for sentencing CRIME2 was modified from
a rule used in CRIME0.

The sentence given for the set of features in CRIME0
was a term of imprisonment of not less than 40 years nor
more than 50 years.  Of this sentence, 25 years could not be
reduced or suspended.

Both of these cases were instances of murder.  CRIME2
was started by the offender; CRIME0 was started by the
victim.

--- This difference resulted in a slight reduction of the
sentence given by the rule, since the eventual victim
started the violence in CRIME2, while the general rule
applies to situations where the offender initiated the
violence.

In both of them, the offender caused the victim to be
```

killed. The offender in CRIME2 acted in response to
falling down, while the one in CRIME0 was responding
to being stabbed.

--- This led to a moderate increase in the CRIME2
sentence because the offender in that case responded to a
lesser degree of violence than the rule accounts for.

The final actions in both crimes were interpreted to be
escalated retaliation.

The rule used in CRIME2 inherited the features of the
rule used in CRIME0, with the following exceptions:

    ---   FOR HARMING INITIAL-AGGRESSOR
    ---   FOR RESPONDING TO HARM AT KNOCK-DOWN LEVEL

Thus, the sentence given for the set of features in
CRIME2 was a term of imprisonment of not less than 45 years
nor more than 50 years. Of this sentence, 25 years could
not be reduced or suspended.

4.17   The Effect of Ordering on Learning

Because the JUDGE system stores its cases as experiences in memory and
occasionally forms general rules for giving sentences in similar situations, the
order in which it receives cases is crucial. The program does not always give
the same sentences to crimes when they are presented in a different sequence,
nor does it necessarily form the same rules or generalize rules that relate to
the same crimes. Both the sentences that it gives and the rules that it forms
depend on what is retrieved from memory, and when. Thus, if memory is
arrayed differently, the system will retrieve different cases, which will cause
its behavior to change.

In fact, we reversed the order of presentation of 20 cases we gave to the
system to observe the effects. The outcome of this reversal was that the
system made generalizations in different places. For example, when running
the cases from CRIME0 through CRIME19, a generalization was made as a
result of processing CRIME9 and CRIME10. CRIME13 was sentenced by an
intact version of this rule (i.e., no differentiation from the CRIME9-CRIME10
rule was necessary). In the backward condition, on the other hand, CRIME12

formed a general sentencing rule with CRIME13. CRIME11 was then sentenced by a differentiated version of the rule, and later, crimes 10 and 9 were sentenced by the original version of the CRIME12-CRIME13 rule.

The significance of order of case presentation on the process of sentencing might be demonstrated experimentally with human judges.[7] For example, two groups of judges could be asked to sentence the 55 cases that JUDGE has processed (without the benefit of any additional information, such as the prior record of the offender in each case). One group would receive cases in the order they were given to JUDGE (i.e., CRIME0 through CRIME54); the other judges would receive the same cases in the reverse sequence (i.e., CRIME54 through CRIME0). We would expect that the sentences of the first group would be more similar to JUDGE's forward-condition sentences, and that those of the second group would be more similar to JUDGE's reverse-sequence sentences, than either group's sentences would be to those of JUDGE running in the opposite order.

What is certain in this sequence-dependent processing is that one cannot be reminded of something that one has not yet seen; furthermore, how similar the most similar case available in memory would be would probably change between these conditions. Thus, any sentencing differences between the two conditions could depend not only on different remindings, but on the different degrees to which previous sentences might have to be modified to fit a new case. A statistically higher correlation between the sentences of each group and the program running in the same direction, compared with the correlation between each group's sentences and those of the program running in the opposite order, would support the conclusion that recent similar experiences have an observable effect on human decision-making. This conclusion lends psychological validity to the case-based methodology used in developing JUDGE.

4.18 Extending JUDGE

Although a great deal of knowledge was trimmed from the cases that the system sees, some of that which judges use could be added to the system without much trouble. For example, certain statutes in the Connecticut Penal Code indicate a mechanical process for accounting for an offender's prior record. The rules which relate to these data suggest that for certain specified types of prior offenses the judge may use a harsher minimum and maximum for sentencing the current offense. Crimes in general are divided up in the statutes into categories which carry standard punishments (e.g., Class A, B, C, and D

---

[7]This idea is due to Bob Abelson, personal communication.

felonies). Thus, finding the appropriate new level of punishment for a repeat offender is trivial.

What is not clear, however, is that judges use this algorithm consistently to determine sentences. Instead, they seem to have a "feel" for determining sentence length which they then often translate into legal mechanisms to impose. Because JUDGE does not construe sentencing as a means of punishing offenders and teaching them lessons, the best it might do would be to use some straightforward process for increasing sentences for repeat offenders, such as altering the base level minima and maxima use for sentencing a crime.

Another extension to the program, which might be more doable, would be to deal with multiple statutory violations by the same offender. It is frequently the case that by one violative action an offender is charged and convicted of committing more than one crime. The mechanisms already present in the program could deal with this because judges are allowed to impose sentences on multiple counts which run either consecutively or concurrently. Thus, if by modifying a previous sentence the system came up with a sentence which was longer than the maximum for any one of the charges, it could still try to impose the sentence. It would do this by dividing the sentence up by the number of counts and giving consecutive sentences for each count. Similarly, concurrency allows for reducing a sentence for multiple violations to less than the sum of the minimum sentences for each charge.

5

Micro JUDGE

5.1 Introduction

In this chapter, we present a miniature version of the JUDGE program. This miniature starts with an empty case base. We give it a new case describing a fight, with a criminal sentence already attached. Then we give it two more cases, without sentences, and it creates their sentences by adapting the cases in memory.

5.2 Implementing Micro JUDGE

As with the other miniatures, micro JUDGE is implemented primarily by its MOPs. Most of the Lisp code is used to define abstraction, calculation, and adaptation functions. The top-level function to run JUDGE is very short, and appears in Listing 5.1

(JUDGE *slot-list*) finds or creates a case under M-CRIME with the given slots and returns it. The call to GET-FILLER forces the calculation of the role SENTENCE, which in turn forces the calculation of a number of intermediate roles, such as the motives and escalation values of each events.

```
(DEFUN JUDGE (SLOTS)
 (LET ((INSTANCE (SLOTS->MOP SLOTS '(M-CRIME) T)))
  (AND (GET-FILLER 'SENTENCE INSTANCE)
       INSTANCE)))
```

Listing 5.1: Top-Level Micro JUDGE Function

```
(DEFMOP I-M-AL (M-ACTOR) INSTANCE)
(DEFMOP I-M-CHUCK (M-ACTOR) INSTANCE)
(DEFMOP I-M-DAVID (M-ACTOR) INSTANCE)
(DEFMOP I-M-RANDY (M-ACTOR) INSTANCE)
(DEFMOP I-M-TED (M-ACTOR) INSTANCE)
(DEFMOP I-M-TIM (M-ACTOR) INSTANCE)

(DEFMOP M-FREQUENCY (M-ROOT) (SEVERITY NIL))
(DEFMOP I-M-ONCE (M-FREQUENCY) (SEVERITY 0))
(DEFMOP I-M-SEVERAL-TIMES (M-FREQUENCY) (SEVERITY 1))
(DEFMOP I-M-REPEATEDLY (M-FREQUENCY) (SEVERITY 2))

(DEFMOP M-MOTIVE (M-ROOT))
(DEFMOP M-JUSTIFIED (M-MOTIVE))
(DEFMOP M-UNJUSTIFIED (M-MOTIVE))
(DEFMOP I-M-SELF-DEFENSE (M-JUSTIFIED) INSTANCE)
(DEFMOP I-M-RETALIATION (M-UNJUSTIFIED) INSTANCE)
(DEFMOP I-M-UNPROVOKED (M-UNJUSTIFIED) INSTANCE)

(DEFMOP M-CRIME-TYPE (M-ROOT))
(DEFMOP I-M-HOMICIDE (M-CRIME-TYPE) INSTANCE)
```

Listing 5.2: Micro JUDGE Basic MOPs

Listing 5.2 defines MOPs for actors, event frequencies, motives, and crime types. The (SEVERITY *integer*) slot is used to attach levels of "badness" to frequencies, actions, physical states, and so on. The bigger the number, the more serious is the object.

Listing 5.3 defines a general set of abstraction functions and MOPs for specifying pattern MOPs that cover ranges of numbers. A specialization of M-RANGE with an (ABOVE *m*) slot is satisfied by any number strictly greater than *m*. A specialization with a (BELOW *n*) is satisfied by any number strictly less than *n*. A specialization with both slots is satisfied by any number between *m* and *n*.

Listing 5.4 defines MOPs used to build events and outcomes. An event has an actor, action, and object, and an outcome has a physical state and an object in that state. The actions are subdivided into two classes, M-HURT-ACT and the more serious M-WOUND-ACT.

Listing 5.5 defines MOPs for M-CRIME, the main MOP in JUDGE, for

```
(DEFMOP RANGE-CONSTRAINT (CONSTRAINT-FN))
(DEFMOP M-RANGE (M-PATTERN)
   (ABST-FN RANGE-CONSTRAINT))

(DEFUN RANGE-CONSTRAINT (CONSTRAINT FILLER SLOTS)
 (AND (NUMBERP FILLER)
      (LET ((BELOW (ROLE-FILLER 'BELOW CONSTRAINT))
            (ABOVE (ROLE-FILLER 'ABOVE CONSTRAINT)))
        (AND (OR (NULL BELOW) (< FILLER BELOW))
             (OR (NULL ABOVE) (< ABOVE FILLER))))))
```

Listing 5.3: Range Constraints

groups of events, outcomes, escalations, and motives, and for the functions that calculate fillers for roles in M-CRIME. It is assumed that any input crime description will already have fillers for CRIME-TYPE, DEFENDANT, VICTIM, EVENTS, and OUTCOMES.

Listing 5.6 defines the Lisp code for the functions in Listing 5.5 that calculate the escalations and motives of the events in the case.

(CALC-ESCALATIONS *pattern mop*) takes the group of events in *mop* and calculates a group of corresponding escalations. The escalation of an event is the severity of the current event minus the severity of the preceding event. The escalation of the first event is just its severity.

(CALC-MOTIVES *pattern mop*) takes the group of events in *mop* and calculates a group of corresponding motives. Motives are more complex to calculate than escalations. The motive of an event depends on the escalation of the event and the motive of the previous event. This knowledge is stored in calculation MOPs (M-CALC's) defined in Listing 5.7 and retrieved with MOP-CALC.

(MOP-CALC *slot-list*) finds the specialization of M-CALC with the given slots and returns its VALUE filler. Basically M-CALC MOPs represent rules, organized into an abstraction hierarchy, and MOP-CALC is the rule applier.

Listing 5.7 defines the MOPs used by CALC-MOTIVES in Listing 5.6. Each MOP describes some possible constraints on the current event's escalation level and the previous event's motive, and the VALUE role specifies the appropriate motive. The situations are:

- If the current event is more severe than the preceding event (escalation is positive), the motive is retaliation.

- If the current event is not more severe than the preceding event, and the

```
(DEFMOP M-FIGHT-ACT (M-ACT) (SEVERITY NIL))
(DEFMOP M-HURT-ACT (M-FIGHT-ACT)
    (SEVERITY M-RANGE (BELOW 5)))
(DEFMOP I-M-SLAP (M-HURT-ACT) (SEVERITY 1))
(DEFMOP I-M-HIT (M-HURT-ACT) (SEVERITY 1))
(DEFMOP I-M-STRIKE (M-HURT-ACT) (SEVERITY 2))
(DEFMOP I-M-KNOCK-DOWN (M-HURT-ACT) (SEVERITY 3))
(DEFMOP I-M-SLASH (M-HURT-ACT) (SEVERITY 4))

(DEFMOP M-WOUND-ACT (M-FIGHT-ACT)
    (SEVERITY M-RANGE (ABOVE 4)))
(DEFMOP I-M-STAB (M-WOUND-ACT) (SEVERITY 5))
(DEFMOP I-M-SHOOT (M-WOUND-ACT) (SEVERITY 5))
(DEFMOP I-M-BREAK-SKULL (M-WOUND-ACT) (SEVERITY 5))

(DEFMOP M-STATE (M-ROOT))
(DEFMOP M-PHYS-STATE (M-STATE) (SEVERITY NIL))
(DEFMOP I-M-BRUISED (M-PHYS-STATE) (SEVERITY 1))
(DEFMOP I-M-KNOCKED-DOWN (M-PHYS-STATE) (SEVERITY 2))
(DEFMOP I-M-CUT (M-PHYS-STATE) (SEVERITY 3))
(DEFMOP I-M-DEAD (M-PHYS-STATE) (SEVERITY 5))

(DEFMOP M-OUTCOME (M-ROOT))
(DEFMOP M-FIGHT-OUTCOME (M-OUTCOME)
    (STATE M-PHYS-STATE) (ACTOR M-ACTOR))

(DEFMOP M-FIGHT-EVENT (M-EVENT) (ACTION M-FIGHT-ACT))
```

Listing 5.4: Micro JUDGE Event MOPs

```
(DEFMOP M-EVENT-GROUP (M-GROUP) (1 M-EVENT))
(DEFMOP M-OUTCOME-GROUP (M-GROUP) (1 M-OUTCOME))
(DEFMOP M-ESCALATION-GROUP (M-GROUP) (1 M-RANGE))
(DEFMOP M-MOTIVE-GROUP (M-GROUP) (1 M-MOTIVE))

(DEFMOP CALC-ESCALATIONS (M-FUNCTION))
(DEFMOP CALC-MOTIVES (M-FUNCTION))
(DEFMOP ADAPT-SENTENCE (M-FUNCTION))
(DEFMOP CALC-SENTENCE (M-FUNCTION))

(DEFMOP M-CRIME (M-CASE)
    (CRIME-TYPE M-CRIME-TYPE)
    (DEFENDANT M-ACTOR)
    (VICTIM M-ACTOR)
    (EVENTS M-EVENT-GROUP)
    (OUTCOMES M-OUTCOME-GROUP)
    (ESCALATIONS M-PATTERN (CALC-FN CALC-ESCALATIONS))
    (MOTIVES M-PATTERN (CALC-FN CALC-MOTIVES))
    (SENTENCE M-PATTERN (CALC-FN ADAPT-SENTENCE)))
```

Listing 5.5: Micro JUDGE Top-Level MOP

```
(DEFUN CALC-ESCALATIONS (PATTERN MOP)
 (FORMAT T "~&----------------")
 (FORMAT T "~&Calculating escalations in ~S" MOP)
 (LIST->GROUP
   (LET ((PREV-SEVERITY 0))
     (FOR (EVENT :IN (GROUP->LIST
                       (ROLE-FILLER 'EVENTS MOP)))
       :SAVE (LET ((THIS-SEVERITY
                     (PATH-FILLER '(ACTION SEVERITY)
                                  EVENT)))
               (LET ((RESULT (- THIS-SEVERITY
                                PREV-SEVERITY)))
                 (SETF PREV-SEVERITY THIS-SEVERITY)
                 RESULT))))))

(DEFUN CALC-MOTIVES (PATTERN MOP)
 (FORMAT T "~&----------------")
 (FORMAT T "~&Calculating motives in ~S" MOP)
 (LIST->GROUP
   (LET ((PREV-MOTIVE 0))
     (FOR (ESCALATION :IN (GROUP->LIST
                            (GET-FILLER 'ESCALATIONS
                                        MOP)))
       :SAVE (SETF PREV-MOTIVE
                   (MOP-CALC
                     '((ROLE MOTIVE)
                       (ESCALATION ,ESCALATION)
                       (PREV-MOTIVE ,PREV-MOTIVE)
                       )))))))

(DEFUN MOP-CALC (SLOTS)
 (LET ((INSTANCE (SLOTS->MOP SLOTS '(M-CALC) NIL)))
   (AND INSTANCE
        (GET-FILLER 'VALUE INSTANCE))))
```

Listing 5.6: Micro JUDGE Role Calculation Functions

```
(DEFMOP MOTIVE (M-ROLE) INSTANCE)

(DEFMOP M-CALC (M-ROOT))

(DEFMOP M-CALC-MOTIVE (M-CALC)
    (ROLE MOTIVE) (VALUE NIL))

(DEFMOP M-CALC-ESCALATION-MOTIVE (M-CALC-MOTIVE)
    (ESCALATION M-RANGE (ABOVE 0))
    (VALUE I-M-RETALIATION))

(DEFMOP M-CALC-SELF-DEFENSE-MOTIVE (M-CALC-MOTIVE)
    (ESCALATION M-RANGE (BELOW 1))
    (PREV-MOTIVE M-UNJUSTIFIED)
    (VALUE I-M-SELF-DEFENSE))

(DEFMOP M-CALC-RETALIATION-MOTIVE (M-CALC-MOTIVE)
    (ESCALATION M-RANGE (BELOW 1))
    (PREV-MOTIVE M-JUSTIFIED)
    (VALUE I-M-RETALIATION))
```

Listing 5.7: Micro JUDGE Calculation MOPs

previous event was unjustified (defined in Listing 5.2), the motive is self defense.

- If the current event is not more severe than the preceding event, but the previous event was justified the motive is retaliation.

These rules have roughly the same function as those given in Figure 4.1 in Chapter 4.

Listing 5.8 defines the functions that adjust a sentence, taking into account how different the input crime was from the retrieved crime. The formula used is basically the same as that described in Section 4.15.

(ADJUST-SENTENCE *pattern mop*) is called by the sentence calculation MOPs in Listing 5.11 to adjust the sentence appropriately. The slots in *mop* contain the old sentence, a weighting factor (between 0.00 and 0.50) that says how critical the difference is, an index (between 0 and the number of events in the shortest fight) that says how close the difference was to the final act,

```
(DEFUN ADJUST-SENTENCE (PATTERN MOP)
  (FORMAT T "~&---------------")
  (FORMAT T "~&~S applied, ~S events from the end"
          MOP (GET-FILLER 'INDEX MOP))
  (ADJUST-FN
      (GET-FILLER 'OLD-SENTENCE MOP)
      (GET-FILLER 'WEIGHT MOP)
      (GET-FILLER 'INDEX MOP)
      (GET-FILLER 'DIRECTION MOP)))

(DEFUN ADJUST-FN (X Y INDEX DIRECTION)
  (+ X (* X (+ Y (COND ((< INDEX 2) 0.25) (T 0.0)))
          DIRECTION)))
```

Listing 5.8: Micro JUDGE Adjustment Functions

and a direction (1 or -1) that says which case is worse, the old one (-1) or the new one (1).

(ADJUST-FN *sentence weight index direction*) determines the value of the new sentence, based on the old sentence, using the formula

$$sentence + (sentence \times (weight + closeness) \times direction)$$

where *closeness* is 0.25 if *index* is 0 or 1, i.e., the last or second last events differed, or 0.00 if *index* $>= 1$.

Listing 5.9 defines the adaptation function that derives a sentence for a case. It does this by comparing the events, motives, and outcomes in the case with those in a related case. The comparison starts with the last event, motive, and outcome in each case, and works backwards, on the grounds that the events closest to the final criminal act are more relevant than events occurring at the start of the fight. As soon as a difference is found, the sentence in the retrieved case is adjusted accordingly and assigned to the input case.

(ADAPT-SENTENCE *pattern mop*) gets another case with the same immediate abstraction as *mop*, and compares the actions, motives, and outcomes in the two cases, working backwards, until a difference is found and an adjusted sentence is calculated. The comparison and adjustment are done using the calculation MOPs defined in Listings 5.12 and 5.13.

(CRIME-COMPARE-SLOTS *mop n role-list*) returns a list of slots, where the first role in *role-list* is filled with the action of the *n*th-last event, the second

```
(DEFUN ADAPT-SENTENCE (PATTERN MOP)
 (LET ((OLD-MOP (GET-FILLER 'OLD MOP)))
  (LET ((OLD-SIZE (GROUP-SIZE
                    (GET-FILLER 'EVENTS OLD-MOP)))
        (SIZE (GROUP-SIZE (GET-FILLER 'EVENTS MOP)))
        (OLD-SENTENCE (GET-FILLER 'SENTENCE OLD-MOP)))
   (FORMAT T "~&----------------")
   (FORMAT T "~&Adapting the sentence in ~S" OLD-MOP)
   (OR (FOR (OLD-POS :IN (MAKE-M-N OLD-SIZE 1))
            (POS :IN (MAKE-M-N SIZE 1))
         :FIRST
           (MOP-CALC
             '((ROLE SENTENCE) (INDEX ,(- SIZE POS))
               (OLD-SENTENCE ,OLD-SENTENCE)
               ,@(CRIME-COMPARE-SLOTS OLD-MOP OLD-POS
                   '(OLD-ACTION OLD-MOTIVE
                     OLD-SEVERITY))
               ,@(CRIME-COMPARE-SLOTS MOP POS
                   '(THIS-ACTION THIS-MOTIVE
                     THIS-SEVERITY)))))
       (PROGN (FORMAT T "~&----------------")
              (FORMAT T "~&No major difference found")
              (FORMAT T "~&Using old sentence")
              OLD-SENTENCE)))))

(DEFUN CRIME-COMPARE-SLOTS (MOP POS ROLES)
 (LET ((PATHS '((EVENTS ,POS ACTION)
                (MOTIVES ,POS)
                (OUTCOMES ,POS STATE SEVERITY))))
  (INSIST CRIME-COMPARE-SLOTS
          (EQL (LENGTH ROLES) (LENGTH PATHS)))
  (FOR (ROLE :IN ROLES) (PATH :IN PATHS)
    :SAVE (MAKE-SLOT ROLE (PATH-FILLER PATH MOP)))))
```

Listing 5.9: Micro JUDGE Adaptation Functions

role with the *n*th-last motive, and the third role with the severity of the *n*th-last outcome. These are the factors used to compare two crimes.

Listing 5.10 defines a general set of abstraction functions and MOPs for

```
(DEFMOP COMPARE-CONSTRAINT (CONSTRAINT-FN))

(DEFMOP M-COMPARE (M-PATTERN)
    (ABST-FN COMPARE-CONSTRAINT) (TO M-ROLE)
    (COMPARE-FN M-FUNCTION))

(DEFMOP EQL (M-FUNCTION))
(DEFMOP < (M-FUNCTION))

(DEFMOP M-EQUAL (M-COMPARE) (COMPARE-FN EQL))
(DEFMOP M-LESS-THAN (M-COMPARE) (COMPARE-FN <))

(DEFUN COMPARE-CONSTRAINT (CONSTRAINT FILLER SLOTS)
  (FUNCALL (GET-FILLER 'COMPARE-FN CONSTRAINT)
           FILLER
           (INDIRECT-FILLER 'TO CONSTRAINT SLOTS)))

(DEFUN INDIRECT-FILLER (ROLE MOP SLOTS)
  (GET-FILLER (GET-FILLER ROLE MOP) SLOTS))
```

Listing 5.10: Comparison MOPs

specifying pattern MOPs that compare the fillers of two roles. The comparison function can be any two argument function, such as EQL or <.

M-COMPARE is the MOP for patterns that compare MOPs against other MOPs. A specialization of M-COMPARE with a (TO *role*) slot and (COMPARE-FN *function*) slot is satisfied by a MOP *mop* if (*function mop filler*) returns true, where *filler* is the filler of *role* in the MOP whose slots are being tested.

M-EQUAL and M-LESS-THAN are comparison MOPs for equality and being less than, respectively. Their abstraction functions are Common Lisp's EQL and <, respectively.

(COMPARE-CONSTRAINT *constraint filler slots*) applies the comparison function in *constraint* to *filler* and the filler of *role* in *slots*, where *role* is the role that fills the TO slot in *constraint*.

(INDIRECT-FILLER *role mop slots*) gets the filler of *role* in *mop*, which should be a role, and gets the filler of that role in *slots*.

Listings 5.11, 5.12, and 5.13 define the calculation MOPs used by the function ADAPT-SENTENCE (Listing 5.9) to find differences between two cases. The MOPs compare corresponding events, motives, and outcomes from the

```
(DEFMOP SENTENCE (M-ROLE) INSTANCE)
(DEFMOP OLD-SEVERITY (M-ROLE) INSTANCE)

(DEFMOP ADJUST-SENTENCE (M-FUNCTION))

(DEFMOP M-ADAPT-SENTENCE (M-CALC)
    (ROLE SENTENCE)
    (VALUE M-PATTERN (CALC-FN ADJUST-SENTENCE)))
```

Listing 5.11: Micro JUDGE MOPs for Adaptation

input and retrieved cases. The INDEX field is set to an integer representing how many steps back from the end of the fight these items occur. Each M-ADAPT-SENTENCE MOP describes some possible difference, which determine the WEIGHT and DIRECTION slots. When the MOP-CALC call in ADAPT-SENTENCE asks for the VALUE slot, ADJUST-SENTENCE is inherited and constructs the sentence. If none of the M-ADAPT-SENTENCE MOPs apply, MOP-CALC returns NIL and ADAPT-SENTENCE tries again, with an earlier pair of crime events.

The differences recognized are:

- The old event involved extreme force (M-WOUND-ACT) and the new event did not, and neither were justified. The weight is 0.50 and the direction is -1.

- The new event involved extreme force (M-WOUND-ACT) and the old event did not, and neither were justified. The weight is 0.50 and the direction is 1.

- The new event was justified, but the old one wasn't, and both were of comparable severity. The weight is 0.25 and the direction is -1.

- The old event was justified, but the new one wasn't, and both were of comparable severity. The weight is 0.25 and the direction is 1.

- The new event is less severe than the old one, but unjustified, while the old one was justified. The weight is 0.00 and the direction is -1.

- The old event is less severe than the new one, but unjustified, while the new one was justified. The weight is 0.00 and the direction is 1.

The JUDGE equivalent of these rules can be found in Section 4.15.

```
(DEFMOP M-ADAPT-EXTREME-FORCE-OLD (M-ADAPT-SENTENCE)
    (OLD-ACTION M-WOUND-ACT)
    (THIS-ACTION M-NOT (OBJECT M-WOUND-ACT))
    (OLD-MOTIVE M-UNJUSTIFIED)
    (THIS-MOTIVE M-UNJUSTIFIED)
    (WEIGHT 0.50) (DIRECTION -1))

(DEFMOP M-ADAPT-EXTREME-FORCE-NEW (M-ADAPT-SENTENCE)
    (OLD-ACTION M-NOT (OBJECT M-WOUND-ACT))
    (THIS-ACTION M-WOUND-ACT)
    (OLD-MOTIVE M-UNJUSTIFIED)
    (THIS-MOTIVE M-UNJUSTIFIED)
    (WEIGHT 0.50) (DIRECTION 1))

(DEFMOP M-ADAPT-WORSE-MOTIVE-OLD (M-ADAPT-SENTENCE)
    (OLD-SEVERITY NIL)
    (THIS-SEVERITY M-EQUAL (TO OLD-SEVERITY))
    (OLD-MOTIVE M-UNJUSTIFIED)
    (THIS-MOTIVE M-JUSTIFIED)
    (WEIGHT 0.25) (DIRECTION -1))

(DEFMOP M-ADAPT-WORSE-MOTIVE-NEW (M-ADAPT-SENTENCE)
    (OLD-SEVERITY NIL)
    (THIS-SEVERITY M-EQUAL (TO OLD-SEVERITY))
    (OLD-MOTIVE M-JUSTIFIED)
    (THIS-MOTIVE M-UNJUSTIFIED)
    (WEIGHT 0.25) (DIRECTION 1))
```

Listing 5.12: Micro JUDGE Force and Motive Adaptation MOPs

```
(DEFMOP M-ADAPT-MIXED-OLD (M-ADAPT-SENTENCE)
    (OLD-SEVERITY NIL)
    (THIS-SEVERITY M-LESS-THAN (TO OLD-SEVERITY))
    (OLD-MOTIVE M-JUSTIFIED)
    (THIS-MOTIVE M-UNJUSTIFIED)
    (WEIGHT 0.00) (DIRECTION -1))

(DEFMOP M-ADAPT-MIXED-NEW (M-ADAPT-SENTENCE)
    (THIS-SEVERITY NIL)
    (OLD-SEVERITY M-LESS-THAN (TO OLD-SEVERITY))
    (OLD-MOTIVE M-UNJUSTIFIED)
    (THIS-MOTIVE M-JUSTIFIED)
    (WEIGHT 0.00) (DIRECTION 1))
```

Listing 5.13: Micro JUDGE Mixed Comparison Adaptation MOPs

Listings 5.14, 5.15, and 5.16 define three cases for testing JUDGE. *CASE1* is a base case, giving a crime and a sentence. *CASE2* and *CASE3* are input cases, with crimes but no sentences assigned yet.

Listing 5.17 defines the JUDGE demo function. (JUDGE-DEMO) calls JUDGE with the three sample cases. If any of them returns NIL, something went wrong and the demo stops immediately.

```
(SETF *CASE1*
     '((CRIME-TYPE I-M-HOMICIDE)
       (DEFENDANT I-M-TED) (VICTIM I-M-AL)
       (EVENTS M-GROUP
                (1 M-FIGHT-EVENT
                   (ACTION I-M-SLASH)
                   (ACTOR I-M-TED) (OBJECT I-M-AL)
                   (FREQ I-M-ONCE))
                (2 M-FIGHT-EVENT
                   (ACTION I-M-SLASH)
                   (ACTOR I-M-AL) (OBJECT I-M-TED)
                   (FREQ I-M-ONCE))
                (3 M-FIGHT-EVENT
                   (ACTION I-M-STAB)
                   (ACTOR I-M-TED) (OBJECT I-M-AL)
                   (FREQ I-M-REPEATEDLY)))
       (OUTCOMES M-GROUP
                (1 M-FIGHT-OUTCOME
                   (STATE I-M-CUT) (ACTOR I-M-AL))
                (2 M-FIGHT-OUTCOME
                   (STATE I-M-CUT) (ACTOR I-M-TED))
                (3 M-FIGHT-OUTCOME
                   (STATE I-M-DEAD) (ACTOR I-M-AL)))
       (SENTENCE 40)))
```

Listing 5.14: Micro JUDGE First Test Case

```
(SETF *CASE2*
      '((CRIME-TYPE I-M-HOMICIDE)
        (DEFENDANT I-M-RANDY) (VICTIM I-M-CHUCK)
        (EVENTS M-GROUP
          (1 M-FIGHT-EVENT
             (ACTION I-M-STRIKE)
             (ACTOR I-M-RANDY) (OBJECT I-M-CHUCK)
             (FREQ I-M-REPEATEDLY))
          (2 M-FIGHT-EVENT
             (ACTION I-M-STRIKE)
             (ACTOR I-M-CHUCK) (OBJECT I-M-RANDY)
             (FREQ I-M-REPEATEDLY))
          (3 M-FIGHT-EVENT
             (ACTION I-M-SLASH)
             (ACTOR I-M-RANDY) (OBJECT I-M-CHUCK)
             (FREQ I-M-ONCE))
          (4 M-FIGHT-EVENT
             (ACTION I-M-SLASH)
             (ACTOR I-M-CHUCK) (OBJECT I-M-RANDY)
             (FREQ I-M-ONCE))
          (5 M-FIGHT-EVENT
             (ACTION I-M-STAB)
             (ACTOR I-M-RANDY) (OBJECT I-M-CHUCK)
             (FREQ I-M-REPEATEDLY)))
        (OUTCOMES M-GROUP
          (1 M-FIGHT-OUTCOME
             (STATE I-M-BRUISED) (ACTOR I-M-CHUCK))
          (2 M-FIGHT-OUTCOME
             (STATE I-M-BRUISED) (ACTOR I-M-RANDY))
          (3 M-FIGHT-OUTCOME
             (STATE I-M-CUT) (ACTOR I-M-CHUCK))
          (4 M-FIGHT-OUTCOME
             (STATE I-M-CUT) (ACTOR I-M-RANDY))
          (5 M-FIGHT-OUTCOME
             (STATE I-M-DEAD) (ACTOR I-M-CHUCK)))))
```

Listing 5.15: Micro JUDGE Second Test Case

```
(SETF *CASE3*
     '((CRIME-TYPE I-M-HOMICIDE)
       (DEFENDANT I-M-TIM) (VICTIM I-M-DAVID)
       (EVENTS M-GROUP
         (1 M-FIGHT-EVENT
            (ACTION I-M-SLAP)
            (ACTOR I-M-DAVID) (OBJECT I-M-TIM)
            (FREQ I-M-SEVERAL-TIMES))
         (2 M-FIGHT-EVENT
            (ACTION I-M-STRIKE)
            (ACTOR I-M-TIM) (OBJECT I-M-DAVID)
           (FREQ I-M-SEVERAL-TIMES))
         (3 M-FIGHT-EVENT
            (ACTION I-M-KNOCK-DOWN)
            (ACTOR I-M-DAVID) (OBJECT I-M-TIM)
            (FREQ I-M-ONCE))
         (4 M-FIGHT-EVENT
            (ACTION I-M-STAB)
            (ACTOR I-M-TIM) (OBJECT I-M-DAVID)
            (FREQ I-M-SEVERAL-TIMES)))
       (OUTCOMES M-GROUP
         (1 M-FIGHT-OUTCOME
            (STATE I-M-BRUISED) (ACTOR I-M-TIM))
         (2 M-FIGHT-OUTCOME
            (STATE I-M-BRUISED) (ACTOR I-M-DAVID))
         (3 M-FIGHT-OUTCOME
            (STATE I-M-KNOCKED-DOWN) (ACTOR I-M-TIM))
         (4 M-FIGHT-OUTCOME
            (STATE I-M-DEAD) (ACTOR I-M-DAVID)))))
```

Listing 5.16: Micro JUDGE Third Test Case

```
(DEFUN JUDGE-DEMO ()
 (RUN-JUDGE *CASE1* '*CASE1*)
 (RUN-JUDGE *CASE2* '*CASE2*)
 (RUN-JUDGE *CASE3* '*CASE3*))

(DEFUN RUN-JUDGE (CASE CASE-NAME)
 (FORMAT T "~&----------------")
 (FORMAT T "~&Sentencing ~S in ~S"
          (ROLE-FILLER 'DEFENDANT CASE) CASE-NAME)
 (LET ((INSTANCE (JUDGE (FORMS->SLOTS CASE))))
  (INSIST JUDGE-DEMO (NOT (NULL INSTANCE)))
  (FORMAT T "~&Sentence in ~S is ~S years"
           INSTANCE (ROLE-FILLER 'SENTENCE INSTANCE))
  INSTANCE))
```

Listing 5.17: Micro JUDGE Demo

5.3   Running the JUDGE Demo

To run the micro JUDGE demo, you need the code in the Listings in Chapter
3 and this chapter. Follow these steps:

1. Load all DEFUN, DEFMACRO, SETF, DEFINE-FOR-KEY, and DEFINE-TABLE
   forms, in the order in which they appear in the Listings.

2. Execute the function call (CLEAR-MEMORY).

3. Load all the DEFMOP forms, in the order in which they appear in the
   Listings.

4. Execute the function call (JUDGE-DEMO).

   After Step 3, the abstraction hierarchy printed by (DAH 'M-ROOT) should
look like the following, except for the numbers on the MOPs.

```
(M-ROOT
    (M-CALC
        (M-ADAPT-SENTENCE
            (M-ADAPT-MIXED-NEW)
            (M-ADAPT-MIXED-OLD)
            (M-ADAPT-WORSE-MOTIVE-NEW)
            (M-ADAPT-WORSE-MOTIVE-OLD)
            (M-ADAPT-EXTREME-FORCE-NEW)
            (M-ADAPT-EXTREME-FORCE-OLD))
        (M-CALC-MOTIVE
            (M-CALC-RETALIATION-MOTIVE)
            (M-CALC-SELF-DEFENSE-MOTIVE)
            (M-CALC-ESCALATION-MOTIVE)))
    (M-OUTCOME (M-FIGHT-OUTCOME))
    (M-CRIME-TYPE (I-M-HOMICIDE))
    (M-MOTIVE
        (M-UNJUSTIFIED
            (I-M-UNPROVOKED)
            (I-M-RETALIATION))
        (M-JUSTIFIED (I-M-SELF-DEFENSE)))
    (M-FREQUENCY
        (I-M-REPEATEDLY)
        (I-M-SEVERAL-TIMES)
        (I-M-ONCE)))
```

```
(M-FAILED-SOLUTION)
(M-ROLE (OLD-SEVERITY) (SENTENCE) (MOTIVE))
(M-CASE (M-CRIME))
(M-PATTERN
    (M-PATTERN.24)
    (M-COMPARE
        (M-LESS-THAN (M-LESS-THAN.29))
        (M-EQUAL (M-EQUAL.27)))
    (M-PATTERN.20)
    (M-PATTERN.19)
    (M-PATTERN.18)
    (M-RANGE
        (M-RANGE.22)
        (M-RANGE.21)
        (M-RANGE.17)
        (M-RANGE.16))
    (M-NOT (M-NOT.25))
    (M-PATTERN.15))
(M-FUNCTION
    (ADJUST-SENTENCE)
    (<)
    (EQL)
    (CALC-SENTENCE)
    (ADAPT-SENTENCE)
    (CALC-MOTIVES)
    (CALC-ESCALATIONS)
    (GET-SIBLING)
    (CONSTRAINT-FN
        (COMPARE-CONSTRAINT)
        (RANGE-CONSTRAINT)
        (NOT-CONSTRAINT)))
(M-GROUP
    (M-MOTIVE-GROUP)
    (M-ESCALATION-GROUP)
    (M-OUTCOME-GROUP)
    (M-EVENT-GROUP)
    (M-EMPTY-GROUP (I-M-EMPTY-GROUP)))
(M-ACTOR
    (I-M-TIM)
    (I-M-TED)
    (I-M-RANDY)
```

```
            (I-M-DAVID)
            (I-M-CHUCK)
            (I-M-AL))
      (M-ACT
          (M-FIGHT-ACT
              (M-WOUND-ACT
                  (I-M-BREAK-SKULL)
                  (I-M-SHOOT)
                  (I-M-STAB))
              (M-HURT-ACT
                  (I-M-SLASH)
                  (I-M-KNOCK-DOWN)
                  (I-M-STRIKE)
                  (I-M-HIT)
                  (I-M-SLAP))))
      (M-STATE
          (M-PHYS-STATE
              (I-M-DEAD)
              (I-M-CUT)
              (I-M-KNOCKED-DOWN)
              (I-M-BRUISED)))
      (M-EVENT (M-FIGHT-EVENT)))
```

After Step 4, you should see something very close to the following output, except for the numbers on the MOPs:

```
----------------
Sentencing I-M-TED in *CASE1*
Sentence in I-M-CRIME.39 is 40 years
----------------
Sentencing I-M-RANDY in *CASE2*
I-M-CRIME.52:OLD <= I-M-CRIME.39
----------------
Adapting the sentence in I-M-CRIME.39
----------------
Calculating motives in I-M-CRIME.39
----------------
Calculating escalations in I-M-CRIME.39
I-M-CRIME.39:ESCALATIONS <= I-M-GROUP.53
I-M-CRIME.39:MOTIVES <= I-M-GROUP.57
----------------
```

```
Calculating motives in I-M-CRIME.52
----------------
Calculating escalations in I-M-CRIME.52
I-M-CRIME.52:ESCALATIONS <= I-M-GROUP.58
I-M-CRIME.52:MOTIVES <= I-M-GROUP.64
----------------
No major difference found
Using old sentence
I-M-CRIME.52:SENTENCE <= 40
Sentence in I-M-CRIME.52 is 40 years
----------------
Sentencing I-M-TIM in *CASE3*
I-M-CRIME.78:OLD <= I-M-CRIME.52
----------------
Adapting the sentence in I-M-CRIME.52
----------------
Calculating motives in I-M-CRIME.78
----------------
Calculating escalations in I-M-CRIME.78
I-M-CRIME.78:ESCALATIONS <= I-M-GROUP.79
I-M-CRIME.78:MOTIVES <= I-M-GROUP.84
----------------
I-M-CALC.86 applied, 1 events from the end
I-M-CALC.86:VALUE <= 30.0
I-M-CRIME.78:SENTENCE <= 30.0
Sentence in I-M-CRIME.78 is 30.0 years
```

5.4 Extensions

5.4.1 Ordering of Cases

Bain [1986] discusses how JUDGE's memory differs if cases are encountered in a different order. Try running micro JUDGE with *CASE3* before *CASE2*. Does it make a difference? What does the result suggest about micro JUDGE's adjustment formula?

5.4.2 Frequency of Actions

Currently, our rules for calculating escalations ignore the FREQ frequency slot on actions, so that hitting someone several times after they hit you once is not seen as escalatory. Modify CALC-ESCALATIONS in Listing 5.6 to take frequencies into account.

5.4.3   Outcomes of Actions

Our rules do not take the outcome of each event into account. In the real JUDGE, the outcome of an event was used to rate how serious the event was. If a person died from being knocked down, then the knocking down was clearly more serious than if the person was only bruised. On the other hand, JUDGE also had to take into account how predictable the outcome was, given the event that caused it. It is predictable that shooting someone may kill them, and hence, the person who does the shooting is more culpable. It is less predictable that knocking someone down will kill them, and hence, the person who does the knocking down is, comparatively, less culpable, even though they are still clearly responsible for the death. Try incorporating this kind of reasoning in micro JUDGE. Read [Bain, 1986] for some guidance, then try to formulate your own rules making these kinds of comparisons.

5.4.4   Consistency of Sentences

JUDGE used several crimes to check the consistency of its sentences. If the crime retrieved by an input case had a sentence that was itself derived from some other even older crime, then JUDGE would first adapt the sentence from the retrieved crime to fit the input, then compare the input case to the older crime and see if the adapted sentence was consistent with the second comparison. For example, suppose the input case is judged worse than some crime CRIME-1, and CRIME-1 was previously judge less serious than CRIME-0. If the input case is also judged less serious than CRIME-0, then, to be consistent, the sentence for the input case should be harsher than the sentence in CRIME-1, but not as harsh as the sentence in CRIME-0. The adjustment rules will take care of making the new sentence harsher than CRIME-1's, but extra processing might be necessary to make it more lenient than CRIME-0's. Experiment with averaging techniques to keep the order of sentences consistent with the seriousness of crimes.

5.4.5   Adapting Closest Cases

The function GET-SIBLING in Listing 3.22 picks MOPs for adaptation. It picks an instance that shares an immediate abstraction with the input instance and that is not a known failure, but, if more than one such instance is available, it does not pick the instance that is most similar to the input case. Using the terminology of Section 2.4 in Chapter 2, finding the immediate abstractions for the input instance is the indexing phase of case retrieval. What we need is the matching phase. We already have some of the knowledge we need: the abstraction hierarchies tell us how similar primitive MOPs are. For example, in micro JUDGE, I-M-RETALIATION and I-M-UNPROVOKED are more similar to each other than they are to I-M-SELF-DEFENSE because the former share an abstraction, namely M-UNJUSTIFIED.

We also need to tell micro JUDGE which slots are more important in the match. In Section 4.9, the slots for statute, who started the fight, results, and actions, are weighted from heaviest to lightest. "Who started the fight" is a calculated slot: it should be I-M-DEFENDANT or I-M-VICTIM, depending on whether the the actor of the first event is the same as the defendant in the input case or not.

Matching two crimes to determine similarity is a complex process that involves calculating motivations and so on. Fortunately, most of it is already being done, albeit simplistically, by ADJUST-SENTENCE in Listing 5.9. This should not be surprising, since the similarity of two crimes determines how much adjustment in sentences is necessary. So, one way to change micro JUDGE so that it uses the most similar case when creating sentences is to change it so that all sibling instances are compared against the input case, using the existing rules to calculate a sentence adjustment for each case. Only a case with the smallest adjustment however would be actually used to assign the final sentence. Try doing this. Also, try adding a slot for "who started the fight" and modifying the sentence adjustment calculation to take that into account.

6

CHEF

Kristian J. Hammond[1]

6.1   Case-based Planning

Case-based planning is the idea of planning as remembering. When a surgeon approaches an operation, he does not build his course of action piece by piece out of a set of primitive steps. He recalls past operations from similar situations and modifies his behavior to suit the new situation. When an architect starts a new design for a client, he does not go back to first principles and try all possible combinations of sub-plans. Instead he recalls past plans and changes them to fit his current needs. And when you get into your car to go home tonight, you will not create a new plan for buckling up, starting the car and finding a route home. You will just recall the plan that has worked before and make use of it directly.

Planning from cases means remembering failures so that they can be avoided; remembering successes so that they can be reused; and remembering repairs so that they can be reapplied. Case-based planning is entirely different from rule-based planning. Questions of memory organization, indexing, and plan modification are important in case-based planning because a case-based planner must make extensive use of memory. Learning is central to case-based planning because a case-based planner must reuse its own experiences to build new plans and to avoid past errors.

A planning task is, in essence, a memory problem. A plan for a set of goals is not built up piece by piece from the individual plans for each goal. It

---

[1]The material in this chapter has been excerpted from *Case-Based Planning: Viewing Planning as a Memory Task*, Kristian J. Hammond (Academic Press, 1989), which contains a more detailed exposition of the CHEF system.

is instead constructed by modifying a plan from memory that already satisfies or partially satisfies many if not all of the planner's goals. Plan failures
are not only planning problems; they are expectation failures that have to be
remembered so that the faulty expectations can be changed. They are indi-
cations that the knowledge the planner has of the world is faulty and should
be altered in much the same way as the plan is altered. And plans are not
disposable items that should be built and then discarded. They are valuable
commodities that can be stored and recalled for later use.

Thus, a case-based planner uses memory in two ways. It uses past failures
to anticipate problems and past solutions as the bases for future solutions.
Likewise, it stores two kinds of information in memory. It stores failures for
future anticipation, and solutions for future modification and use.

6.2   A New Theory of Planning

If we view planning problems as memory problems, a number of basic features
of most theories of planning must be altered:

1. Rather than planning for individual goals and then merging the results,
   a case-based planner must search its memory for plans that satisfy many
   of its goals at once.

2. Rather than recovering from planning errors and then forgetting the
   results of that recovery, a case-based planner must treat these errors
   as opportunities to learn and to recall more about its domain and the
   problems that arise in it.

3. Rather than discarding the plans that it builds, a case-based planner
   has to save them in memory for later use in similar circumstances.

Planning and learning form a closed loop, in which planning errors lead
the planner to learn more about what causes them, which gives it a better
understanding of how to avoid them.

Most of the issues involved in case-based planning are not confined to
planning in the strictest sense of the word. Except for plan modification and
validation, the issues are ones of memory, indexing, and learning.

In order to plan from past experience, a planner must have a rich understanding of that experience and a clear method for organizing it and incorporating it into memory. The memory structures and learning mechanisms
needed to support a case-based planner must have the ability to integrate past
failures and successes into memory so that the former can be avoided and the
latter reused.

Case-based planning differs from other approaches to planning and problem solving [Fikes and Nilsson, 1971; Korf, 1982; Sacerdoti, 1977; Sussman, 1975; Tate, 1977; Wilensky, 1980] in three areas: in initial plan building, in the reaction to plan failures, and in the vocabulary for describing and storing plans. There is a great deal of overlap in these areas. The initial choice of a plan affects the way in which it is debugged, and the way in which debugged plans are stored affects the way in which they are chosen for later use. Still it is important to separate these areas and understand how different planners handle them.

6.2.1   Building an Initial Plan

A case-based planner builds new plans out of old plans. Past planning experiences are organized in an episodic memory by two sorts of indexes: goals to be satisfied and failures to be avoided. Plans are indexed by the goals they satisfy and the problems they avoid.

In order to use this memory organization, a case-based planner must take the input set of goals and note potential goal interaction problems. By doing this, it can anticipate any failure that it has experienced before and use this anticipation to search for a plan that solves the problem it has predicted. For example, a case-based planner should be able to infer from the fact that it is raining that it will get wet if it goes outside and thus it should find a plan that avoids that problem, if one exists, instead of building and having to repair a faulty plan that does not.

> The case-based approach to finding an initial plan is to *anticipate* problems so the planner can find plans that *avoid* them.

By organizing plans around planning failures as well as goals, a planner can avoid problems it has encountered before. The planner can use the prediction of a failure that results from a goal interaction to find a plan that avoids it. This idea of using a prediction mechanism along with a memory organization that can make use of these predictions to *anticipate and avoid* planning problems contrasts strongly with the *create and debug* paradigm that has been the thrust of machine planning over the past fifteen years. The main difference between these approaches is that the *anticipate and avoid* approach tries to predict problems and then avoid them by finding plans in memory that deal with them, whereas the *create and debug* approach debugs failures only after they arise during the planning process.

6.2.2   Debugging Failed Plans

A case-based planner can anticipate and avoid failures having to do with plan interactions. It can only do this, however, with interactions it has seen before. In order to plan effectively it must be able to recover and learn from failures that it hasn't seen before and isn't able to anticipate. So, like *create and debug* planners, it has to have knowledge of how to identify and repair faulty plans that have failed due to unforeseen interactions between steps.

Although there are technical differences between the way plan failures are handled by a case-based planner and the way programs such as NOAH [Sacerdoti, 1977] or PANDORA [Wilensky, 1980] deal with them, the most important difference between them is that a case-based planner treats its mistakes as *expectation* failures as well as *planning* failures. Planning is a test of understanding the world. Planning failures indicate where that understanding has broken down and where it has to be fixed. They tell the planner when it needs to learn.

A planning failure occurs when a plan does not satisfy some goal that it was designed to deal with. For example, if a planner puts together a plan to get a newspaper on a rainy day that is a simple "go outside, get paper, come back" plan, it will end up getting wet. Because the planner is wet and doesn't want to be, it has had a planning failure. But because it did not expect to get wet, it has also had an expectation failure. An *expectation* failure is different from a *planning* failure. It occurs when an expected event does not take place or when an unexpected event occurs. In the newspaper situation, the *expectation* failure occurs at the same time as the planning failure, but the response to the planning failure is the alteration of a plan whereas the response to the expectation failure has to be the alteration of the planner and its understanding of the world.

A planner should respond to *planning* failures by building a causal explanation of why the failure has occurred and then using that explanation to access replanning strategies designed for the situation in general. It should respond to *expectation* failures by again using that explanation to add new inference rules that will allow it to anticipate the problem that it previously was unable to foresee. It should first ask itself, "What went wrong with the plan?" and then ask "What went wrong with the planning?" In other words, a planner has to repair its expectations about the world when those expectations lead to plans that fail. Plan repair is one capability which sets case-based planning apart from other theories of planning.

> A case-based planner responds to planning failures by repairing both the faulty plan and its own faulty knowledge base that allowed it to build the plan incorrectly.

The notion of learning from expectation failures is not a new one. Schank has argued that learning occurs when an understander is confronted by expectation failures [Schank, 1982].

6.2.3 Storing Plans for Later Use

To store a plan in memory, a planner has to know when it will be appropriate to use again. For most planners this has meant storing plans in relation to the goals they satisfy. For a case-based planner that tries to anticipate problems and find the plans that avoid them, this is not enough. To access a plan that avoids a certain problem, the plan must have been indexed so as to allow such a connection. The basic vocabulary of plan indexing is necessarily the vocabulary of the planner's domain, and of the goals of the domain. But this vocabulary is not sufficient to allow a planner to avoid actively the problems that it anticipates. Plans must also be stored by *descriptions of the negative goal interactions they avoid*. A plan to go outside with an umbrella has to be indexed by the fact that it gets the planner outside, but also by the fact that it does so while protecting him from the rain. It also has to be indexed by the fact that it avoids the problem of the planner getting wet. This is so it can later be accessed when the need for such a plan is inferred. As with any vocabulary item based on a plan satisfying a goal, the fact that a plan successfully avoids a problem must be used to index it for later use when a goal to avoid the same or similar problems arises.

> Plans are indexed by the goals they satisfy and by the problems they avoid. This allows a planner to find plans that achieve the goals it is planning for while avoiding the problems it predicts will arise while doing so.

6.3 Learning from Planning

A case-based planner is also a learning system because it reuses its own experiences. The learning done by a case-based planner is learning by remembering, rather than inductive *concept learning* [Lebowitz, 1980; Michalski, 1983; Winston, 1975] or *explanation-based learning* [Mitchell *et al.*, 1986; DeJong and Mooney, 1986]. The learning in case-based planning breaks down into three types: *plan learning, expectation learning,* and *critic learning.*

Plan learning is the creation and storage of new plans as the result of planning for situations that the planner has never encountered before. The planner has to build a new plan and decide what features are best for indexing it in memory. Any new plans are stored in memory, indexed by the positive goals they satisfy as well as by the negative effects they avoid. For example, a plan for going outside in the rain to get a paper would be indexed by the fact that it is a plan to retrieve a paper and by the fact that it allows the planner to avoid getting wet.

Expectation learning means learning the features in a domain that are predictive of negative interactions between plan steps. This predictive ability is used to anticipate particular problems and then to search for plans in memory designed to avoid them. These features are learned by building causal explanations of planning failures and marking the states and steps that lead to the failures as predictive of them. The fact that it is raining and the planner has a goal to pick up his paper would be marked as predictive of the problem of getting wet. Once predicted, this problem could be planned for by finding a plan that avoids it. Once one of these predictions is activated, they can be avoided by searching memory for a plan that takes it into account.

Critic learning occurs when a problem in a plan can be traced back to a specific object or prop rather than to an interaction between steps. Any repair that is made to a plan because of an idiosyncratic object can be saved and associated with the object. The fix to a specific problem can become a general repair that can be applied in later cases of the problem. Even if an overall plan to avoid a problem cannot be found, the repair can still be reapplied to fix a plan that satisfies other goals. This would be like predicting that the rain would get someone wet in any plan for going outside and then applying the repair of using an umbrella to a plan for going outside that does not already include this fix.

Case-based planning involves three types of learning:

- Learning new plans that avoid problems.
- Learning the features that predict the problems.
- Learning the repairs that have to be made if those problems arise again in different circumstances.

All three of these types of learning are supported by a planning vocabulary that describes plans in terms of the direct goals they satisfy and the interactions they deal with. Storing plans in terms of the goals they satisfy is not enough if the planner wants to reuse them. They also have to be stored in terms of the problems they avoid. This makes it possible for the planner to rediscover these past plans when it predicts the same problems again in a different planning situation.

6.4 Building it from the Bottom

The following sections will look at the nature of case-based planning in general, arguing why planning should make use of the case-based paradigm and then looking at what it takes to build such a planner. To do this we will start with the simplest possible case-based planner — a plan retriever — and expand it with the additions required to do plan repair and problem anticipation.

6.4.1 Why Case-based?

The argument for case-based planning is straightforward: we want a planner that can learn and recall complex plans rather than having to repeat work it has already done. In the case of a single plan for building a car or a house, the number of steps involved is huge. Although such plans can be built up *ab initio* from a set of rules or from plan abstractions each time the planner needs them, it is more economical to save entire plans and recall them for reuse when situations that require their use arise.

It is always useful for a planner to save the plans it creates, especially in those situations where a plan includes information about how to avoid problems that the planner's initial base of rules tended to lead into. For any planning task involving the reuse of information, the best approach is to make use of a detailed representation of the experience itself. Given that all planning tasks make use of past information, this argues that the best approach to planning in general is to find and modify past plans rather than rebuild from a set of rules each time.

> The functional justification for case-based planning is the need to learn from experience.

6.4.2 Plan Retrieval

At its simplest, a case-based planner is a memory that returns to a past plan whenever it is given a new set of goals. If it cannot find a plan that satisfies all of the goals it has been handed, it returns a plan that meets most or many of them. It is trying to find the *best match* between the current situation and some situation in the past for which it has a plan. There is no guarantee that the best match will actually be the best possible plan for use in the current situation, but our effort is to construct a memory organization that will aim in that direction. We will call this basic component of the planner the RETRIEVER. Its input is a set of goals to be achieved and its output is a plan from its memory that achieves as many of these goals as is possible.

Since RETRIEVER uses the input goals to index past instances in memory, planning episodes have to be indexed and stored by the goals they have satisfied. We also need to use the generalizations of these goals as well. An episode in which a planner flies to London should be indexed as a plan to get to London and also as a plan to get to someplace distant. An episode in which the planner removes an inflamed appendix should be indexed as satisfying that goal but also by the more general result of removing an diseased organ. The simple plan of calling down to the hotel desk for a wake-up call has to be indexed by the fact that it satisfies the goal of getting you up in the morning. A planner has to be able to discriminate between plans on the basis of all of the goals it is trying to accomplish.

Along with goals, a planner must also know what the plan execution environment is. Plans are designed for particular situations, not just particular goals. For example, a plan using an umbrella while retrieving a newspaper from the porch when it is raining should be indexed not only by the goal that it satisfies, i.e., getting the newspaper, but also by the conditions under which it is appropriate to use, i.e., when it is raining. Likewise, the plan to call down to the hotel desk for a wake-up call should be indexed both by the goal to wake-up at a specific time in the morning and by the situation of being in a hotel. This means that there will be a number plans in memory that satisfy the same goal or goals but are distinguished by different situations.

When no plan satisfies all goals exactly, RETRIEVER picks the plan whose goals are the best match for the current goals. If there is no plan to get to London, try the plan for getting to Paris. If there is no plan for designing three-story houses, try the plan for a two-story houses. To determine best matches, a planner needs some notion of similarity between goals. This similarity can be expressed by placing similar goals into sets, by building them into an ISA hierarchy, or by dynamically evaluating their similarity on the basis of individual features. Paris and London may both be considered as foreign cities, a gall bladder and an appendix are both organ, and so on. No matter what the method, there has to be some metric for the similarity of goals that a planner can use to judge partial matches.

If goals all had the same value, the best plan would be the one that satisfied the largest number of goals. But normally some goals are more important than others. The RETRIEVER has to know about the relative value of goals and find a plan that matches best on the most important goals. The goals fit into a *value hierarchy* that is used to determine the relative utility of different plans with respect to a set of goals. It is important to distinguish this from the *abstraction hierarchy* that is used to determine the similarity between plans. The abstraction hierarchy tells the RETRIEVER if a plan partially satisfies a goal; the value hierarchy tells it how much that goal is worth. The source of this hierarchy is not important. What is important is the notion of deciding between competing plans on the basis of their relative utility, no matter how that utility is determined.

For example, imagine a memory with two plans: one for a two-story building of glass and steel and one for a five-story building of brick. Imagine also that the input goals ask for a five-story building of steel and glass. All other factors being equal, a planner would have to decide which plan would be the best to modify, the one using the same materials, or the one with the same number of stories. In this domain, it is easier to adapt the two-story building plan, because adding stories requires less changes than redesigning with new materials. In other words, the choice depends on what kinds of changes are easiest to make. The goal value hierarchy is linked to the planner's abilities. Goals that are easier to incorporate into existing plans are less important, as far as determining plan similarity, than goals that are more difficult to satisfy.

In short, to get a plan that is the *best match* for a set of goals, a planner needs three kinds of knowledge (Figure 6.1):

- A memory of plans indexed by the goals they satisfy.

- A similarity metric for judging the similarity of goals that is required for determining partial matches.

- A value hierarchy of goals used to judge the relative utility of plans with respect to a set of goals.

To integrate this knowledge, the RETRIEVER first uses the input goals and their abstractions to discriminate through memory and then uses its knowledge of the relative value of the different goals to decide between the overall value of competing plans. This defines a basic case-based planner that takes a set of goals and recalls a plan from memory which satisfies as many of the most important goals as possible.

> To get a *best match*, the RETRIEVER needs a plan memory, a goal similarity metric and a goal value hierarchy.

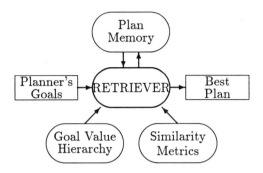

Figure 6.1: The RETRIEVER

This conception of RETRIEVER isn't complete. It can find past plans on the basis of similarities between surface level goals, but it cannot find past plans on the basis of interactions between those goals. A planner also needs a vocabulary that describes similarities between situations not captured by the surface features alone. This problem will be examined after some discussion of the repair mechanisms from which this vocabulary emerges.

6.4.3   Plan Modification

The RETRIEVER only finds and suggests past plans for new situations; it doesn't modify these plans to fit the new goals. This is the job of the MODI-FIER.

In order to modify a plan, the MODIFIER uses a library of modification rules that specify what steps to add to particular plans, given particular goals. The rules do not have to give complete plans for achieving any particular goal. They can just be the modifications that are needed to alter an existing plan to achieve that goal. The MODIFIER also needs to have information about items in its domain that tells it how to change those items to meet the conditions required by the more general modification rules. This information, in the form of special purpose critics, tailor the general modifications of a plan to the specific needs of the items required to achieve particular goals. Finally, the MODIFIER needs to know about what the plans it is modifying are supposed to be doing in general. This is needed so that it doesn't violate the goals of the overall plan when it modifies it to satisfy a specific goal.

> To alter old plans to meet new goals, the MODIFIER needs a set of modification rules, critics with knowledge of goal specific requirements, and general plan specifications.

For example, in the architectural domain, to add a window to an existing design, the MODIFIER would have to know the goal (add a window), the type of design (office, apartment or house), and the features of the particular window (the type of glass, the size, or the shape). The changes required for adding a window to the design for an apartment building are different from those that have to be made to a plan for a standard house. By storing modifications in terms of both the goal to be added and the type of plan begin altered, a MODIFIER can be sensitive to these differences. By also storing idiosyncratic steps that deal with the features of particular items in a domain, it can deal with those items within the context of a more general process of plan alteration.

Another example is in the domain of automotive design. Suppose the system wants different parts of a car it is designing to be colored red. If the part is an exterior metal piece, the alteration to the initial plan will involve changing the color of the paint that is used to cover the part. If the part is an interior plastic part, the change will involve altering the pigments used in the initial mixing of the plastic. The different initial plans determine different alterations in response to the same goal. No one plan for changing the color will do. Different alterations, associated with the different initial plans, have to be used for the different situations.

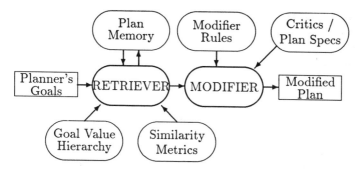

Figure 6.2: The MODIFIER

The RETRIEVER and MODIFIER together make up a basic case-based planner. The RETRIEVER takes a set of goals and finds the past plan that best satisfies them. The MODIFIER takes this plan and the goals that it fails to meet and modifies the plan to satisfy all of the input goals. To do this it needs to have plan modification rules, rules on actions that have to be performed in order to use certain items, and general information about the goals that types of plans are supposed to satisfy (Figure 6.2). For a given set of goals, then, the RETRIEVER finds a good plan and MODIFIER makes it better.

6.4.4   Plan Storage

The original justification for case-based planning was learning. We want the planner's abilities to improve, based on its own experience. Within the confines of the planner that we have built so far, only one kind of learning is really possible. This is learning by remembering, i.e., by storing a plan that has been built in the planner's memory. This is sometimes called *caching* the plan.

The features that are used to store a plan must be the same as those used to access it. The knowledge that a planner needs to store a plan is exactly parallel to the knowledge it needs to find one. The indexes used to store plans, then, are the goals that the plan it is storing satisfies and the circumstances in which the goals occurred that affected plan choice.

The STORER stores in memory the results of the work done by the RE-TRIEVER and the MODIFIER. The STORER does nothing to help in the building of a present plan. Storing plans helps the planner save time when solving similar problems in the future. Later we'll see how these stored plans also help the planner learn from failure.

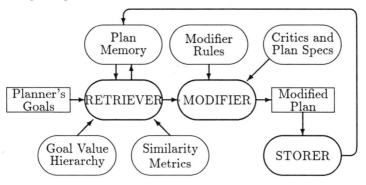

Figure 6.3: The STORER

To place new plans in memory, the STORER needs to index them under the same features that the RETRIEVER uses to find them: the goals that they satisfy and the situations in which they are appropriate.

6.4.5   Plan Repair

Many planning systems stop once a plan has been generated. In the real world, this is impractical, because even the best-laid plans will fail once in a while. A real planner has to be able to repair failed plans. No matter how good the planner is, at one time or another it will have to confront problems that arise out of its own lack of knowledge and the limits of its own heuristics. Given that the planner is going to make mistakes, we have to give it some mechanism for repairing the faulty plans it builds. This mechanism will be called the REPAIRER.

The input to the REPAIRER has two parts: a faulty plan and some description of the fault. The fault is either a desired state that was not achieved or an undesired state that arose during the plan execution. How a planner gets this information can vary. It can actually run its plans and examine the results. It can run simulations of the plans and use this to diagnose errors. It can even ask an outside source if the plan will do what it wants it to. But no matter how it does it, a planner has to be able to notice and respond to its own failures.

To do its job, the RETRIEVER also needs to know *why* the fault arose. It needs a causal explanation of the failure. For example, the problem might be "The engine failed to start when I turned the key." The causal explanation might be "The engine failed to start because a wire leading to the starter has shorted out on the body where it passes behind the side-mounted air-filter. The heat exchange from the air-filter melts the insulation on the wire." The explanation is important because it specifies which states and actions participated in the failure. This in turn suggests which parts of a design have to be changed. Even if a specific method for fixing the particular problem doesn't already exist, one can be generated out of a method for dealing with the general problem (a side effect of one part violating the maintenance conditions of another) and the particular states (the side effect is excess heat, the maintenance condition is the fact of the insulation and so on). This could be used to suggest possible general kinds of repair, e.g., "recover from side effect" (find a way to drain off the heat from the air-filter), or "protect from side effect" (use a heat resistant insulation on the wire), or "bypass side effect" (reroute the wire).

So, along with a vocabulary for describing plan execution failures, the REPAIRER needs a set of repair methods that can be accessed with that vocabulary. These methods should be organized such that the description of a given failure will access only those repair methods that have a chance of repairing that particular plan fault. This relationship between problem and repair is like the relationship between goals and plans. Plans are indexed under the goals they satisfy and repair methods are indexed under the types of failures that they deal with.

When a plan is repaired, the result is not only a plan that satisfies a set of goals, it is also a plan that avoids a particular problem. The original goals and plans interacted and caused a problem. The repaired plan is designed to cope with that interaction and to avoid the failure altogether. The REPAIRER therefore tells the STORER about the goals that the repaired plan satisfies and the failures that it avoids along the way. With this information, the STORER can index repaired plans in memory in such a way that the RETRIEVER can find them when a similar combination of goals occurs again.

> With the addition of the REPAIRER, the STORER can now index plans by the problems that they avoid as well as the goals that they satisfy.

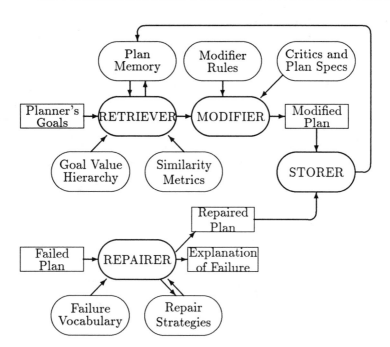

Figure 6.4: The REPAIRER

To summarize, the REPAIRER is invoked only when a plan fails. Its task is to repair the plan and tell the STORER how to characterize it so that it can be found again in a similar problem situation. The REPAIRER requires a vocabulary for describing plan execution problems and a set of strategies that are indexed by the problems that they solve. The repaired plan is given to the STORER to place in memory, indexed by the goals that the plan satisfies and the problems it avoids (Figure 6.4).

> To repair failed plans and describe them to the STORER, the REPAIRER requires a vocabulary of plan failures and repair strategies that are indexed by that vocabulary.

6.4.6 Learning from Failure

Even though STORER indexes a repaired plan by the problems it avoids, there is still a stumbling block to reusing that plan for similar problems in the future. This is the RETRIEVER's inability to figure out when the problem is going to arise again. The fact that a plan solves a particular problem is not useful unless the planner can anticipate that problem in the appropriate circumstances and use that prediction to find the plan in memory. Having a plan that solves a problem does the planner no good if it cannot recognize the circumstances in which that problem will arise.

The ability to predict when a problem is going to arise in the future rests on the ability to figure out why it happened in the past. To do that the planner needs a function that can decide which *input* features of a failed plan caused the failure to occur. Given these features, it can predict when the problem will arise again. This function, which assigns blame to features, is called the ASSIGNER. The job of the ASSIGNER is to look at a failed plan and decide what circumstances will be predictive of that failure in the future. The knowledge the ASSIGNER uses can vary in much the same way that the knowledge used by the REPAIRER can vary: it can be simple and unreliable or complex and robust.

> To decide which features in a situation are to blame for a failure, the ASSIGNER needs to be able to describe the causes of the failure. The more extensive its vocabulary for this description, the more exact its credit assignment will be.

Take for example a situation in which John misses a free ride with Bill from the airport to the hotel because John has to wait for his baggage to come off the plane. Many factors led to the missed ride, including the haste with which Bill had to leave, but the main feature of *John's plan* that is

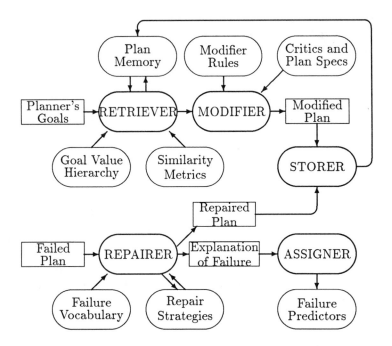

Figure 6.5: The ASSIGNER

involved is the fact that he checked his baggage while traveling with others. When later performing a similar plan, that is, taking a flight with other people and checking baggage, John should recall the failure and plan for it by, say, taking only carry-on luggage.

So, the ASSIGNER's task is to mark features in a situation as predictive of the problems that arose in that situation. Like the STORER, the ASSIGNER has no effect on problems that the planner is currently working on. Instead, its job is to assure that the planner is able to predict when the current problem is going to arise again in later circumstances. Its output can be a set of inference rules that are to be checked in the early stages of planning, links going from surface goals to predictions, or a table of effects that matches features to predictions. The form of the output is not the issue here. The issue is that the planner, because the ASSIGNER is able to identify the features that predict a problem, is now able to anticipate that problem and use the goal of avoiding it to find a plan that does so (Figure 6.5).

6.4.7 Problem Anticipation

The ASSIGNER determines which features led to the failure. Another module, the ANTICIPATOR, uses this information to predict problems when new goals and situations come in, *before* any other planning is done. The ANTICIPATOR tells the RETRIEVER about these potential problems, so that the RETRIEVER can try to find a plan that avoids them (Figure 6.6).

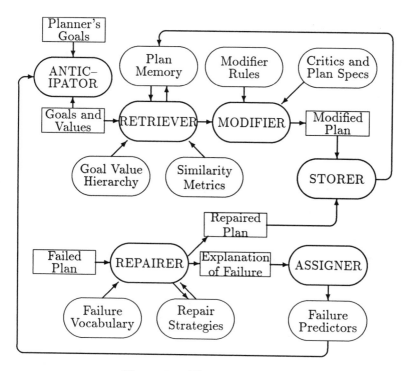

Figure 6.6: The ANTICIPATOR

> To anticipate a problem on the basis of surface features, the ANTICIPATOR needs the base of information built by the ASSIGNER

For example, consider again poor John, who missed a ride because he had to wait for his baggage. The next time he travels, his ANTICIPATOR should remember the problems caused by waiting for luggage, and the RETRIEVER should either find a past plan that deals with the problem or alter another plan to do so, *before* John misses another ride.

Note the relationship between the ANTICIPATOR, ASSIGNER, and RETRIEVER. Once a problem plan has been repaired, it is stored in memory, indexed by the fact that it deals with a particular problem. The ANTICIPATOR is needed to enable the RETRIEVER to find the repaired plan when the same potential problem arises again. The ASSIGNER is needed to find out what the ANTICIPATOR should look for.

> With the addition of the ANTICIPATOR, the RETRIEVER can search for plans on the basis of the problems that they avoid as well as the goals they satisfy

6.4.8   The Final Package

The basic case-based planner that grows out of the need to reuse plans and adapt them for new goals functions as follows: A set of goals is handed to the planner and sent directly to the ANTICIPATOR. The ANTICIPATOR, based on the knowledge built up by the ASSIGNER, makes any predictions of planning problems that it thinks will arise out of the current goals. The goals are then handed to the RETRIEVER along with the ANTICIPATOR's predictions of problems that have to be avoided. The RETRIEVER uses both to search for a plan in memory that best satisfies the goals it is trying to achieve and avoids any problems that have been anticipated. The result is a past plan that matches some or all of the goals now being planned for.

This plan is sent to the MODIFIER, which adds or substitutes new steps to the plan in order to make it satisfy any of the planner's goals that it does not yet achieve. Once modified, the plan is run and the results checked against the goals of the planner. If there is a failure, either because a desired goal has not been achieved or because an undesired state has resulted from the plan, the plan is given to the REPAIRER.

The REPAIRER builds a characterization of the failure and uses this to find and apply one of its repair methods. The repaired plan, along with a description of the problems that had to be solved along the way, are then sent to the STORER for placement into memory. The STORER indexes the new plan by the goals it achieves and the problems it avoids. Now the plan can be used again in similar circumstances in the future.

While the REPAIRER is repairing the plan, the ASSIGNER is deciding which input features interacted to cause the failure to occur. Once it has done this, it marks these features as predictive of the problem so that the

ANTICIPATOR can anticipate the problem if it encounters the goals in a later input.

This planner does two things as it builds a plan. It is trying to satisfy a set of goals using its model of what plans are appropriate for different situations. But it is also testing that model of the appropriateness of those plans against the real world so that later planning will be easier and more reliable.

To serve its first function, the planner has to react to failures by repairing the present plan. To serve its second function, it has to alter its view of the world by adding new plans indexed by the problems they solve and by altering its predictions so that it can anticipate those problems and find the plans that avoid them.

The fact that planning and learning are so intimately connected in case-based planning is no accident. The power of a case-based planner is directly dependent on its ability to reuse plans, and the only way to reuse plans effectively is to take seriously the notion of learning which features in a planning situation determine when they are appropriate to use.

A case-based planner learns by remembering plans and deciding which features are important for indexing plans. The learning is not in the building of plans but in the storing and indexing of them.

> A case-based planner learns by correctly indexing its planning experiences in memory.

Memories of past planning experience can also be helpful to a planner in dealing with the situation in which it predicts a failure but is unable to find a plan that deals with it. In these situations, the memory of a repair used to fix a past plan with a similar failure can often be used to repair the current plan before it is run. plan is being devised. Of course, not all repairs can be transferred between plans, just as not all old plans can be transferred to new situations.

In all three of these learning situations, the main task of the learner is to figure out which features a piece of information should be indexed under. Any generalization that is done takes the form of generalizing these features without changing the specificity of the information being stored. The plans that are placed in memory are the actual plans created by the planner. They are not generalized versions of these plans. The goals that are used to index them, however, are generalized so that the plans can be found in situations that are similar if not identical to those in which they were originally constructed.

The theory of case-based planning presented here is a theory of learning in each of these three areas. It is a theory of learning new plans, new problems

and new solutions. It is a theory of learning within the context of active
planning.

> A case-based planner learns new plans, the features that pre-
> dict failures and past repairs to faulty plans that it can reuse.
> This learning is accomplished by saving the different results of
> the planner's own experience.

6.5   CHEF: A Case-based Planner

CHEF is a case-based planner whose primary domain is Szechwan cooking.
CHEF creates new recipes, i.e., cooking plans, from old ones, in response to
requests for dishes with particular ingredients and tastes. CHEF has to build
one plan that satisfies a number of goals simultaneously. In this, CHEF's job
is much harder than many other planners, which can create a simple sequence
of plans to satisfy several goals. The need to satisfy many goals at once occurs
in many design domains, such as industrial design or circuit construction.

Here is an example of CHEF planning for the problem of building a stir fry
dish with beef and broccoli. CHEF has three goals: to have a stir-fried dish,
to include beef, and to include broccoli. Instead of searching for individual
plans that satisfy each of the goals separately and then merging them, as most
hierarchical planner's would do, CHEF searches its memory for a single plan
that matches, or partially matches, as many of the goals as possible. If there
are several such plans that match equally well, CHEF chooses one at random.

```
Searching for plan that satisfies -
    Include beef in the dish.
    Include broccoli in the dish.
    Make a stir-fry dish.

Found recipe -> REC2 BEEF-WITH-GREEN-BEANS

Recipe exactly satisfies goals ->
    Make a stir-fry dish.
    Include beef in the dish.

Recipe partially matches ->
    Include broccoli in the dish.
            in that the recipe satisfies:
                    Include vegetables in the dish.
```

> CHEF begins planning by finding a plan that satisfies as many
> of its active goals as possible.

Once the base-line plan is found, it is modified to match whatever goals
it doesn't already satisfy. The modification rules are specific to the kind of
dish (STIR-FRY), and by the goal of the modification (to include broccoli).
This kind of knowledge in cooking is similar to the knowledge in other design
domains such as architecture. In architecture, instead of knowing how to
modify STIR-FRY plans, an expert knows how to alter plans for houses and
apartment buildings. Likewise, instead of knowing how to add broccoli or beef
to an existing recipe, an expert would know how to add windows or doors to
an existing plan.

In this case, the partial match between the target goal, including broccoli,
and an object in the existing recipe, green beans, tells the planner that it
can replace the broccoli for the green beans directly. Other structures, called
object critics then change the cooking time of the vegetables to account for
the difference between the requirements of green beans and broccoli, and add
a step to chop the broccoli before stir frying it.

```
Building new name for copy of BEEF-WITH-GREEN-BEANS
Calling recipe BEEF-AND-BROCCOLI

Modifying recipe: BEEF-AND-BROCCOLI
to satisfy: Include broccoli in the dish.

Placing some broccoli in recipe BEEF-AND-BROCCOLI

- Considering ingredient-critic:
    Before doing step: Stir fry the -Variable-
    do: Chop the broccoli into pieces the size of chunks.
- ingredient-critic applied.
```

> CHEF alters old plans to satisfy new goals using a set of mod-
> ification rules and a set of *object critics*.

Once these modifications are made, the planner has a plan that should
satisfy all of the initial goals it was given.

BEEF-AND-BROCCOLI

```
A half pound of beef
Two tablespoons of soy sauce
One teaspoon of rice wine
A half tablespoon of corn starch
One teaspoon of sugar
A half pound of broccoli
One teaspoon of salt
One chunk of garlic
```

```
Chop the garlic into pieces the size of matchheads.
Shred the beef.
Marinate the beef in the garlic, sugar, corn starch,
rice wine and soy sauce.
Chop the broccoli into pieces the size of chunks.
Stir fry the spices, rice wine and beef for one minute.
Add the broccoli to the spices, rice wine and beef.
Stir fry the spices, rice wine, broccoli and beef
for three minutes.
Add the salt to the spices, rice wine, broccoli and beef.
```

CHEF knows more than just the steps of this plan. It also knows what goals should be satisfied when it is run. These goals are derived from its knowledge of stir-frying and its understanding of what items are important in this recipe. In particular, executing this plan should result in the following:

```
The beef is now tender.      The dish now tastes salty.
The dish now tastes savory.  The dish now tastes sweet.
The broccoli is now crisp.   The dish now tastes like garlic.
```

> CHEF derives the goals that a plan should satisfy from general plan specifications and the particulars of the current plan.

But not all plans work the first time. In this plan, the goal to have the broccoli crisp will fail, because it is being stir fried with the beef and is cooked in the liquid that the beef produces.

6.5.1   When Plans Fail

CHEF discovers the failure by simulating the execution of the plan. This simulation is the program's equivalent of real world execution. The simulator uses a set of inference rules to determine the outcome of each step of the plan. CHEF looks for any failures to achieve its positive goals as well as any occurrences of negative states that it would like to avoid.

```
Checking goals of recipe -> BEEF-AND-BROCCOLI

Recipe -> BEEF-AND-BROCCOLI has failed goals.

The goal: The broccoli is now crisp.
is not satisfied.
It is instead the case that: The broccoli is now soggy.

Unfortunately: The broccoli is now a bad texture.
In that: The broccoli is now soggy.

Changing name of recipe BEEF-AND-BROCCOLI
to BAD-BEEF-AND-BROCCOLI
```

> CHEF checks the goals of a plan against the results of a simulation of the plan that is its equivalent of the real world.

A plan failure means two things to CHEF. First, it must repair the plan. Second, it has to repair its understanding of the world. For both of these tasks CHEF needs to understand exactly why the failure has come about. It is not enough that it can point to the fact that the broccoli isn't crisp and call this a failure. It must also be able to explain why this particular failure has happened. What series of steps and states that led to the failure? CHEF uses the explanation to find the appropriate repair strategies. Because a causal explanation is used to describe the problem, a set of fixes that are aimed at altering the causality behind the failure can be used, instead of weaker methods such as back-tracking or total replanning.

6.5.2 Explaining Plan Failures

An explanation describes the failure, the step that caused it, and the conditions that had to be true for it to come about. CHEF also knows what goals were being served by the steps and states that caused the failure. With this knowledge, CHEF identifies what has to be changed in the plan to solve the present problem and also identifies what has to be changed in the planner's knowledge of the world so that the failure will not occur again.

CHEF diagnoses the failure by "asking" itself a sequence of questions. The answers to these questions organize the information about the cause of the failure. There is a significant simplification in the failure explanation process in CHEF. The simulation rules that test the recipe leave a record of all the causal connections. The simulation does not just report "the broccoli is soggy." It also reports that "water in the pan made the broccoli soggy," "cooking the meat left water in the pan," and so on. In other words, the real-world simulator and CHEF's causal model of the world are one and the same. This is clearly not the way things work in real life, but a model of explanation is way beyond the scope of this research. (See Collins in this volume for an example of how complicated causal explanation can become.)

```
Explaining the following failures:
 It is not the case that: The broccoli is now crisp.
in that: The broccoli is now soggy.
 The broccoli is now a bad texture.
in that: The broccoli is now soggy.
In: BAD-BEEF-AND-BROCCOLI

ASKING THE QUESTION: 'What is the failure?'

ANSWER-> The failure is:  It is not the case that:  The
            broccoli is now crisp.

ASKING THE QUESTION: 'What is the preferred state?'

ANSWER-> The preferred state is: The broccoli is now crisp.

ASKING THE QUESTION:
   'What was the plan to achieve the preferred state?'

ANSWER-> The plan was:  Stir fry the sugar, soy sauce, rice
            wine, garlic, corn starch, broccoli and beef for
            three minutes.

ASKING THE QUESTION:
   'What were the conditions that led to the failure?'

ANSWER-> The condition was:  There is thin liquid in the
            pan from the beef equaling 4.8 teaspoons.

ASKING THE QUESTION:
   'What caused the conditions that led to the failure?'
```

```
ANSWER-> There is thin liquid in the pan from the beef
         equaling 4.8 teaspoons was caused by:  Stir fry
         the sugar, soy sauce, rice wine, garlic, corn
         starch, broccoli and beef for three minutes.

ASKING THE QUESTION:
   'Do the conditions that caused the failure satisfy any
   goals?'

ANSWER-> The condition:  There is thin liquid in the pan
         from the beef equaling 4.8 teaspoons is a side
         effect only and meets no goals.

ASKING THE QUESTION:
   'What goals does the step which caused the condition
   enabling the failure satisfy?'

ANSWER-> The step:  Stir fry the sugar, soy sauce, rice
         wine, garlic, corn starch, broccoli and beef for
         three minutes.
         enables the satisfaction of the following goals:
         The dish now tastes savory.
         The beef is now tender.
```

CHEF explains the failures that it encounters through a causal
description of why they have occurred.

6.5.3   Plan Repair Strategies and TOPs

At this point, then CHEF knows what steps and states combined to cause the
current failure. It also knows which goals were being pursued in taking the
actions and creating the states that led to its failure.

This explanation serves two functions. First, it describes the planning
problem in a general causal vocabulary that can be used to access some equally
general repair strategies. Second, the explanation points out which features
in the domain interact to cause this sort of failure to occur, and hence which
features should be watched out for in the future.

Repair strategies are indexed under goal interaction structures called *Thematic Organization Packets* or TOPs [Schank, 1982]. TOPs are similar in

function to the critics found in HACKER [Sussman, 1975] and NOAH [Sacerdoti, 1977]. Each TOP is indexed by a particular type of planning problem and organizes a set of strategies for dealing with that type of problem. These strategies take the form of general repair rules such as REORDER steps and RECOVER from side effects. Each general strategy is filled in with the specifics of the particular problem to build a description of a change in the plan that would solve the current problem. This description is used as an index into a library of plan modifiers in the cooking domain. The modifications found are then tested against one another using rules concerning the efficacy of the different changes, and the one that is most likely to succeed is chosen.

The idea behind TOPs is simple. There is a great deal of planning information that is related to the *interactions* between plans and goals. This information cannot be tied to any individual goal or plan but is instead tied to problems that rise out of their combination. Each TOP corresponds to a planning problem due to the causal interaction between the steps and the states of a plan. When a problem arises, a causal analysis of it identifies the TOP and hence locates the repair strategies needed to fix the problem.

This explanation of the failure in this example indexes to the TOP SIDE-EFFECT:DISABLED-CONDITION:CONCURRENT (SE:DC:C), a memory structure related to the interaction between concurrent plans in which a side effect of one violates a precondition of the other. This is because the side effect of liquid coming from the stir-frying of the beef is disabling a precondition attached to the broccoli stir-fry plan that the pan being used is dry.

CHEF knows about 20 TOPs. Besides SE:DC:C, there is another one, DESIRED-EFFECT:DISABLED-CONDITION:SERIAL (DE:DC:S), that describes a situation in which the desired effect of a step interferes with the satisfaction conditions of a later step. CHEF recognizes that the current situation is a case of SE:DC:C rather than DE:DC:S, because it has determined that no goal is satisfied by the interfering condition (the liquid in the pan). Had the liquid in the pan satisfied a goal, the situation would have been recognized as a case of DE:DC:S, and different repair strategies would be needed.

```
Found TOP TOP1 -> SIDE-EFFECT:DISABLED-CONDITION:CONCURRENT
TOP -> SIDE-EFFECT:DISABLED-CONDITION:CONCURRENT has 3
       strategies associated with it:
          SPLIT-AND-REFORM
          ALTER-PLAN:SIDE-EFFECT
          ADJUNCT-PLAN
```

> CHEF uses its causal description of a problem to find a TOP
> that has strategies which will solve it.

This TOP has three strategies associated with it: SPLIT-AND-REFORM
suggests breaking a problematic step into several separate steps, ALTER-
PLAN:SIDE-EFFECT suggests replacing the problematic step with a different
plan, and ADJUNCT-PLAN suggests adding a new step to counteract the
effects of the problematic step. CHEF tries to apply each strategy to the
current example. It can only instantiate SPLIT-AND-REFORM. The other
strategies turn out not to fit the current situation, given CHEF's limited
knowledge base.

```
Applying TOP -> SIDE-EFFECT:DISABLED-CONDITION:CONCURRENT
to failure it is not the case that: The broccoli is now
                                    crisp.
in recipe BAD-BEEF-AND-BROCCOLI

Asking questions needed for evaluating strategy:
    SPLIT-AND-REFORM

ASKING -> Can plan
            Stir fry the sugar, soy sauce, rice wine,
            garlic, corn starch, broccoli and beef for
            three minutes.
          be split and rejoined

Found plan: Instead of doing step: Stir fry the sugar,
  soy sauce, rice wine, garlic, corn starch, broccoli
  and beef for three minutes
  do:
  S1 = Stir fry the broccoli for three minutes.
  S2 = Remove the broccoli from the result of action S1.
  S3 = Stir fry the sugar, soy sauce, rice wine, garlic,
  corn starch and beef for three minutes.
  S4 = Add the result of action S2 to the result of action
       S3.
  S5 = Stir fry the result of action S4 for a half minute.

Asking questions needed for evaluating strategy:
    ALTER-PLAN:SIDE-EFFECT

ASKING -> Is there an alternative to
            Stir fry the sugar, soy sauce, rice wine,
            garlic, corn starch, broccoli and beef for
```

                    three minutes.
                    that will enable
                    The dish now tastes savory.
                    which does not cause
                    There is thin liquid in the pan from the
                    beef equaling 4.8 teaspoons.

No alternate plan found

Asking questions needed for evaluating strategy:
    ADJUNCT-PLAN

ASKING -> Is there an adjunct plan that will disable
                    There is thin liquid in the pan from the beef
                    equaling 4.8 teaspoons.
                    that can be run with
                    Stir fry the sugar, soy sauce, rice wine, garlic,
                    corn starch, broccoli and beef for three minutes.

No adjunct plan found

Deciding between modification plans suggested by
strategies:
    Only one modification can be implemented
    -> SPLIT-AND-REFORM

Implementing plan -> Instead of doing step: Stir fry the
    sugar, soy sauce, rice wine, garlic, corn starch,
    broccoli and beef for three minutes.
    do: S1 = Stir fry the broccoli for three minutes.
        S2 = Remove the broccoli from the result of action S1.
        S3 = Stir fry the sugar, soy sauce, rice wine, garlic,
        corn starch and beef for three minutes.
        S4 = Add the result of action S2 to the result of
            action S3.
        S5 = Stir fry the result of action S4 for a half
            minute.
Suggested by strategy SPLIT-AND-REFORM.

> CHEF tries to implement the strategies suggested by the TOP
> by searching for the actual plan modifications that the strate-
> gies define.

6.5.4 Anticipating Failures

After changing the plan to solve immediate problems, CHEF also changes its
understanding of the world so that it will be able to anticipate and avoid
similar problems in the future. To do this, CHEF must figure out what it
was that caused the failure in the first place. It must decide which features
in the initial situation contributed to the failure so that later requests for
similar goals can be planned for. Here CHEF again makes use of the causal
explanation that it has for the failure to back-chain to the features that can be
used to predict this kind of problem. These features are then generalized to
the highest level of description allowed by the rules that explain the situation.
BEEF is generalized to MEAT in the example, because the rule that explains
the liquid in the pan states that stir frying *any* meat will have this result. The
resulting descriptions are marked as predictive of this problem. Once this is
done, CHEF is able to predict and plan for a problem of this kind whenever
it encounters a similar situation.

```
                Building demons to anticipate failure.

    Building demon: DEMON0 to anticipate interaction between
    rules:
    "Meat sweats when it is stir-fried."
    "Stir-frying in too much liquid makes vegetables soggy."

    Indexing demon: DEMON0 under item: MEAT
    by test:
        Is the item a MEAT.

    Indexing demon: DEMON0 under item: VEGETABLE
    by test:
        Is the item a VEGETABLE.
    and Is the TEXTURE of item CRISP.

    Goal to be activated = Avoid failure of type
    SIDE-EFFECT:DISABLED-CONDITION:CONCURRENT
    exemplified by the failure 'The broccoli is now soggy'
```

```
in recipe BEEF-AND-BROCCOLI.
```

```
Building demon: DEMON1 to anticipate interaction between
rules:
"Liquids make things wet."
"Stir-frying in too much liquid makes vegetables soggy."
```

```
Indexing demon: DEMON1 under item: SPICE
by test:
    Is the TEXTURE of item LIQUID.
```

```
Indexing demon: DEMON1 under item: VEGETABLE
by test:
    Is the item a VEGETABLE.
and Is the TEXTURE of item CRISP.
```

```
Goal to be activated = Avoid failure of type
SIDE-EFFECT:DISABLED-CONDITION:CONCURRENT
exemplified by the failure 'The broccoli is now soggy' in
recipe BEEF-AND-BROCCOLI.
```

> CHEF uses its explanation of why a failure has occurred to build links that will allow it to predict the failure later, in similar circumstances.

Once a plan is debugged and the sources of any problem are marked as predictive of that problem, CHEF stores the plan using two types of features. The first is the standard vocabulary of goals met by the plan, such as what foods and tastes are included in it, as well as what type of dish it is. These features are generalized so that plans which only partially satisfy a set of goal requests can be accessed in the absence of exact matches. The generalizations allowed depend on the modification rules available. Since CHEF knows how to replace one vegetable with another, a recipe with green beans can be indexed as a recipe with a vegetable.

The second vocabulary indexes repaired plans by the failures they avoid. By storing plans this way, it is possible for the planner to use the prediction of a previously encountered problem to find a plan that solves that problem. CHEF can avoid past errors by predicting them and then finding a plan that deals with them. In the case of the beef and broccoli, the plan is indexed by the fact that it deals with the interaction between the meat sweating and the need to have a dry pan while cooking crisp vegetables.

CHEF uses its new knowledge of what went wrong in the making the BEEF-AND-BROCCOLI recipe to anticipate and avoid the same problem in making a later one. We test this by next asking CHEF for a stir-fried dish with chicken and snow peas. The output shows CHEF predicting the possibility of the snow peas getting soggy if cooked with the chicken.

```
Searching for plan that satisfies -
    Include chicken in the dish.
    Include snow pea in the dish.
    Make a stir-fry dish.

  Collecting and activating tests.

  Fired: Is the dish STYLE-STIR-FRY.

  Fired: Is the item a MEAT.

  Fired: Is the item a VEGETABLE.
         Is the TEXTURE of item CRISP.

    Chicken + Snow Pea + Stir frying = Failure
    "Meat sweats when it is stir-fried."
    "Stir-frying in too much liquid makes vegetables
    soggy."
    Reminded of BEEF-AND-BROCCOLI.
    Fired demon: DEMON0

Based on features found in items: snow pea, chicken and
                                  stir fry
Adding goal: Avoid failure of type
SIDE-EFFECT:DISABLED-CONDITION:CONCURRENT exemplified by
the failure 'The broccoli is now soggy' in recipe
BEEF-AND-BROCCOLI.
```

> CHEF uses its understanding of past failures to anticipate problems that will arise in new situations.

Once a problem has been anticipated, CHEF can use the prediction of the problem to find a plan that avoids it. It does this by adding a goal to avoid the problem to the list of goals it is using to search for a plan. The BEEF-AND-BROCCOLI plan is indexed in memory by the fact that it satisfies the goal of avoiding the problem of the interaction between meat and vegetable.

```
Searching for plan that satisfies -
   Include chicken in the dish.
   Include snow pea in the dish.
   Make a stir-fry dish.
   Avoid failure of type
     SIDE-EFFECT:DISABLED-CONDITION:CONCURRENT
   exemplified by the failure 'The broccoli is now soggy'
   in recipe BEEF-AND-BROCCOLI.

Found recipe -> REC9 BEEF-AND-BROCCOLI

Recipe exactly satisfies goals ->
     Avoid failure of type
       SIDE-EFFECT:DISABLED-CONDITION:CONCURRENT
     exemplified by the failure 'The broccoli is now soggy'
     in recipe BEEF-AND-BROCCOLI.
   Make a stir-fry dish.

Recipe partially matches ->
     Include chicken in the dish.
             in that the recipe satisfies: Include meat in the
                                           dish.

Recipe partially matches ->
     Include snow pea in the dish.
       in that the snow pea can be substituted for the
       broccoli

Building new name for copy of BEEF-AND-BROCCOLI based on its
  goals.
Calling recipe CHICKEN-STIR-FRIED

Modifying recipe: CHICKEN-STIR-FRIED
to satisfy: Include chicken in the dish.
   Placing some chicken in recipe CHICKEN-STIR-FRIED

Modifying recipe: CHICKEN-STIR-FRIED
to satisfy: Include snow pea in the dish.
   Placing some snow pea in recipe CHICKEN-STIR-FRIED
```

Created recipe CHICKEN-STIR-FRIED

CHICKEN-STIR-FRIED

A half pound of chicken
Two tablespoons of soy sauce
One teaspoon of rice wine
A half tablespoon of corn starch
One teaspoon of sugar
A half pound of snow pea
One teaspoon of salt
One chunk of garlic

Bone the chicken.
Chop the garlic into pieces the size of matchheads.
Shred the chicken.
Marinate the chicken in the garlic, sugar, corn starch,
rice wine and soy sauce.
Chop the snow pea into pieces the size of chunks.
Stir fry the snow pea for three minutes.
Remove the snow pea from the pan.
Stir fry the spices, rice wine and chicken for three
minutes.
Add the snow pea to the spices, rice wine and chicken.
Stir fry the spices, snow pea, rice wine and chicken
for a half minute.
Add the salt to the spices, snow pea, rice wine and
chicken.

> CHEF uses its anticipation of a problem to find a plan that
> avoids it.

When CHEF decides to use the beef and broccoli recipe as its starting point, it passes up other recipes in memory that might appear to have more in common with the input goals. It has, for example, a recipe with chicken and green beans that, in the absence of the beef and broccoli experience, it would have been happy to modify to account for the chicken and snow peas. But it prefers a plan that fixes the predicted problem, because the interaction between plan steps has a greater effect on the final structure of the plan than the goals to include certain ingredients.

The lesser goals are not ignored, however. If CHEF were asked for a stir fry dish with chicken and bean sprouts after storing its new CHICKEN-

STIR-FRIED plan in memory, it would anticipate the problem with the bean sprouts getting soggy, but would start with CHICKEN-STIR-FRIED, rather than BEEF-AND-BROCCOLI, because CHICKEN-STIR-FRIED deals with the problem of stir frying meats and crisp vegetables together *and* has more surface features in common with the current situation. Once a failure is anticipated, it becomes one of the features that is used to find a plan, but not the only one.

6.6   Learning Plans

A case-based planner learns plans in the sense that it stores the new plans it creates in its plan memory. Learning, in this context, means figuring out the features that should be used index the plan in memory and then storing the plan using them. The task is to organize experience such that it can be retrieved and reused at the appropriate time.

> A case-based planner stores the most obvious result of planning, the plan itself, in a plan memory.

The stored plan is a series of steps and list of ingredients that has been built to satisfy some particular set of goals. This plan is not generalized in any way. To do so would be to lose information that could be used again, without gaining anything in terms of more general applicability.

For example, it's as easy for CHEF to modify STRAWBERRY-SOUFFLE to use kirsch instead of strawberries as it would be for CHEF to use a generalized version of the same recipe. But if CHEF is asked for strawberry soufflé, perhaps with something else, then it can use the stored recipe directly, without having to adapt a generalized plan.

While a case-based planner need not generalize the plans it stores, it does need to generalize the features that are used to index them. Because of this, the plan can be suggested for use in a wide range of situations and can still retain the specific information that makes it more useful when applied to situations in which the goals that are being planned for are completely satisfied by the plan itself. By generalizing the indexes rather than the plan, a case-based planner is able to avoid much of the tradeoff between generality and power of application. The general indexes makes it applicable in many situations and the specificity of the plan makes it a powerful tool in those situations in which the match between the current goals and those satisfied by the plan is a good one.

> In storing a plan in memory, a case-based planner does not
> generalize the plan itself. It instead generalizes the features
> that are used to index the plan in memory.

A case-based planner indexes plans by the goals that they satisfy and the problems that they avoid. The goals that a plan satisfies are states that have to be true once the plan has been run. The problems that a plan avoids are causal interactions that need to be overcome.

CHEF's goals include the ingredients, their final tastes, and textures, and the type of dish. These are the initial features that are used in indexing the plan. Problems that a plan avoids are represented by the TOP that describes the abstract causal situation linked to the specific failure state. In CHEF, a plan may solve several problems, just as it may satisfy several goals. These two sets of items are combined into a single list of features that will be used to index the plan in memory.

The fact that a plan avoids a particular problem can be treated by a case-based planner as a *goal* to avoid that failure that the plan associated with it satisfies. These goals to avoid failures can be treated as any other goal for use in indexing of plans in memory. They are considered more important than most other goals, however, because it is often easier to alter a plan to satisfy a new goal than to make the changes required to deal with an interaction between goals.

A plan is indexed in memory, then, by the goals that it satisfies and the problems that it avoids. It also has to be indexed by the features of a situation that are independent of the goals but do direct the planner to one plan or another. As mentioned before, the plan to call the front desk for a wake-up call is a good plan to get the planner up in the morning, but only in certain circumstances. These circumstances, which can be reduced to states that describe the world, also have to be used to index plans in memory.

In the CHEF program, plans are stored in a discrimination net [Charniak *et al.*, 1987]. These goals and problems are ordered by their importance, with the higher priority features used at the higher levels of discrimination. Once the features are ordered, a plan is placed in a discrimination net, using the features as indexes. The ordering of features allows CHEF to somewhat limit the branching in this net by allowing discrimination from any one node to be made only on the basis of features of less importance than the last one used to index to it.

As each goal is used to place a plan in memory, more general versions of the goals are also used. BEEF-AND-BROCCOLI is indexed by the fact that it includes beef and broccoli, but it is also indexed by the fact that it includes meat and vegetables in general. The level of generality of the goals used to index plans is preset and corresponds to the level of generality that is used in defining the modification rules used in substituting one ingredient for another in a plan. As a result, the goal to include one type of ingredient can be used to find a plan for a similar ingredient.

> CHEF stores new plans indexed by the goals that they satisfy and the problems that they avoid.

Once a plan is placed in memory this way it can be accessed by the planner when it is searching for a plan that satisfies similar goals and for a plan that avoids failures that it predicts may appear and wants to avoid.

For example, in building a strawberry soufflé recipe, CHEF has to deal with the fact that the liquid from the fruit prevents the soufflé from rising. It deals with this by adding more egg white to the recipe, reestablishing the relationship between liquid and leavening that the fruit unbalanced. The final recipe satisfies a set of goals having to do with making a soufflé, including strawberries, making the soufflé taste sweet and like berries and having a fluffy texture. These goals come from the input request and some are generated by the planner out of its understanding of what this type of plan should be like in general (Figure 6.7). The plan also has a token associated with it that indicates that it deals with the problem of the added liquid from the fruit interfering with the baking (Figure 6.8).

```
Created recipe STRAWBERRY-SOUFFLE

If this plan is successful, the following should be true:

        The batter is now baked.
        The batter is now risen.
        The dish now tastes like berries.
        The dish now tastes sweet.

The plan satisfies -
        Include strawberry in the dish.
        Make a souffle.
```

Figure 6.7: Goals Satisfied by STRAWBERRY-SOUFFLE

These goals are collected and used to index the plan in memory, the goal to make a soufflé and the goals to avoid the failure taking priority over all others.

These are then used to insert the plan into CHEF's plan memory. The only generalization that goes on is with the goal to include the strawberries, which is generalized up to the level of FRUIT. There are no other goals that can be further generalized.

```
Created recipe STRAWBERRY-SOUFFLE

        The plan avoids the failure of type
        SIDE-EFFECT:DISABLED-CONDITION:BALANCE
        exemplified by the failure 'The batter is now flat'
        in recipe STRAWBERRY-SOUFFLE.


        Token = SIDE-EFFECT:DISABLED-CONDITION:BALANCE0
```

Figure 6.8: Avoidance Goal under STRAWBERRY-SOUFFLE

6.7 Learning to Predict Failures

The problem of learning to predict failures so as to anticipate and avoid them is a problem of figuring out which features of an existing situation have caused a current failure so that these links can be created.

> A case-based planner saves memories of failures, indexed by the features that predict them. It uses these memories to anticipate problems when these features arise again in new situations.

When reminded of a failure, the planner needs to recall the token that has been built to represent the failure and to index the plan that avoids it in memory. By having the planner be reminded of the same representation of the failure that was used to index the plan which avoids it in memory, it can use the reminding of the failure directly in searching for the appropriate plan.

CHEF, for example, indexes STRAWBERRY-SOUFFLE by the fact that it avoided a particular problem of too much liquid and too little leavening. A case-based planner that does any sort of causal analysis of a problem in order to repair it has a powerful tool for figuring out which features in a situation have to take the blame for causing a problem. The explanation of *why* a failure has occurred points out which features are responsible in a current situation for the problem. These features will be predictive of the problem in later situations. In fact, these features can be generalized, by a process I call *generalizing to the level of the rules*. This means generalizing an object in an explanation up to the highest level of generality that is possible while still staying within the confines of the rules that explain the failure.

The difference between this notion of explanation and that suggested by other theories of explanation-driven learning [Mitchell *et al.*, 1986; DeJong and Mooney, 1986] lies in what is learned. Within case-based planning, the explanation of why a plan has failed is used to figure out the features that will later predict similar failures. In other theories of explanation-driven learning, explanations of why a plan has been successful are used to weed out the steps that are irrelevant and generalize those that are too specific. Explanation of failures is far more constrained a task in that only a single anomalous state has to be accounted for and the planner is not trying to generalize the plan it is building at all. It is only trying to generalize its understanding of the circumstances in which that plan can be used.

> A case-based planner uses the explanation of a failure to iden-
> tify the features that will predict it. It generalizes these fea-
> tures to the highest level of description allowed by the rules in
> the explanation.

In the example of the failed strawberry soufflé plan, where too much liquid caused the soufflé to fall, part of the explanation was that that the liquid came from the chopped strawberries. A simple way to avoid this failure in the future would be for the planner to mark strawberries as predictive of it and be reminded of the failure and the repaired plan whenever it is asked to make a strawberry soufflé. But the rule that explains the added liquid as a side effect of chopping the strawberries does not require that the the object of the chopping be strawberries at all. It actually says that chopping *any* fruit will produce this effect. So, instead using STRAWBERRY as the predictive feature, CHEF can use FRUIT (Figure 6.9).

In some cases, the rule that explains a link in the causal chain leading to a failure does have specific requirements. For example, in explaining the soggy broccoli in the BEEF-AND-BROCCOLI plan, CHEF uses a rule that explains that stir frying any crisp vegetable in liquid will make it soggy. In this case, BROCCOLI is too specific a feature to look for, and VEGETABLE is too general. To deal with this, CHEF uses the tests on the rule itself to control the activation of the failure prediction. These tests are associated with the general ingredient type that the rule tests for, VEGETABLE, and tests for the features that are required for the rule to apply, (TEXTURE = CRISP).

```
Building demons to anticipate failure.

Building demon: DEMON2 to anticipate interaction between
rules:
"Chopping fruits produces liquid."
"Without a balance between liquids and leavening the
 batter will fall."

Indexing demon: DEMON2 under item: FRUIT
by test: Is the item a FRUIT.

Indexing demon: DEMON2 under style: SOUFFLE

Goal to be activated = Avoid failure of type
SIDE-EFFECT:DISABLED-CONDITION:BALANCE
exemplified by the failure 'The batter is now flat' in
recipe STRAWBERRY-SOUFFLE.
```

Figure 6.9: Marking FRUIT and SOUFFLE as Predictive of Problems

This means that each time the planner has to deal with stir frying vegetables it will test their texture and partially activates the memory of the failure if they are crisp.

In most situations, it is not a single feature but a set of features that combine to cause a failure. The BEEF-AND-BROCCOLI situation is one of these because the failure is not the result of either stir frying the beef or stir frying the broccoli but of stir frying them together. In these situations, a single feature alone should not activate the prediction of the failure. It is only when all of the features are together, (stir-fry, meat, and crisp vegetable), that the prediction should be made. To deal with this, the activation of a single feature that is linked to a failure only partially activates the memory. It is only when all features send a signal that they are present that the memory of the failure is itself activated and the planner is warned of the impending problem. CHEF does not anticipate a problem when it plans for crisp vegetables alone. It only does so when it is asked to plan for stir frying crisp vegetables along with other goals that will combine with the first to cause the problem again.

> When multiple features are required to predict a failure, all of
> them are linked to the memory of the failure. This memory is
> not activated unless all of the linked features are present.

In tracing back through the explanation of a failure to the initial causes, a planner passes through states that those original causes have created. These states are the ones that are the more proximate causes of the problems but not the first causes in terms of the recipe. The liquid from chopping the strawberries is the actual cause of the problem with the strawberry soufflé but it is not the initial cause, the goal to include strawberries itself.

Although these states are not the initial causes of the problems that the planner has to deal with, they can still be used to predict the problems in later situations. A planner has to handle these intermediate states in the same way as it handles the ingredients it has to mark as predictive of problems. It generalizes them up to the level of the rules that explain the failure and link them to the token representing the failure. If other conditions are also required for the failure to occur, they are also linked to the memory of the failure so that the one feature alone will not predict the failure when it is inappropriate.

The CHEF program responds to the failure of the strawberry soufflé by marking the goal to include any liquid spice in a soufflé as predictive of that soufflé falling (Figure 6.10). This is implemented by placing a test on the concept SPICE that checks for the texture and partially activates the memory of the failure when the test is true.

> Intermediate states that serve as links in the causal chain that
> led to a failure are also linked to the memory of the failure and
> can be used to predict it if they arise in a later situation.

When a set of features that combine to predict a failure is present, a case-based planner is reminded of the memory of the failure itself. In CHEF, the request for a soufflé with raspberries in it reminds the planner of the problem of extra liquid in a soufflé and allows it to find and modify the STRAWBERRY-SOUFFLE plan that deals with it. It also allows CHEF to be reminded of it when planning for a kirsch soufflé, in which the added liqueur would have the same effect as the liquid from the chopped fruit. This is a plan that the planner would not have used had it not been for the prediction of the failure. The fact that the ASSIGNER has earlier established these links between features and failures allows it to find and make use of plans that otherwise would have not interesting features in common.

```
Building demons to anticipate failure.


Building demon: DEMON3 to anticipate interaction between
rules:
"Liquids make things wet."
"Without a balance between liquids and leavening the
 batter will fall."

Indexing demon: DEMON3 under item: SPICE
by test: Is the TEXTURE of item LIQUID.

Indexing demon: DEMON3 under style: SOUFFLE

Goal to be activated = Avoid failure of type
SIDE-EFFECT:DISABLED-CONDITION:BALANCE
exemplified by the failure 'The batter is now flat' in
recipe STRAWBERRY-SOUFFLE.
```

Figure 6.10: Marking LIQUID and SOUFFLE as Predictive of Problems

Before closing the discussion of learning to predict failures, there is one point that has to be made about indexing in a case-based planner. A case-based planner indexes its plans by the fact that they avoid particular problems. It also indexes memories of these problems by the features that predict them. Given this fact, the question that arises is why not just index the plans by the features that predict the problem that they solve directly.

There are two answers to this question. First, because a single class of problems can have many specific causes, it is just more efficient to index the plan under a single characterization of the problem and have the problem be predicted independently instead of indexing the plan by all possible circumstances that might cause the problem. Problems can be predicted with only a few features. There is little interaction between them that would lead to the need for a complex indexing system. But adding these features to the those already used to index plans would increase the complexity of plan indexing dramatically.

But efficiency is not the only argument. A more compelling argument is that indexing the plans that solve problems by the features that predict them, without marking those features in any way, doesn't work. As was pointed out earlier in this chapter it is often the case that the best plan for a situation is not the one that has the closest match in terms of low level features.

In CHEF, for example, the prediction of the "soggy vegetable" failure allowed the program to find the beef and broccoli plan that avoided it. Without this prediction, however, the planner would have to rely on finding a plan using only the features of the initial goals. Because the planner does have a plan for CHICKEN-AND-PEANUTS in memory, this would be taken as the base-line plan. But this plan, when modified for the current goals, will lead to soggy snow peas while a modified BEEF-AND-BROCCOLI will not.

The fact that a case-based planner indexes plans by the problems they solve and then predicts these problems for use in search allows it to recover them in situations where the low level features of the current goals will lead it to less appropriate plans.

6.8   Learning Critics

Aside from storing plans and failures, a case-based planner also stores some of the repairs that it makes to plans so that they can be used again. These repairs, stored in the form of critics, allow a planner to repair plans it knows to be faulty *before* it runs them. A planner would run into this situation when it predicts a problem, but cannot find a plan of the proper type to deal with that problem. This can happen if the only plans in memory that solve this problem are too different from what the input goals ask for the modification rules to handle. Remember that modification rules are not all-purpose complete planning rules. When this occurs, the case-based reasoner uses a plan that it knows to be faulty and then change it with the same patch it used to repair another faulty plan in the past.

> A case-based planner stores some of the repairs that it makes, indexed by the problems that they solve.

As with learning plans, the task of the learner is not to build the repair that is going to be stored, but only to decide how it is going to be indexed so that it can be accessed at the right time. There is a difference, however, in that not all repairs can be saved. Some repairs, because they involve interactions between many parts of a plan are too complex to transfer to new problems. Others are also linked to the type of plan that is being built, so there is never a possibility that the problem is predicted but no plan of the dish type needed can be found. Aside from deciding where to store the repair, the learner also has to decide which repairs can be saved at all.

The decision to save a repair as a critic is based on the repair strategy that is used to build the specific repair and on the cause of the failure in the first place. Some failures are the product of multiple ingredients interacting, so no one ingredient can be blamed for the problem, and no one ingredient can be given the necessary critic. The first test for turning a repair into a critic, then, is whether it relates to a single ingredient. The second test depends on the complexity of the repair itself. Some strategies, such as ALTER-PLAN:PRECONDITION, ALTER-PLAN:SIDE-EFFECT, and SPLIT-AND-REFORM depend on specific steps being present in a plan and their changes cannot reliably be reused. On the other hand, strategies such as REORDER and REMOVE-FEATURE create simple changes that can be added to most plans. For example, CHEF created one recipe with duck that was too greasy. This was repaired by the REMOVE-FEATURE strategy which suggested removing the fat from the duck before cooking. This repair can be added to any plan involving duck. CHEF created another recipe that marinated shrimp before shelling, making the shelling process very difficult. This was repaired by the REORDER strategy which suggested shelling the shrimp first. This repair can be applied to any case where two steps are misordered.

> A case-based planner can only save those repairs that can be transferred to any plan in which the problem that they repair arises.

In turning a repair into critic, a case-based planner has to store the specific change suggested by the strategy under the ingredient that it relates to. This is again so the prediction of a problem can lead to finding the repair that will fix it. By doing this, the past repair can be suggested when and only when the problem it relates to is noticed or predicted.

In CHEF, for example, a repair that the planner creates that adds the step of removing the fat from the duck is stored under the concept duck itself. Unlike other repairs that take the form of critics, however, these new critics are indexed by the problem that they solve. To activate them, then, CHEF has to anticipate the problem and then fail to find a plan that solves it. This restriction prevents CHEF from applying a repair to a plan that has already been fixed. It only applies the new critic when the features predicting the problem are anticipated and the plan that is used by the planner fails to deal with it.

Building a critic out of a repair requires that the planner only put together the pieces that have already been built or identified. The explanation that is used to repair the plan in the first place identifies where the critics should be stored. The critic itself is the actual repair that was built by the strategy to patch the plan in the first place.

> CHEF builds new critics out of current repairs and then in-
> dexes them by the description of the problem being repaired.

```
Applying TOP -> SIDE-FEATURE:GOAL-VIOLATION
to failure The bunch of dumplings is now greasy.
in recipe BAD-DUCK-DUMPLINGS

Implementing plan -> After doing step: Bone the duck
                   do: Clean the fat from the duck.
Suggested by strategy REMOVE-FEATURE
```

Figure 6.11: Repairing DUCK-DUMPLINGS with REMOVE-FEATURE

```
Building critic to avoid failure: The bunch of dumplings
is now greasy.
caused by condition: The duck is now fatty.

Critic =
After doing step: Bone the duck
               do: Clean the fat from the duck
          because: The duck is now fatty.
Storing critic under DUCK
Indexing by SIDE-FEATURE:GOAL-VIOLATIONO
```

Figure 6.12: Storing New Critic under DUCK

An example of this notion arises when the CHEF program has to confront
the problem of the grease from duck fat. In dealing with the fat from the duck
making the dish greasy, CHEF repairs the plan using the strategy REMOVE-
FEATURE (Figure 6.11). Because the repair is a simple one having to do
with only one ingredient, it can then go on to store it as a critic under DUCK,
indexed so that the prediction of the problem will activate the critic for use
in a different plan (Figure 6.12). When it later has to make a duck pasta dish
and cannot use its DUCK-DUMPLINGS, it is in the position of predicting
a problem that it does not solve with a complete plan. During modification,
it activates the critics and adds the step that removes the fat from the duck

(Figure 6.13). Even though it could not find a complete plan to deal with the problem then it is able to avoid it before running its new plan by using its earlier repair.

```
Problem predicted - SIDE-FEATURE:GOAL-VIOLATION0

Considering critic:
After doing step: Bone the duck
             do: Clean the fat from the duck
        because: The duck is now fatty. - Critic applied.
```

Figure 6.13: Using New DUCK Critic

As with the other aspects of a case-based planner's learning, the stress in learning new critics is not on the construction of the critics themselves. The stress is on how they are to be stored so that they can be accessed at the appropriate time. By indexing the patches to a plan under the prediction that it will fail, a case-based planner can activate those patches only when the features that predict the failure are present and avoid them before the plan is run.

6.9 How Learning from Planning is Different

Learning for a case-based planner is a by-product of planning, so the needs of the planner determine what is going to be learned, when it is going to be learned and how it is going to be learned. Other learners that learn categories or plans in the absence of a use for what they learn are concerned with creating new structures but have little interest in how they are stored and managed for use in an active memory. A learner associated with a planner, on the other hand, does not do any building on its own. It is instead concerned with how to organize the results, both positive and negative, of its planner in a dynamic memory of experience that the planner can use.

Learning is the organization of experience. As a result, the core issues of learning are memory organization and indexing. The most important problem in learning is deciding how to describe and store an experience so that it can be used again. In a planner that learns, this means finding a way to organize the planner's results so they can be used again in the appropriate situations.

Because a case-based planner makes use of existing plans to create new ones, the most natural thing for it to be learning is new plans so that it can adapt them for later use. A case-based planner plans by finding the "best match" between new goals and old plans that satisfy them so it also makes sense that the most important issue in learning plans is indexing them so that they can be found at the appropriate time. A case-based planner must predict problems so that it can find plans that avoid them, so it makes sense for it to learn the features that predict the problem it encounters. Because it is possible to predict a problem that cannot be handled with an existing plan, it also makes sense for a planner to to learn specific fixes that can be applied to repair the plan it has to use. The needs of the planner decide what is going to be learned: plans, problems, and repairs.

Planning is a test of the planner's knowledge. When that knowledge fails, the planner can see through its own experience that it needs to learn some new way to discriminate between the situation it thought it was in and the one it is actually in.

Because a planner is able to test its knowledge of the world by building new plans, its planning experiences can tell it when it has to learn something from those experiences. When a case-based planner builds a successful plan, it knows to store it for later use. Because it knows in what sense the plan is successful, in that it knows the goals it satisfies and the problems it avoids, it also knows how to index it in memory. When a case-based planner fails, it knows to mark the features that caused the failure as predictive of it so that it can anticipate it in the future. The failure itself tells the planner that its knowledge has a gap, and that the gap has to be filled with the prediction of a problem that the planner was not able to anticipate before. And when a case-based planner repairs a plan, it knows that this repair is a patch that fixes a failure created by its own modification process. In response, the planner adds this patch to the knowledge used by that process. The planner determines when the learner is turned on: when the planner succeeds, fails, and repairs.

Finally, the planner itself provides the learner with the content of what is learned. It builds the plans that are stored in memory. It builds the explanation that is used to assign blame for a failure. It even builds the patch that is stored as a new ingredient critic. The learner does not create what is learned, the planner does. In every case, the task of the learner is the task of collecting the features that should be used to index the planner's work and then store that work away for later use.

The planner does the reasoning. The learner examines that reasoning and decides how it should be stored in memory such that it can be recalled again when needed. Unlike systems that do nothing but learn and as a result do nothing with what they learn, a case-based planner that learns is managing a dynamic memory of experience in service of planning.

> Learning means storing the different results of the planner's activity, indexed by the features that determine their usefulness.

6.10 How Learning from Planning is Better

A case-based planner must build functional categories that allow it to anticipate problems and then react to them. This is as opposed to programs that build definitional categories that are no more than lists of necessary and sufficient features. The notion of learning not only a plan, but the features that it should be indexed by is an improvement over other learners that are aimed at plan learning. A planner is concerned with the reuse of its plans while other systems are not. It is not satisfied with just having the plan in hand, it has to understand when it should be used and where it should be stored.

A case-based planner can use its knowledge as a planner to guide the credit assignment decisions it makes in marking features as predictive of problems so it does not run into the difficulties associated with inductive learning algorithms. It only has to see one instance of a problem to learn the features that predict it. It ignores extraneous features. It uses the explanation of a situation to determine the level of generality that those features will be pushed to. And it does not have to rely on a tutor to hand it the correct set of examples for generalization. By using the knowledge of what it is learning to guide it, a case-based planner can replace credit assignment through repetition with an more powerful credit assignment through relevance.

A planner knows when to learn. Unlike learning systems that do nothing but learn, a planner actually has a motivation for learning: the improvement of its planning abilities. Because it learns in response to the needs of the planner, it learns when and only when the planner requires it to. Because it learns in order to improve the planner, its learning is constrained to be only that which will help the planner with later efforts. The stress of the learning is on the use of what is learned instead of on the moment of learning itself.

> Learning from planning is an improvement over other types of learning in that it uses the knowledge of the planner to determine what it learns, how to index it and when to learn it at all.

All of these improvements come for the basic idea that learning is not separate from planning. Learning is the management of the planner's memory of its own experience so that it can plan more effectively and avoid the problems that it has encountered before. Learning does not just involve memory, learning is memory.

7

Micro CHEF

7.1 Introduction

In this chapter, we present a miniature version of the CHEF program. This miniature has two parts. One part generates recipes and the other part repairs them. Micro CHEF starts with a case base containing two recipes, plus some information on how to debug a certain kind of failure. We give micro CHEF a partial recipe with ingredients and other characteristics, but no steps, and it returns a full recipe with steps filled in, formed by adapting the steps in one of the stored recipes. Next we give it a "failure report" containing a problem with the recipe it generated. Micro CHEF explains the problem (in a trivial way) and creates a new recipe that avoid the problem. Finally we test micro CHEF's ability to predict when the failure might arise again, by giving it two more partial recipes. The first one is similar to the problematic case. Micro CHEF handles it by adapting the *repaired* recipe. The second input does not have the failure-causing features. Micro CHEF handles it by adapting one of the *original* stored recipes.

7.2 Implementing Micro CHEF

The top-level function to run CHEF is very short, and appears in Listing 7.1.

(CHEF *slot-list*) finds or creates a case under M-RECIPE with the given slots and returns it. The call to GET-FILLER forces the calculation of the role STEPS. (DPH (ROLE-FILLER 'STEPS *recipe*)) will print a readable version of the steps in the recipe returned by CHEF.

Listing 7.2 defines MOPs for ingredients, tastes, and recipe types.

Listing 7.3 defines the MOPs for constructing cooking steps. A cooking step has an action and an object. The object might be an ingredient or a

```
(DEFUN CHEF (SLOTS)
 (LET ((INSTANCE (SLOTS->MOP SLOTS '(M-RECIPE) T)))
  (AND (GET-FILLER 'STEPS INSTANCE)
       INSTANCE)))
```

Listing 7.1: Top-Level Micro CHEF Function

group of objects.

Listing 7.4 defines MOPs for representing the steps in a recipe. One piece of cooking knowledge that CHEF needs to know is the order in which steps should be done. Stir-fry recipes usually follow the order: remove bones, chop, marinate, cook, and serve, so we define a recipe steps MOP, M-RECIPE-STEPS, with this fixed order. This makes it simpler for the code that has to add steps during adaptation.

Listing 7.5 defines a general substitution function for creating a new MOP from an old one by replacing some element of the old MOP with a new element throughout. Substitution is of obvious use to CHEF which has to do things like replace all occurrences of I-M-CHICKEN with I-M-BEEF. Substitution in lists is fairly easy to define:[1]

```
(DEFUN SUBST (NEW OLD L)
 (COND ((EQL L OLD) NEW)
       ((ATOM L) L)
       (T (CONS (SUBST NEW OLD (CAR L))
                (SUBST NEW OLD (CDR L)))))))
```

The expression (SUBST 'A 'B '(A B (C (D B E)) F)) would return (A A (C (D A E)) F). Note that both occurrences of B are replaced, including the nested one.

Substitution in MOPs, however, is a little trickier, because changing a piece of a MOP may create a non-MOP. For example, suppose we are turning a chicken recipe into a beef recipe, and we substitute beef for chicken in the cooking step with the slots ((ACTION I-M-BONE) (OBJECT I-M-CHICKEN)). The resulting ((ACTION I-M-BONE) (OBJECT I-M-BEEF)) is not a MOP, because beef is not an bony ingredient. Therefore the result of substituting beef for chicken in this case causes a step to disappear.

Even if substitution does not create a non-MOP, it may create a MOP with very different abstractions. Chopping broccoli may be classified as a

---

[1]Common Lisp comes with a better definition SUBST, but this one is simpler.

```
(DEFMOP M-INGRED (M-ROOT))
(DEFMOP M-MEAT (M-INGRED))
(DEFMOP M-VEGETABLE (M-INGRED))
(DEFMOP M-CRISP-VEGETABLE (M-VEGETABLE))
(DEFMOP M-STURDY-VEGETABLE (M-VEGETABLE))

(DEFMOP M-LARGE-INGRED (M-INGRED))
(DEFMOP M-SMALL-INGRED (M-INGRED))

(DEFMOP M-BONELESS-MEAT (M-MEAT))
(DEFMOP I-M-BEEF (M-BONELESS-MEAT M-LARGE-INGRED)
       INSTANCE)

(DEFMOP M-BONY-MEAT (M-MEAT))
(DEFMOP I-M-CHICKEN (M-BONY-MEAT M-LARGE-INGRED)
       INSTANCE)

(DEFMOP I-M-BROCCOLI
       (M-CRISP-VEGETABLE M-LARGE-INGRED) INSTANCE)
(DEFMOP I-M-SNOW-PEAS
       (M-CRISP-VEGETABLE M-SMALL-INGRED) INSTANCE)
(DEFMOP I-M-GREEN-BEANS
       (M-STURDY-VEGETABLE M-SMALL-INGRED) INSTANCE)
(DEFMOP I-M-GREEN-PEPPERS
       (M-STURDY-VEGETABLE M-LARGE-INGRED) INSTANCE)
(DEFMOP I-M-PEANUTS
       (M-STURDY-VEGETABLE M-SMALL-INGRED) INSTANCE)

(DEFMOP M-SPICES (M-INGRED))
(DEFMOP I-M-SPICES (M-SPICES) INSTANCE)

(DEFMOP M-RECIPE-STYLE (M-ROOT))
(DEFMOP I-M-STIR-FRIED (M-RECIPE-STYLE) INSTANCE)

(DEFMOP M-TASTE (M-ROOT))
(DEFMOP I-M-HOT (M-TASTE) INSTANCE)
(DEFMOP I-M-MILD (M-TASTE) INSTANCE)

(DEFMOP M-RULE (M-ROOT))
```

Listing 7.2: Micro CHEF Basic MOPs

```
(DEFMOP M-COOK-ACT (M-ACT))
(DEFMOP I-M-BONE (M-COOK-ACT) INSTANCE)
(DEFMOP I-M-CHOP (M-COOK-ACT) INSTANCE)
(DEFMOP I-M-LET-STAND (M-COOK-ACT) INSTANCE)
(DEFMOP I-M-STIR-FRY (M-COOK-ACT) INSTANCE)
(DEFMOP I-M-SERVE (M-COOK-ACT) INSTANCE)

(DEFMOP M-STEP (M-EVENT) (ACTION M-ACT))
(DEFMOP M-COOK-STEP (M-STEP) (ACTION M-COOK-ACT))
(DEFMOP M-BONE-STEP (M-COOK-STEP)
    (ACTION I-M-BONE) (OBJECT M-BONY-MEAT))
(DEFMOP M-CHOP-STEP (M-COOK-STEP)
    (ACTION I-M-CHOP) (OBJECT M-LARGE-INGRED))
(DEFMOP M-LET-STAND-STEP (M-COOK-STEP)
    (ACTION I-M-LET-STAND) (OBJECT NIL))
(DEFMOP M-STIR-FRY-STEP (M-COOK-STEP)
    (ACTION I-M-STIR-FRY) (OBJECT NIL))
(DEFMOP M-SERVE-STEP (M-COOK-STEP)
    (ACTION I-M-SERVE) (OBJECT NIL))
```

Listing 7.3: Micro CHEF Event MOPs

```
(DEFMOP M-INGRED-GROUP (M-GROUP) (1 M-INGRED))
(DEFMOP M-STEP-GROUP (M-GROUP) (1 M-COOK-STEP))
(DEFMOP I-M-EMPTY-GROUP (M-STEP-GROUP) INSTANCE)

(DEFMOP M-RECIPE-STEPS (M-ROOT)
    (BONE-STEPS M-STEP-GROUP)
    (CHOP-STEPS M-STEP-GROUP)
    (LET-STAND-STEPS M-STEP-GROUP)
    (STIR-FRY-STEPS M-STEP-GROUP)
    (SERVE-STEPS M-STEP-GROUP))
```

Listing 7.4: Micro CHEF Recipe Steps MOP

hard step, but if green peppers is substituted, the step may be classified as easy. The function RAISE-ABST is used to move a substituted MOP up the hierarchy to an appropriate abstraction.

(MOP-SUBST mop_1 mop_2 mop_3) returns a new MOP that is like mop_3. except that all occurrences of mop_2 have been replaced with mop_1. The result may be NIL if such a MOP as mop_3 doesn't fit in memory. If the slots in a group have changed, LIST->GROUP is used to renumber the slots correctly.

(SLOTS-SUBST mop_1 mop_2 *slot-list*) returns a new list of slots with mop_1 replacing mop_2 in each filler of *slot-list*. Slots with NIL fillers after substitution are not included in the result.

(RAISE-ABST *slot-list* *mop*) searches the abstractions of *mop* until it finds one where it can put a MOP with the slots in *slot-list*. It returns the MOP with *slot-list* or NIL, if there is no abstraction that can hold *slot-list*.

The functions in Listing 7.6 define functions and MOPs for building new MOPs using pieces of old MOPs. For example, in Listing 7.7, we define a MOP that takes any large ingredient and builds an instance of M-CHOP-STEP whose object is that ingredient.

(MAKE-MOP *pattern* *mop*) builds a MOP, where *pattern* provides the template and *mop* provides some of the pieces. The MOP role of *pattern* says what kind of MOP to build, e.g., M-COOK-STEP, and the other slots in *pattern* say what slots the new MOP should have. If a slot in *pattern* is filled with the name of a role, then the filler of that role in *mop* is used.

(REPLACE-SLOTS *slot-list* *mop*) returns *slot-list*, with every filler that is a role name replaced by the filler of that role in *mop*. Note that in order for REPLACE-SLOTS to know that something is a role name, it must have been defined to be an instance of M-ROLE.

Although the functions in Listing 7.5 can replace ingredients in a recipe and remove unnecessary steps, such as boning beef, we need other functions to *add* steps. For example, if we replace green beans with broccoli, we will need to add a "chop broccoli" step, because green beans did not need chopping in the original recipe. Such additional steps are called *preconditions*, and are handled by the functions and MOPs in Listing 7.7.

(GET-PRECONS *ingred*) returns a MOP similar in form to M-RECIPE-STEPS, containing those steps that *ingred* requires.

M-BONY-INGRED-PRECONS says that bony ingredients need a boning step.

M-LARGE-INGRED-PRECONS says that large ingredients need a chopping step.

Listing 7.8 defines several general functions for manipulating groups.

(GROUP-MEMBER *mop* *group*) returns true if *mop* is a member of *group*.

(GROUP-SPLICE *mop-list* *mop* *group*) returns a new group MOP with all

```
(DEFUN MOP-SUBST (NEW OLD MOP)
 (COND ((EQL MOP OLD) NEW)
       ((NULL (MOP-SLOTS MOP)) MOP)
       (T (LET ((SLOTS (MOP-SLOTS MOP)))
           (LET ((NEW-SLOTS
                  (SLOTS-SUBST NEW OLD SLOTS)))
             (COND ((EQUAL NEW-SLOTS SLOTS) MOP)
                   ((GROUPP MOP)
                    (LIST->GROUP
                      (FOR (SLOT :IN NEW-SLOTS)
                        :SAVE (SLOT-FILLER SLOT))))
                   (T (RAISE-ABST
                       (FORMS->SLOTS NEW-SLOTS)
                       MOP)))))))))

(DEFUN SLOTS-SUBST (NEW OLD SLOTS)
 (FOR (SLOT :IN SLOTS)
    :FILTER
      (LET ((FILLER
              (MOP-SUBST NEW OLD (SLOT-FILLER SLOT))))
        (AND FILLER
             (MAKE-SLOT (SLOT-ROLE SLOT) FILLER)))))

(DEFUN RAISE-ABST (SLOTS MOP)
 (LET ((ABST (FOR (ABST :IN (MOP-ALL-ABSTS MOP))
               :WHEN (SLOTS-ABSTP ABST SLOTS)
               :FIRST ABST)))
   (AND ABST (SLOTS->MOP SLOTS (LIST ABST) NIL))))
```

Listing 7.5: Substitution Functions

```
(DEFUN MAKE-MOP (PATTERN MOP)
 (LET ((SLOTS (FOR (SLOT :IN (MOP-SLOTS PATTERN))
                   :WHEN (NOT (EQL (SLOT-ROLE SLOT) 'MOP))
                   :SAVE SLOT)))
   (SLOTS->MOP (REPLACE-SLOTS SLOTS MOP)
               (LIST (GET-FILLER 'MOP PATTERN))
               T)))

(DEFUN REPLACE-SLOTS (SLOTS MOP)
 (FOR (SLOT :IN SLOTS)
    :SAVE '(,(SLOT-ROLE SLOT)
            ,(LET ((FILLER (SLOT-FILLER SLOT)))
               (COND ((ABSTP 'M-ROLE FILLER)
                      (ROLE-FILLER FILLER MOP))
                     (T FILLER)))))))

(DEFMOP MAKE-MOP (M-FUNCTION))
(DEFMOP M-MAKE-MOP (M-PATTERN) (CALC-FN MAKE-MOP))
```

Listing 7.6: Dynamic MOP-making Functions

```
(DEFUN GET-PRECONS (INGRED)
 (FORMAT T "~&---------------")
 (FORMAT T "~&Getting preconditions for ~S" INGRED)
 (AND INGRED
      (SLOTS->MOP '((INGRED ,INGRED))
                 '(M-PRECONS)
                 NIL)))

(DEFMOP INGRED (M-ROLE) INSTANCE)

(DEFMOP M-PRECONS (M-ROOT))

(DEFMOP M-BONY-INGRED-PRECONS (M-PRECONS)
    (INGRED M-BONY-MEAT)
    (BONE-STEPS M-MAKE-MOP (MOP M-BONE-STEP)
                (OBJECT INGRED)))

(DEFMOP M-LARGE-INGRED-PRECONS (M-PRECONS)
    (INGRED M-LARGE-INGRED)
    (CHOP-STEPS M-MAKE-MOP (MOP M-CHOP-STEP)
                (OBJECT INGRED)))
```

Listing 7.7: Calculating Preconditions

```
(DEFUN GROUP-MEMBER (MOP GROUP)
  (AND (GROUPP GROUP)
       (FOR (SLOT :IN (MOP-SLOTS GROUP))
            :FIRST (EQL (SLOT-FILLER SLOT) MOP))))

(DEFUN GROUP-SPLICE (NEW OLD GROUP)
  (LIST->GROUP
    (FOR (MOP :IN (GROUP->LIST GROUP))
      :SPLICE (COND ((EQL MOP OLD) NEW)
                    (T (LIST MOP)))))))

(DEFUN GROUP-INSERT (MOP GROUP)
  (COND ((NULL MOP) GROUP)
        ((GROUP-MEMBER MOP GROUP) GROUP)
        (T (LIST->GROUP (APPEND (GROUP->LIST GROUP)
                                (LIST MOP)))))))
```

Listing 7.8: Precondition Functions

the elements of *group*, except that *mop* is replaced with the elements of *mop-list*. Note that a NIL *mop-list* returns a group with *mop* removed.

(GROUP-INSERT *mop group*) returns a new group MOP with all the elements of *group* plus *mop*, added at the end.

Listing 7.9 defines the functions that merge the steps in the MOP returned by GET-PRECONS with the steps in an old recipe.

(ADD-PRECONS *precon-mop slot-list*) merges the slots of *precon-mop* with *slot-list*.

(MERGE-STEP *precon-mop slot*) adds the filler of slot to the group MOP in the corresponding slot in *precon-mop*, unless it is already there.

Listing 7.10 defines the functions that adapt an old recipe to use new ingredients. This requires comparing the corresponding ingredient roles in the old and new recipes. The following possibilities can hold with each role:

- The old and new recipes have the same ingredient: The old recipe needs no changes.

- The new recipe has NIL: It inherits the old ingredient and the old recipe needs no changes.

```
(DEFUN ADD-PRECONS (PRECON-MOP STEPS-SLOTS)
 (COND ((NULL PRECON-MOP) STEPS-SLOTS)
       (T
        (FORMAT T "~&Adding preconditions to recipe")
        (FOR (SLOT :IN STEPS-SLOTS)
           :SAVE (MERGE-STEP PRECON-MOP SLOT)))))

(DEFUN MERGE-STEP (PRECON-MOP SLOT)
 (LET ((ROLE (SLOT-ROLE SLOT))
       (OLD-FILLER (SLOT-FILLER SLOT)))
  (LET ((NEW-FILLER
         (GROUP-INSERT (GET-FILLER ROLE PRECON-MOP)
                       OLD-FILLER)))
    (COND ((EQL NEW-FILLER OLD-FILLER) SLOT)
          (T (MAKE-SLOT ROLE NEW-FILLER))))))
```

Listing 7.9: Micro CHEF Precondition Merging Functions

- The old recipe has NIL: The preconditions for the new ingredient have to be added to the old recipe.

- The old and new recipes have different ingredients: The old ingredient has to be replaced with the new one, and the preconditions for the new ingredient have to be added.

(ADAPT-STEPS *pattern mop*) fills the STEPS slot of *mop* by adapting the *STEPS* slot of a sibling instance of *mop*. The :ALWAYS in the FOR means that ADAPT-STEPS will return NIL immediately if the set of steps becomes NIL.

(SUBST-INGRED *ingred₁ ingred₂ pattern slot-list*) first replaces $ingred_2$ with $ingred_1$ in the fillers of the slots in *slot-list*, and then adds any preconditions of $ingred_1$ not in the modified list. Note that the substitution process removes steps such as boning a non-bony meat. The modified list of slots is returned.

Listing 7.11 defines M-RECIPE, the recipe MOP in CHEF. It doesn't have a (VEGE2 M-VEGETABLE) slot because that slot is optional.

Listings 7.12 and 7.13 give two base recipes to be used for adaptation.

```
(DEFUN ADAPT-STEPS (PATTERN MOP)
 (LET ((RECIPE (GET-FILLER 'OLD MOP)))
  (FORMAT T "~&---------------")
  (FORMAT T "~&Adapting the steps in ~S" RECIPE)
  (LET ((STEPS (MOP-SLOTS (GET-FILLER 'STEPS RECIPE))))
   (AND (FOR (INGRED-ROLE :IN '(MEAT VEGE VEGE2))
         :ALWAYS
          (SETF STEPS
                (SUBST-INGRED
                  (GET-FILLER INGRED-ROLE MOP)
                  (GET-FILLER INGRED-ROLE RECIPE)
                  STEPS)))
        (SLOTS->MOP STEPS '(M-RECIPE-STEPS) NIL)))))

(DEFUN SUBST-INGRED (NEW-INGRED OLD-INGRED STEPS)
 (COND ((OR (NULL NEW-INGRED)
            (EQL NEW-INGRED OLD-INGRED))
        STEPS)
       (T (ADD-PRECONS (GET-PRECONS NEW-INGRED)
          (COND ((NULL OLD-INGRED) STEPS)
                (T (FORMAT T "~&Substituting ~S for ~S"
                              NEW-INGRED OLD-INGRED)
                   (SLOTS-SUBST NEW-INGRED
                                OLD-INGRED
                                STEPS)))))))
```

Listing 7.10: Micro CHEF Adaptation Functions

```
(DEFMOP ADAPT-STEPS (M-FUNCTION))

(DEFMOP M-RECIPE (M-CASE)
    (MEAT M-MEAT) (VEGE M-VEGETABLE)
    (STEPS M-PATTERN (CALC-FN ADAPT-STEPS)))
```

Listing 7.11: Micro CHEF Top-Level MOP

```
(DEFMOP I-M-BEEF-AND-GREEN-BEANS (M-RECIPE)
    (MEAT I-M-BEEF) (VEGE I-M-GREEN-BEANS)
    (STYLE I-M-STIR-FRIED)
    (STEPS M-RECIPE-STEPS
        (BONE-STEPS I-M-EMPTY-GROUP)
        (CHOP-STEPS M-STEP-GROUP
            (1 M-CHOP-STEP (OBJECT I-M-BEEF)))
        (LET-STAND-STEPS M-STEP-GROUP
            (1 M-LET-STAND-STEP
                (OBJECT M-INGRED-GROUP
                    (1 I-M-BEEF) (2 I-M-SPICES))))
        (STIR-FRY-STEPS M-STEP-GROUP
            (1 M-STIR-FRY-STEP
                (OBJECT M-INGRED-GROUP
                    (1 I-M-BEEF) (2 I-M-SPICES)))
            (2 M-STIR-FRY-STEP
                (OBJECT M-INGRED-GROUP
                    (1 I-M-BEEF)
                    (2 I-M-GREEN-BEANS)
                    (3 I-M-SPICES))))
        (SERVE-STEPS M-STEP-GROUP
            (1 M-SERVE-STEP
                (OBJECT M-INGRED-GROUP
                    (1 I-M-BEEF)
                    (2 I-M-GREEN-BEANS)
                    (3 I-M-SPICES))))))
```

Listing 7.12: Micro CHEF Beef and Green Beans Recipe

```
(DEFMOP I-M-CHICKEN-AND-PEANUTS (M-RECIPE)
    (MEAT I-M-CHICKEN) (VEGE I-M-GREEN-PEPPERS)
    (VEGE2 I-M-PEANUTS)
    (TASTE I-M-HOT) (STYLE I-M-STIR-FRIED)
    (STEPS M-RECIPE-STEPS
        (BONE-STEPS M-STEP-GROUP
            (1 M-BONE-STEP (OBJECT I-M-CHICKEN)))
        (CHOP-STEPS M-STEP-GROUP
            (1 M-CHOP-STEP (OBJECT I-M-CHICKEN))
            (2 M-CHOP-STEP (OBJECT I-M-GREEN-PEPPERS)))
        (LET-STAND-STEPS M-STEP-GROUP
            (1 M-LET-STAND-STEP
                (OBJECT M-INGRED-GROUP
                        (1 I-M-CHICKEN)
                        (2 I-M-SPICES))))
        (STIR-FRY-STEPS M-STEP-GROUP
            (1 M-STIR-FRY-STEP
                (OBJECT M-INGRED-GROUP
                        (1 I-M-CHICKEN)
                        (2 I-M-GREEN-PEPPERS)
                        (3 I-M-PEANUTS)
                        (4 I-M-SPICES))))
        (SERVE-STEPS M-STEP-GROUP
            (1 M-SERVE-STEP
                (OBJECT M-INGRED-GROUP
                        (1 I-M-CHICKEN)
                        (2 I-M-GREEN-PEPPERS)
                        (3 I-M-PEANUTS)
                        (4 I-M-SPICES))))))
```

Listing 7.13: Micro CHEF Chicken and Peanuts Recipe

```
(DEFUN CHEF-REPAIR (SLOTS)
 (LINK-ABST (ROLE-FILLER 'SOLUTION SLOTS)
            'M-FAILED-SOLUTION)
 (LET ((INSTANCE (SLOTS->MOP SLOTS '(M-REPAIR) T)))
  (AND (GET-FILLER 'REPAIRED-SOLUTION INSTANCE)
       INSTANCE))))
```

Listing 7.14: Micro CHEF Top-Level Repair Function

7.3 Implementing Repair in Micro CHEF

Repair in CHEF is handled with a top-level function that takes as input a partially specified M-REPAIR MOP. This is a MOP that has slots for a solution that failed, an explanation of the failure, a repair, and a repaired solution. The explanation is a MOP that has slots for the failure (some bad state), the cause (some step in the failing solution), and the inference rule that explains why the causal step led to the failure state.

Our example in Listing 7.23 mimics the repair of the beef and soggy broccoli recipe described in Chapter 7. We don't do any simulation or explanation. The input repair MOP already has the failed solution (the beef and broccoli recipe) and the explanation filled in. The explanation has a FAILURE slot with "broccoli is soggy," a CAUSE slot with the "stir-fry beef and broccoli together" step, a RULE slot with an inference rule that says "cooking meat and crisp vegetables together makes the vegetable soggy," and a MAPPING slot that says that beef and broccoli are the meat and vegetable referred to in the rule, respectively. The MAPPING information is used to index the repaired solution, as described in Section 7.4.

The top-level function for repair is very similar to the top-level function for recipe generation. (CHEF-REPAIR *slot-list*) finds or creates a case under M-REPAIR with the given slots and returns it. We first mark the solution as a failure, to avoid using it in future adaptations (see Listing 3.22).

Listing 7.15 gives the failure and explanation MOPs we need for our example failure. The abstraction M-SIDE-EFFECT-EXPLANATION abstracts those explanations where the cause of the failure is an action on a group of objects. This abstraction will lead us to the repair "split up the action."

Listing 7.16 defines MOPs and constraints for rule mappings. We will not represent rules in MOPs in this book, because we do not make enough use of rules to demonstrate the advantage of one form over another. However, we assume that a rule would have IF part that is a standard pattern MOP. When

```
(DEFMOP M-BAD-STATE (M-STATE))

(DEFMOP I-M-SOGGY (M-BAD-STATE) INSTANCE)

(DEFMOP M-FAILURE (M-ROOT) (STATE M-BAD-STATE))

(DEFMOP M-EXPLANATION (M-ROOT) (FAILURE M-FAILURE))

(DEFMOP M-SIDE-EFFECT-EXPLANATION (M-EXPLANATION)
    (CAUSE M-STEP (OBJECT M-GROUP)))
```

Listing 7.15: Micro CHEF Explanation MOPs

a rule matches an instance, we need a way to represent which elements of the pattern MOP matched which elements of the instance. This is done with a *map group.*

(ISA-CONSTRAINT *constraint filler slot-source*) returns true if the filler of *role* in *slot-source* is an abstraction of *filler*, where *role* is the filler of the ROLE slot of *constraint*. In other words, the constraint is true if *filler* is a specialization of the filler of the role pointed to by *constraint*.

An M-MAP-GROUP is a group, each of whose elements is an M-MAP. An M-MAP has two roles, ABST and SPEC, filled with the corresponding elements of the abstract pattern and specialized instance, respectively. The SPEC filler is constrained to be a specialization of the ABST filler.

Listing 7.17 defines a general function for creating a new MOP from an old one by changing the filler of a role. Note the differences between this function and ADD-ROLE-FILLER in Listing 3.7.

(RESET-ROLE-FILLER *role mop filler*) returns a new MOP with the slots of *mop* changed to include (*role filler*).

Listing 7.18 defines the functions CHEF uses to generate the repair for the soggy broccoli recipe and apply that repair to create a new recipe.

(SPLIT-STEP *pattern mop*) returns a group of steps that should be used in place of the step that caused the failure. It assumes that the step (found in the CAUSE slot of the EXPLANATION) has a group filling its OBJECT slot. SPLIT-STEP generates two steps. The first one applies the step's action to just the ingredients that ended up in a failure state, and the second one applies the action to the remaining ingredients. In our example, SPLIT-STEP will return a group MOP with a step that stir fries the broccoli step, and a step that stir fries the beef and other ingredients.

```
(DEFMOP ISA-CONSTRAINT (CONSTRAINT-FN))

(DEFUN ISA-CONSTRAINT (CONSTRAINT FILLER SLOTS)
  (ABSTP (ROLE-FILLER (ROLE-FILLER 'ROLE CONSTRAINT)
                      SLOTS)
         FILLER))

(DEFMOP ABST (M-ROLE) INSTANCE)

(DEFMOP M-MAP (M-ROOT)
    (ABST M-ROOT)
    (SPEC M-PATTERN
         (ABST-FN ISA-CONSTRAINT) (ROLE ABST)))

(DEFMOP M-MAP-GROUP (M-GROUP) (1 M-MAP))
```

Listing 7.16: Rule Mappings

```
(DEFUN RESET-ROLE-FILLER (ROLE MOP NEW-VALUE)
  (LET ((OLD-VALUE (ROLE-FILLER ROLE MOP)))
   (INSIST RESET-ROLE-FILLER (NOT (NULL OLD-VALUE)))
   (COND ((EQL OLD-VALUE NEW-VALUE) MOP)
         (T (RAISE-ABST
              (FOR (SLOT :IN (MOP-SLOTS MOP))
                 :SAVE (COND ((EQL (SLOT-ROLE SLOT)
                                   ROLE)
                              (MAKE-SLOT ROLE
                                         NEW-VALUE))
                             (T SLOT)))
              MOP)))))
```

Listing 7.17: Role Resetting Function

```
(DEFUN SPLIT-STEP (PATTERN MOP)
 (LET ((STEP (PATH-FILLER '(EXPLANATION CAUSE) MOP))
       (OBJECT
          (PATH-FILLER '(EXPLANATION FAILURE OBJECT)
                       MOP)))
  (LET ((STEP-OBJECT (ROLE-FILLER 'OBJECT STEP)))
   (LIST->GROUP
     (LIST
       (RESET-ROLE-FILLER 'OBJECT STEP OBJECT)
       (RESET-ROLE-FILLER 'OBJECT STEP
         (GROUP-SPLICE NIL OBJECT STEP-OBJECT)))))))

(DEFUN APPLY-REPAIR (PATTERN MOP)
 (LET ((REPAIR (GET-FILLER 'REPAIR MOP))
       (CAUSE (PATH-FILLER '(EXPLANATION CAUSE) MOP))
       (RECIPE (ROLE-FILLER 'SOLUTION MOP)))
  (LET ((STEPS (ROLE-FILLER 'STEPS RECIPE)))
   (RESET-ROLE-FILLER 'STEPS RECIPE
     (FOR (SLOT :IN (MOP-SLOTS STEPS))
       :WHEN (GROUP-MEMBER CAUSE (SLOT-FILLER SLOT))
       :FIRST (RESET-ROLE-FILLER (SLOT-ROLE SLOT)
                 STEPS
                 (GROUP-SPLICE (GROUP->LIST REPAIR)
                   CAUSE
                   (SLOT-FILLER SLOT)))))))))
```

Listing 7.18: Micro CHEF Role Calculation Functions

(APPLY-REPAIR *pattern mop*) takes the group of steps in the REPAIR slot of *mop* and puts them in the recipe in place of the step that caused the failure. APPLY-REPAIR first has to find which group of steps in the recipe contained the bad step, then it splices in the new steps.

Listing 7.19 defines the M-REPAIR MOPs which control the repair process described above.

```
(DEFMOP SPLIT-STEP (M-FUNCTION))
(DEFMOP APPLY-REPAIR (M-FUNCTION))

(DEFMOP M-REPAIR (M-ROOT) (EXPLANATION M-EXPLANATION))

(DEFMOP M-SPLIT-REPAIR (M-REPAIR)
    (EXPLANATION M-SIDE-EFFECT-EXPLANATION)
    (REPAIR M-PATTERN (CALC-FN SPLIT-STEP))
    (REPAIRED-SOLUTION M-PATTERN
                        (CALC-FN APPLY-REPAIR)))
```

Listing 7.19: Micro CHEF Top-Level Repair MOP

7.4   Indexing Repairs in Micro CHEF

After the recipe has been repaired, CHEF has one more job to do. It has to generalize the repair so that future recipes will be based on the repaired recipe, when appropriate. The generalization is based on the rule that explained the failure. In particular, it is based on the map group that says what parts of the input matched the rule. In our example, the map group says that beef matched the pattern M-MEAT and broccoli matched the pattern M-CRISP-VEGETABLE. Any time we have ingredients matching those patterns, we will run into the same failure unless we use the repaired recipe as the basis for adaptation.

Therefore, we want to build a recipe abstraction with M-MEAT in the MEAT role and M-CRISP-VEGETABLE in the VEGE role. We then want to put the repaired recipe under this MOP. We'll also need new MOPs to put those recipes that don't fit this abstraction. Any recipe that doesn't have a meat, and any recipe that doesn't have a crisp vegetable, should be classified separately.

(GENERALIZE-REPAIR *repair-mop role-list*) uses the mapping in *repair-mop* and the slots referred to by *role-list* to form an abstraction and its negations. These are then used to reorganize the solution and its siblings in *repair-mop*. *role-list* should specify those roles that are given as input to the problem solver.

(GENERALIZE-SLOTS *solution-mop role-list map-group*) returns a list of generalized slots, one for each role in *role-list*. The fillers are the corresponding fillers in *solution-mop*, generalized according to *map-group*.

(GENERALIZE-SLOT *role mop map-group*) returns a *role* slot, with *mop* generalized according to *map-group*.

(GENERALIZE-MOP *mop map-group*) looks in *map-group* for a mapping

```
(DEFUN GENERALIZE-REPAIR (REPAIR INPUT-ROLES)
 (LET ((SOLUTION
         (GET-FILLER 'REPAIRED-SOLUTION REPAIR)))
  (LET ((SLOTS (GENERALIZE-SLOTS SOLUTION INPUT-ROLES
                   (PATH-FILLER '(EXPLANATION MAPPING)
                                REPAIR)))
        (ABSTS (MOP-ABSTS SOLUTION)))
   (FOR (SLOT :IN SLOTS)
     :DO (SLOTS->MOP
            (FORMS->SLOTS
              '((,(SLOT-ROLE SLOT)
                M-NOT
                (OBJECT ,(SLOT-FILLER SLOT)))))
            ABSTS T))
   (SLOTS->MOP SLOTS ABSTS T))))

(DEFUN GENERALIZE-SLOTS (MOP ROLES MAPS)
 (FOR (ROLE :IN ROLES)
   :FILTER (GENERALIZE-SLOT ROLE
                         (ROLE-FILLER ROLE MOP)
                         MAPS)))

(DEFUN GENERALIZE-SLOT (ROLE MOP MAPS)
 (AND MOP
      (LET ((ABST (GENERALIZE-MOP MOP MAPS)))
       (AND ABST (MAKE-SLOT ROLE ABST)))))

(DEFUN GENERALIZE-MOP (MOP MAPS)
 (FOR (SLOT :IN (MOP-SLOTS MAPS))
   :WHEN (EQL (ROLE-FILLER 'SPEC (SLOT-FILLER SLOT))
              MOP)
   :FIRST (ROLE-FILLER 'ABST (SLOT-FILLER SLOT))))
```

Listing 7.20: Micro CHEF Generalization Functions

with *mop* in the SPEC slot. If it finds one, it returns the corresponding ABST filler.

Listing 7.21 defines the function that "explains" the soggy broccoli failure. All it really does is build an instance of a predefined explanation that has

```
(DEFUN CHEF-EXPLAIN (MOP)
 (SLOTS->MOP
   '(INSTANCE
     (FAILURE ,MOP)
     (CAUSE ,*BAD-STEP*)
     (RULE M-RULE)
     (MAPPING
       ,(SLOTS->MOP
          (FORMS->SLOTS
            '((1 M-MAP INSTANCE
                 (ABST M-MEAT) (SPEC I-M-BEEF))
              (2 M-MAP INSTANCE
                 (ABST M-CRISP-VEGETABLE)
                 (SPEC I-M-BROCCOLI))))
          '(M-MAP-GROUP)
          T)))
   '(M-EXPLANATION)
   T))
```

Listing 7.21: MOP Instances for CHEF Examples

the information needed to make the example work. It does not do any real explanation.

(CHEF-EXPLAIN *mop*) takes a failure MOP and returns an explanation for the failure. The step blamed for the failure is taken from *BAD-STEP*, which is set by CHEF-DEMO (Listing 7.24).

Note that CALC-TYPE's rules for default types (Listing 3.17) do the wrong thing here. Even though the filler of the RULE slot of an explanation is a rule pattern (an empty rule in this case), the MOP formed should be an instance of an explanation, not an abstraction. Likewise, the mapping with the abstraction M-MEAT in its ABST slot is an instance of a mapping. This is why we coded SLOTS->MOP to accept a MOP type as the first element of the slot list.

Listing 7.22 defines a function for running CHEF and printing the steps in the recipe created.

(RUN-CHEF *slot-list*) calls CHEF with the given slots. If it returns a recipe, the steps are printed and the recipe is returned.

Listing 7.23 defines a set of five functions, to be called in order, to run the CHEF demo. CHEF1 creates the beef and broccoli recipe. CHEF2 invokes an

```
(DEFUN RUN-CHEF (SLOTS)
 (LET ((RECIPE (CHEF SLOTS)))
  (AND RECIPE
       (PROGN (FORMAT T "~&----------------")
              (FORMAT T "~&The steps in ~S are:"
                      RECIPE)
              (DPH (ROLE-FILLER 'STEPS RECIPE))
              RECIPE)))))
```

Listing 7.22: Micro CHEF Test Function

instance of a canned explanation for the broccoli getting soggy because it was cooked with the beef. Note that the CAUSE slot of this explanation is inserted dynamically by taking the first stir fry step from the recipe CHEF1 made. CHEF3 repairs the recipe created by CHEF1. CHEF4 uses the repair created by CHEF3 to reorganize the recipes, distinguishing them by whether they contain a meat and crisp vegetable or not. CHEF5 and CHEF6 can be called in either order. CHEF5 creates a recipe by adapting the repaired recipe, while CHEF6, which does not involve a crisp vegetable, uses one of the original recipes.

Listing 7.24 defines CHEF-DEMO, which is the master program that runs through the tests defined in Listing 7.23.

7.5 Running the CHEF Demo

To run the micro CHEF demo, you need the code in the Listings in Chapter 3 and this chapter. Follow these steps:

1. Load all DEFUN, DEFMACRO, SETF, DEFINE-FOR-KEY and DEFINE-TABLE forms, in the order in which they appear in the Listings.

2. Execute the function call (CLEAR-MEMORY).

3. Load all the DEFMOP forms, in the order in which they appear in the Listings.

4. Execute the function call (CHEF-DEMO).

After Step 3, the abstraction hierarchy printed by (DAH 'M-ROOT) should look like the following, except for the numbers on the MOPs.

```
(DEFUN CHEF1 ()
  (SETF *BAD-RECIPE*
        (RUN-CHEF '((MEAT I-M-BEEF) (VEGE I-M-BROCCOLI)
                    (TASTE I-M-HOT)
                    (STYLE I-M-STIR-FRY))))
  (SETF *BAD-STEP*
        (PATH-FILLER '(STEPS STIR-FRY-STEPS 1)
                     *BAD-RECIPE*))
  *BAD-RECIPE*)

(DEFUN CHEF2 ()
  (SETF *BAD-RECIPE-EXPLANATION*
        (CHEF-EXPLAIN
          (SLOTS->MOP '((STATE I-M-SOGGY)
                        (OBJECT I-M-BROCCOLI))
                     '(M-FAILURE)
                     T))))

(DEFUN CHEF3 ()
  (SETF *RECIPE-REPAIR*
    (CHEF-REPAIR
      '((SOLUTION ,*BAD-RECIPE*)
        (EXPLANATION ,*BAD-RECIPE-EXPLANATION*))))
  (SETF *GOOD-RECIPE*
        (ROLE-FILLER 'REPAIRED-SOLUTION
                     *RECIPE-REPAIR*)))

(DEFUN CHEF4 ()
  (GENERALIZE-REPAIR *RECIPE-REPAIR*
                     '(MEAT VEGE VEGE2 TASTE STYLE)))

(DEFUN CHEF5 ()
  (RUN-CHEF '((MEAT I-M-CHICKEN) (VEGE I-M-SNOW-PEAS)
              (STYLE I-M-STIR-FRY))))

(DEFUN CHEF6 ()
  (RUN-CHEF '((MEAT I-M-BEEF) (VEGE I-M-GREEN-PEPPERS)
              (STYLE I-M-STIR-FRY))))
```

Listing 7.23: Micro CHEF Test Cases

```
(DEFUN CHEF-DEMO ()
  (FORMAT T "~&----------------")
  (FORMAT T "~&Beef and broccoli recipe")
  (INSIST CHEF-DEMO (CHEF1))
  (FORMAT T "~&----------------")
  (FORMAT T "~&Kludging soggy broccoli failure")
  (LINK-ABST *BAD-RECIPE* 'M-FAILED-SOLUTION)
  (FORMAT T "~&Cause is ~S" *BAD-STEP*)
  (FORMAT T "~&Kludging explanation")
  (INSIST CHEF-DEMO (CHEF2))
  (FORMAT T "~&Explanation is ~S"
          *BAD-RECIPE-EXPLANATION*)
  (FORMAT T "~&----------------")
  (FORMAT T "~&Trying to repair ~S" *BAD-RECIPE*)
  (INSIST CHEF-DEMO (CHEF3))
  (FORMAT T "~&Repaired beef and broccoli recipe is ~S"
          *GOOD-RECIPE*)
  (FORMAT T "~&----------------")
  (FORMAT T "~&The repaired steps are:")
  (DPH (ROLE-FILLER 'STEPS *GOOD-RECIPE*))
  (FORMAT T "~&----------------")
  (FORMAT T "~&Generalizing repair")
  (INSIST CHEF-DEMO (CHEF4))
  (FORMAT T "~&New hierarchies:")
  (DAH 'M-RECIPE)
  (DAH 'M-FAILED-SOLUTION)
  (FORMAT T "~&----------------")
  (FORMAT T "~&Chicken and snow-peas recipe")
  (INSIST CHEF-DEMO (CHEF5))
  (FORMAT T "~&----------------")
  (FORMAT T "~&Beef and green peppers recipe")
  (INSIST CHEF-DEMO (CHEF6)))
```

Listing 7.24: Micro CHEF Demo

```
(M-ROOT
    (M-REPAIR (M-SPLIT-REPAIR))
    (M-MAP)
    (M-EXPLANATION (M-SIDE-EFFECT-EXPLANATION))
    (M-FAILURE)
    (M-PRECONS
        (M-LARGE-INGRED-PRECONS)
        (M-BONY-INGRED-PRECONS))
    (M-RECIPE-STEPS
        (I-M-RECIPE-STEPS.47)
        (I-M-RECIPE-STEPS.32))
    (M-RULE)
    (M-TASTE
        (I-M-MILD)
        (I-M-HOT))
    (M-RECIPE-STYLE (I-M-STIR-FRIED))
    (M-INGRED
        (M-SPICES (I-M-SPICES))
        (M-SMALL-INGRED
            (I-M-PEANUTS)
            (I-M-GREEN-BEANS)
            (I-M-SNOW-PEAS))
        (M-LARGE-INGRED
            (I-M-GREEN-PEPPERS)
            (I-M-BROCCOLI)
            (I-M-CHICKEN)
            (I-M-BEEF))
        (M-VEGETABLE
            (M-STURDY-VEGETABLE
                (I-M-PEANUTS)
                (I-M-GREEN-PEPPERS)
                (I-M-GREEN-BEANS))
            (M-CRISP-VEGETABLE
                (I-M-SNOW-PEAS)
                (I-M-BROCCOLI)))
        (M-MEAT
            (M-BONY-MEAT (I-M-CHICKEN))
            (M-BONELESS-MEAT (I-M-BEEF))))
    (M-FAILED-SOLUTION)
    (M-ROLE
        (ABST)
```

```
        (INGRED))
    (M-CASE
        (M-RECIPE
            (I-M-CHICKEN-AND-PEANUTS)
            (I-M-BEEF-AND-GREEN-BEANS)))
    (M-PATTERN
        (M-PATTERN.51)
        (M-PATTERN.50)
        (M-PATTERN.49)
        (M-PATTERN.18)
        (M-MAKE-MOP
            (M-MAKE-MOP.17)
            (M-MAKE-MOP.16))
        (M-COMPARE
            (M-NOT-EQUAL)
            (M-EQUAL))
        (M-NOT)
        (M-PATTERN.15))
    (M-FUNCTION
        (APPLY-REPAIR)
        (SPLIT-STEP)
        (ADAPT-STEPS)
        (MAKE-MOP)
        (NOT-EQL)
        (EQL)
        (GET-SIBLING)
        (CONSTRAINT-FN
            (ISA-CONSTRAINT)
            (COMPARE-CONSTRAINT)
            (NOT-CONSTRAINT)))
    (M-GROUP
        (M-MAP-GROUP)
        (M-PATH)
        (M-STEP-GROUP
            (I-M-STEP-GROUP.46)
            (I-M-STEP-GROUP.43)
            (I-M-STEP-GROUP.40)
            (I-M-STEP-GROUP.37)
            (I-M-STEP-GROUP.34)
            (I-M-STEP-GROUP.31)
            (I-M-STEP-GROUP.28)
```

```
            (I-M-STEP-GROUP.23)
            (I-M-STEP-GROUP.20)
            (I-M-EMPTY-GROUP))
        (M-INGRED-GROUP
            (I-M-INGRED-GROUP.41)
            (I-M-INGRED-GROUP.38)
            (I-M-INGRED-GROUP.26)
            (I-M-INGRED-GROUP.21))
        (M-EMPTY-GROUP (I-M-EMPTY-GROUP)))
  (M-ACTOR)
  (M-ACT
      (M-COOK-ACT
          (I-M-SERVE)
          (I-M-STIR-FRY)
          (I-M-LET-STAND)
          (I-M-CHOP)
          (I-M-BONE)))
  (M-STATE
      (M-BAD-STATE (I-M-SOGGY)))
  (M-EVENT
      (M-STEP
          (M-STEP.48)
          (M-COOK-STEP
              (M-SERVE-STEP
                  (I-M-SERVE-STEP.45)
                  (I-M-SERVE-STEP.30))
              (M-STIR-FRY-STEP
                  (I-M-STIR-FRY-STEP.42)
                  (I-M-STIR-FRY-STEP.27)
                  (I-M-STIR-FRY-STEP.25))
              (M-LET-STAND-STEP
                  (I-M-LET-STAND-STEP.39)
                  (I-M-LET-STAND-STEP.22))
              (M-CHOP-STEP
                  (I-M-CHOP-STEP.36)
                  (I-M-CHOP-STEP.35)
                  (I-M-CHOP-STEP.19))
              (M-BONE-STEP (I-M-BONE-STEP.33))))))))
```

After Step 4, you should see something very close to the output that follows, except for the numbers on the MOPs:

```
----------------
Beef and broccoli recipe
I-M-RECIPE.52:OLD <= I-M-CHICKEN-AND-PEANUTS
----------------
Adapting the steps in I-M-CHICKEN-AND-PEANUTS
----------------
Getting preconditions for I-M-BEEF
Substituting I-M-BEEF for I-M-CHICKEN
Adding preconditions to recipe
I-M-PRECONS.53:CHOP-STEPS <= I-M-CHOP-STEP.19
----------------
Getting preconditions for I-M-BROCCOLI
I-M-PRECONS.66:CHOP-STEPS <= I-M-CHOP-STEP.67
Substituting I-M-BROCCOLI for I-M-GREEN-PEPPERS
Adding preconditions to recipe
I-M-RECIPE.52:STEPS <= I-M-RECIPE-STEPS.76
----------------
The steps in I-M-RECIPE.52 are:
(I-M-RECIPE-STEPS.76
    (BONE-STEPS I-M-EMPTY-GROUP)
    (CHOP-STEPS I-M-GROUP.69
                (1 I-M-CHOP-STEP.19
                   (OBJECT I-M-BEEF))
                (2 I-M-CHOP-STEP.67
                   (OBJECT I-M-BROCCOLI)))
    (LET-STAND-STEPS I-M-STEP-GROUP.23
                     (1 I-M-LET-STAND-STEP.22
                        (OBJECT I-M-INGRED-GROUP.21
                                (1 I-M-BEEF)
                                (2 I-M-SPICES))))
    (STIR-FRY-STEPS I-M-GROUP.72
                    (1 I-M-STIR-FRY-STEP.71
                       (OBJECT I-M-GROUP.70
                               (1 I-M-BEEF)
                               (2 I-M-BROCCOLI)
                               (3 I-M-PEANUTS)
                               (4 I-M-SPICES))))
    (SERVE-STEPS I-M-GROUP.75
                 (1 I-M-SERVE-STEP.74
                    (OBJECT I-M-GROUP.70
                            (1 I-M-BEEF)
```

```
                              (2 I-M-BROCCOLI)
                              (3 I-M-PEANUTS)
                              (4 I-M-SPICES)))))
----------------
Kludging soggy broccoli failure
Cause is I-M-STIR-FRY-STEP.71
Kludging explanation
Explanation is I-M-EXPLANATION.81
----------------
Trying to repair I-M-RECIPE.52
I-M-REPAIR.82:REPAIR <= I-M-GROUP.86
I-M-REPAIR.82:REPAIRED-SOLUTION <= I-M-RECIPE.89
Repaired beef and broccoli recipe is I-M-RECIPE.89
----------------
The repaired steps are:
(I-M-RECIPE-STEPS.88
    (BONE-STEPS I-M-EMPTY-GROUP)
    (CHOP-STEPS I-M-GROUP.69
                (1 I-M-CHOP-STEP.19
                  (OBJECT I-M-BEEF))
                (2 I-M-CHOP-STEP.67
                  (OBJECT I-M-BROCCOLI)))
    (LET-STAND-STEPS I-M-STEP-GROUP.23
                  (1 I-M-LET-STAND-STEP.22
                     (OBJECT I-M-INGRED-GROUP.21
                        (1 I-M-BEEF)
                        (2 I-M-SPICES))))
    (STIR-FRY-STEPS I-M-GROUP.86
                  (1 I-M-STIR-FRY-STEP.83
                     (OBJECT I-M-BROCCOLI))
                  (2 I-M-STIR-FRY-STEP.85
                     (OBJECT I-M-GROUP.84
                        (1 I-M-BEEF)
                        (2 I-M-PEANUTS)
                        (3 I-M-SPICES))))
    (SERVE-STEPS I-M-GROUP.75
                  (1 I-M-SERVE-STEP.74
                     (OBJECT I-M-GROUP.70
                        (1 I-M-BEEF)
                        (2 I-M-BROCCOLI)
                        (3 I-M-PEANUTS)
```

```
                          (4 I-M-SPICES)))))
----------------
Generalizing repair
New hierarchies:
(M-RECIPE (M-RECIPE.94 (I-M-RECIPE.52)
                       (I-M-RECIPE.89))
          (M-RECIPE.93 (I-M-BEEF-AND-GREEN-BEANS)
                       (I-M-CHICKEN-AND-PEANUTS))
          (M-RECIPE.91))
(M-FAILED-SOLUTION (I-M-RECIPE.52))
----------------
Chicken and snow-peas recipe
I-M-RECIPE.95:OLD <= I-M-RECIPE.89
----------------
Adapting the steps in I-M-RECIPE.89
----------------
Getting preconditions for I-M-CHICKEN
I-M-PRECONS.96:CHOP-STEPS <= I-M-CHOP-STEP.35
Substituting I-M-CHICKEN for I-M-BEEF
Adding preconditions to recipe
I-M-PRECONS.96:BONE-STEPS <= I-M-BONE-STEP.33
----------------
Getting preconditions for I-M-SNOW-PEAS
Substituting I-M-SNOW-PEAS for I-M-BROCCOLI
I-M-RECIPE.95:STEPS <= I-M-RECIPE-STEPS.118
----------------
The steps in I-M-RECIPE.95 are:
(I-M-RECIPE-STEPS.118
    (BONE-STEPS I-M-STEP-GROUP.34
                (1 I-M-BONE-STEP.33
                   (OBJECT I-M-CHICKEN)))
    (CHOP-STEPS I-M-GROUP.112
                (1 I-M-CHOP-STEP.35
                   (OBJECT I-M-CHICKEN)))
    (LET-STAND-STEPS I-M-STEP-GROUP.40
                     (1 I-M-LET-STAND-STEP.39
                        (OBJECT I-M-INGRED-GROUP.38
                                (1 I-M-CHICKEN)
                                (2 I-M-SPICES))))
    (STIR-FRY-STEPS I-M-GROUP.114
                    (1 I-M-STIR-FRY-STEP.113
```

```
                        (OBJECT I-M-SNOW-PEAS))
                   (2 I-M-STIR-FRY-STEP.104
                      (OBJECT I-M-GROUP.103
                              (1 I-M-CHICKEN)
                              (2 I-M-PEANUTS)
                              (3 I-M-SPICES))))
      (SERVE-STEPS I-M-GROUP.117
                   (1 I-M-SERVE-STEP.116
                      (OBJECT I-M-GROUP.115
                              (1 I-M-CHICKEN)
                              (2 I-M-SNOW-PEAS)
                              (3 I-M-PEANUTS)
                              (4 I-M-SPICES)))))
----------------
Beef and green peppers recipe
I-M-RECIPE.119:OLD <= I-M-BEEF-AND-GREEN-BEANS
----------------
Adapting the steps in I-M-BEEF-AND-GREEN-BEANS
----------------
Getting preconditions for I-M-GREEN-PEPPERS
I-M-PRECONS.120:CHOP-STEPS <= I-M-CHOP-STEP.36
Substituting I-M-GREEN-PEPPERS for I-M-GREEN-BEANS
Adding preconditions to recipe
I-M-RECIPE.119:STEPS <= I-M-RECIPE-STEPS.129
----------------
The steps in I-M-RECIPE.119 are:
(I-M-RECIPE-STEPS.129
    (BONE-STEPS I-M-EMPTY-GROUP)
    (CHOP-STEPS I-M-GROUP.55
                (1 I-M-CHOP-STEP.19
                   (OBJECT I-M-BEEF))
                (2 I-M-CHOP-STEP.36
                   (OBJECT I-M-GREEN-PEPPERS)))
    (LET-STAND-STEPS I-M-STEP-GROUP.23
                (1 I-M-LET-STAND-STEP.22
                   (OBJECT I-M-INGRED-GROUP.21
                           (1 I-M-BEEF)
                           (2 I-M-SPICES))))
    (STIR-FRY-STEPS I-M-GROUP.124
                (1 I-M-STIR-FRY-STEP.25
                   (OBJECT I-M-INGRED-GROUP.21
```

```
                        (1 I-M-BEEF)
                        (2 I-M-SPICES)))
              (2 I-M-STIR-FRY-STEP.123
                  (OBJECT I-M-GROUP.122
                          (1 I-M-BEEF)
                          (2 I-M-GREEN-PEPPERS)
                          (3 I-M-SPICES)))))
  (SERVE-STEPS I-M-GROUP.127
              (1 I-M-SERVE-STEP.126
                  (OBJECT I-M-GROUP.122
                          (1 I-M-BEEF)
                          (2 I-M-GREEN-PEPPERS)
                          (3 I-M-SPICES)))))))
```

7.6 Extensions

7.6.1 Constraints on Optional Fillers

Our M-RECIPE MOP had no constraint on the VEGE2 slot, because we wanted
to allow for the absence of a second vegetable. A more correct approach would
be to define a constraint that said that the filler of VEGE2 should either be NIL
or some vegetable different from the one filling the VEGE slot. One way to
specify this slot constraint that would be fairly general is:

```
(VEGE2 M-PATTERN (ABST-FN OPTIONAL-AND-DIFFERENT)
       (ROLE VEGE) (TYPE M-VEGETABLE))
```

ROLE specifies the slot with the filler to be avoided, and TYPE specifies the
type the filler should be, if any. Define the appropriate MOPs and functions
to allow the above to be used.

7.6.2 MOP-SUBST

The definition of MOP-SUBST in Listing 7.5 has a bug. It will go into an endless
loop if its third argument is, or contains, a MOP that packages itself. Fix this.
Hint: DPH in Listing 3.20 does not have this bug.

7.6.3 Merging Steps

Sometimes, when steps are added to a recipe, they can be merged with existing
steps. If, for example, we add a second vegetable to a recipe, it will require

a stir fry step. Normally, there will already be a stir fry step in the recipe and the vegetable should simply be added to the other ingredients being fried. Micro CHEF, however, will add a new stir fry step.

Fix ADAPT-STEPS to merge steps when possible. Not all kinds of steps should be merged. For example, it is not physically possible to bone more than one ingredient at a time, so merging boning steps is not sensible. On the other hand, marinating, i.e., LET-STAND, is a perfectly reasonable candidate for merger. You should also have some way of deciding what to do when there is more than one step to merge with. For example, the repaired beef and broccoli recipe has two stir fry steps, one cooking the broccoli and one cooking the meat and other ingredients. If we view the meat step as the primary one, and the broccoli step as a secondary offshoot, then a default rule might be to put the new ingredient in with the primary step. A very smart system, perhaps too smart to be a good model of the average cook, would note that the secondary step was generated to avoid making the broccoli soggy, and would put the new ingredient in the primary or secondary step, depending on whether the new ingredient was a crisp vegetable. As you can see, the apparently simple task of merging steps raises all sorts of complex issues.

7.6.4   Including Cooking Times

We deliberately left cooking times out of our representation of recipes to avoid many of the complexities of merging and splitting cooking steps. Many real planning domains unfortunately require adding a lot of knowledge about time. To add time, you need to add DURATION role to each cooking step in a recipe, indicating how long, in minutes, the step is supposed to last. You'll also need information to each ingredient MOP specifying how long it takes to cook. The functions for adding, splitting, and merging steps will have to keep track of the total cooking time for each ingredient.

7.6.5   Adding New Kinds of Steps

Another simplification we made was to structure recipe steps so that different kinds of steps, e.g., boning steps versus chopping steps, were put in different slots. This made it relatively easy to write code to add new steps, but it also means that if a new kind of step is added, e.g., shelling shrimp, then our master recipe steps MOP will have to have a shelling slot added somewhere. The explicit slot solution is preferable to the standard planning approach of ordering solely to satisfy precondition constraints, e.g., don't chop chicken before you bone it. Recipes have a fairly standardized order, which goes beyonds the needs of preconditions. An interesting extension would be to be able to add a recipe with a new kind of step, e.g., a shrimp recipe, and have the memory extend the recipe steps MOP to include the new slot, in the same position that it appears in the input recipe.

7.6.6 Adapting Closest Cases

In one of the extensions to micro JUDGE in Chapter 5, we discussed the problem of extending the function GET-SIBLING in Listing 3.22 to pick the most similar instance for adaptation, rather than just any sibling instance. The same issue comes up in micro CHEF. Currently, if the siblings for an input request for a beef recipe are a beef recipe and a chicken recipe, there is no preference for adapting the beef recipe. In micro JUDGE, the easiest solution was to try adapting each case and pick the one that needed the least adjustment. This won't work in CHEF for two reasons. First, generating a recipe in CHEF is much more expensive than generating a sentence in JUDGE. Second, there is no easy way of measuring how much "adjustment" adapting a recipe required. The issue is not how close the adapted recipe is to the recipe it was adapted from, but how much work was involved in adapting it.

Fortunately, input requests in CHEF are much simpler than input crimes in JUDGE. CHEF's requests are basically simple lists of desired ingredients and tastes. Hence it is reasonable to pursue the problem of matching them against retrieved cases, prior to attempting adaptation. As in the real CHEF, our notion of similarity is defined by the goal of adaptation. We want our similarity rules to predict which retrieved case will need the least adaptation. One reason is because our adaptation rules are limited in how drastically they can change things, e.g., no rules exist for changing a stir fry recipe into a casserole. Another reason is simply to avoid unnecessary work. In fact, avoiding extra work is why CHEF creates a new MOP for recipes involving a meat and a crisp vegetable. The MOP helps CHEF avoid the work of repairing recipes producing soggy vegetables.

We want our rules for matching an input request against a stored recipe to be based on things such as how hard it is to substitute one ingredient for another, or how hard it is to change a taste, e.g., to make a hot dish milder. Many of these rules can be pretty general, e.g., it is harder to substitute beef into a chicken dish than a pork one, because chicken is a bony meat with a skin, which beef and pork are not. When adapting a chicken recipe to a beef recipe, CHEF has to remove the steps for removing skin and bones. When adapting a pork recipe, no steps have to be changed.

Define some rules, using M-CALC MOPs (Chapter 5) if you wish, for calculating a measure of how easy or hard it is to substitute different kinds of ingredients for each other. You may want to add more information about the different ingredients to make things realistic. Currently our MOP definitions in Listing 7.2 suggest that green beans and peanuts are very much alike!

7.6.7   Simulation

This exercise, and the two following it, replace the explanation kludge in CHEF2 in Listing 7.23 with something a bit more interesting.

Add a simulator to micro CHEF. A simulator determines the states produced by each step in a recipe. In the cooking domain, the states describe the properties of the various ingredients, e.g., their size, cookedness, texture, taste, and so on. How a step affects an ingredient often depends on what state the ingredient was in when the step is performed. in effect when the step was executed. For example, a "stir fry broccoli" step will cook the broccoli if the broccoli is in small chunks, but not if it still in one large piece.

The simulator should take two inputs: a recipe and a set of ingredient states. It should "execute" each step in order, creating a new set of states to reflect the effects of each step. The output should list each step, the states it produces, and a set of mappings. We'll discuss the mappings shortly.

For example, the state

```
(M-STATE (STATE I-M-SOGGY) (OBJECT I-M-BROCCOLI))
```

among others, should be produced when the first beef and broccoli recipe is simulated. Initially, the ingredients beef and broccoli are uncooked and large. The simulator would then step through each line of the recipe, changing the set of ingredient states appropriately. Some steps have simple effects, e.g., "chop broccoli" makes the piece size of the broccoli small. Some steps are more complex. In particular, "stir fry beef and broccoli" cooks both ingredients, but it also makes the broccoli soggy. In the real CHEF program, this was because cooking the beef produced water in the pan, and cooking the broccoli in the pan with the water made the broccoli soggy. In your first attempt at a simulator, you may want to simplify this to just say that cooking meat with a crisp vegetable makes it soggy.

You should represent the knowledge of how steps affect states with MOPs. For example, one possible form, not necessarily the best one, is

```
(DEFMOP M-CHOP-EFFECT (M-EFFECT)
    (STEP M-CHOP-STEP (OBJECT M-INGRED))
    (EFFECT M-MAKE-MOP (MOP M-STATE)
            (STATE I-M-SMALL)
            (OBJECT M-PATH (1 STEP)
                           (2 OBJECT)))))
```

This is intended to say that the effect of an M-CHOP-STEP is to make the ingredient small. To make this representation work, you will have to change REPLACE-SLOTS in Listing 7.6 to handle M-PATH fillers, and you will have to define STEP and OBJECT to be instances of M-ROLE.

The simulator needs to keep track of the current set of states, and, for each step, retrieve any M-EFFECT MOPs that match it. Each EFFECT should replace any state with the same STATE and OBJECT. Thus, given the step

```
(M-CHOP-STEP (OBJECT I-M-BROCCOLI))
```

the simulator should replace

```
(M-STATE (STATE I-M-LARGE) (OBJECT I-M-BROCCOLI))
```

in the input states with

```
(M-STATE (STATE I-M-SMALL) (OBJECT I-M-BROCCOLI))
```

In addition, the simulator needs to record the mapping between the input step and the STEP filler. In this case, the mapping is

```
(M-MAP-GROUP
   (1 M-MAP INSTANCE
         (ABST M-INGRED) (SPEC I-M-BROCCOLI)))
```

For our purposes, the simulator only needs to record those mappings where a filler matched a non-NIL abstraction. This information is used when generalizing the repair, in Listing 7.20. Note in particular the mapping produced by CHEF-EXPLAIN in Listing 7.21.

7.6.8 Evaluation

Once you've created the simulator in the previous exercise, you can design the evaluator. The evaluator determines whether or not a recipe succeeds or fails. It does this by looking at the final states of the recipe, as generated by the simulator. There are two kinds of goals: explicit goals, given in the input request, and implicit goals, true in every recipe. It is unlikely that micro CHEF's recipes will violate the few explicit goals it is given, which say what ingredients should be there and whether the dish should be hot or not, but its first beef and broccoli recipe does violate the implicit goal that broccoli should be crisp.

Add an evaluator that will take a recipe and return a (possibly empty) list of M-FAILURE MOPs, representing violated goals. In particular, the evaluator should make an M-FAILURE MOP for the soggy broccoli state returned by the simulator, as was done by the function CHEF2 in Listing 7.23. Use MOPs to represent the implicit goals, such as that ingredients should be cooked and crisp vegetables should still be crisp.

7.6.9 Explanation

The job of the explainer module is to link the failures that the evaluator found to the steps in the recipe that generated them. The explainer uses the output from the simulator to make these links. Finding the right step to blame is called the *credit assignment* problem, and is a major AI research topic. For micro CHEF we propose a very simplistic algorithm. Given a bad final state, such as soggy broccoli, search backward in the list of steps and states, until you find the step before which the bad state did not exist. Blame that step. In our beef and broccoli example, this will correctly blame the stir fry step, not the serving step, even though the broccoli is soggy after both steps.

The output should be an M-EXPLANATION MOP like the one produced by CHEF-EXPLAIN in Listing 7.21. Note that the mappings produced by the simulator should be included in the M-EXPLANATION MOP.

7.6.10 Other Kinds of Recipes

All of our recipes are stir fry recipes. The real CHEF program however also did a few dessert recipes. Try implementing the strawberry soufflé example discussed briefly in Chapter 6 and at length in [Hammond, 1989].

8

Plan Creation

Gregg C. Collins[1]

8.1 Introduction

Learning is one of the most difficult problems facing researchers in artificial intelligence. There appear to be two reasons for this. First, it is difficult to specify the problem in functional terms, such as the search for a process that will associate a set of possible inputs with a set of desired outputs. Since the "output" in this case is a modification of the system itself, and since the meaning of such a modification can only be determined by reference to a reasonably well-specified theory of how that system carries out its other tasks, the general lack of well-specified theories of how intelligent systems do things is a serious obstacle. Second, it seems quite possible that there will not be *a* theory of learning, but will instead be a number of distinct theories of learning. There is no *a priori* reason to doubt that there might be several different processes that could be employed to modify a complex mechanism in the direction of improved performance.

In what follows, I will look at one particular modification process: the process of plan creation. The process of plan creation is fundamental, in the sense that other learning processes follow from the drive to create new plans. This is because intelligent agents are goal-pursuers, and plans are the mechanism of goal pursuit. Without the idea of an agent pursuing some set of goals, the reason for learning, and in fact the notion of "improvement," would be missing.

---

[1]The material in this chapter has been edited from [Collins, 1987]

8.1.1   Examples of Plan Creation

Human planners produce plans not only by chaining old plans together, e.g., plans for going to the store, buying milk, and getting home, but also by applying general strategic principles to modify plans that are not performing as desired. We can look for examples in any situation where a planner, who has been pursuing one plan, suddenly stops, reconsiders the situation, and decides to employ a radically different plan in place of the one he has been pursuing.

Going Out: Bob and Susan were going out for the evening. Susan wanted to see the new Tom Cruise movie. Bob wanted to have dinner at the *nouvelle* American restaurant that had just opened downtown. Bob figured that they would have to leave by 8:30 to make either the movie or their reservation at the restaurant, but at 8:25 the argument was still raging. It occurred to Bob that he had to get the car out of the parking lot and get some cash no matter which decision they made, so he decided to do those things first, which left more time to make the decision.

Making Coffee: Dave was measuring water for coffee. Dave takes his coffee seriously, so he wanted to be precise. However, he found that unless he ran the water very slowly, it splashed in the container so much that he could not tell how much water he had added. Dave gave up on this plan. Instead, he splashed water in to about the right level, checked it, threw a little out, checked it again, splashed in a bit more, and so on, until he was close enough to the mark to add the rest slowly.

Football: Bruce was a natural for his football team's defensive line, but he had yet to learn the position. When he was blocked, he would push as hard as he could until he felt resistance give way in one direction or the other, in which case he would slide that way and push some more. After several plays where he got a good opening to one side, only to realize that he had taken himself out of the play, which was going the other direction, he realized that his opponent was deliberately allowing him an opening on one side to influence him to move in the wrong direction. After that, Bruce was more concerned about keeping open his option of going either way than with getting by his man.

Buying Clothes: As a graduate student, John got in the habit of buying his clothes at a local discount store, a place that buys up overstocks of brand-name clothing and sells it for much less than the usual retail price. When John needed an item of clothing, he would go to the store, find the best example of this item, and buy it. However, this plan was often frustrated at the discount store's buying policies. What they had in stock was often not what he needed. Finally, it occurred to him that he had the wrong plan. The answer was to go regularly and buy the best of whatever they had. This would mean that over the long haul he would have the best possible clothing in each category, and things would even out.

John was reminded of the way professional football teams pick players. Each year, the pro teams have a "draft," in which they engage in an orderly selection process to choose new players from the group that is coming out of college. Most teams draft by determining what they need and looking for players to fill those positions, but some teams, such as John's favorite team, Dallas, simply choose the "best available athlete," regardless of the team's current strengths or weaknesses.

Here, we have four different examples in which the same basic event occurs: a planner notices a problem in a plan, and alters the plan in such a way that the problem disappears or is mitigated. In each case, the change that is carried out seems to be tailor-made to solve the exact problem in question. The construction of the solution seems to follow directly from an analysis of the problem. It is not the result of a process of trial-and-error, or of induction over instances. The analysis of the problem in each case seems to be sufficient to produce a strategy for solving that problem.

Furthermore, in each case, the strategy for fixing the problem appears to be quite general. In the *going out* example, for instance, we can see that any time a planner is facing a decision between two plans, and those plans share steps, and the time required to perform those steps is a factor in determining the deadline for making the decision, then the decision can be postponed by factoring out these shared steps and performing them before the decision is made. In the *making coffee* example, the change is from steady monitoring of the approach of some quantity toward a threshold, to a plan of *successive approximation*. In principle, it is always possible to substitute a successive approximation method in such a situation, although the cost (due to the risk of overshooting) may be high. It matters not at all what the quantity in question is. It could equally well be the tension on a guitar string, for instance.

In the *football* example we have a shift from a decision-making policy that is essentially *hillclimbing*, in that the path of least resistance is always taken, to one that strives to keep options open rather than make the biggest possible advance at each point. Any hillclimbing situation is susceptible to the problem of traps. In general the way to avoid a trap is to plan to conserve available options. The *buying clothes* example gives two radically different situations in which the strategy of "stockpile the best" applies. Furthermore, it is clear that such a strategy will apply any time a process of resource selection is encountered where certain conditions hold true of the selection process.

There are three key observation that I'd like to make:

- Associated with planning problems are strategies for repair.

- These strategies take the form of *transformation rules*, that alter a plan with problems to produce a plan that avoids those problems, while preserving as many essential characteristics of the original plan as possible.

- Solution strategies may be generalized to the point of making no reference to the physical world whatsoever, beyond basic notions of time and space.

The third point will be argued for shortly.

These three points constitute the fundamental claim of this research. They imply that there exists a set of strategies for solving planning problems that are completely *domain-independent*, in the above-mentioned sense of not referring to the physical world, and that these strategies take the form of *plan transformation rules*. The remainder of this section will examine the mechanisms through which these strategies are employed, and characterize a number of particular strategies.

8.1.2   Models of Plan Creation

This section compares four general approaches to plan generation. First, there is the *Generalize and Store Model*, which is used in most current AI planners.[2] Such planners create one-shot plans. A one-shot plan is a set of directions, tailored specifically to the exact situation at hand, that will never be used again. Charniak and McDermott [1985] compare this kind of plan to a shopping list. Each time you go shopping, you generate a new list.

The components from which particular plans are built are stored plans, generalized for repeated use. They are adapted to whatever particular situation they are used in. It may be necessary to specify parameters, fill in

---

[2]See [1975], Tate [1977], McDermott [1978], and Wilkins [1984]. The theory is generally referred to as *non-linear planning*, a term due to Sacerdoti.

subplans for subgoals, or connect a number of stored plans together to achieve a complex goal. It is the task of the planner to do these things when building a new plan. Thus, the AI planner is almost a learning model already; it lacks only a mechanism for storing the plans it builds for future use. The obvious extension of the model is to generalize the one-shot plans it creates and store them away.

There are a number of interesting aspects to the *Generalize and Store* model of learning. Many of them are addressed in Schank's work on MOP learning [Schank, 1982]. Schank discusses how people may build up "scripts" for dealing with certain circumstances by, in effect, accreting a generalization by overlaying different episodes that occur in a similar circumstance, saving the commonalities between the episodes and dismissing the variances. The important issues here include how "similar circumstances" are be defined for this purpose, how new and old episodes are matched up, and how and when the system should decided to break apart a single generalization into alternative versions.

It will often be the case, however, that a *Generalize and Store* planner will be unable to accomplish its goals by stringing together stored plans.[3]. When this happens, we need a model of plan creation in *Response to Problems*.

Minimally, a *Response to Problems* model must account for the detection and characterization of planning problems, and the use of these characterizations for guiding plan repair. The key to constructing such a model is to relate planning problems to solution strategies. There must, at some point, be a rule that says "in order to fix a problem like *this*, make a change like *that*."

Consider the *going out* example again. The first step is to notice a problem. The basis for noticing execution problems is monitoring the constraints that described the original plan. In this case, the constraint of interest is the deadline associated with the decision of where to go. The planner notices that this deadline is likely to fail by extrapolating the time it is taking to make progress in the decision and comparing it with the time available. I assume that any model of this process will involve anticipating problems, since this is much more useful than simply reporting them after they have occurred.

Once the problem is detected, the planner must characterize the problem situation. In this case, some relevant features are:

- A decision is in danger of missing its deadline

- The alternatives in question share a step

---

[3]Notice that this failure may arise either as an inability of the planning algorithm to construct a plan, or the failure of the plan that was constructed by the planner to succeed in execution. I am trying to be as general as possible here, although I am mainly interested in the latter case

- These steps could be merged without much increased cost

- At least one of the shared steps is a factor in in the deadline for the decision, in the sense that time has been allowed for the execution of that step after the decision is executed

It seems reasonable that the first two features could serve as indexes to retrieve potential plan transformation rules. The other two features would be tested for explicitly by the rules retrieved.

These features, if true, as they are here, mean that the rule I will call **factor precondition** applies. This rule merges the shared step of the two plans and schedules them *before* the decision.

Responding to problems is the primary model of plan creation that I will be discussing here. There are, however, two other models that deserve mention. First, there is the *Notice Opportunities Model*, as seen in DeJong's [1981] model of learning new plans by observing other agents performing tasks in unexpected ways.

The fundamental issue here is that of recruiting causal knowledge as planning knowledge. If an understander determines that A causes B, it is always possible that bringing about A may be a practical way to achieve B. Since we all know many interconnected causal relationships, an open problem is how to search through them in some computationally tractable way. By doing a bit of "mucking about" in the causal structures, the understander may occasionally hit upon the key to a new plan. We must postulate rules that direct this mucking about in the first place.

Another problem is designing a planner that can even notice the relevance of some piece of new knowledge to its plans. Part of the effort in discovering that a piece of knowledge in hand at the moment relates to a desired plan lies in searching through the inferences rules; part of it lies in storing the memory that the plan is needed in a way that makes it likely to be found. This problem is analogous to the general problem of implementing *opportunism* [Birnbaum, 1985; Birnbaum, 1986], in which outstanding goals must be indexed so that they will be recalled in the presence of opportunities for fulfilling them. This is a major research issue.

The other model of plan creation that I would like to mention is the *Serendipity Model*. This is the sort of thing that occurs when you add tarragon to your spaghetti sauce by mistake, discover that you like the result better than the sauce you intended to make, and incorporate the accident into a new plan that achieves the unexpectedly good result. In general, the determination of whether the accidental plan should be stored depends on whether the circumstances that made it work are likely to arise, or are easy to bring about, in the future. To take a somewhat facetious example, if you are trying to defuse a bomb, and you accidentally drop it, causing some component to dislodge and accomplishing the task, it is unlikely that you want to simply store this as a new bomb-defusing technique.

In addition, the unexpected success of the accidental plan does not necessarily indicate that it is the best plan for the circumstances. It may, in fact, indicate that the circumstances were not as you envisioned them originally, and that you chose the wrong plan in the first place. The right plan might be more effective than the serendipitous one.

The model that seems to provide the best viewpoint for making these determinations is *failure-driven learning* [Schank, 1982]. This may at first seem somewhat perverse, since the keynote here seems to be unexpected *success*. However, failure in this model means *expectation* failure, not goal failure. The response should be to note the expectation that failed, and attempt to explain what circumstances caused it to fail. Schank's model involves three main steps:

- Notice an expectation failure

- Explain the failure

- Alter memory structures to avoid the failure in the future

To this we can add another step:

- Look for ways in which the failure might indicate that the system could improve its plans

A number of things might occur as part of this step. For example, if an expectation failure represents a problem for the planner, the explanation of it might suggest a basis for a way to predict that problem well in advance, something that might well be very useful. Note how this differs from the issue of avoiding making the wrong prediction. It is one thing to avoid falsely predicting that a bad result will not occur, and another thing to predict that bad result in advance.

The point of this step for our purposes is, of course, that it is here that the planner may consider the fact that the expectation failure in question is associated with the serendipitous success of the plan. In this case, the response of the planner should be to consider if the pleasant result might be recreated by means of a plan. This method of learning can be viewed as an aspect of expectation-failure-driven learning.

The sections that follow present a catalog of domain-independent strategies for plan transformation in service of the *Response to Problems* model of plan creation. By domain-independent, I mean that the problem situation associated with the strategy is independent of the physics of the world. The

existence of these domain-independent transformation rules support Newell's
[1981] position that there is a knowledge level of description that deals with
agents and rational goal-plan behavior.

8.2   Replanning and Planning

Now it is time to consider in more detail what a plan transformation rule
really is. Since the point of such rules is to fix planning problems, the obvious
place to start is with the nature of planning problems. What is a planning
problem? If we reconsider the four examples of Section 8.1.1, we have four
different answers: a deadline is threatened, a plan proceeds too slowly, a plan
consistently fails to meet a goal that it is in service of, and a plan over time
produces less benefit than was potentially available from the situation.

These examples provide us the beginnings of a taxonomy of possible planning problems. Roughly, we can generalize them as follows: A plan cannot
be executed as specified, it can but it costs too much, it doesn't achieve the
goal, or it achieves the goal but achieves less than it could have in the given
situations. To these we can add another possible problem, which is that a
plan achieves its goal but produces a bad side effect. This is the "toxic waste"
problem.

If we clean these up a little, we arrive at the following taxonomy of planning
problems:

1. **Failed constraint**—some explicit constraint in the original plan specification cannot be met.

2. **Excessive cost**—a plan uses more resources than its result is worth, or,
   more subtly, uses more resources than the planner has come to expect
   this class of plans to use (as for example when one refuses to employ a
   service because it charges more than the going rate).

3. **Failed result**—a plan does not achieve the goal that it was in service
   of.

4. **Bad side effect**—a plan has a side effect that is costly to the planner
   in some way.

5. **Global suboptimality**—a plan does not perform as well over the long
   run as *post hoc* analysis would suggest. For example, if you have a
   scheme for choosing stocks that you employ for a year, and if, looking
   back, you see that by choosing a different set of stocks you would have
   done much better than you did, you might consider your plan to be a

poor one (although the fact that you could in principle have done better does not mean that *a priori* you could have developed a plan that would in fact do better).

The implication of this taxonomy is that the planner should be monitoring its plan with an eye toward detecting any of these problems. We will go into more detail about the mechanisms by which these things must be monitored later.

We can expect our rules to be indexed by particular examples of these problems that can be solved by particular transformations. For example, the rule that applies to the case of Bob and Susan going out for the evening is indexed by the problem "unmeetable constraint." The planning situations that can be fixed with this rule are those where a) the constraint in question is a deadline, and b) the plan step that will not meet its deadline is a decision. In general, the problem description associated with a transformation rule will be a restricted subclass of one of the above problem classes.

The rest of this section addresses the following questions:

1. How transformation rules relate to the planning process

2. Why planning *requires* transformation rules for fixing planning problems

3. How fixing a problem in a plan relates to the issue of plan creation

8.2.1 Planning as Decision Making

The first order of business is to characterize very roughly the standard theory of planning in AI, which is usually called *non-linear planning*[Sacerdoti, 1975].[4] A planner starts with a goal and makes a series of choices that lead to the construction of a set of steps—the plan—that should achieve that goal when executed. The choices for the most part boil down to deciding which plan steps to choose to satisfy a goal, and deciding when to schedule a plan step to avoid undoing the desired effects of previous plan steps. Plan steps have *preconditions* which must be true before the steps can be performed, so choosing a plan step usually leads to subgoals that must be achieved in service of the main goals.

We can view constructing a plan as a case of search. Since the point of each decision is to add another element to a partially completed plan, the search space is the space of partial plans. This is a common way to view the process of planning (cf. [McDermott, 1978]).

---

[4][Chapman, 1985] has an elegant formal statement of the non-linear planning model.

There cannot be a guarantee that the plan is in fact workable. We are particularly interested in those cases where a plan has problems during execution *and* the planner could have chosen differently and produced a plan that would have worked. In these cases, *the planning problem can be associated with a bad decision that was made during the construction of the plan.*

Transformation rules have the job of recognizing when a particular decision was made badly, and rectifying the mistake. Consider, for instance, the example of Dave and the coffee maker. Dave chose a plan for filling the container that involved continuous monitoring of a changing quantity. This took too long so he switched to a successive approximation plan. Since Dave could have chosen this plan in the first place, we can say that Dave's original decision to use continuous monitoring was a bad one, and he reversed himself and used successive approximation instead.

Our transformation rule says that *if a plan based on continuous monitoring is too slow, change to a plan using successive approximation.* Now, we could have an equivalent planning rule that says *if continuous monitoring* will be *too slow, use successive approximation.* It could have been applied when Dave originally constructed his plan, if he had realized at that point that the plan would be too slow. These are the same rule. In fact,

---

transformation rules are simply rules about decision-making formulated to be applied after the fact.

The reason for transformation rules is that the information required by a decision rule may be unavailable, or too costly to obtain, at planning time. Since this information may become available at execution time, and may serve as evidence that the decision was made incorrectly, the knowledge captured by the decision rule should be kept available during execution. Transformation rules are a way of formulating this knowledge for application.

Undoing a decision that was made previously is, of course, a somewhat different proposition than making that decision in the first place. The reason is that a number of decisions may have been made subsequently, and these may depend on the problematic decision. However, we do not want the planner to simply return to the problematic decision and start planning from scratch from that point; many of the subsequent decisions are still perfectly reasonable. For example, after deciding on a continuous monitoring plan for getting coffee water, Dave may have put a lot of effort into finding a source of water and so on. Some elements of his subsequent planning may depend upon the initial decision of which approach to take; some may not. In undoing his decision, he must also change those subsequent decisions that were contingent on the bad decision, but he would like to leave unrelated decisions alone. The job of the transformation rule is to compile in an understanding of how this entire process must be performed.

> The purpose of the transformation component of a rule is to save the planner from having to replan from scratch after a bad decision.

8.2.2 Implicit Decisions

Warning! The notion of a "decision" is not a simple one, and the bland assumption that we can explicitly identify all of the decisions that the program is making, and characterize the planning algorithm as a search through the space of these decisions, is likely to mislead us without further analysis.

The problem is that many decisions are implicit. Consider a few examples:

- You are choosing a restaurant for dinner. You want to spend under ten dollars, and you want to walk there. The only restaurant that meets these criteria is *Mañana*, which is Mexican. Thus, you have chosen Mexican cuisine, even though you did not recognize that you were making such a choice.

- You have an ordinary week, during which you do not once think about Bangkok, Thailand. At the end of the week you have of course not visited Bangkok. You have implicitly *chosen* not to visit Bangkok.

- You have a habit of pandering to people in authority. Presumably you learned to do this because it relaxed them and made them seem more friendly to you. However, you are not *aware* that you are pandering, you have never *considered* that you might be pandering, and you would be *appalled* at the thought that you should do such a thing. Nonetheless, you have chosen to pander.

Now, the above examples may seem somewhat perverse. The explicit consideration of a choice by the planner is a big part of our notion of what a decision is in the first place. In the examples, the planner is innocent of any such explicit consideration. However, for our purposes these qualify as decisions, on the grounds of two criteria:

1. The results in question are predictable outcomes of the planner's plans

2. Subsequent problems encountered by the planner may be tied to these decisions

The latter point is the interesting one, since it implies that during replanning we may want to identify the decision in question, despite the fact that it did not occur explicitly. For example, suppose that we take Grandma to *Mañana*, and she gets indigestion, as she *always* does, when she eats hot, spicy food. Obviously it was a mistake to choose Mexican, and we had better not make that choice again when Grandma visits. We *didn't* make that choice, you want to say—but we *did*, and in fact that is the only reasonable way to characterize the error in question. Similarly, a friend may say, "You should have come to Bangkok last week! You would have had the time of your life!" If we analyze missing the putative time of our lives as a planning problem, this can only be blamed on the phantom decision not to go to Thailand. If someone says, "Stop brown-nosing! You're embarrassing me!" we must conclude that our mistake was in choosing this strategy for dealing with persons in authority.

Implicit decisions will occur constantly in the course of planning. We can generalize the three examples above into a descriptive taxonomy of such decisions:

- **Contingent decisions:** The decisions made in the course of constructing a plan are causally related, and tend to be mutually constraining. By making one decision, we may force choice in another.

- **Negative decision:** As planners, we have any number of options that we could employ at almost any time. I *could* get a cup of coffee. I *could* go and run a few miles. I could go to Bangkok. We are constantly making the decision *not* to do any of these things, simply because we do not in fact decide to do them.

- **Unanalyzed decisions:** Some plans contain choices that were made arbitrarily or in a simple way when the plan was first tried. The plans work and so are never altered. Some plans are copied or learned directly from other people. In either case, there are many decisions implicit in the plan that the planner is unaware of.

What we really have here are three very general points about decision making that are all, in some sense, quite well known. The point about contingency of decisions is of course exactly the idea that underlies constraint-propagation models of reasoning (cf., e.g., [Waltz, 1975]). The point about deciding *not* to do things is a special case of Wittgenstein's [1953] point about implicit knowledge.

The upshot of these considerations is the following fact:

> Transformation rules must be able to recognize the circumstances in which a decision is being made, even if it is being made implicitly; they cannot rely on the explicit specification of the decisions involved in a plan.

Note though that this situation can be to the planner's advantage, since it saves the cost of worrying about certain options except in cases where feedback from execution shows that the plan will not succeed without exercising one of these options.

8.2.3 Plan Repair and Learning

In the *Generalize and Store* model, plans for commonly encountered circumstances are compiled and stored for future use. This model seems reasonable as a way to avoid unnecessary planning effort. However, there is a more urgent reason for storing specific plans. In some circumstances it may be the case that the planner's normal decision-making machinery produces the wrong plan for a certain situation, but it is not clear how to change the planner's general decision rules to avoid the problem without adversely affecting planning for other situations. When this happens, it is particularly critical that the planner should store the *right* plan for the circumstances in such a way that it will be reused in the future. This will short-circuit the (incorrect) planning process.

Here, finally, we come to the relationship between replanning and learning.

> It is critical that when an error is detected, and fixed by a transformation rule, that the fix is stored at as general a level as possible, so that in the future the same error will not be repeated *in the planning process.*

In effect, the planner needs to store such inferences to short-circuit the general decision-making process of the planner, which has been shown by experience to produce the wrong plan for cases of the type in question.

8.3 Learning in a Competitive Domain

I have chosen to look at the game of football as an example domain. Football teams operate by utilizing a set of standard plans, called *plays*. It is the creation of these plays that I am interested in. Like chess, football is a game, and hence highly constrains the set of situations we have to worry about. Unlike chess, however, football requires reasoning about time and space, and,

most importantly, about *opponents and how they reason about your strategies.*
Planning and counterplanning [Carbonell, 1981] are fundamental to football.
One major problem with football is that it not an easy domain to experiment
in. Novices and fledgling AI programs don't get to coach football teams.

Instead, in this section, I will describe and analyze a set of "just so" stories
about the creation and development of several standard plays in football. I
will then show how these stories can be explained in the transformation-rule
paradigm I have presented. I have three main purposes in presenting these
examples:

1. To provide an illustration of the ideas I have presented so far

2. To illustrate the way in which domain-specific plans relate to general
   strategic knowledge

3. To provide a basis for considering what kinds of processes must be available in order to apply plan transformation rules to real problems

By "strategic knowledge" I mean knowledge about global plan patterns,
such as has appeared in the transformation rules given so far. **Successive
Approximation** is a strategy that contrasts with the alternative strategy of
continuous monitoring, and *choose the best available resource* is a strategy
that contrasts with *choose the most needed resource.*

8.3.1   Forced Choice and Generalized Problem Descriptions

Let us consider a particular example of a general planning problem: the problem of *forced choice.* Forced choice arises when a planner can retrieve only one
plan for a goal. In any domain, it can be a serious problem, because it leaves
no alternatives open if the plan fails. This is standard strategic knowledge.
Keep your options open. Cover your bets. Don't paint yourself into a corner.
All of these aphorisms argue for *flexibility* in plan creation.

Therefore, when a planner encounters a situation where only one plan is
available, it may indicate the need to add new plans, or to avoid the situation
in question due to the danger inherent in having only one option, or, at the
very least, it may suggest the need to make that particular plan especially
immune to failure.

In a competitive situation, it is even more important that such a situation
be diagnosed, because if your opponent can determine what your forced choice
is, then he or she can counterplan much more effectively.

The problem of *forced choice* is an important organizing concept for planners. It is also an abstract kind of problem, not involving the physics of the real-world, beyond that of time. We call such a thing a *generalized problem description.* These problem descriptions are useful organizing concepts for knowledge about possible solutions, about prediction and avoidance of the problem, and, in a competitive domain, about techniques for forcing an opponent into the situation.

8.3.2 The Football Domain

The particular example of forced choice that I want to consider occurs in the football domain. To present this example I will have to describe the rules of football briefly for the benefit of readers who do not know the game. I will get most of this description out of the way at once. Readers familiar with football can skip or skim this information. Many many details have been omitted.

Football is played by two teams of eleven men each, with one ball, on a 100-yard-long field. There is a *end zone* at each end of the field, and one is assigned to each team. During most of the game, the ball is at some position on the field between the end zones, called the *line of scrimmage*, and in the *possession* of one of the teams. The team that has the ball is called the *offense.* The team that doesn't is called the *defense.* The goal of the offense is to score points by carrying the ball into the defense's end zone for a *touchdown.* The goal of the defense is to stop them. The winning team is the one that scores the most points before an allotted period of time runs out.

When a team first gets possession of the ball, it gets four chances, called *downs*, to either get the ball into the defense's end zone, and thereby score, or move the ball's position at least 10 yards closer to that end zone, in which case it has made a *first down* and gets four new chances. If it fails to do either, the defense gets possession of the ball, and hence becomes the new offense.

At the start of each down, the offense secretly chooses a plan, or *play.* A play allocates tasks, such as running and blocking (see below), for each player. The defense also picks a play. Then the teams line up facing each other at the line of scrimmage. Play begins when the offense team *hikes* the ball, which means that one player on the offensive team hands or passes it backwards to another player. We'll assume all hikes go the player called the *quarterback.* The down is over when either the defense stops the offense in one of a number of prescribed ways, or the offense scores.

Most of the time, the offense is too far from the end zone to score directly, and its main goal is to *gain yardage* and eventually make a first down. There are two ways to gain yardage. A *run* means that the quarterback, or another player to whom the quarterback has handed the ball, carries the ball *downfield* toward the defense's end zone. A *pass* means that one or more offensive players, called *receivers*, first run downfield without the ball, and then the quarterback throws the ball to the one that is most in the clear.

If an offensive player is running with the ball, the defense can stop him by *tackling* him, i.e., knocking him to the ground, or forcing him off the side of the field. In this case, the down ends and the ball's new position is where the tackle occurred. If the tackle occurs behind the line of scrimmage, then the offense *loses* yardage and may be in the difficult position of having more than just ten yards to gain for a first down. If the quarterback passes the ball, then the defense tries to catch it in mid-air, called an *interception*, or at least prevent the receivers from catching it. In the former case, the down ends and the defense is given possession of the ball. In the latter case, the pass is *incomplete* and the down ends with the position of the ball unchanged.

The plays, defensive and offensive, assign specific tasks to each of the eleven men on a team. Defensive plays assign some men to run after the man with the ball and others to spread out over the field to watch for passes. In particular, *linebackers* are defensive men who line up on the line of scrimmage immediately in front of the offense. They may either try to get past the offensive players and tackle the quarterback (or whoever has the ball), or stay where they are and prevent runners from passing them. Offensive plays assign most most of the players to *blocking*, i.e., physically impeding the defensive linebackers from getting to the quarterback. We shall focus on the offensive plays and how they are designed to deal with particularly successful defensive plays.

8.3.3 The Blitz

Which play the offense picks depends on how far it has to go to make a first down. Runs are pretty good for short distances, up to three yards or so, but get much worse after that. Passes can gain greater distances, but are riskier. If the offense has one down left and five yards to go, it will probably pass, but if it has only two yards to go, it can run.

When many yards need to be gained, the offense has a forced choice; it must pass. A normal defensive play in this situation is to have some men run after the quarterback, while the rest cover the field to try to stop the pass at the receiving end. There is an alternative defense, however, called the *blitz*, where most of the defensive linebackers charge directly at the quarterback as soon as the play starts, hoping to tackle him before he can throw the pass.

When this occurs, execution of the pass play begins normally but is almost immediately interrupted by a hoard of linebackers charging all-out toward the quarterback. One of them usually tackles him, the down ends, and yards are lost.

Imagine a novice coach who has never encountered the blitz before, trying to characterize the problem. One thing he can infer is that this defensive play was selected because the defense knew that his choice was forced. An obvious plan transformation to apply when an opponent is optimizing his response to your forced choice is to do the unexpected thing, such as run when a pass is clearly called for.

Unfortunately, however, this more than likely will fail. It turns out that the blitz is not really much worse against the run than the standard defense. The only reason the blitz isn't the standard defense is that when it fails, it fails big. This is because if a runner makes it past the blitzing linebackers, then he is pretty much out in the open and can gain more yardage than a run usually gains. This doesn't happen too often, however.

Another possibility is assign more offensive men to block the increased number of defensive attackers. This is known as "picking up" the blitz.

Yet another possibility is to speed the play up, so that the pass is thrown before the defenders reach the quarterback. In this plan, the receivers only run downfield 5 or 10 yards or so, and the quarterback throws the ball almost immediately. Normally this would be an ineffective use of passing, since little yardage is gained by the pass itself, but since most of the defense is committed to the quarterback, any pass that is completed has a good chance of doing well after the ball is caught, because, again, the receiver is now in the clear.

Finally, there is another possible counterplan, but it requires more consideration. The blitz often causes a loss of yardage, or even loss of possession of the ball, and sometimes injury (mental as well as physical) to the quarterback. It would be nice to find a counterplan that would reduce how much damage the blitz does when it succeeds, i.e., it would be nice if the coach could "hedge his bets."

One way to accomplish this is to find some escape plan that the quarterback can select at the last minute, if need be, to reduce the yardage lost if a tackle seems inevitable. For example, near the quarterback (who is normally chosen for his passing abilities), we could put a good runner. If the quarterback got in trouble, he would toss the ball to the runner. While the blitzers were changing course, the runner would have a chance of moving forward before he is caught. This is called a "safety valve" in real football.

8.3.4 Analyzing the Examples

In the above example we have seen the creation of four new plans, namely:

- Running in a passing situation

- Picking up the blitz

- Throwing a quick pass

- Setting up a "safety valve"

We will now look at the plan transformation rules involved in creating these plans. To make the rules more readable, "I" and "me" will refer to the planner, "you" will refer to the opponent, and "we" refers to the two of "us."

Be Unpredictable:

If:

- We are competing
- I have a forced choice
- You know this
- You have an effective counterplan to this choice

Then I should:

- select a plan option that would normally be considered unworkable in this situation.

This is one of the simplest transformation rules, because it is really a "shot in the dark" kind of strategy. It does not really deal directly at all with the opponent's plan. It assumes that picking an unexpected plan has a chance solely because the opponent is planning for something else.

Aggressive counterplan:

If:

- We are competing
- You have a forced choice
- I have an effective counterplan to this choice

Then I should:

- dedicate most of my resources to this counterplan.

This rule deals with the reverse situation of the previous rule. Although it is obviously useful for helping an opportunistic planner recognize and take advantage of an opponent's dilemma, it is also useful for a *Response to Problems* planner, in that one way to recover from a problem is to find a weakness in the opponent and exploit it.

Hold the fort:

If:

- We are competing
- I have a forced choice
- You have an aggressive counterplan to that choice
- That counterplan will only work for a limited period of time
- I can delay your plan

Then I should:

- dedicate a few of my resources to delaying your plan.

This rule brings up two basic aspects of competitive reasoning. First, such reasoning is often recursive. By putting myself in your shoes, I can see when you may apply the "Aggressive Counterplan" transformation. This means that *for me* the "Hold the Fort" transformation may become relevant. Second, such reasoning also depends heavily on time. In general, time becomes important in planning when deadlines are involved, and a competitor who is trying to do something before you do is a common source of deadlines. This second point comes up again in our next rule.

Beat them to the punch:

If:

- We are competing
- I have a forced choice
- You have an aggressive counterplan to that choice
- That counterplan will only work for a limited period of time
- I can do my plan faster

Then I should:

- do my plan faster.

The "hold the fort" strategy slows down the opponent's attack so that the plan can go forward. The obvious counterpart to this strategy is to speed up the plan.

Hedge your bets:

If:
- I have a plan with the risk of a big loss
- I have a plan for detecting the imminence of such a loss
- I have a plan for mitigating the loss

Then I should:
- devote some resources to the detection plan, and prepare to switching to the mitigating plan, if necessary.

Note that competition and forced choice is not involved in this last rule, which underlies the safety valve pass. Instead we have the more general problem of a plan that risks heavy losses in certain circumstances. When a planner finds himself in this position, one response is to try to "hedge his bets," that is, find a way to avoid the big loss when things go wrong, even at the cost of reducing the payoff from or the odds of getting the big win.

8.3.5   Applying Plan Transformations

A strategic plan transformation rule is a blueprint, specifying what must be achieved by the domain-specific plan. Applying the transformation may be quite complex, or even impossible, in some cases. In our football examples, however, things are relatively straightforward. Take the **Be unpredictable** rule. It has to find an alternative to passing. There are only four things you can do with the football after you hike it, excluding dropping it. You can run with it, pass it, punt it, i.e., kick it into the possession of the other team, or try for a field goal, i.e., kick the ball into the end zone for points. Punting loses possession of the ball, and field goals are only possible if you are near the end zone, so running is the only alternative left.

Holding the fort turns into "picking up" the blitz with blockers fairly directly. In football, blocking is the most straightforward known plan for impeding the physical advance of a defender. To implement this plan, we simply need to designate an offensive man to block each defensive man who will be blitzing. This means taking some resources away from the pass plan, namely making some potential receivers into blockers, but that is always the tradeoff involved in holding the fort.

Turning **beating them to the punch** into the "quick pass" play involves more consideration of the physics of the domain, but is still not too bad. We have to design our pass play in such a way that the pass can be thrown almost immediately. The physics of football say that we should send a receiver to a place that is both close to where he starts from, so that he can get there quickly, and close to the quarterback, so that the quarterback can spot him and throw the ball quickly.

Turning **hedging your bets** into the "safety valve" play is the hardest example and the most creative. It is easy to determine that the quarterback can detect if loss is imminent, but hard to find the plan that mitigates this loss, namely the plan of stationing someone else near enough to catch a quick toss, but not too near to be in the path of the attacking linebackers. In Section 8.5.2, we'll analyze some of the complexities of applying a similar rule, called **the Fork**.

The most important point about plan creation based on plan transformations is this: *the physics of the domain is important only insofar as it is needed to carry out domain-independent strategies.*

8.3.6   Problem Analysis

To get to the transformation rules described in Section 8.3.4, the planner has to generate a *problem description* when problems are detected, using the problem taxonomy of Section 8.2. This process of *problem analysis* is needed because the features tested for by the transformation rules, such as "You have an aggressive counterplan to a forced choice of mine," are not present in the raw input, in the same way that a feature like "my quarterback was tackled 3 yards behind the line of scrimmage" is present.

Problem analysis is an explanation process, which is basic to much of learning [Schank, 1986]. The planner seeks answers to two questions:

- What caused the observed problem?

- How does this cause affect my plans?

There are a number of specific strategies for detecting planning problems. However, they all come down to plan expectation failures. The problem, of course, is that often the failure that is noticed is actually the result of some earlier failure. The first task for the analysis process, then, is to find the "real" failure.

For example, we expect the pass play to go as follows:

1. the center hikes the ball to the quarterback

2. the quarterback moves back from the line of scrimmage

3. he waits until he sees a receiver in the clear

4. he passes the ball to that receiver

5. the receiver catches the ball

6. the receiver runs with the ball until he is tackled or reaches the end zone

But when the defense uses the blitz play, the fourth step fails to occur. Instead, our quarterback is tackled by one of the defensive linebackers while still looking for a receiver.

Being good counterplanners, we study the failure to see if we can explain our mistake. In particular, we search the inference chain that led to the incorrect expectation and look for a weak link. Obviously this technique relies on keeping track of the inference rules that were used to form expectations in the first place. Knowledge structures indicating these relationships are known as *data dependencies* [Rieger, 1975; Doyle, 1979].

We can suggest the following as a simple model for explanation: when the failure of an expectation is detected, we ask if the failure is the fault of the rule that spawned the expectation, or of one of the preconditions of the rule? If the answer is that the rule failed, the process stops. If, however, it is determined that one of the preconditions failed, then the rule is absolved, and the problem of finding the explanation for the failure becomes a problem of finding an explanation for the failure of the precondition.

This simple model has to be modified to account for the fact that many preconditions are implicit, just as many planning decisions are implicit. Many preconditions are implicit because they are true by default. They become false only when certain known events and states occur or are mentioned. For example, being able to see is an implicit precondition. "John read the paper" seems perfectly plausible, unless it is explicitly falsified by a sentence, such as "John is blind." In the football domain, we'll assume that "the play continues" is true by default, and falsified by the occurrence of a tackle. Thus, we infer that the tackle was responsible for the pass failing to occur.

Is this an explanation? Yes and no. In everyday parlance, it is because it explains what happened. But for a planning purposes, it is not because there is no stored repair indexed by this explanation. There is no plan that simply accomplishes the goal "don't get tackled." If a defensive man gets close enough to make a tackle, he will do so, and that's about all there is to it.

We need to know why this unexpected tackle occurred, if we are to prevent it from happening in the future. To do this, we must examine the preconditions of the tackle. There are two: the defensive man must be near the offensive man, and the offensive man must be holding the ball.

We know why our quarterback had the ball (it's part of our plan), but we don't know why the defensive man was there. So now our explanation is "the play failed because there was a defensive man near my quarterback."

Now we ask "why did I expect that defensive man to *not* be there?" In football, there are only a few reasons why a defensive man is expected not to be at a given location:

- He will be blocked by an offensive man

- His original position is too far away

- He has another assignment in the defensive play

The last assumption applies here. In the normal defensive play that we expected, this defensive man does not attack the quarterback. Our mistake was in predicting the normal defensive play, rather than a blitz.

Once we understand how the blitz foiled the particular pass play we ran, we must consider the general circumstances in which this play might work. This process is similar to Mitchell et al.'s work on explanation-based learning [1983] where he randomly applies integration rules to a problem until some sequence works, then computes the condition under which that sequence will work in general and stores it as a plan for integration. In our case, we ask ourselves whether this tackle would succeed again, if the blitz is used when we have a forced choice pass play. The answer is *yes*: we have no plan for stopping the defensive man and can identify no condition which might generally prevent him from tackling the quarterback. The verification that this defense will work in general with no conditions is a signal that we must counterplan against it.

Having created a characterization of the problem, we can now use it to index the four plan transformation rules given in Section 8.3.3.

8.4 A Catalog of Plan Transformations

The real test of this model is whether a good set of plan transformation rules can be developed. To be a "good set," the rules must be specific ("accomplish main goal" is not a good rule), applicable to many domains, and manageable in number (more like 100 than 1,000). I have already presented four such rules. I will now present several more. [Collins, 1987] lists about two dozen in all and discusses them in more detail. I have divided these rules into three groups: *scheduling transformations, information-processing transformations*m and *resource allocation transformations.* Examples from the first two groups are given below.

Though there are certainly many more rules to be discovered, the breadth of coverage of each rule suggests that a very workable set should be possible with less than 100 rules. This is of course in addition to the many many rules needed to represent the physics of a particular domain.

The descriptions below should be self-explanatory for the most part. I continue to use the "me versus you" notation of Section 8.3.4. Note that there is a discussion of the *tradeoffs* involved with each rule. As discussed in Section 8.2.2, a transformation rule alters both explicit and implicit planning decisions, and hence we need to take into account tradeoffs between alternative courses of action that are implied by these decisions.

8.4.1   Scheduling Transformations

> **Reschedule:**
>
> If:
>
> - I have or will have a problem with a plan step
> - The problem is likely to not be present at some other time
>
> Then I should:
>
> - reschedule the plan step for that other time.

Examples: Because of the simplicity, and consequent generality, of this transformation, examples are numerous. Phoning someone, getting no answer, and deciding to try again later is an example. Trying to start your car, having it not start, waiting a while and trying again is another. Going to a store, finding it closed, and coming back some other time is a third.

Discussion: One form of rescheduling is postponement. If something isn't working, try it later. It may be that we just be hope that conditions will change, or it may be that we intend to do something in the meantime to remove the problem.

We may also consider rescheduling a plan step for an earlier time for similar reasons. We may be trying to get the step done before the problem arises, or we may be able to do something now to enable the step that may not work for very long.

When to consider rescheduling may best be summarized as this: if we can explain the problem and demonstrate that it will not go away, then don't bother rescheduling. Otherwise, postponement is a viable option.

Tradeoffs: Two benefits of postponing a step are fine-tuning and opportunism [Birnbaum, 1986]. In real life, any step in a plan may undergo further elaboration, have its parameters altered, or even be abandoned entirely, right up until the time it is scheduled to be executed. The later the scheduled execution of a plan step, the more information will generally be available to the planner before it is executed. This can lead to the fine tuning of that step to suit the particular goal it is in service of. For example, if the plan step is "get money," then the later it is scheduled, the more likely it is that we will know exactly how much money we will need. In addition, the later the plan step is scheduled, the greater the chance that an opportunity to execute the step at a particularly low cost will arise before the scheduled time. It is for this reason that we get upset when we buy an item only to find it on sale shortly afterwards.

There are, however, two costs to postponing steps. First, executing the plan step earlier allows more opportunity to adjust the results or even recover from failure. Second, the more things are postponed, the more the planner's time is "booked up." Goals may come along that cannot be pursued because of limitations on the planner's time.

To summarize, schedule plan steps that are more likely to fail early, schedule steps that could benefit from fine tuning later, and schedule steps that are neutral on all other counts early to keep the planner's time clear.

Factor Precondition:

If:

- I have two plans to choose between
- The plans share a step before diverging
- I have a deadline for deciding
- I have a problem meeting the deadline
- The deadline would be delayed if the shared step of the plan were done first

Then I should:

- schedule the shared step before the decision.

Examples: A straightforward example is our story where Bob and Susan were having trouble deciding where to go for the evening, and gave themselves more time to make the decision by doing several errands that had to be performed in either case, before making the decision.

Discussion: This transformation, along with the next two we will discuss, represents a specific way of postponing, or (in reverse) moving up the scheduling of a DECIDE plan step *without* replanning from scratch. The problems that the transformation addresses, however, are essentially the same. We may want to postpone a decision for all the reasons we may want to postpone a plan step in general, and we have all the same reasons for expecting that doing so will be an efficacious plan. One difficulty is determining what steps, if any, are shared between two plans. We can't assume that two steps have the same name, or are exactly identical structures.

Tradeoffs: One cost to this transformation is that by scheduling the shared step earlier, we lose the ability to fine tune it. In particular, we lose useful information about what alternative will be pursued. In the example above, for instance, we considered factoring out the step of getting dressed to go out. However, dressing for dinner and dressing for a movie are not necessarily the same. Of course, we can make one style of dress suit both occasions, but then we are very definitely giving up something in order to allow factoring.

The benefit of the **Factor Preconditions** strategy is that it extends the deadline for a decision; the cost is the loss of the ability to adjust plan steps optimally for the particular plan they are in service of. We need to consider how sensitive a given precondition step is to the context in which it is performed. Some actions, like getting money or getting gas, are fairly standardized and as a result cannot generally be optimized that much to fit a particular situation. Hence they are good candidates for factoring.

Merge Conjuncts:

If:

- I have several independent plans
- There is a plan step shared between them

Then I should:

- create a conjoined plan merging that plan step into one plan.

Examples: The standard examples here involve running errands with many transportation subgoals, e.g., go to the store, go to the post office, etc. Different "errand" goals will share plan steps at a number of levels, from "get in car" to "go to shopping center," creating many possibilities for merging. A human planner wouldn't think of running one errand without considering whether some of its steps can be merged with other errands.

Discussion: The **Factor Preconditions** transformation discussed above was aimed at *disjunctive* preconditions associated with alternative results of a single decision. An analogous technique can be applied to *conjunctive* plans that are independent. By merging steps, we can accomplish identical subgoals with a single action. Failing to execute this transformation will not give rise to a fatal execution error, but will simply result in wasted effort. Detection involves the planner noticing that he is executing the same action over and over, regardless of the fact that no fatal error has occurred.

This transformation is a way of approaching the problem of *plan-time*, as opposed to *execution-time* opportunism. The latter means that, while executing other plans, we would like our planner to notice opportune situations for pursuing other goals. Doing this requires situational feedback. Noticing opportunities at plan-time means that we would like our planner to notice during planning when two goals were going to be pursued anyway have actions that can be merged.

Apart from the issue of determining whether any two particular plans steps can be merged (and what result the combination should achieve), there is a basic problem of deciding when to consider doing this. This transformation, possibly more than any other, seems to require top-down processing for its application. The planner must look for opportunities to apply it. This is because, as I mentioned, the result of *not* performing the transformation is not really a failure, in the sense of a planner not achieving a goal he thought he had planned for successfully. What must be noticed, instead, is needless repetition. This means that the best model of detecting a *problem* would seem to be that the planner stores a memory of executing a given plan step, and if he later executes the same plan step with more or less the same parameters, without too much time separating the two, then he should recall the previous execution and consider whether the two could have been merged.

One last point concerning the application of this transformation is its relationship to the notion of *goal subsumption* [Wilensky, 1983]. Goal subsumption is the strategy of acquiring a large amount of a resource when it can be predicted that possessing a certain amount of that resource will be a subgoal that comes up often. For example, when a postage stamp is needed, an intelligent planner will probably want to buy a number of stamps at once, in anticipation of future situations where stamps will again be needed. Needs that might have spawned subgoals in the future, e.g., to go and buy a stamp, are obviated—or *subsumed* —by the planner's action of stockpiling them previously.

Subsumption is both a specialization of **Merge Conjuncts**, in that it applies only to preconditions involving the acquisition of a resource, and a generalization of it, in that it involves factoring preconditions that have not been scheduled yet. It is based on the anticipation that actions of a certain sort will be scheduled in the future, though the particular plans which they will be a part of are specified either vaguely or not at all at the present time.

Tradeoffs: Merging has the same cost as factoring in that it cuts down on the planner's ability to fine tune plan steps to specific situations. We also face a (potentially) much bigger cost, which is the constraint on the timing of the two plans whose steps are merged.

To see this problem, suppose that you are picking up some wine to take to dinner at a friend's house, and the liquor store is in the same shopping center as your grocery store. You have already decided to merge getting the wine with going to the dinner, but, on the way, you realize that you need milk. If getting milk is merged with getting wine, you'll have some milk that needs to be kept cold. If you leave the milk in the car during dinner, it will spoil. You could fix this by taking it inside and putting it in your friend's refrigerator, but this might be embarrassing, and it adds a cost in the very real possibility that you will forget to take it home. You could get the milk and simply drive home. That would leave the "get milk" plan undisturbed by the merger, but it would disturb the "get to dinner" plan instead, because going home might make you late. Going home would also add a cost in driving that is approximately equal to what the merger saved you in the first place. So, merging getting milk with getting wine in this case is a bad idea.

Find Middle Path:

If:

- I have two plans to choose between
- I have a problem with the decision
- The plans differ only by the target value of some variable that they eventually achieve
- Going toward one target value does not prevent subsequently going toward the other target value

Then I should:

- delay my decision as long as possible by using a plan that first goes for a value between the two target values.

Examples: An obvious source of examples comes from movement in two-dimensional space. Suppose I have to choose between going to one of two locations, but which is better is not yet clear. This transformation says I should follow the path that approaches both equally, postponing my decision until any further movement has to go one way or the other.

More concretely, consider games that involve running on a field or court. Often, a defensive player is assigned to cover more than one possible move that the offense may make, and these different possibilities may involve being in different places. Commonly, a player who is not sure what to do will run in a direction that splits the difference of the two points.

Discussion: If a decision can be characterized as a choice of achieving one of a number of possible values of a quantity, we can view the plans for achievement as *functions* (called *delta functions* in [Schank and Abelson, 1977]) that will lead, at the end of some time interval, to the quantity having the desired value. The kinds of quantities involved may be temperatures, or distances, or locations (which will be vectors, of course, but which will still be susceptible to the delta function approach). This point of view is particularly useful when the planner has a nearly continuous ability to alter the direction of the change in a quantity (or vector), and is limited only by the rate at which change can be effected.

Tradeoffs: The tradeoff here is quite straightforward: by pursuing an intermediate path, the planner must pursue a *longer* path than is involved in going straight to whichever destination value is chosen The tradeoff is the benefit of extra decision time versus the cost of the extra distance traveled.

8.4.2 Information Processing Transformations

Reduce Variance:

If:

- We are competing
- I have to choose between plans
- You will try to diagnose what decision I've made from my actions

Then I should:

- make my observable actions as ambiguous as possible.

Examples: Football offers a particularly good example of the use of this strategy. Most teams arrange their offense so that all of their plays—perhaps forty or so—begin with one of four or five opening sequences. This means that the initial movements made on a play never indicate uniquely that a particular play is about to be executed. The quarterback will practice making the same movements after receiving the hike, turning in the same way, taking the same number of steps, even though the action he is ultimately going to perform, such as handing the ball of to another player, or throwing a pass, is different in different cases. These movements *could* be optimized for each instance, but that would be a shortsighted strategy. Instead great pains are taken to make them as alike as possible.

Discussion: We can assume that in general an opponent will try to diagnose as quickly as possible what decision the planner has made, in order to counterplan against that particular plan. The more accurately and quickly the opponent can make this diagnosis, more likely he is to counterplan effectively. Anything that the planner can do to *reduce* the speed and accuracy of the opponent's diagnostic process will make plan he chooses more effective. One way of accomplishing this is to reduce the amount of *variance* between the observable features of the likely alternatives.

Applying this transformation resembles the process of factoring preconditions in that steps in alternative plans are made more similar. The difference is that in this case the purpose is not to postpone the decision, but only to hide it from the opponent.

Tradeoffs: The tradeoff with this transformation is also essentially the same as with factor preconditions: a price is paid in the loss of flexibility to adapt to the situation, and in not having plan steps which are fine-tuned to the particular plan involved. In general, if the planner believes he can simply overpower his opponent, he may decide that the ability to fine-tune the plan is more important than disguising it.

Delegate:

If:

- I have several plans to choose from
- I have a problem making the decision
- The plans will be executed by another agent

Then I should:

- tell the agent the rules for making the decision, and have the agent be responsible for both the decision and the execution.

Examples: In football, coaches often call the plays, which are then communicated to the field either by hand signals or by shuffling players in and out carrying the information to the quarterback. The communication takes some time, and is sometimes faulty. As a result many teams allow the quarterback to call the plays on the field. Obviously, a prerequisite to this is to teach the quarterback in great detail what kind of play should be called in what circumstance.

Robotics is a whole field devoted to developing devices that will allow decisions to be delegated where they never have been before. Sometimes, the problem is that decisions have to be made too quickly or too often, as on high-speed assembly lines. Other times, the problem is with the communications, as with the vehicles exploring the Martian surface, where it may take hours for messages to reach their destination.

Discussion: The strategy of delegating tasks to another planner is well known. Schank and Abelson [1977], for example, refer to this as the *delta agency* plan. One of the most interesting aspects of getting another agent to carry out one's intentions is to delegate a *decision* to that agent.

There are two major reasons to delegate a decision. First, the decision may simply be problematic; it may be that the planner has too many other tasks scheduled, or lacks some facility which is necessary to make the decision well, or is inefficient at making decisions such as the one in question. Second, another agent may be in a better position to *implement* the decision.

The process of delegation involves the communication of how to make the decision in question. The specification of the method may take a number of forms. Most generally, it might involve simply communicating to the agent to whom the decision is being delegated (let us refer to him as the planner's *representative*), what the goals of the planner are in the situation, and relying on the representative to take the best possible course. Obviously this is the easiest way to do things, but it is not always realistic to assume that the representative has the requisite knowledge to take this responsibility. In this case, it may be possible to communicate a general set of evaluation criteria for a possible choice, along with a way of generating or recognizing such possible choices. This may become complex, however, because of the attempt at generality. The complexity can be overcome by communicating a strict rule of choice for a specific set of alternatives.

Tradeoffs: The main cost of delegating is a loss of accuracy and control. If the decision rule is complex, it is not likely to be understood perfectly by the second agent, or will have to be oversimplified to be communicated. Also, you lose the chance to change your mind in the light of unexpected later events. A benefit of delegation is the savings in time realized by not having to communicate a decision at the time of execution. By moving the necessary communication to a point at the very beginning of the plan, the planner sidesteps any time-pressure on the communication, since this can be scheduled an arbitrary amount of time in advance.

Successive Approximation:

If:

- I need to achieve a target value of a quantity within some margin of error
- I need to achieve it quickly
- I have plans that are accurate enough but too slow
- I have plans that are fast enough but too inaccurate

Then I should:

- do the fast plans first, followed at the end by the more accurate ones.

Examples: In the days before the computerization of consumer appliances, audio and video tuners often had two tuning knobs, one of which was known as the "fine" tuner. Both knobs tuned, but a few turns of the tuning knob would cover the entire dial, while a few turns of the fine tuning knob would only cover a small part of the dial. You would turn the main knob to get close to the desired station quickly, then turn the fine tuning know to get the station as clearly as possible.

Another example is painting a house. Big brushes and rollers are fast, but sloppy; small brushes are neat but slow; obviously, you paint with a big brush or roller first, then fill in with a small brush. The example of filling a coffee pot from Section 8.1 is another example.

Discussion: The use of such a multi-stage process in lieu of a single-stage process is one way of dealing with the tradeoff that is commonly known as *speed vs. accuracy.* We can view the implementation of multi-stage processing as a plan transformation that deals with the speed/accuracy tradeoff by using a fast, inaccurate process to get close to the goal state, and then uses a slower, more accurate one to traverse the presumably much reduced distance to the goal.

This strategy can be generalized into a string of attempts at a process, each one beginning where the last left off, and each more precise but slower than the one previous. This strategy is known in general as **Successive Approximation**.

Tradeoffs: The basic tradeoff behind this strategy is the cost of maintaining multiple processes with different parameters, where one might have served. Obviously, this is often manifest in the cost of the equipment being used: extra tuning dials and extra brushes cost money, and add to the complexity of the operations in which they are involved in various ways (for example, it makes adjunct plan steps like cleaning up after painting a bit more complicated).

Another cost associated with this strategy arises if undoing a step costs more than doing it. For example, if we want to put five gallons of gas in our car, we shouldn't quickly put in more than five, then siphon out (and still pay for) the excess. Likewise, if we are cutting a piece of paper to a certain size, we don't want to cut off too much, and then try to glue or tape pieces back on.

8.5 A Detailed Example

I will now present an extended example of the formation of a new plan. The focus will be on the complexities involved in using domain physics to implement domain-independent strategies. I have two goals here. First, I want to give the flavor of how strategies are implemented. Second, I hope that the complexities involved in the domain physics will convince the reader of the necessity of top-down guidance by simpler domain-independent strategies.

The plan in question is a football play called "the quarterback option," or, simply, "the option." Historically, the option play was a major advance in football strategy. It was devastatingly effective from the beginning, and it was quickly copied by other coaches to the point where today any halfway serious football team has at least a version of it available. Teams that built their offenses around the option and its variations dominated college football for nearly two decades after its invention. Certainly, if we want to be sure that our model of plan invention is actually capable of inventing truly novel plans in principle, then this is as good an example as any to study.

It might be argued that the option play is *too* novel and that a planner capable of coming up with it must be exploring too many possibilities for it to be useful in real domains. I believe that this is not really the case, for two reasons. As I will show, while the option play is a particularly neat example, it uses very normal techniques, useful for *un*-novel plans. I believe that the option play took so long to invent mainly because, up until that time, it was assumed that football players should not make decisions during play. Highly detailed plays were designed in advance to make things run smoother. Even the idea of allowing the quarterback to call plays in the huddle was a serious controversy for many years. So the option play may have gone uninvented for

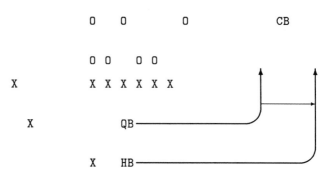

Figure 8.1: Sweep, Bootleg Run, and Option Play

so long because it violated an axiom of football planning in general. Support for this comes from the fact that subsequent to the acceptance of the option play many other areas in football have been "optioned," including choosing the location of a run, choosing the type of pass pattern to be run by a receiver, and even the choice of whom to block. New option plays are turning up right and left, and they are not very novel anymore. Yet, the process of creating a new option play is just as complex. It is only the decision to *consider* it that has changed.

8.5.1   The Design of the Play

We will begin with some background knowledge that will be helpful in understanding the design of the option play. In particular, we will look at a couple of simpler plays that are related to the option: the SWEEP and the BOOTLEG RUN. Consider the diagram in Figure 8.1.

The X's in this diagram represent offensive players and the O's represent defensive players as they line up before a play begins. The lines represent (in an extremely impoverished way) the action involved in the two plays we are discussing. The upper line indicates the path of the quarterback running around the end with the ball, which is the way the BOOTLEG RUN play works. The lower line similarly represents the halfback's course, having taken the ball from the quarterback and running with it, in the SWEEP play. Notice that in both instances the defensive man marked CB (which stands for "cornerback") is in the area where the play is directed. The cornerback, as you might expect, is the defensive player most responsible for stopping either the SWEEP or the BOOTLEG RUN.

The offense tries to prevent this by assigning a man to *block* the cornerback. Unfortunately, the cornerback is particularly hard to block in this situation, because he is a long way from where these plays start, and can see both the play and the man assigned to block him coming for some time. In addition, he is out in the open, and not crowded in among other players who would limit his freedom of movement. Hence, a good cornerback can often avoid the offensive blocker and stop the two plays under consideration.

The option play is designed to neutralize the power of the defensive cornerback. The play starts with the quarterback running the ball to the outside. The halfback runs a few yards behind him. The quarterback watches the cornerback. If the cornerback makes a move to tackle the quarterback, the quarterback pitches the ball, using what is called a *lateral pass*, to the halfback who then runs with it. This is indicated by the thin arrow in Figure 8.1. If the cornerback makes a move toward the halfback, or makes no move at all, the quarterback simply keeps the ball and runs with it himself. Regardless of his skill, it is essentially impossible for the cornerback to stop this play as long as the offense runs it properly.

8.5.2 The Fork

While the option play itself may have been novel, the strategy behind it is in fact quite common. Consider, for instance, a different planning problem that is involved in playing the game tic-tac-toe. Anyone who plays tic-tac-toe discovers early on that any time a single threat of two in a row is mounted, the opponent will invariably detect and block that threat. The only chance to win this game is to make a move that keeps alive two threats, i.e., two lines of two in a row, at once. The opponent is then forced to choose one of the two available counterplans, leaving the other threat to carry through unopposed.

In negotiations, one tactic is to force your opposition to commit themselves to some position first. In fact, any domain in which there is competition involved is likely to produce a circumstance where this particular bit of strategic reasoning is usefully applicable. Of course, this is exactly the point of the model of plan creation that I have outlined. Since strategies like "fork" are so likely to be useful in a new domain, it only makes sense for the planner to be, in some sense, looking for opportunities to apply them. The model accounts for the invention of the option play by saying that the planner recognized a circumstance in football where the fork strategy would reasonable apply, and created the option as an implementation of the fork strategy for football.

Fork:

If:

- We are competing
- I have to decide between two plans
- You pick a counterplan by detecting what my choice is
- You can only do one counterplan
- There is a deadline on when you have to choose

Then I should create a new plan which has these steps:

- the steps shared by the alternatives, if any
- a modified form of one of the alternatives, which can be executed until your deadline forces you to make a decision
- a step to detect which choice you made
- a step to decide whether to keep doing the current alternative or not
- a step to crossover to the second alternative, if necessary
- a modified form of the second alternative, which can pick up from the crossover point.

An important factor here is that once you have started executing a plan, you are committed to that plan.

Note that another potentially applicable transformation to this situation, where you pick your counterplan by detecting what my decision was, is to **Reduce Variance**, which means that I should make it hard for you detect what my choice is, until it is too late.

8.5.3   Representing Plans

We will represent a *plan* as a causal network of events and states, as in [Schank and Abelson, 1977]. Events can cause states, and states can enable events.

In particular, in football, the basic actions are linked to the states that enable them, and the states that they result in. For example, a short sideways pass from player X to player Y, written as LATERAL(X,Y), is enabled by the state POSSESS-BALL(X) and results in the state POSSESS-BALL(Y). A play (plan) is a sequence of actions done by particular players.

We use the packaging and abstraction hierarchical relationships of [Schank, 1982] to link plays together. A play plan *packages* particularized football actions. The SWEEP play, for example, packages the state POSSESS-BALL(QB) ("the quarterback has the ball"), which enables the action LATERAL(QB,HB) ("the quarterback throws a lateral pass to the halfback"), which results in the state POSSESS-BALL(HB) ("the halfback has the ball"). An action, state, or play can have more general versions or *abstractions*. For example, the state POSSESS-BALL(QB) has the abstraction POSSESS-BALL(OM) ("an offensive man has the ball").[5].

Information derived from packaging relationships is predictive, while information derived from abstractions is background. By this I mean that if we have an instance of POSSESS-BALL(QB) packaged in SWEEP, we *predict* the action LATERAL(QB,HB), but we also know that, in principle, the quarterback could do anything that is enabled by the abstraction POSSESS-BALL(OM).

The top-level plan is PLAY-FOOTBALL, which packages a loop consisting of CHOOSE-PLAY, RUN-PLAY, and EVALUATE-RESULTS actions. The selected plays in turn package specific states and actions. The SWEEP play is outlined in Figure 8.2.

This representation is crude in a number of ways. The temporal order of events is represented simply by the order of items in the list. The goal of the play is simply the last state achieved. Variable elements, e.g., "a defensive man," are not distinguished from constant elements, e.g., "the halfback." All this would need to be corrected in a more formal treatment or in a program. We use the notation above for human readability only.

Note that the final state, i.e., the yardage gained, is the causal result of two actions, joined with the word UNTIL, which represents that the first action continues until the second action occurs. The final state is a net result of this complex action. Goal failure in this domain will usually be signaled by a net result that is less than expected.[6].

---

[5]Packaging and abstraction are for events and states what PART-OF and ISA are for objects

[6]It would be an *expectation* failure to gain 10 yards, and perhaps worth pursuing (is this team's defense weak in some way?), but not a goal failure

PLAY: SWEEP
  HIKE(C, QB)   center hikes to the quarterback
  POSSESS-BALL(QB)   quarterback has the ball
  LATERAL(QB,HB)   lateral pass to the halfback
  POSSESS-BALL(HB)   the halfback has the ball
  RUN-TO-HOLE(HB)   the halfback runs to hole in defense
  AT-HOLE(HB)   the halfback is at the hole
  RUN-DOWNFIELD(HB)   the halfback runs downfield until
    UNTIL TACKLE(DM,HB)   a defensive man tackles him
  GAIN-YDG(3-5)   3 to 5 yards gained

Figure 8.2: The SWEEP Play

8.5.4   Recognizing the situation

The planner has the expectation that the defense will detect whatever play is chosen and choose some corresponding counterplan (the details of which are not known). Figure 8.3 outlines the abstract cycle of choosing and running plays in football. Basically, I run a play until you stop it. In order to stop it, you have to determine what it is, pick a response, and execute it. Because this information is in the abstraction, it is not predicted for execution of the SWEEP, but it is available for understanding what might be going wrong when the SWEEP fails.

Assume that both SWEEP and BOOTLEG-RUN are failing frequently, and that I have packaged these two plays together as two choices for a given situation, both of which you can stop. This means that I have a partial match to **The Fork**. To determine that picking one counterplan commits you to it, I note that the same player, the defensive cornerback, is involved in both counterplans, that the counterplans involve tackles in different locations, and that one player can't be in two places at once.

8.5.5   Applying the Fork

The first step in applying **The Fork** to SWEEP and BOOTLEG-RUN is to conjoin the initial shared steps of the two plays, if any. In this case, these steps are the hike to the quarterback and his turning toward the appropriate side of the field. The two plays now diverge, depending on the value of the mutually exclusive state of who carries the ball to the side, the quarterback or the halfback. So far in the planning, there is no need to decide who it should be, but I note that since the quarterback already has the ball, it would be

```
PLAY-FOOTBALL:
   CALL-PLAY:
      DECIDE(PLAY,POCKET-PASS)                         a play is chosen
         OR DECIDE(PLAY,BOOTLEG-RUN)
         OR DECIDE(PLAY,SWEEP)
         OR DECIDE(PLAY,DRAW)
         OR DECIDE(PLAY,OFF-TACKLE)
         . . .
   RUN-PLAY:
      RUN(OFFENSE,PLAY)                              I run the selected play
         UNTIL
            SOME-OBSERVABLE-STATE(PLAY)           it has visible effects
            DETECT(DEFENSE,PLAY)                      you detect them
            KNOW(DEFENSE,PLAY)                       you know my plan
            DECIDE(DEFENSE,COUNTERPLAN)    you pick a counterplan
            INTEND(DEFENSE,COUNTERPLAN)        you intend to do it
            RUN(DEFENSE,COUNTERPLAN)                    you run it
         SOME-STOP-STATE(PLAY)                       it stops my play
```

Figure 8.3: Choosing and Running Football Plays

simpler if he kept it.

Now I have to create the crossover plan. This plan has to change the mutually exclusive "possession of the ball" state from one value to the other. In football, the lateral pass is the standard plan for transferring the ball. Now I have another constraint on who should have the ball. It should be someone who can pass. This is yet another reason to prefer having the quarterback carry the ball, because his specialty is passing.

Now I have to instantiate the detection step that determines what choice the opponent makes. What observable state will indicate that the opponent is committed to one plan or other? The obvious place to search for such states is by looking at implications of each counterplan you, as the opponent, might execute. In particular, what preconditions do you have to achieve for each counterplan? The two counterplans are TACKLE(CB,QB) and TACKLE(CB,HB), i.e., your cornerback will tackle either my quarterback or halfback, depending on who has the ball. The only *necessary* preconditions TACKLE are that the cornerback is near the player with the ball. I already know who has the ball, so the question is whether we will be able to detect to which location your man has chosen to go.

The cornerback will get to the location using PTRANS (Physical TRANSfer), one of Schank's Conceptual Dependency Primitives [Schank, 1975]. One abstraction of the PTRANS action is INCREMENTAL-APPROACH, which is any action that reaches a target value for a variable, like location, by continuously incrementing the value of the variable. The detection plan for INCREMENTAL-APPROACH is to set a threshold value for the distance between the current value and the target value. The threshold must be far enough from the target to allow enough time to take whatever action depends on the detection. The physics of football says that a lateral pass takes about half a second, so the threshold distance between the cornerback and the quarterback must be such that the cornerback will not be able to cross it in less than half a second. More football physics determines that a player can cover about 2 yards in half a second. Hence, our plan says that the crossover plan will need to be executed when the cornerback approaches within 2 yards of the quarterback. The lateral pass is reliable at 5 yards, so we pick that value as a safe place to put the halfback.

Our new plan, then, which is known as "the option play," looks like this:

- the quarterback takes the hike,

- he and the halfback run toward the outside of the line, keeping about five yards apart,

- he watches the cornerback

- if the cornerback comes within 2 yards, he laterals the ball to the halfback, who then runs with it

- if the cornerback does not come within 2 yards, the quarterback runs with the ball himself.

8.6 Conclusions

When a plan fails on a performance yardstick, the planner knows two things: first, that the plan is probably suboptimal, and second that this problem is probably worth correcting. This is of interest because it forces a reevaluation of what it is worth to reconsider possible alternatives. The failure of a plan focuses the attention of the planner on aspects of that plan's construction. It makes it worthwhile to search for evidence that is costly to dig up, make some implicit decisions explicit, and make some distinctions finer, in order to find a better alternative. There are two different times when a planner is motivated to evaluate a decision: when the decision is being made, and when it is implicated in a planning problem. The second time around, there is more motivation to work on the problem than there is initially.

Successfully reopening the design of a plan requires three things. First, since most plans result from a large number of decisions, the planner needs knowledge specialized to determining *which* decision caused the problem. Second, since some decisions were implicit during the original selection of the plan, the planner needs to be able to evaluate the tradeoffs involved at problem time. Third, since a lot of work went into constructing the original plan, the planner needs knowledge specialized to changing planning decisions with the minimal amount of "undoing" of the rest of the plan. Generalized problem descriptions and the plan transformation strategies that they index were proposed as a way of satisfying these three needs.

A central implication of this work is that most human planning is neither novel nor optimal. Instead, it is mainly a matter of employing rote constructions in ways that suffice to do an adequate job in most cases. This is a point that Schank has pursued for many years in various directions [Schank and Abelson, 1977; Schank, 1982], although usually from the standpoint of modeling story understanding.

Creativity does not arise during normal planning. When first solving a problem, the average planner does not look for the most optimal, cleverest solution. The planner instead adapts an old solution that was used for a problem most like the current one. One cannot afford to be clever all the time. It makes sense to wait until it is apparent that cleverness is *required*. It is during *replanning* that creativity is most called for, and it is in this stage that we would expect to see novel plans invented.

In football it is clearly the case that conservatism in planning is the order of the day. It is expensive to get a plan working with the efficiency required to have some chance of success, and it can be disastrous to execute a single ill-conceived play. Furthermore, most of the components of a play, such as blocking schemes, directions of movement, and so on, have been worked out very carefully over the years. The result of all of this is that in general if a new play is considered, it is considered from the perspective of making a change in an old one that will address a certain problem or take advantage of a certain opportunity.

What is being put forth here is a fundamentally conservative view of the process of plan creation. It is based on the idea that plan creation is something that the planner is driven to by the inadequacy of his current set of plans. The transformation rules presented can be applied to common planning problems in a wide variety of planning domains. The *hard* part of fixing problems is knowing where the problems lie. This is why it makes more sense for a planner to wait until they show up, and apply his knowledge of how to fix them at that point, than to try to employ that knowledge in the first place, with the aim of preventing any problem that could in principle be avoided given his current knowledge.

9

Micro COACH

9.1 Introduction

In this chapter, we present a miniature version of the COACH program. Like CHEF, COACH tries to repair a failing plan, but in a very different way. Plan repair in CHEF is guided by the explanation of a plan failure. If the broccoli got soggy because it was cooked with the beef, then don't cook it with the beef! In COACH, the explanations are not adequate to suggest a repair that works. The bootleg run play fails because the defensive cornerback tackles the quarterback. Possible repairs, such as assigning a blocker to the cornerback, or running a different way, don't work. The cornerback is too far from any available blocker, and running another way would just cause the quarterback to be tackled by some other defensive man. The sweep play fails because the defensive cornerback tackles the halfback. Again, the available repairs for stopping a tackle don't work.

Instead, micro COACH's plan repair is guided by considering both failing plays together. Both cases involve a cornerback tackle. Since he cannot tackle both the quarterback and the halfback, one possibility is to create a new play that has elements from both plays. The real COACH generates the option play, a kind of fork, where the decision as to who will carry the ball to the goal is delayed until the cornerback moves in one direction or the other. Micro COACH generates a simpler alternative, where the ball is not passed from the quarterback to the halfback until the cornerback has committed himself to pursuing the quarterback.

Note that micro COACH is still a case-based planner, like micro CHEF, in that its repair strategies do not start from scratch, but rather adapt an existing set of plans. It would not be hard to write rules for generating plans of the complexity that micro COACH deals with, but this would be missing the point. Micro COACH's plays could be made more complex, e.g., they

```
(DEFUN COACH (SLOTS)
  (LET ((INSTANCE (SLOTS->MOP SLOTS '(M-STRATEGY) T)))
    (AND (GET-FILLER 'NEW-SOLUTION INSTANCE)
         INSTANCE)))
```

Listing 9.1: Top-Level Micro COACH Function

could assign tasks to the other offensive players, such as whom to block or where to run to, with only a relatively small increment in the complexity of the adaptation rules. The adaptation rules would assume that whatever worked before, outside of the steps specifically labeled as problematic, will probably still work and should just be copied into the new plan. A rule-based system that tried to create the entire play from scratch, generating reasonable tasks for 11 players, would be quite complex and slow. A case-based system like COACH that makes small changes to existing plays avoids at least some of these problems.

9.2 Implementing Micro COACH

The top-level function to run COACH is very short and appears in Listing 9.1.

(COACH *slot-list*) finds or creates a case under M-STRATEGY with the given slots and returns it. The call to GET-FILLER forces the calculation of the filler for the slot NEW-SOLUTION. (DPH (ROLE-FILLER 'NEW-SOLUTION *strategy*)) will print a readable version of the solution in the strategy instance returned by COACH.

Listing 9.2 defines MOPs for objects, locations, players and actions in football. Micro COACH's knowledge of football is exceedingly limited. For example, it only knows about four players: three offensive (center I-M-C, halfback I-M-HB, and quarterback I-M-QB) and one defensive (cornerback I-M-CB). We also define three basic Conceptual Dependency primitive acts: grasping (M-GRASP-ACT), gaining information (M-MTRANS-ACT), and physical motion (M-PTRANS-ACT). We'll use these primitives later to define football actions such as running and tackling.

Listing 9.3 defines a general set of abstraction functions and MOPs for specifying pattern MOPs that compare the fillers of two roles. These definitions are upwardly compatible extensions of the definitions in Listing 5.10. Paths, represented as groups of roles, can be specified, for both the current

```
(DEFMOP M-OBJECT (M-ROOT))
(DEFMOP I-M-BALL (M-OBJECT) INSTANCE)

(DEFMOP M-LOCATION (M-ROOT))
(DEFMOP I-M-OFFENSIVE-GOAL (M-LOCATION) INSTANCE)
(DEFMOP I-M-DEFENSIVE-GOAL (M-LOCATION) INSTANCE)
(DEFMOP I-M-SCRIMMAGE (M-LOCATION) INSTANCE)

(DEFMOP M-DISTANCE (M-ROOT))
(DEFMOP I-M-SHORT (M-DISTANCE) INSTANCE)
(DEFMOP I-M-LONG (M-DISTANCE) INSTANCE)

(DEFMOP M-PLAYER (M-ACTOR))
(DEFMOP M-DEFENSIVE-PLAYER (M-PLAYER))
(DEFMOP M-OFFENSIVE-PLAYER (M-PLAYER))

(DEFMOP I-M-CB (M-DEFENSIVE-PLAYER) INSTANCE)

(DEFMOP I-M-C (M-OFFENSIVE-PLAYER) INSTANCE)
(DEFMOP I-M-HB (M-OFFENSIVE-PLAYER) INSTANCE)
(DEFMOP I-M-QB (M-OFFENSIVE-PLAYER) INSTANCE)

(DEFMOP I-M-GRASP-ACT (M-ACT) INSTANCE)
(DEFMOP I-M-MTRANS-ACT (M-ACT) INSTANCE)
(DEFMOP I-M-PTRANS-ACT (M-ACT) INSTANCE)
```

Listing 9.2: Micro COACH Basic MOPs

slot filler and the slot it is being compared against. The comparison function can be any two argument function. We use the standard Common Lisp comparison function EQL and the nonstandard NOT-EQL. COMPARE-CONSTRAINT is the abstraction function that does the comparisons.

A specialization of M-COMPARE with a (TO *to-path*) slot, (ROLE *role-path*) slot, and (COMPARE-FN *function*) slot is satisfied by MOP *mop* if (*function submop filler*) returns true, where *submop* is the filler of *role-path* in *mop* and *filler* is the filler of *to-path* in the MOP whose slots are being tested.

M-EQUAL and M-NOT-EQUAL are comparison MOPs for equality and inequality respectively.

M-PATH is the MOP for representing paths as groups of roles.

(COMPARE-CONSTRAINT *constraint filler slots*) applies the comparison function in *constraint* to the filler of *role-path* in *filler* and the filler of *to-path* in *slots*.

(INDIRECT-FILLER *path mop slots*) gets the filler of *path* in *mop*, which should be either a role or an M-PATH, and gets the filler of that role or path in *slots*.

(NOT-EQL *exp₁ exp₂*) returns true if exp_1 is not EQL to exp_2.

Listing 9.4 defines the MOPs for football events. Using the Conceptual Dependency primitive acts, we define event detection, passing, running, and tackling. Passing events are subdivided into short passes, which include hikes and laterals, and long passes. Our example plays do not involve any long passes. We put a dummy (ACTOR NIL) slot on M-LATERAL to keep it from being a slotless abstraction. (Slotless abstractions are discussed in Chapter 3.) Running is subdivided into running to the line of scrimmage, to the goal, or after another player.

Listing 9.5 defines three simple football plays. A play is simply a list of football event patterns. The definitions for the bootleg run and sweep plays are relatively straightforward. The main difference between the definition of I-M-SWEEP in this Listing and that in Figure 8.2 is that the states resulting from the actions are omitted, as is the notion of running until tackled.

The defending cornerback has one plan: run after and tackle whoever got the ball.

Micro COACH represents time by clustering actions into groups called *time cycles*. Every event in one time cycle is considered to have happened at roughly the same time. Ordering is important only in so far as an event must come before any event that it enables, e.g., the quarterback has to get the ball before he can pass it to someone else. A set of time cycles makes up one *down*.

When an offensive play and a defensive play are executed, a down is produced. Listing 9.6 defines hand-simulated results of executing the bootleg run

```
(DEFMOP EQL (M-FUNCTION))
(DEFMOP NOT-EQL (M-FUNCTION))
(DEFMOP COMPARE-CONSTRAINT (CONSTRAINT-FN))

(DEFMOP M-COMPARE (M-PATTERN)
    (ABST-FN COMPARE-CONSTRAINT)
    (COMPARE-FN M-FUNCTION))

(DEFMOP M-EQUAL (M-COMPARE) (COMPARE-FN EQL))
(DEFMOP M-NOT-EQUAL (M-COMPARE) (COMPARE-FN NOT-EQL))

(DEFMOP M-PATH (M-GROUP) (1 M-ROLE))

(DEFUN COMPARE-CONSTRAINT (CONSTRAINT FILLER SLOTS)
 (FUNCALL (GET-FILLER 'COMPARE-FN CONSTRAINT)
          (INDIRECT-FILLER 'ROLE CONSTRAINT FILLER)
          (INDIRECT-FILLER 'TO CONSTRAINT SLOTS)))

(DEFUN INDIRECT-FILLER (ROLE MOP SLOTS)
 (LET ((PATH-MOP (GET-FILLER ROLE MOP)))
  (PATH-FILLER (COND ((NULL PATH-MOP) NIL)
                     ((ABSTP 'M-PATH PATH-MOP)
                      (GROUP->LIST PATH-MOP))
                     (T (LIST PATH-MOP)))
              SLOTS)))

(DEFUN NOT-EQL (X Y) (AND X Y (NOT (EQL X Y))))
```

Listing 9.3: Extended Comparison MOPs

```
(DEFMOP ACTOR (M-ROLE) INSTANCE)

(DEFMOP M-FOOTBALL-EVENT (M-EVENT) (ACTOR M-PLAYER))

(DEFMOP M-DETECT (M-FOOTBALL-EVENT)
    (ACTION I-M-MTRANS-ACT)
    (TO M-EQUAL (TO ACTOR))
    (INFO M-FOOTBALL-EVENT))

(DEFMOP M-PASS (M-FOOTBALL-EVENT) MOP
    (ACTION I-M-PTRANS-ACT) (ACTOR M-OFFENSIVE-PLAYER)
    (OBJECT I-M-BALL) (TO M-OFFENSIVE-PLAYER))

(DEFMOP M-SHORT-PASS (M-PASS) MOP
    (DISTANCE I-M-SHORT))

(DEFMOP M-HIKE (M-SHORT-PASS) MOP (ACTOR I-M-C))
(DEFMOP M-LATERAL (M-SHORT-PASS) MOP (ACTOR NIL))

(DEFMOP M-RUN (M-FOOTBALL-EVENT)
    (ACTION I-M-PTRANS-ACT)
    (OBJECT M-EQUAL (TO ACTOR)))

(DEFMOP M-RUN-TO-GOAL (M-RUN) MOP
    (TO I-M-OFFENSIVE-GOAL))

(DEFMOP M-RUN-TO-SCRIMMAGE (M-RUN) MOP
    (TO I-M-SCRIMMAGE))

(DEFMOP M-RUN-TO-PLAYER (M-RUN) MOP
    (TO M-PLAYER))

(DEFMOP M-TACKLE (M-FOOTBALL-EVENT) MOP
    (ACTION I-M-GRASP-ACT))
```

Listing 9.4: Micro COACH Event MOPs

```
(DEFMOP M-PLAY (M-GROUP) (1 M-FOOTBALL-EVENT))

(DEFMOP M-OFFENSIVE-PLAY (M-PLAY) MOP
    (1 M-HIKE (ACTOR I-M-C) (TO I-M-QB)))

(DEFMOP I-M-BOOTLEG-RUN (M-OFFENSIVE-PLAY)
    (1 M-HIKE (ACTOR I-M-C) (TO I-M-QB))
    (2 M-RUN-TO-SCRIMMAGE (ACTOR I-M-QB))
    (3 M-RUN-TO-GOAL (ACTOR I-M-QB)))

(DEFMOP I-M-SWEEP (M-OFFENSIVE-PLAY)
    (1 M-HIKE (ACTOR I-M-C) (TO I-M-QB))
    (2 M-LATERAL (ACTOR I-M-QB) (TO I-M-HB))
    (3 M-RUN-TO-SCRIMMAGE (ACTOR I-M-HB))
    (4 M-RUN-TO-GOAL (ACTOR I-M-HB)))

(DEFMOP M-DEFENSIVE-PLAY (M-PLAY) MOP
    (1 M-FOOTBALL-EVENT (ACTOR M-DEFENSIVE-PLAYER)))

(DEFMOP M-CB-DEFEND (M-DEFENSIVE-PLAY)
    (1 M-DETECT (ACTOR I-M-CB) (INFO M-PASS))
    (2 M-RUN (ACTOR I-M-CB) (TO M-OFFENSIVE-PLAYER))
    (3 M-TACKLE (ACTOR I-M-CB)
                (OBJECT M-OFFENSIVE-PLAYER)))
```

Listing 9.5: Micro COACH Play MOPs

```
(DEFMOP M-TIME-CYCLE (M-GROUP) (1 M-EVENT))
(DEFMOP M-DOWN (M-GROUP) (1 M-TIME-CYCLE))

(DEFMOP I-M-RUN-BOOTLEG (M-DOWN) INSTANCE
    (1 M-TIME-CYCLE
        (1 M-HIKE (ACTOR I-M-C) (TO I-M-QB))
        (2 M-RUN (ACTOR I-M-QB) (TO I-M-SCRIMMAGE))
        (3 M-DETECT (ACTOR I-M-CB)
                    (INFO M-HIKE (ACTOR I-M-C)
                                 (TO I-M-QB)))
        (4 M-RUN (ACTOR I-M-CB) (TO I-M-QB)))
    (2 M-TIME-CYCLE
        (1 M-RUN-TO-GOAL (ACTOR I-M-QB))
        (2 M-TACKLE (ACTOR I-M-CB) (OBJECT I-M-QB))))

(DEFMOP I-M-RUN-SWEEP (M-DOWN) INSTANCE
    (1 M-TIME-CYCLE
        (1 M-HIKE (ACTOR I-M-C) (TO I-M-QB))
        (2 M-LATERAL (ACTOR I-M-QB) (TO I-M-HB))
        (3 M-RUN (ACTOR I-M-HB) (TO I-M-SCRIMMAGE))
        (4 M-DETECT (ACTOR I-M-CB)
                    (INFO M-LATERAL (ACTOR I-M-QB)
                                    (TO I-M-HB)))
        (5 M-RUN (ACTOR I-M-CB) (TO I-M-HB)))
    (2 M-TIME-CYCLE
        (1 M-RUN-TO-GOAL (ACTOR I-M-HB))
        (2 M-TACKLE (ACTOR I-M-CB) (OBJECT I-M-HB))))
```

Listing 9.6: Micro COACH Execution Result MOPs

and sweep plays. (Section 9.4.3 describes how these were generated.)

In the first time cycle of I-M-RUN-BOOTLEG, the quarterback gets the ball and runs toward the line of scrimmage, while the defensive cornerback detects and runs toward the quarterback. In the next time cycle, the quarterback runs for the goal and the cornerback tackles him.

In the first time cycle of I-M-SWEEP, the quarterback gets the ball and laterals it to the halfback, who runs toward the line of scrimmage. The cornerback sees the lateral pass and pursues the halfback. In the next time cycle, the halfback runs for the goal and the cornerback tackles him.

```
(DEFMOP M-BAD-STATE (M-STATE))
(DEFMOP M-BAD-CYCLE (M-TIME-CYCLE M-BAD-STATE)
        (1 M-FOOTBALL-EVENT))

(DEFMOP M-FAILURE (M-ROOT) (STATE M-BAD-STATE))
(DEFMOP M-EXPLANATION (M-ROOT) (FAILURE M-FAILURE))

(DEFMOP I-M-BOOTLEG-XP (M-EXPLANATION) INSTANCE
 (FAILURE M-FAILURE
          (STATE M-BAD-CYCLE
                 (1 M-RUN-TO-GOAL (ACTOR I-M-QB))
                 (2 M-TACKLE (ACTOR I-M-CB)
                             (OBJECT I-M-QB))))
 (CAUSE I-M-RUN-BOOTLEG)
 (RULE M-CB-DEFEND))

(DEFMOP I-M-SWEEP-XP (M-EXPLANATION) INSTANCE
 (FAILURE M-FAILURE
          (STATE M-BAD-CYCLE
                 (1 M-RUN-TO-GOAL (ACTOR I-M-HB))
                 (2 M-TACKLE (ACTOR I-M-CB)
                             (OBJECT I-M-HB))))
 (CAUSE I-M-RUN-SWEEP)
 (RULE M-CB-DEFEND))
```

Listing 9.7: Micro COACH Failure and Explanation MOPs

An offensive play is considered to have failed if a tackle occurs before (in an earlier time cycle) or during (in the same time cycle) as the run for the goal. Both downs in Listing 9.6 are thus failures for the offense, because the tackle occurs in the same time cycle as the run for the goal.

Listing 9.7 defines MOPs for failure and explanations of failure. Note that the definitions of M-BAD-STATE, M-FAILURE, and M-EXPLANATION are the same as those in Listing 7.15. For micro COACH, the failing state is simply the cycle in which the tackle occurred, the cause of the state is the down in which the cycle occurred, and the rule explaining the failure is the play the defender chose.

Listing 9.8 defines the MOPs for the (unsuccessful) attempts to repair the bootleg run and sweep plays. Being unsuccessful, they have no filler for their

```
(DEFMOP M-REPAIR (M-ROOT) (EXPLANATION M-EXPLANATION))

(DEFMOP I-M-BOOTLEG-REPAIR (M-REPAIR) INSTANCE
    (SOLUTION I-M-BOOTLEG-RUN)
    (EXPLANATION I-M-BOOTLEG-XP))

(DEFMOP I-M-SWEEP-REPAIR (M-REPAIR) INSTANCE
    (SOLUTION I-M-SWEEP)
    (EXPLANATION I-M-SWEEP-XP))
```

Listing 9.8: Micro COACH Repair MOPs

REPAIRED-SOLUTION slots. These SOLUTION slot of these repair MOPs contains the failed offensive play, while the EXPLANATION slot contains the simulation and the successful defensive play.

Listing 9.9 defines the MOPs for strategies for creating new plays, i.e., for things like "fork," "hedge bets," and so on. In particular, we define a variant of the fork called M-DECEIVE. This strategy is very similar to the "reduce variance" strategy, described in Chapter 8. M-DECEIVE looks at the failures in two repairs. If the causes of the two failures are mutually exclusive and involve the detection of some offensive action, then a "deceptive" play is created by merging the two plays. The actual mechanics of doing this are represented in Lisp code in the listings that follow.

Listings 9.10 and 9.12 define the functions and MOPs for determining when two sequences of events are mutually exclusive. In particular, we are interested in finding cases where actions by a defensive player are mutually exclusive.

(REPAIR-1-EXCLUSION-P *constraint filler slots*) returns true if *filler* is a repair MOP that contains a time cycle that is mutually exclusive with a corresponding time cycle in the filler of the REPAIR-1 slot of *slots*.

(CYCLE-EXCLUSION-P *time-cycle$_1$ time-cycle$_2$*) returns true if any action by a defensive player in *time-cycle$_1$* is mutually exclusive with any action by the same actor in *time-cycle$_2$*.

(EVENT-EXCLUSION-P *event$_1$ event$_2$*) returns true if *event$_1$* and *event$_2$* have the same defensive player as actor and are mutually exclusive. Mutual exclusiveness is represented in the MOPs in Listing 9.12.

Listing 9.11 defines a general set of pattern MOPs and functions for specifying a conjunction of constraints. A M-AND MOP has an OBJECT slot filled with an M-CONSTRAINTS MOP. M-CONSTRAINTS is an M-GROUP of constraints. The M-AND pattern is satisfied if all of the constraints in the group are satisfied.

```
(DEFMOP REPAIR-1 (M-ROLE) INSTANCE)
(DEFMOP REPAIR-2 (M-ROLE) INSTANCE)
(DEFMOP EXPLANATION (M-ROLE) INSTANCE)
(DEFMOP CAUSE (M-ROLE) INSTANCE)

(DEFMOP REPAIR-1-EXCLUSION-P (CONSTRAINT-FN))
(DEFMOP GET-DETECTED-EVENT (M-FUNCTION))
(DEFMOP MAKE-DECEPTION (M-FUNCTION))

(DEFMOP M-GET-DETECTED-STEP (M-PATTERN)
    (CALC-FN GET-DETECTED-EVENT))

(DEFMOP M-STRATEGY (M-ROOT))

(DEFMOP M-DECEIVE (M-STRATEGY)
    (REPAIR-1 M-REPAIR)
    (REPAIR-2 M-PATTERN
            (ABST-FN REPAIR-1-EXCLUSION-P))
    (DETECTED-EVENT-1
       M-GET-DETECTED-STEP (ROLE REPAIR-1))
    (DETECTED-EVENT-2
       M-GET-DETECTED-STEP (ROLE REPAIR-2))
    (NEW-SOLUTION
       M-PATTERN (CALC-FN MAKE-DECEPTION)))
```

Listing 9.9: Micro COACH Strategy MOPs

```
(DEFUN REPAIR-1-EXCLUSION-P (CONSTRAINT FILLER SLOTS)
 (LET ((DOWN-1
         (PATH-FILLER '(EXPLANATION CAUSE) FILLER))
        (DOWN-2
         (PATH-FILLER '(REPAIR-1 EXPLANATION CAUSE)
                       SLOTS)))
   (FORMAT T "~&---------------")
   (FORMAT T "~&Checking for mutual exclusions")
   (FORMAT T "~&  between ~S and ~S" DOWN-1 DOWN-2)
   (FOR (SLOT-1 :IN (MOP-SLOTS DOWN-1))
        (SLOT-2 :IN (MOP-SLOTS DOWN-2))
     :FIRST (CYCLE-EXCLUSION-P
               (GROUP->LIST (SLOT-FILLER SLOT-1))
               (GROUP->LIST (SLOT-FILLER SLOT-2)))))))

(DEFUN CYCLE-EXCLUSION-P (CYCLE-1 CYCLE-2)
 (FOR (EVENT-1 :IN CYCLE-1)
   :FIRST
     (FOR (EVENT-2 :IN CYCLE-2)
       :FIRST (EVENT-EXCLUSION-P EVENT-1 EVENT-2))))

(DEFUN EVENT-EXCLUSION-P (EVENT-1 EVENT-2)
 (LET ((ACTOR (GET-FILLER 'ACTOR EVENT-1)))
   (AND (ABSTP 'M-DEFENSIVE-PLAYER ACTOR)
        (EQL (GET-FILLER 'ACTOR EVENT-2) ACTOR)
        (SLOTS->MOP '((THIS-EVENT ,EVENT-1)
                       (THAT-EVENT ,EVENT-2))
                    '(M-EXCLUSION)
                    NIL)
        (PROGN (FORMAT T "~&~S excludes ~S"
                       EVENT-1 EVENT-2)
               T))))
```

Listing 9.10: Micro COACH Exclusion Functions

```
(DEFMOP ANDP (CONSTRAINT-FN))
(DEFMOP M-AND (M-PATTERN) (ABST-FN ANDP))
(DEFMOP M-CONSTRAINTS (M-GROUP))

(DEFUN ANDP (CONSTRAINT FILLER SLOTS)
  (FOR (SLOT :IN
       (MOP-SLOTS (ROLE-FILLER 'OBJECT CONSTRAINT)))
   :ALWAYS (SATISFIEDP (SLOT-FILLER SLOT)
                       FILLER SLOTS)))
```

Listing 9.11: Conjoined Constraints

Listing 9.12 defines the MOPs representing which pairs of events are mutually exclusive. There are two such pairs in micro COACH. You can't run to two different places and you can't pass the ball to two different people. These restrictions only apply to a time cycle. The pass restriction, for example, does not rule out passing the ball twice, in separate time cycles.

Listing 9.13 defines the function for finding an offensive action detected by an defensive player.

(GET-DETECTED-EVENT *pattern mop*) finds the first M-DETECT event by a defensive player in *mop* and returns the filler of the INFO slot. *mop* should be a repair MOP containing an explanation with a CAUSE filled with a group of time cycles.

(DEFENSIVE-DETECT-INFO *event*) returns the filler of the INFO slot if *event* is a defensive M-DETECT event.

The M-DECEIVE strategy constructs a new play by merging two plays and delaying as long as possible the detectable step that would tell the defense which play is being executed. Listing 9.14 defines the functions that delay a step as long as possible.

(DELAY-STEP *step play*) returns a copy of *play*, by copying every step in *play* up to *step*, and then calling UNTIL-ENABLE to insert *step* as late as possible in the remainder of the play.

(DELAYED-INSERT *step play*) returns a copy of *play*, with *step* inserted when a step in *play* is reached that is enabled by *step*.

(ENABLESP $step_1$ $step_2$) returns true if $step_1$ enables $step_2$. Enablement conditions are represented in the MOPs in Listing 9.15.

Listing 9.15 defines the MOPs representing which steps enable which other steps. There are two such pairs in micro COACH. Passing a ball to someone enables that player to run to the goal, and hiking the ball enables every other

```
(DEFMOP THIS-EVENT (M-ROLE) INSTANCE)
(DEFMOP TO (M-ROLE) INSTANCE)

(DEFMOP M-EXCLUSION (M-ROOT))

(DEFMOP M-RUN-EXCLUSION (M-EXCLUSION)
    (THIS-EVENT M-RUN)
    (THAT-EVENT M-AND
      (OBJECT M-CONSTRAINTS
              (1 M-RUN)
              (2 M-NOT-EQUAL (ROLE TO)
                 (TO M-PATH (1 THIS-EVENT) (2 TO))))))

(DEFMOP M-PASS-EXCLUSION (M-EXCLUSION)
    (THIS-EVENT M-PASS)
    (THAT-EVENT M-AND
      (OBJECT M-CONSTRAINTS
              (1 M-PASS)
              (2 M-NOT-EQUAL (ROLE TO)
                 (TO M-PATH (1 THIS-EVENT) (2 TO))))))
```

Listing 9.12: Micro COACH Exclusion MOPs

```
(DEFUN GET-DETECTED-EVENT (PATTERN MOP)
 (FORMAT T "~&----------------")
 (LET ((CAUSE (PATH-FILLER '(EXPLANATION CAUSE)
                 (INDIRECT-FILLER 'ROLE PATTERN MOP))))
  (FORMAT T "~&Looking for a detected event in ~S"
          CAUSE)
  (LET ((EVENT
          (FOR (SLOT :IN (MOP-SLOTS CAUSE))
            :FIRST (FOR (SUBSLOT :IN
                          (MOP-SLOTS
                            (SLOT-FILLER SLOT)))
                     :FIRST (DEFENSIVE-DETECT-INFO
                              (SLOT-FILLER SUBSLOT)))))))
    (AND EVENT
       (PROGN (FORMAT T "~&Detected event found")
              EVENT)))))

(DEFUN DEFENSIVE-DETECT-INFO (EVENT)
 (AND (ABSTP 'M-DETECT EVENT)
      (ABSTP 'M-DEFENSIVE-PLAYER
             (ROLE-FILLER 'ACTOR EVENT))
      (ROLE-FILLER 'INFO EVENT)))
```

Listing 9.13: Micro COACH Detected Event Function

```
(DEFUN DELAY-STEP (STEP PLAY)
 (COND ((NULL PLAY) NIL)
       ((EQL (CAR PLAY) STEP)
        (DELAYED-INSERT STEP (CDR PLAY)))
       (T (CONS (CAR PLAY)
                (DELAY-STEP STEP (CDR PLAY))))))

(DEFUN DELAYED-INSERT (STEP PLAY)
 (OR (AND (OR (NULL PLAY)
              (ENABLESP STEP (CAR PLAY)))
          (CONS STEP PLAY))
     (CONS (CAR PLAY)
           (DELAYED-INSERT STEP (CDR PLAY)))))

(DEFUN ENABLESP (EVENT NEXT-EVENT)
 (SLOTS->MOP '((ANTE ,EVENT) (CNSQ ,NEXT-EVENT))
             '(M-ENABLE) NIL))
```

Listing 9.14: Micro COACH Delay Functions

step, that is, play doesn't start until the ball is hiked.

Listing 9.16 defines the functions that merge two plays, and delay some step to avoid detection.

(MERGE-PLAYS *play*$_1$ *play*$_2$ *step*) creates a new play that is the merger of *play*$_1$ and *play*$_2$, with *step* delayed as long as possible.

(MERGE-STEPS *step-list*$_1$ *step-list*$_2$) returns the steps in *step-list*$_1$, minus its final "run to goal" step, followed by the steps in *step-list*$_2$, minus any steps in *step-list*$_1$.

(REMOVE-GOAL-STEP *step-list*) removes the last "run to goal" step from *step-list*.

Listing 9.17 defines the functions that test to see if a detected event in a time cycle can be delayed until the next time cycle. Such a delay would change the time cycle in which the tackle occurs, if the tackle is based on the detection.

(DELAYABLEP *event down*) returns true if *event* can be delayed until the next time cycle. This is true if *event* does not enable any events that follow it in the time cycle it occurs in.

(NEXT-EVENTS *event down*) returns the events that follow *event* in whatever time cycle it occurs in.

```
(DEFMOP ANTE (M-ROLE) INSTANCE)

(DEFMOP M-CAUSAL (M-ROOT))
(DEFMOP M-ENABLE (M-CAUSAL))

(DEFMOP M-PASS-ENABLE-RUN-TO-GOAL (M-ENABLE)
    (ANTE M-PASS)
    (CNSQ M-AND
          (OBJECT M-CONSTRAINTS
                  (1 M-RUN-TO-GOAL)
                  (2 M-EQUAL (ROLE ACTOR)
                          (TO M-PATH (1 ANTE) (2 TO))))))

(DEFMOP M-HIKE-ENABLE-ALL (M-ENABLE)
    (ANTE M-HIKE)
    (CNSQ M-FOOTBALL-EVENT))
```

Listing 9.15: Micro COACH Enablement MOPs

Listing 9.18 defines the functions that merge two plays to form a deceptive play that looks like both of them.

(MAKE-DECEPTION *pattern mop*), takes *mop*, a strategy containing two repairs, and tries to make either the first play look like the second or vice versa.

(CALC-DECEPTION *role₁ role₂ role₃ mop*) takes three roles and a strategy MOP. *role₂* and *role₃* retrieve the two repairs, and *role₁* retrieves the event in the execution of the repair in *role₂* that was detected by the defense. CALC-DECEPTION first checks to see if the detected event is delayable. If so, then it gets the step in the original play that generated the detected event and calls MERGE-PLAYS to generate a play that starts out like the play in the *second* repair, but ends like the play in the *first* repair, with the detectable step delayed as long as possible.

(GET-ABST-IN-GROUP *mop group*) returns the first member of *group* that is an abstraction of *mop*.

Listing 9.19 is the master program that runs through an example of merging the bootleg run and the sweep plays to generate a new play that has steps from both plays, but delays the lateral in the sweep until after the quarterback and halfback have run to the line of scrimmage. Since we have not defined a football simulator, we can't test out this new play, but it would in fact do

```
(DEFUN MERGE-PLAYS (PLAY-1 PLAY-2 STEP)
 (FORMAT T "~&----------------")
 (FORMAT T "~&Merging plays")
 (LIST->GROUP
   (DELAY-STEP STEP
     (MERGE-STEPS (GROUP->LIST PLAY-1)
                  (GROUP->LIST PLAY-2)))))

(DEFUN MERGE-STEPS (STEPS-1 STEPS-2)
 (LET ((NEW-STEPS (REMOVE-GOAL-STEP STEPS-1)))
   (APPEND NEW-STEPS
           (FOR (STEP :IN STEPS-2)
                :WHEN (NOT (MEMBER STEP NEW-STEPS))
                :SAVE STEP))))

(DEFUN REMOVE-GOAL-STEP (STEPS)
 (FOR (STEP :IN STEPS)
   :WHEN (NOT (ABSTP 'M-RUN-TO-GOAL STEP))
   :SAVE STEP))
```

Listing 9.16: Micro COACH Play Merging Functions

```
(DEFUN DELAYABLEP (EVENT DOWN)
  (FORMAT T "~&----------------")
  (FORMAT T "~&Seeing if ~S can be delayed" EVENT)
  (COND ((FOR (NEXT-EVENT :IN (NEXT-EVENTS EVENT DOWN))
             :ALWAYS (NOT (ENABLESP EVENT NEXT-EVENT)))
         (FORMAT T "~&~S can be delayed" EVENT)
         T)
        (T (FORMAT T "~&~S can not be delayed" EVENT)
           NIL)))
```

```
(DEFUN NEXT-EVENTS (EVENT DOWN)
  (CDR
    (FOR (SLOT :IN (MOP-SLOTS DOWN))
      :FIRST (MEMBER EVENT
               (GROUP->LIST (SLOT-FILLER SLOT)))))))
```

Listing 9.17: Micro COACH Delay Testing Functions

what we want, given the primitive physics of football we have assumed here.

9.3 Running the COACH Demo

To run the micro COACH demo, you need the code in the Listings in Chapter 3 and this chapter. Follow these steps:

1. Load all DEFUN, DEFMACRO, SETF, DEFINE-FOR-KEY and DEFINE-TABLE forms, in the order in which they appear in the Listings.

2. Execute the function call (CLEAR-MEMORY).

3. Load all the DEFMOP forms, in the order in which they appear in the Listings.

4. Execute the function call (COACH-DEMO).

After Step 3, the abstraction hierarchy printed by (DAH 'M-ROOT) should look like the following, except for the numbers on the MOPs..

```
(DEFUN MAKE-DECEPTION (PATTERN MOP)
 (FORMAT T "~&----------------")
 (FORMAT T "~&Trying M-DECEIVE")
 (OR (CALC-DECEPTION
        'DETECTED-EVENT-1 'REPAIR-1 'REPAIR-2 MOP)
     (CALC-DECEPTION
        'DETECTED-EVENT-2 'REPAIR-2 'REPAIR-1 MOP)))

(DEFUN CALC-DECEPTION (DETECTED-ROLE ROLE-1 ROLE-2 MOP)
 (LET ((EVENT (GET-FILLER DETECTED-ROLE MOP))
       (REPAIR-1 (GET-FILLER ROLE-1 MOP))
       (REPAIR-2 (GET-FILLER ROLE-2 MOP)))
  (LET ((DOWN (PATH-FILLER '(EXPLANATION CAUSE)
                            REPAIR-1))
        (PLAY-1 (GET-FILLER 'SOLUTION REPAIR-1))
        (PLAY-2 (GET-FILLER 'SOLUTION REPAIR-2)))
   (FORMAT T "~&----------------")
   (FORMAT T "~&Trying to make ~S look like ~S"
            PLAY-2 PLAY-1)
   (AND (DELAYABLEP EVENT DOWN)
        (MERGE-PLAYS PLAY-2 PLAY-1
            (GET-ABST-IN-GROUP EVENT PLAY-1))))))

(DEFUN GET-ABST-IN-GROUP (MOP GROUP)
 (FOR (SLOT :IN (MOP-SLOTS GROUP))
   :WHEN (ABSTP (SLOT-FILLER SLOT) MOP)
   :FIRST (SLOT-FILLER SLOT)))
```

Listing 9.18: Micro COACH Deception Making Functions

```
(DEFUN COACH-DEMO ()
 (LET ((INSTANCE
          (COACH '((REPAIR-1 I-M-BOOTLEG-REPAIR)
                   (REPAIR-2 I-M-SWEEP-REPAIR)))))
   (INSIST COACH-DEMO (NOT (NULL INSTANCE)))
   (FORMAT T "~&---------------")
   (FORMAT T "~&The new play is ")
   (DPH (ROLE-FILLER 'NEW-SOLUTION INSTANCE))
   (FORMAT T "~&---------------")
   INSTANCE))
```

Listing 9.19: Micro COACH Demo

```
(M-ROOT
    (M-CAUSAL
        (M-ENABLE
            (M-HIKE-ENABLE-ALL)
            (M-PASS-ENABLE-RUN-TO-GOAL)))
    (M-EXCLUSION
        (M-PASS-EXCLUSION)
        (M-RUN-EXCLUSION))
    (M-STRATEGY (M-DECEIVE))
    (M-REPAIR
        (I-M-SWEEP-REPAIR)
        (I-M-BOOTLEG-REPAIR))
    (M-EXPLANATION (I-M-SWEEP-XP) (I-M-BOOTLEG-XP))
    (M-FAILURE (I-M-FAILURE.56) (I-M-FAILURE.52))
    (M-DISTANCE (I-M-LONG) (I-M-SHORT))
    (M-LOCATION
        (I-M-SCRIMMAGE)
        (I-M-DEFENSIVE-GOAL)
        (I-M-OFFENSIVE-GOAL))
    (M-OBJECT (I-M-BALL))
    (M-FAILED-SOLUTION)
    (M-ROLE
        (ANTE)
        (TO)
        (THIS-EVENT)
        (CAUSE)
```

```
        (EXPLANATION)
        (REPAIR-2)
        (REPAIR-1)
        (ACTOR))
    (M-CASE)
    (M-PATTERN
        (M-AND (M-AND.72) (M-AND.68) (M-AND.64))
        (M-PATTERN.60)
        (M-PATTERN.57)
        (M-GET-DETECTED-STEP
            (M-GET-DETECTED-STEP.59)
            (M-GET-DETECTED-STEP.58))
        (M-COMPARE
            (M-NOT-EQUAL (M-NOT-EQUAL.62))
            (M-EQUAL (M-EQUAL.70) (M-EQUAL.16)))
        (M-NOT)
        (M-PATTERN.15))
    (M-FUNCTION
        (MAKE-DECEPTION)
        (GET-DETECTED-EVENT)
        (NOT-EQL)
        (EQL)
        (GET-SIBLING)
        (CONSTRAINT-FN
            (ANDP)
            (REPAIR-1-EXCLUSION-P)
            (COMPARE-CONSTRAINT)
            (NOT-CONSTRAINT)))
    (M-GROUP
        (M-CONSTRAINTS
            (M-CONSTRAINTS.71)
            (M-CONSTRAINTS.67)
            (M-CONSTRAINTS.63))
        (M-DOWN (I-M-RUN-SWEEP) (I-M-RUN-BOOTLEG))
        (M-TIME-CYCLE
            (M-BAD-CYCLE
                (I-M-BAD-CYCLE.55)
                (I-M-BAD-CYCLE.51))
            (I-M-TIME-CYCLE.48)
            (I-M-TIME-CYCLE.45)
            (I-M-TIME-CYCLE.38)
```

```
            (I-M-TIME-CYCLE.35))
    (M-PLAY
        (M-DEFENSIVE-PLAY (M-CB-DEFEND))
        (M-OFFENSIVE-PLAY
            (I-M-SWEEP)
            (I-M-BOOTLEG-RUN)))
        (M-PATH (I-M-PATH.69) (I-M-PATH.61))
        (M-EMPTY-GROUP (I-M-EMPTY-GROUP)))
(M-ACTOR
    (M-PLAYER
        (M-OFFENSIVE-PLAYER
            (I-M-QB)
            (I-M-HB)
            (I-M-C))
        (M-DEFENSIVE-PLAYER (I-M-CB))))
(M-ACT
    (I-M-PTRANS-ACT)
    (I-M-MTRANS-ACT)
    (I-M-GRASP-ACT))
(M-STATE
    (M-BAD-STATE
        (M-BAD-CYCLE
            (I-M-BAD-CYCLE.55)
            (I-M-BAD-CYCLE.51))))
(M-EVENT
    (M-FOOTBALL-EVENT
        (M-FOOTBALL-EVENT.26)
        (M-TACKLE
            (M-TACKLE.29
                (I-M-TACKLE.47)
                (I-M-TACKLE.37)))
        (M-RUN
            (M-RUN.28 (I-M-RUN.44) (I-M-RUN.34))
            (M-RUN-TO-PLAYER
                (I-M-RUN.44)
                (I-M-RUN.34))
            (M-RUN-TO-SCRIMMAGE
                (I-M-RUN-TO-SCRIMMAGE.24)
                (I-M-RUN-TO-SCRIMMAGE.20))
            (M-RUN-TO-GOAL
                (I-M-RUN-TO-GOAL.25)
```

```
                    (I-M-RUN-TO-GOAL.21)))
        (M-PASS
            (M-SHORT-PASS
                (M-LATERAL (I-M-LATERAL.23))
                (M-HIKE (I-M-HIKE.18))))
        (M-DETECT
            (M-DETECT.27
                (I-M-DETECT.43)
                (I-M-DETECT.33))))))
```

After Step 4, you should see something very close to the output that follows, except for the numbers on the MOPs:

```
----------------
Checking for mutual exclusions
  between I-M-RUN-SWEEP and I-M-RUN-BOOTLEG
I-M-RUN.44 excludes I-M-RUN.34
----------------
Trying M-DECEIVE
----------------
Looking for a detected event in I-M-RUN-BOOTLEG
Detected event found
I-M-STRATEGY.73:DETECTED-EVENT-1 <= I-M-HIKE.18
----------------
Trying to make I-M-SWEEP look like I-M-BOOTLEG-RUN
----------------
Seeing if I-M-HIKE.18 can be delayed
I-M-HIKE.18 can not be delayed
----------------
Looking for a detected event in I-M-RUN-SWEEP
Detected event found
I-M-STRATEGY.73:DETECTED-EVENT-2 <= I-M-LATERAL.23
----------------
Trying to make I-M-BOOTLEG-RUN look like I-M-SWEEP
----------------
Seeing if I-M-LATERAL.23 can be delayed
I-M-LATERAL.23 can be delayed
----------------
Merging plays
I-M-STRATEGY.73:NEW-SOLUTION <= I-M-GROUP.84
----------------
```

```
The new play is
(I-M-GROUP.84 (1 I-M-HIKE.18
                 (ACTOR I-M-C)
                 (TO I-M-QB))
              (2 I-M-RUN-TO-SCRIMMAGE.20
                 (ACTOR I-M-QB))
              (3 I-M-RUN-TO-SCRIMMAGE.24
                 (ACTOR I-M-HB))
              (4 I-M-LATERAL.23
                 (ACTOR I-M-QB)
                 (TO I-M-HB))
              (5 I-M-RUN-TO-GOAL.25 (ACTOR I-M-HB)))
----------------
```

9.4 Extensions

9.4.1 Correcting M-CB-DEFEND

The MOP M-CB-DEFEND in Listing 9.5 is not restrictive enough. It would match a play where the cornerback sees the halfback get the ball, but the cornerback still chases the quarterback. Fix the definition of this MOP to only accept cases where the cornerback chases and tackles the receiver of the detected pass.

9.4.2 Recognizing Failing Plays

Define a pattern MOP that would recognize when a down contains a failing offensive play.

9.4.3 A Football Play Simulator

Define a function that takes an offensive and a defensive play and returns an M-DOWN representing the events that occur when these two plays are run together. In particular, given I-M-BOOTLEG-RUN and M-CB-DEFEND, the function should generate the time cycles found in I-M-RUN-BOOTLEG, which we generated by hand. Given I-M-SWEEP and M-CB-DEFEND, it should generate the cycles in I-M-RUN-SWEEP.

First, we copy steps from the offensive play into the first time cycle. We classify M-FOOTBALL-EVENT's into long and short events. Detections, and short passes are short events, while runs, tackles, and long passes are long events. Our rule is that each player can do any number of short events in a time cycle,

but at most one long event. Thus, the quarterback can lateral the ball to the
halfback and run toward the line of scrimmage in one time cycle, and the
cornerback can detect the lateral and run toward the halfback in that same
cycle. In simulating I-M-SWEEP, we can therefore copy the first three steps
into the first time cycle, ending with the halfback running toward the line of
scrimmage.

Next we copy steps from the defensive play into the same time cycle. The
same rule about long and short events applies. The two sets of events form
one time cycle. We repeat this process to generate the next time cycle, until
a cycle is generated with either a tackle or run to goal event.

Detection events require extra work, because they contain patterns. The
M-DETECT in M-CB-DEFEND has a pattern in its INFO slot for a pass to an
offensive player. What we want to put in the time cycle is the particular
pass the cornerback sees. The first cycle of M-SWEEP has two passes, a hike
and a lateral. Our rule for detection *for defenders* is to take the latest event
in the current time cycle that matches the INFO pattern. Thus in this case,
the detection *step* becomes the detection *event* "cornerback sees lateral to
halfback." In addition, since the corrected version of M-CB-DEFEND from the
earlier exercise says that the next step is to pursue the receiver of the pass,
the next step becomes the event "cornerback runs toward the halfback."

Although it doesn't come up here, our detection rule *for offenders* is to
take the latest event in the previous time cycle that matches the INFO pattern.
Thus, looking ahead to the next exercise, the quarterback can detect that the
cornerback is going toward the halfback in the time cycle after the cornerback
starts running.

9.4.4   Generating the Option Play

The play generated by M-DECEIVE is not the option play because the quarterback always laterals the ball to the halfback. If we added a new defensive play
where the cornerback simply ran after and tackled the halfback, the quarterback would toss the ball to the halfback just in time for him to get tackled.

What's missing is a detection event for the quarterback. If the quarterback
detects the cornerback running toward him, he should toss the ball to the
halfback. Otherwise, the quarterback should keep the ball and run toward the
goal.

You need a representation for conditional steps in plays. One possibility
is an M-SELECT MOP with a CHOICES slot filled with a group of M-CHOICE
MOPs. Each M-CHOICE would have two slots, IF and THEN. For example, in
the option play, the conditional step might be represented thus:

```
M-SELECT
    (CHOICES M-CHOICE-GROUP
        (1 M-CHOICE
            (IF M-DETECT (ACTOR I-M-QB)
                (INFO M-RUN
                    (ACTOR I-M-CB) (TO I-M-QB)))
            (THEN M-OFFENSIVE-PLAY
                (1 M-LATERAL
                    (ACTOR I-M-QB) (TO I-M-HB))
                (2 M-RUN-TO-GOAL
                    (ACTOR I-M-HB))))
        (2 M-CHOICE
            (IF M-DETECT (ACTOR I-M-QB)
                (INFO M-RUN
                    (ACTOR I-M-CB)
                    (TO M-NOT (OBJECT I-M-QB))))
            (THEN M-RUN-TO-GOAL (ACTOR I-M-QB))))
```

You'll need to change the simulator to know about conditional steps. This isn't too hard. You'll also have to create an M-FORK strategy, similar to M-DECEIVE, capable of adding this conditional step. This is harder, since it involves some inferencing we glossed over in M-DECEIVE. The conditional step should switch between the two plays being merged, i.e., M-BOOTLEG-RUN and M-SWEEP. You can tell where the switch has to occur because the quarterback can't run to the goal and also lateral the ball to the halfback running to the goal. (Our interpretation of running to the goal implies carrying the ball.) You'll have to add this kind of exclusion knowledge to the micro COACH. This will take care of the THEN slots in the M-CHOICE's. As for the IF slots, it's clear that an M-DETECT is involved, since that's the only action we're using to influence choices, but who should do the detecting, and what should he be looking for? The detector should be whoever has the ball, since they're in control. The event being looked for should be whatever event (or events) would enable a tackle of the holder of the ball. You'll have to add this knowledge too.

9.4.5 Adding States

The real COACH had states as well as events. Thus, passing someone the ball meant that the passer no longer had the ball and the receiver did. We've done without states simply to keep our plays short and the number of MOPs in memory small, but they really should be in micro COACH. Representing who has the ball makes it easier to infer who can and can't run to the goal and who can and can't be tackled. Redo micro COACH, using MOPs for possessing the ball and being at a location, as well as the knowledge of what states an event causes, and what events a state enables.

9.4.6   Representing Strategic Knowledge

This is a research problem rather than an exercise, but the simplicity and concreteness of micro COACH may make it easier to approach. One of the main claims of the real COACH system was the existence of domain *independent* strategic planning knowledge. Our M-DECEIVE strategy, however, makes calls to Lisp abstraction and calculation functions that are quite specific to football plays. Ideally, M-DECEIVE (and M-FORK from the exercise above) should contain only domain independent concepts such as mutual exclusion, finding detected events and plan switchover points, and so on. Then there should be separate knowledge mapping these general concepts into the specific domain of football. The way to do this is to "migrate" all the domain-specific knowledge in the Lisp code into MOPs. For example, we've already captured some enablement knowledge in MOPs, so that particular Lisp code would work in any domain, as long as the appropriate enablement MOPs were in memory. Examples of domain-specific functions are EVENT-EXCLUSION-P (Listing 9.10), DEFENSIVE-DETECT-INFO (Listing 9.13), and REMOVE-GOAL-STEP (Listing 9.16). Any time you see a call to ABSTP, you probably are looking at a domain-specific function. Your job is to find ways to move this knowledge out of Lisp and into MOPs.

10

Case-based Parsing

Charles E. Martin

10.1 Introduction

A crucial issue faced by any natural language understander is connecting the input text to the understander's prior knowledge and goals. This cannot be done solely on the basis of the input text. It requires a model in which access to prior knowledge and goals is an integral part of the parsing process. Case-based parsing meets this requirement. This chapter provides an introduction to the theory of case-based parsing and describes current research aimed at implementing a model of case-based parsing in DMAP, the Direct Memory Access Parsing program.

10.1.1 Background

The aim of a case-based parser is to recognize which already-existing memory structures are most relevant to the input, where "most relevant" is determined by the understander's plans and goals. This aim differs from that of traditional models of parsing which attempt to construct a syntactic analysis [Thorne *et al.*, 1968; Bobrow and Fraser, 1969; Woods, 1970; Winograd, 1972; Kaplan, 1975; Periera and Warren, 1980; Marcus, 1980] or a conceptual meaning structure [Wilks, 1973; Wilks, 1975; Riesbeck, 1974; Birnbaum and Selfridge, 1981; Dyer, 1983; Lytinen, 1984] for a text.

> Case-based parsing is primarily a *recognition* process.

Just as research in conceptual analysis questioned the early assumption that a syntactic analysis would be required as the front-end to a complete lan-

319

guage understanding system, we question whether a full conceptual (or syntactic) analysis is required for the successful identification of relevant memory structures. "Why should I care about what this person is saying to me?" becomes the primary concern of the understander. The determination of syntactic or conceptual analyses should serve a secondary, instrumental role.

Since case-based parsing addresses a different goal than previous parsers, the algorithm for a case-based parser is different as well. Certain aspects of the algorithm encode syntactic or conceptual knowledge, but the algorithm as a whole is concerned with providing access to the pre-existing memory structures of the understander at the earliest possible point in natural language processing. It is a claim of our theory that this early access to memory structures is essential to understanding.

10.1.2   Case-based Parsing

At its most basic level, case-based parsing is simply recognizing that the input is the "same old story."

> Most interest rates rose slightly yesterday in sluggish activity.
>
> — *The Wall Street Journal*, July 19, 1988

If you follow the financial pages, this is the kind of statement that you can count on seeing three or four times a week. Most readers flip right past this statement, and for good reason; their response to this kind of text is "same stuff, different day."

Before the reader can flip the page, however, two principles fundamental to case-based parsing have been at work. The first is *memory organization.* This "same old story" is expressed here in terms of "standard headline about interest rates: ignore it." This is a prescriptive memory structure; it directs the understander in the further pursuit of its goals. What does this kind of memory structure look like? What relation does it bear to more standard meaning representations? Case-based parsing attempts to identify relevant memory structures, but they must be memory structures *in memory* for this to work. What kind of memory organization does a case-based parser have?

Memory organization is central to a case-based parser.

The second principle is *memory search.* Given the existence of a suitable memory for case-based parsing, how does the reader locate the relevant memory structures? What clues are available from the text, what clues are available from memory, and how are different sources of information integrated?

A case-based parser must bridge the gap between the primitive lexical items of the input and the prescriptive memory structures identified as the output of the understanding process. What are the requirements and constraints of memory search in a case-based parser?

> Memory search is central to a case-based parser.

10.1.3   Memory Organization

The case-based parsing hypothesis is that the memory structures such as "standard text on interest rates: ignore it" constitute the correct parse of the input text. These memory structure have very little to do with the specific meaning representation which might be built for a text by a conceptual analyzer (Figure 10.1). Rather, their definitions are phrased in terms more suited to the understander's plans and goals: "this is standard, so you don't have to pay attention to it." To this extent, these representations are idiosyncratic; we would expect a bond trader to have a very different memory structure for this particular input, *e.g.*, "call customers looking to buy."

> Case-based parsing relies on the idiosyncratic plans and goals of the understander.

Furthermore, a text can — and should — reference many memory structures, each structure being a different characterization of the input in goal-related terms. The notion of a single meaning for a text is abandoned in case-based parsing.

Figure 10.1 illustrates the different level of representation required by a case-based parser. A case-based parser must recognize a memory structure which makes a coherent whole of the input and the existing structure of plans and goals of the understander. The level of representation afforded by conceptual analysis is simply too impoverished for this task. Case-based parsing in DMAP consists mainly of recognizing which *Memory Organization Packages*, or MOPs, are most relevant to the input. Previous chapters have covered MOPs in detail.

> MOPs are the organizational unit for the memory of a case-based parser.

Case-based parsing requires a change in the notion of what constitutes the *output* of a successful parse. Conventional parsers that construct a representation of the meaning of an input text generally return a representation as the

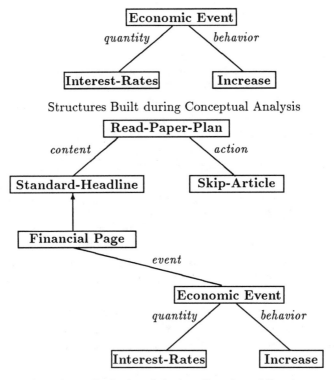

Structures Built during Conceptual Analysis

Structures Referenced during Case-based Parsing

Figure 10.1: Conceptual Analysis versus Case-based Parsing

output of the parsing process. A case-based parser, however, may be called upon to recognize multiple memory structures in the course of processing an input text. What is significant about these memory structures is not their individual representations, but their connections to other memory structures which may also be relevant to the text. The parser's set of expectations and references determine which memory structures will be recognized. It is this set of expectations and references which changes as a result of the parsing process.

The output of a case-based parser can be characterized as *a new state of memory*. Some structures will have been referenced by an input text or inference process, and some will be expected. Although new memory structures will be added when specific information is not already in memory, it is the state of references and expectations which constititute the real output of the system.

> The output of a case-based parser is a new state of memory.

10.1.4 Memory Search

A case-based parser uses linguistic clues such as individual words to direct the memory search process to concepts in memory. The task of memory search is to connect these scattered references by finding the MOPs which best organize the input. Since it is likely that alternative organizational strategies will be possible, the memory search process must be capable of disambiguating between alternative MOPs.

> Case-based parsers must find the most specific MOPs that best organize the input.

The processing knowledge which a case-based parser uses for this task is in the form of *expectations*. Expectations are based on the common-sense idea that people are able to make predictions about what is likely to happen in the future based upon what happened in the past and their previous experience. Expectations have always been a part of natural language systems: syntactic analyzers derived expectations from a grammar of the language, and conceptual analyzers derived expectations from information associated with incomplete conceptual representations [Birnbaum and Selfridge, 1981].

In a case-based parser, expectations are derived from stereotypical examples of language use which point to MOPs in memory. These are the *indexes* for a case-based parser. The text "Milton Friedman says interest rates will rise as a consequence of the monetary explosion," for example, would fit the

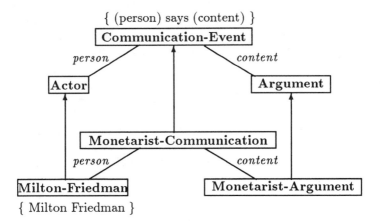

Figure 10.2: Milton Friedman's Argument

index "(some person) says (something)." This is a pretty general index, and
it points to a pretty general MOP. We will write this kind of index as:

$\{$ *(person)* **says** *(content)* $\} \longleftrightarrow$ COMMUNICATION-EVENT

This index ties a particular pattern of language use to a particular memory
structure.

> Case-based parsers use specific examples of language use to
> index memory structures.

Indexes such as this pattern provide the link between higher-level expectations and lower-level concepts derived from the input. To illustrate this
link, suppose the text given above were input to a case-based parser. Further
suppose there exists a high-level expectation that a communication event may
appear in the input. The system finds the index given above and determines
that the first sequential element of the pattern is *(person)*. In Figure 10.2,
this is a reference to the packaging link between the communication event and
person MOPs. The system generates a new expectation pointing to the person
MOP.

The linguistic phrase "Milton Friedman" is a reference to the Milton Friedman MOP, representing the famous University of Chicago economist. In the
abstraction hierarchy of memory, Milton Friedman is a monetarist, a monetarist is an economist, and an economist is a person. The reference to Milton
Friedman is therefore also a reference to an economist and a reference to a

person, which satisfies the expectation for a person. Since the reference was more specific than the expectation, the original expectation for a communication event is subjected to a process called *concept refinement*, which creates a more refined expectation for a monetarist communication (Figure 10.2).

After reading "says," which matches the lexical item **says** in the pattern of the index, the next sequential element of the pattern is *(content)*. Since the high-level expectation has been refined to monetarist communications, the system now expects a monetarist argument. If one is seen, then every element of the pattern will have been recognized. This generates a reference to the monetarist communication MOP, and this reference may in turn satisfy some larger expectation.

This discussion gives a general idea of the way in which MOP-organized memory can make use of language-processing information in the form of particular patterns of language use. As concepts are derived from the input, expectations which point to those concepts within the abstraction hierarchy of memory are satisfied. In addition, new expectations are created, which provide the processing knowledge needed to direct memory search toward connecting these concepts with the most relevant MOPs in memory.

10.1.5   Understander Goals

In the previous discussion, we assumed that there was an initial high-level expectation that a communication event might be implicated in the input. Where did this expectation come from? In the case of a low-level concept such as "communication event," it was probably derived from an index pattern attached to a higher-level concept. Ultimately, however, there must be some top-level expectations which are simply present in the system. These expectations comprise the answer to the understander's question: "Why do I care *at all* about this text?"

One motivation for work on case-based parsing has been the inability of previous analyzers to handle significant amounts of word-sense ambiguity. The obvious solution has always been "bring more knowledge to bear on the situation," in particular, knowledge beyond the conceptual level, at the episodic, MOP-organized level. But actually implementing this solution has been stymied by the memory-parser communication bottleneck. The more knowledge the memory finds relevant, the more messages it has to send to the parser.

Our solution to this bottleneck has two parts. First, we remove the distinction between parsing and searching memory. Parsing *is* memory search, and when search finds something, the parser has it automatically. Second, we control memory search using top-level expectations.

> The understander's goals are its top-level expectations.

For our model case-based reasoner, operating in the domain of economics, a typical goal is to come to a conclusion about a probable future state of the economy; for example, "What will happen to interest rates?" A goal like this generates a number of high-level expectations, such as "Look for economists making predictions about interest rates."

This may seem straightforward, but the important point is that there must be an explicit identification of the memory structures (economists' opinions about interest rates) which are relevant to achieving the system's goal. These memory structures may be abstract, in the sense that communication event, above, is abstract; they constitute expectations which can be refined to more specific levels and serve to disambiguate the input.

10.1.6   Output

Figure 10.3 presents an example of what the "output" of a case-based parser looks like. This is taken from our current implementation, DMAP [Riesbeck and Martin, 1985]. The figure is a selection of some of the MOPs in the computer program's knowledge base which are referred to in the program trace described in section 10.8. Lines with arrowheads denote abstraction relationships; lines without arrowheads denote packaging relationships where the packaged MOP appears below the packaging MOP in the figure. All packaging relationships are labeled.

The text used for the example is: "Donald Regan: On a long-term basis, interest rates are headed down." Most of the MOPs in the figure existed in memory prior to parsing this text. All new MOPs have names with a ".<number>" extension, such as `Support.8`. Eight of the MOPs created in parsing the text appear in the figure.

The essential difference between a case-based parser and previous theories of parsing can be demonstrated by reference to the figure. The MOP `IR-Communication.5`, along with `Donald-Regan` and `IR-Decrease.3`, represents the communication event referred to in the text: a communication took place, in which Donald Regan was the actor of the communication, and the mental object communicated was that interest rates would decrease. This is as far as previous theories of parsing would go in understanding the text.

The remaining thirteen out of sixteen MOPs depicted in the figure demonstrate how a case-based parser integrates the input into its existing knowledge, arriving at a conclusion as to why Regan said what he did.

Based on texts previously parsed, the parser expected Regan to support the argument that interest rates would *increase*. Regan's actual statement

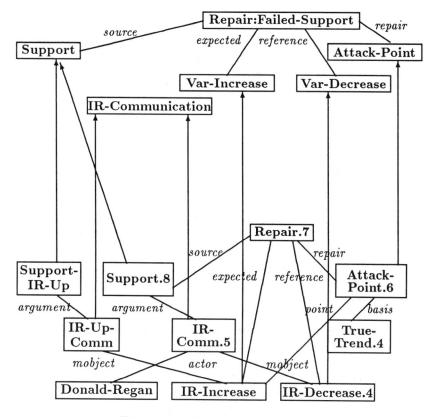

Figure 10.3: Case-based Parsing Output

contradicts this hypothesis, causing the system to *explain* why Regan's actual argument did not match its expectations. The failure of the expectation for an argument support indexes the MOP `Repair:Failed-Support`, which suggests that Regan is instead *attacking* the point that interest rates will rise (`Attack-Point.6`), and claiming that interest rates are actually decreasing (`True-Trend.4`).

Section 10.8 presents a detailed trace of this example. For now, the important point is to note that a case-based parser has a dynamic memory which changes as a result of the parsing process. This new state of memory is the true output of the parsing process; a representation of the "meaning" of the input text alone cannot adequately reflect the impact a text has had on memory and the future behavior of the parser.

10.1.7   History

The fundamental hypothesis of case-based parsing is that access to prior knowledge in the form of domain-specific, dynamic memory structures is crucial to the earliest stages of natural language understanding. Two observations led to this position. The first was the failure of conceptual analyzers ever to change the way in which they understood a sentence. Conceptual analyzers constructed the same representation from the same sentence, where the representations were derived by a fixed lexicon of productions. But people clearly change their understanding on the basis of their experience, their goals, even seemingly low-level considerations such as "did I just see this sentence," which should naturally implicate such memory structures as "why is there repetition here?"

The second observation was that conceptual analysis did not adequately address the problems that had originally motivated the paradigm. Issues such as lexical ambiguity have remained difficult problems for conceptual analyzers. Selectional restrictions and scriptal lexicons, the tools of a conceptual analyzer, have not proven adequate to these tasks.

The theoretical development of dynamic memory [Schank, 1982] led to the recognition that memory structures at a higher level than Conceptual Dependency could organize information necessary for case-based parsing and supply higher-level expectations. Lebowitz's IPP [Lebowitz, 1980] and Kolodner's CYRUS [Kolodner, 1984] were first attempts at using MOPs to organize knowledge for understanding. Lytinen's MOPTRANS [Lytinen, 1984] included a conceptual analyzer that made use of MOPs for disambiguation and concept refinement at a specific level of "actions."

The issue of ambiguity in natural language, however, is more pervasive [Birnbaum, 1986]. What is required is a theory of natural language understanding which integrates the parsing process with memory structures at any level of representation. Quillian [1969] demonstrated the possibility of such a system with his Teachable Language Comprehender (TLC). He integrated memory and parsing by attaching linguistic phrases, called *form tests*, to specific memory structures. An algorithm called *marker passing* was used to connect individual concepts with higher-level structures; the form tests were then used to disambiguate and choose the correct interpretation.

The Direct Memory Access Parser is a case-based parser. DMAP is an attempt to show how ideas from Quillian can be integrated with the Schank's dynamic memory to allow memory structures to influence parsing at all levels of representation.

10.2 The Case-based Parser

Case-based parsing is the idea of parsing by remembering. When headlines about the economy catch our eye, we don't have to construct an entire plausible interpretation of the headline before trying to recall what it could relate to. Talk about the budget deficit in the 1980's instantly recalls the considerable media discussion of this economic problem, as well as a host of ancillary issues such as the possibility of a tax hike, and what positions presidential candidates and congressmen take in an election year.

Parsing from cases means remembering past instances of language use so they can be recognized again, and remembering past conceptualizations so they can be recalled. Case-based parsing is very different from conceptual analysis. Questions of memory organization, indexing, and memory search are of central importance to a case-based parser because a case-based parser must operate within an existing memory model.

The parsing task is a memory search problem. Concepts are not constructed from pieces derived from the input. Instead, concepts already exist which fit most needs of the understander. The task is to use the clues supplied by the task to locate the most relevant concepts and modify them as needed to reflect the differences between what is seen and what is already known. Because a case-based parser makes use of memory, it can make use of expectations derived from that memory. These expectations drive the parsing process.

10.3 A Theory of Case-based Parsing

Previous work in natural language understanding has tackled a number of difficult problems. Some of their constraints and objectives are irrelevant for case-based parsing, but in most cases the knowledge these approaches used must be reflected in the understanding task. If parsing is viewed as a memory problem, the basic features of past natural language systems must find expression in memory structures and process knowledge for memory search.

- Instead of accessing a general grammar of language syntax to determine the related elements of an utterance, a case-based parser captures the idiosyncratic ways in which language is used to reference particular concepts in memory.

- Instead of building conceptualizations to represent the meaning of an input text, a case-based parser makes use of the elements of conceptual analysis to direct the memory search process to concepts which organize those elements.

- Instead of relying on memory to disambiguate possible interpretations after parsing has been performed, a case-based parser uses the goals and expectations in memory to disambiguate the input during the parsing process.

The output of case-based parsing is a state of memory where relevant memory structures have been referenced and possibly extended to reflect new information in the input. In addition, the set of expectations in memory will be changed as index patterns are partially recognized by these references.

The output of case-based parsing includes changes to memory structures and the context of expectations in memory.

This means that a case-based parser's memory organization changes as it parses, both in the long-term structure of memory, and in the short-term influence of memory on parsing through the mechanism of contextual expectations. A case-based parser cannot be expected to parse the same text the same way twice in a row, since the system will be in a different state after the first interpretation.

The following sections expand upon the knowledge sources of a case-based parser, how case-based parsing integrates these sources, and how interpretation changes the memory organization of the parser.

10.3.1   Linguistic Knowledge

Modern linguistic theory seeks to "capture the significant generalizations" in language use. This work has focused almost exclusively on looking for syntactic patterns Case-based parsing, however, is more concerned with characterizing how text refer to concepts. Becker [1975] advanced the thesis that most of language use is highly stereotyped; in such situations, specific phrasal patterns may do a better job of picking out those relevant linguistic units.

Most interest rates rose slightly yesterday in sluggish activity.

For example, this text might usefully be broken down into at least the following phrasal patterns.

1. { interest rates }

2. { *(quantity) (change)* }

3. { *(price-change)* in *(market-exchange)* }

Not only can phrasal patterns organize a text into coherent linguistic units, they can also be represented as and linked to specific memory structures. In other words, since phrasal patterns can be memory structures in their own right, they can be used by the recognition process. The combination of a phrasal pattern and its connection to a MOP memory structure is what we have been calling an *index pattern*.

> Phrasal patterns (as memory structures) can be used to recognize other memory structures.

Becker's conception of phrasal patterns representing specific linguistic knowledge is the basis for the richer knowledge structure of index patterns. Since index patterns are connected to memory structures, they may contain references to the relationships between memory structures. Hence the index pattern for communication events of { *(actor)* says *(concept)* }, which explicitly refers to the *actor* and *concept* packaging relationships of memory.

> Index patterns refer to memory packaging relationships, not specific memory structures.

Since packaging relationships are passed down the abstraction hierarchy, index patterns at a very general level, such as the one for communication events, generate valid expectations after concept refinement to specific levels such as the one for monetarist communication.

10.3.2   Integrating Knowledge Sources

Index patterns represent stereotypical patterns of language use, and MOPs represent general and episodic knowledge. Each index pattern is connected to one or more MOPs in memory.

Index patterns are recognized when all their (sequential) pieces are referenced. If specializations of these pieces are involved, the MOP to which the index pattern is connected is refined to a comparable level of specialization. Whenever an index pattern is recognized and the MOP it is connected to is expected, the MOP becomes referenced.

The case-based parser's attempt to connect input text and references with high-level expectations is reminiscent of Granger's [1980] work on connecting bottom-up and top-down inferences in the ARTHUR program. Granger's research predated work on dynamic memory, and the simple two-step connections between unambiguous input and top-level memory structures made a very simple approach feasible. Case-based parsing can be seen as an attempt to perform the same kind of inferential connection with a structurally complex memory organization and ambiguous input domain.

10.3.3   Dynamic Memory

One motivation for research in case-based parsing was our belief that previous theories of natural language understanding did not reflect our common-sense observation that reading a sentence changes the way future sentences are read. A classic question for natural language parsers is, "Why doesn't your parser get bored reading the same text over and over again?" There is no answer for a conceptual analyzer, since the fact that a text has been read is not represented in the knowledge structures, i.e., the lexicon, used by a conceptual analyzer.

A case-based parser does not have a lexicon in the usual sense. There is no dictionary linking a word to its word senses. Instead, words are linked to the index patterns they appear in. Since these patterns are in turn linked to the very MOPs that the memory search and construction processes affect, a case-based parser's lexicon automatically changes as texts are read. The lexicon is a *dynamic memory* [Schank, 1982] that changes as understanding takes place.

A case-based parser, therefore, is not in the position of a conceptual analyzer which reads the same text fifty times and generates the same conceptual representation all fifty times. Parsing truly influences memory, and a case-based parser has the potential to represent and use knowledge about its own "interactions with text." We say a case-based parser has the potential, because for a case-based parser to truly represent and use this knowledge requires that the memory structures and index patterns of the system be capable of *recognizing* this knowledge.

> Case-based parsers could get bored if they needed to.

What this means is that the system must have expectations which can be satisfied by the situation in question. A future case-based parser, perhaps interacting with many users, might find it useful to recognize when a user is giving it the same text it has already read, since it would be able to devote more resources to its other tasks.

This aspect of case-based parsing allows the exploration of a new level of understanding for texts. For example, summarization has long been a task of story understanders. "Summarization" usually ends up meaning paraphrasing the input or returning a knowledge-structure representing the input such as a *script* [Schank and Abelson, 1977]. But consider the case of a program designed to read articles about the economy. Most articles present conflicting views on the economy; this lack of consensus might lead to "summarizations" which are paraphrases of all the input arguments. This seems unsatisfactory.

What we would really like a "summary" to be is an *opinion* the parser comes to have about the article. Replacing the summarization task with the opinion-formation task, of course, means that we need a theory about how understanders come to hold opinions. Here is one heuristic which might be useful in the economic domain.

Heuristic 1: If one economist corroborates the opinion of another, there is suggestive evidence that the opinion is worth holding.

Some wags might prefer the inverse: that the opinion is worth discarding. Either way, the task of forming an opinion and the above heuristic combine to make it *useful* for the system to recognize when it is reading the same opinion over again. Making this heuristic part of the domain of applicability of the system requires creating memory structures and index patterns which can recognize this situation.

10.4 Modifying Memory

So far, not much has been said about the tasks of the understanding system. In a sense, they are outside the immediate scope of *how* a case-based parser works, but it is certainly incumbent upon a theory of case-based parsing to demonstrate that the theory in fact *will* work on a non-trivial example. Below

we present such a task, and later we demonstrate our approaches to some of
the problems involved.

10.4.1   Opinion Formation in Economics

For our economics domain, opinion formation about the future behavior of the
economy is a reasonable task for an understander. The following article poses
a question about interest rates and then presents multiple viewpoints on the
subject.[1]

> **Which Way Interest Rates? Leading Economists Look at
> Crystal Balls.**
>
> The *New York Times* interviewed 10 of the nation's leading econ-
> omists for their views.
>
> Milton Friedman: Interest rates will rise as an inevitable conse-
> quence of the monetary explosion we've experienced over the past
> year.
>
> John Kenneth Galbraith: My guess is that the Federal Reserve is
> going to have a nasty choice between a renewal of inflation and the
> raising of interest rates
>
> Alan Greenspan: Let me start by stipulating that elements which
> are making up the recovery at this stage aren't substantially interest-
> sensitive, and that a 1 or 2 percent increase will have a very small
> impact on economic growth over the next six months. Having said
> that, you now have a prescription for short-term money tightening
> by the Fed.
>
> Donald Regan: On a long-term basis, rates are headed down.
> There has been some rise in short-term rates over the past few
> weeks, but interest rates always move up or down in a somewhat
> erratic fashion.
>
> Gregory Kipnis: Until we get to the fall at least, we'll see interest
> rates remaining under upward pressure, reflecting partly a concern
> about a tightness in the capital markets and a crowding out of
> borrowers.
>
> Alan Reynolds: Interest rates will be precisely where the Fed wants
> them to be. And I think now the Fed thinks they are a little too
> high.

---

[1] *The New York Times*, August 4, 1983.

> Herbert Stein: I think interest rates are rising and probably will continue to rise a little further.

What counts as understanding for a text such as this? Our feeling is that coming up with isolated meaning representations of these separate texts is not enough. What we are after is the ability to integrate the knowledge referenced by all these texts to come to a summary opinion about the state of interest rates in the economy.

The points made earlier about the idiosyncratic nature of case-based parsing must be repeated here. No conclusion from a complex text such as this could hope to be free of the bias lent by personal experience and understanding. With this stipulation in mind, one target conclusion is the following:

> The future of interest rates is uncertain, but most economists seem to think they will rise, if only to keep inflation low. Donald Regan thinks they will fall, but he has to say that as Secretary of the Treasury.

This is not the actual output of a case-based parser, but an example of one possible opinion for an economic reasoner to come to.

1. The conclusion makes use of knowledge not found in the input (Donald Regan was Secretary of the Treasury).

2. It focuses on those aspects relevant to the task (which way will interest rates move) and ignores details (the economic consequences of a 1 or 2 percent increase in interest rates).

3. Memory structures implicated in the conclusion are organized by relationships which are a wholly outside the input text. For example, Donald Regan's job is cited as part of an *explanation* as to why his statement is at odds with the conclusion.

A case-based parser capable of handling this task must be able to modify its own memory. Further, those modifications must affect the future course of processing. A case-based parser accomplishes this by integrating memory and parsing.

10.4.2   Simple Memory Modification

It is not enough to just recognize structures in memory. A case-based parser has to be able to record "where it has been." For example, if there is no previous memory structure representing Donald Regan's opinion about interest

rates, a more specific version of the general "opinion" concept would have to
be created with the particular information carried in the input. This is the
simplest case of a *specialization failure*.

Specialization failures occur when no refinement exists.

Specialization failures occur when there does not exist an appropriate refinement from a general structure. This is a "failure" for the parser since its
goal is to *recognize* memory structures, and, in this case, there is none. More
complex failures arise when the memory search algorithm has already committed itself to a particular refinement, only to discover that that refinement
does not adequately characterize the input.

The complex case will be discussed in the next section. This section is
concerned with the most general of failures. Ultimately, all failures must
eventually "bottom out" in this general case in which some specification of a
general structure is required.

Specialization failures cause new memory structures to be
built.

The "repair" for this kind of failure is simply to create a new memory
structure, in the same abstraction hierarchy as the general structure and with
packaging links reflecting the specific knowledge derived from the input. This
is directly analogous to the way in which a case-based planner stores new
plans. The location in memory for the new structure is given explicitly by the
general structure and the packaged components.

Memory structures built by a case-based parser are automatically stored in memory.

This method of creating new structures means that determining where
in memory new concepts should go is handled automatically. All concepts
built by a case-based parser are not only in the same representation language
as concepts in memory, they are immediately *organized* in memory with all
other concepts. This means that a case-based parser can create MOPs which
take advantage of the efficiencies of abstraction and packaging relationships
in memory.

10.4.3 Complex Specialization Failures

More complex case of specialization failure occur when:

1. There are multiple refinements for an expectation possible when a reference to a specific concept intersects with an expectation of a more general one.

2. The refined expectation is overspecialized and incorrectly predicts subsequent references.

A case-based planner such as CHEF does not attempt to do concept refinement or retrieval until all features of the input case have been determined. Hence, the second situation can't occur and the first doesn't matter; if several recipes match the input equally well, pick any one and adapt it.

Unfortunately, this least-commitment approach is not a viable approach for a parser. Parsing is inherently a sequential process; solutions of least-commitment would not allow the kind of incremental refinement and retrieval which generate domain-specific expectations during the course of the parsing process.

Another standard solution is to have the parser "back up" and try alternative interpretations [Woods, 1970]. But this won't handle the case where there aren't *any* refinements that adequately characterize the input. For example, a system with a few examples of arguments about interest rates may be confronted with an argument relating interest rates to a new economic quantity. In this situation, no existing refinement will work.

10.4.4 Repairing Failures

A third approach is to have the parser repair the failure and continue. Failure repair is the method of choice for a case-based parser, and for essentially the same reasons that it is useful to a case-based planner. The fundamental idea is that past knowledge structures may contain useful information even if they do not precisely match the input. In such a situation, a case-based planner such as CHEF *adapts* past plans and *repairs* current plan failures. A case-based parser must do the same, but *incrementally* as a parse proceeds.

When a failure occurs in case-based parsing, the following information is available.

- The concept which was referenced.

- The concept which was expected.

- The source of the expectation.

A case-based parser needs to know what was in the input, what was expected by the system, and what role the concept was meant to serve. For example, an input such as "Lester Thurow says interest rates will rise as a consequence of the monetary explosion" may result in a failure, for which the concept referenced in the input is Lester Thurow, the concept expected by the system is Milton Friedman (since this is a monetarist argument), and the source of the expectation is an opinion by an economist about interest rates.

The source of the expectation is important because it constrains what kind of *repairs* will be acceptable. For example, the repair "Lester Thurow agrees with Milton Friedman" is acceptable since it organizes the referenced concept, the expected concept, and provides the knowledge necessary to satisfy the source: Thurow's opinion is, in fact, the same as Friedman's.

Our theory of repairs for a case-based parser is not as complex as those in CHEF or COACH. This is partly because our failures are simpler and partly because we insist on being able to represent repair knowledge in MOPs. Because repair knowledge is in MOPs, the standard process for memory search and construction is capable of searching for and implementing relevant repairs.

Figure 10.3 shows a repair for Donald Regan's argument. Given the preceding texts, the parser expected that the current text would say that interest rates would rise. Instead, Regan predicted a decrease. The structure `Repair:Failed-Support` is a general MOP representing this particular failure. The `Repair.7` structure is the specific version created to reflect the unique application of this general knowledge to this specific cirucmstance. As part of the repair, DMAP infers that Regan is attacking the previous arguments for a rise in interest rates. If there were more MOPs characterizing Regan or this particular argument, the memory search processes might find a different repair to be more relevant.

10.5   Word-sense Ambiguity

A major motivation for this work on case-based parsing has been the inadequate way in which conceptual analysis has faced those problems of natural language understanding which motivated its genesis in the first place. Word-sense ambiguity is a primary example [Birnbaum, 1986]. This occurs when conceptual analyzers are faced with multiple possible representational structures where it is not clear which is the right structure for the specific circumstance.

10.5.1 Selectional Restrictions

Alternatives for handling disambiguation in conceptual analysis primarily involve one of two techniques. Selectional restrictions are taxonomic constraints on which structures can serve as part of another structure. For example, the actor of a communication event may be required to be a person. A word sense which fails such a constraint is ignored.

> Case-based parsers implement selectional restrictions.

When a case-based parser references a concept, only a limited set of expectations may be satisfied. The taxonomic constraints of selectional restrictions come into play as a function of the abstraction relationships within MOP-memory. The reference can only intersect expectations which point to concepts in the same abstraction hierarchy as the referenced concept. This means that expectations which have taxonomic constraints not inclusive of the referenced concept will "miss" being satisfied by the reference. Unsatisfied, the expectation will have no further consequences on processing, and the selectional restriction is implemented automatically.

10.5.2 Scriptal Lexicons

The second technique is that of the scriptal lexicon, which associates certain word senses with words in particular contexts. For example, "home" might be taken to be the pentagonal plate used for batting if and only if the baseball game memory structure is active.

> Case-based parsers extend the scriptal lexicon to include all language use.

The use of scriptal lexicons to predict certain word senses in certain contexts is broadened in a case-based parser to the point where *every* word sense is the product of a scriptal lexicon. Words are connected to word senses (*i.e.*, concepts) by index patterns, and predicting plausible interpretations (*i.e.*, concepts) primes the relevant linguistic phrases. The lexicon of a case-based parser is *dynamic*, and all entries in that lexicon are the product of the current context of predictions in memory.

10.5.3   Beyond Word-sense Ambiguity

One consequence of this scheme is that a case-based parser behaves as if many scripts were simultaneously active. This makes it highly probable that more than one reference for an ambiguous word or concept will satisfy an expectation. This is equivalent to finding multiple interpretations of the same input.

> Case-based parsers have multiple scripts active simultaneously.

This is a problem for conceptual analyzers. The presence of multiple interpretations means that the parser ultimately fails to disambiguate or, under a "choose and back up later" paradigm, probably disambiguates erroneously.

The index patterns of a case-based parser differ from the straightforward idea of the scriptal lexicon in that they contain knowledge of the relationships from concepts to concepts as well as from concepts to lexical items. For example, the index pattern for a communication event references the actor of that event. This means that multiple references are disambiguated by the expectations in memory, regardless of whether those references are at the lexical or conceptual level. Since the expectation generated by index patterns are not necessarily lexical, the technique of disambiguation by these expectations is generally termed "scriptal expectations" rather than "scriptal lexicon."

The consequence for case-based parsing is that the multiple senses from multiple active "scriptal" index patterns are subject to disambiguation by higher-level expectations. Since there is no arbitrary "grain size" of representation being constructed by a case-based parser, there is no requirement that the input be fully disambiguated at any particular level. Multiple references are possible, and only those for which expectations have been generated will affect future processing.

A further augmentation of traditional models of word-sense disambiguation is the fact that selectional restrictions, implemented through the mechanism of the abstraction hierarchy of the memory, can refer to any type of memory structure represented in the hierarchy.

> Case-based parsers disambiguate ambiguity at one level with expectations at a higher level.

It should be noted that references which do not satisfy any expectations are simply discarded, as are expectations which are never satisfied by a reference. References and expectations represent, in effect, the propagation of bottom-up and top-down knowledge through the system; only when there is an intersection is work performed.

The technique of disambiguating by scriptal expectations was proposed in [Riesbeck and Schank, 1976], and was the foundation of the parsing theory in IPP [Lebowitz, 1980]. This system had a memory organized by MOP structures, but the parser was essentially a conceptual analyzer making reference to memory in order to derive scriptal expectations. This limited it by the same constraints of other conceptual analyzers; the lack of a uniform representation for parsing knowledge (case-based parsing's index patterns) and a uniform algorithm for performing memory search allowed only one script to be active at any given time, limiting its power to that of selectional restrictions and scriptal lexicons.

10.6 Implementing a Case-based Parser

How can expectation-based understanding influence parsing at all levels of representation? Basing our work on that of [Quillian, 1969], we decided to implement the memory search process as a marker-passing algorithm. Our DMAP parser uses a marker-passing architecture to identify relevant memory structures from the input text and the expectations in memory. Two kinds of markers are used in the system: *activation* markers, which capture information about the input text and the currently referenced memory structures, and *prediction* markers, which indicate which memory structures may be expected to become referenced.

10.6.1 Marker Passing

If a prediction marker is *passed* to a concept, and an activation marker is subsequently also passed to that concept, there is said to be an *intersection* at that concept. The markers may carry more information than represented by the concept, in which case the concept may be *refined* to a more specific concept. Ultimately, the refined, intersected concept is *recognized*.

One result of this approach is that there is no one structure which can be pointed to as the "result" at any stage of processing. The state of the parser depends upon which markers have been passed to which concepts.

Also note that the marker-passing algorithm makes no explicit reference to the content of MOPs in memory. The uniform application of the marker-passing algorithm to the memory allows the expectations to drive parsing at all levels of representation. The content of those representations controls how markers are passed through memory.

> Memory search is a domain-independent algorithm, controlled
> by domain-dependent knowledge.

10.6.2 Activation Markers

Activation markers are the implementation of *referenced* concepts. Activation markers are passed up the abstraction hierarchy from their associated structures. This is a recursive process; all concepts which receive an activation marker continue to pass it on to their own abstractions. When a memory structure receives an activation marker, that concept is said to have been *activated*; the activation marker contains a pointer to the originally activated concept.

There are three general rules for passing activation markers.

A1: When a word is read, it is given an activation marker. For example, reading "Milton" puts an activation marker on the lexical node MILTON.

A2: When every element of a phrase has received an activation marker, the concept the phrase is attached to receives an activation marker. For example, when both "Milton" and "Friedman" have been read, the phrase { Milton Friedman } is completed and the concept MILTON-FRIEDMAN gets an activation-marker.

A3: When a concept gets an activation marker, it sends copies to its abstractions. For example, when MILTON-FRIEDMAN gets an activation marker, it sends a copy to PERSON.

10.6.3 Prediction Markers

Prediction markers implement *expectations*. Whenever a concept is predicted, prediction markers are created for the first elements of all the index patterns that are connected to that concept. A prediction marker captures the intuition of the "focus of attention" of the parser. A shift of attention corresponds to passing the prediction marker to a new location in memory. This occurs in response to concept activation and intersection of markers.

Prediction markers are passed under two conditions:

P1: When an element of a phrase receives an activation marker, a prediction marker is passed to the next element of the phrase.

P2: When an prediction marker is passed to a concept, all phrase capable of recognizing that concept have prediction markers passed to their first elements.

The latter is a recursive invocation of the marker-passing process at lower levels of representation.

10.6.4 Implementation and Theory

Our DMAP implementation of case-based parsing follows closely our theory about how references and expectations need to interact. This only reflects the early nature of the work on case-based parsing, and is not meant to be taken as evidence that a marker-passing algorithm is the "best" way of implementing a case-based parser.

Marker passing does hold out the attractive possibility of providing the basis for a parallel implementation of the algorithm. Little work has been done in this direction; the considerable degree of non-locality in the markers (in the form of pointers to other memory structures) would make such an implementation difficult at best.

Our particular version of marker passing, however, is distinctly different from many other versions appearing in other research. We feel that this particular implementation illuminates a few theoretical points about case-based parsing when compared to other implementations. We discuss this in the next section.

10.7 Theoretical Issues

There is a renewed interest in marker-passing models for AI [Alterman, 1985; Charniak, 1986; Granger *et al.*, 1984; Norvig, 1987] . Quillian [1969] originally suggested that markers be passed from two concepts in memory in order to find (through intersection) a semantic concept relating both. Although knowledge representation schemes and algorithms have become more sophisticated, his general approach remains exemplary.

Quillian noticed many features true of such schemes in general, such as the uselessness of *isa-plateaus* (markers meeting at common abstractions) and the poor signal-to-noise ratio (many unwanted intersections). Recent work has included Charniak's use of paths as the "backbones" of proofs for interpretations of the input, and Norvig's interesting catalog of *path shapes* which allow explicit analysis of the "syntactic structure" of the marker-passing route.[2]

Quillian's own solution to the problem was to attach "form tests" to concepts in memory; the form tests for a concept specified lexical usage that would

---

[2]Norvig uses marker passing to identify candidate concepts; subsequent validation is the task of another module. Much of Charniak's results are in the form of a general interpretation of paths, and do not depend upon the marker-passing algorithm *per se*.

correctly identify the concept. For example, in evaluating "lawyer's client," Quillian's scheme passed markers from the LAWYER and CLIENT concepts, ultimately intersecting at the EMPLOY concept. Attached to EMPLOY was the form test

{ *(source word)* + 's *(identified word)* }

which would validate "lawyer's client" as a means of identifying the EMPLOY concept. Quillian's scheme may be (drastically) simplified into the following algorithm:

Quillian Algorithm

1. Activate input concepts.

2. Spread markers from these concepts through the network.

3. Identify candidate concepts from marker intersections.

4. Apply form tests to validate the correct interpretation.

The DMAP system differs dramatically from marker-passing research referred to above. In a sense, DMAP is the reverse of Quillian's scheme. Quillian's form tests provide *ex post* validations of marker intersections. DMAP's index patterns provide *ex ante* specifications of where intersections can take place. For example, Quillian's form test could be read as providing DMAP-style marker-passing information:

{ *(professional)* + 's *(employer)* }

This pattern can be *completed* if (1) a marker intersection takes place at a concept which is in the *professional* relationship to the EMPLOY concept, (2) the morphological ending "'s" is seen, and (3) a marker intersection takes place at a concept in the *employer* relationship to EMPLOY.

Marker intersections in DMAP take place when each of two types of markers arrive at a single location. *Prediction* markers signal the expectations of the system, and are passed down relations in the packaging hierarchy. *Activation* markers signal expectations which have been satisfied, and are are passed up the abstraction hierarchy. The DMAP algorithm can be expressed in terms close to that of the Quillian algorithm.

DMAP Algorithm

1. (Quillian step 4) Get index patterns from predicted concepts.

2. (Quillian step 2a) Pass prediction markers as specified by patterns. (Invoke step (1) recursively.)

3. (Quillian step 1) Activate input concepts.

4. (Quillian step 2b) Spread activation markers up abstraction hierarchy.

5. (Quillian step 3) Identify prediction-activation intersections; invoke step (3) if the pattern is completed, otherwise invoke step (2) with remainder of pattern.

The fundamental claim supported by the DMAP implementation of case-based parsing is that many of the problems associated with lexical and explanatory ambiguity derive, not from the inherent qualities of language and understanding, but from the particular ways in which process models have attempted to account for language and understanding.

Broadly stated, the process of finding possible interpretations for an input (lexical or explanatory) and selecting between them *ex post* is replaced with a process of memory-driven recognition, in which hypotheses about the input can be expressed *ex ante*.

The traditional marker-passing model of inference, or conceptual analysis model of language understanding, has the general form: (a) find candidate interpretations, and (b) choose between them. The case-based model, implemented in DMAP, has the general form: (a) use memory to retrieve a likely interpretation based on past experience, and (b) check to see if it's correct.

> Traditional models derive hypotheses about the input; case-based parsing checks hypotheses against the input.

The approach of case-based parsing does not have to deal with the problem of explicitly choosing between alternative interpretations; this choice is made implicitly by the architecture of the memory search algorithm. The other side of this coin is that a case-based parser may miss possible interpretations in its haste to refine its expectations within the memory model. Some of these erroneous refinements will be caught as specialization failures; if the knowledge to recover from these failures is represented in memory, the system can effect some kind of repair. Other errors which are not caught are invisible to the system, and will remain so until knowledge is added which directs the memory search process to watch for and repair these failures.

Our belief is that case-based parsing offers a viable alternative to traditional models of parsing and understanding. Making hypotheses about interpretations explicit in the memory structures seems, in retrospect, to be almost a zero-th order theory of understanding. The DMAP implementation boils down to just such a theory of explicitly represented processing knowledge. Implementing this theory, however, required the kind of uniform memory organization and uniform memory process which we have discussed in this chapter.

10.8   An Example

In this section we will follow the parser through the text of the Donald Regan argument from the economic text cited above. The memory structures referenced by this example reflect one model of an understander's domain knowledge. The bias in the representation to certain interpretations is an essential part of the system; as was stated above, a case-based parser relies on its idiosyncratic organization of memory.

10.8.1   The Context for the Example

At this point in the understanding episode, the parser has already interpreted arguments by Friedman, Galbraith, and Greenspan. That is, the computer implementation has already seen the following:

THE NEW YORK TIMES

WHICH WAY INTEREST RATES ?

THE NEW YORK TIMES INTERVIEWED 10 LEADING ECONOMISTS .

MILTON FRIEDMAN : INTEREST RATES WILL RISE AS AN
INEVITABLE CONSEQUENCE OF THE MONETARY EXPLOSION WE'VE
EXPERIENCED OVER THE PAST YEAR .

JOHN KENNETH GALBRAITH : MY GUESS IS THAT THE FEDERAL
RESERVE IS GOING TO HAVE A NASTY CHOICE BETWEEN A
RENEWAL OF INFLATION AND THE RAISING OF INTEREST RATES
.

ALAN GREENSPAN : LET ME START BY STIPULATING THAT
ELEMENTS WHICH MAKE UP THE RECOVERY AREN'T
SUBSTANTIALLY INTEREST SENSITIVE . A 1 OR 2 PERCENT
INCREASE WILL HAVE A VERY SMALL IMPACT ON ECONOMIC
GROWTH OVER THE NEXT SIX MONTHS . HAVING SAID THAT ,
YOU NOW HAVE A PRESCRIPTION FOR SHORT-TERM MONEY
TIGHTENING BY THE FED .

A case-based parser does not start from a *tabula rasa.* The existing set of MOPs and phrasal patterns reflect only the current state of what is a *dynamic* memory. The system's interpretation of these arguments is now a part of its memory structures and expectations. This will affect the subsequent processing of the Regan argument:

```
DONALD REGAN : ON A LONG TERM BASIS RATES ARE HEADED
DOWN . THERE HAS BEEN SOME RISE IN SHORT-TERM RATES
OVER THE PAST FEW WEEKS BUT INTEREST RATES ALWAYS MOVE
UP OR DOWN IN A SOMEWHAT ERRATIC FASHION .
```

10.8.2 Knowledge Representation

Forming an opinion from these complex texts requires several distinct kinds of knowledge. There must be knowledge of the economics domain, knowledge of how texts are presented in this domain, and knowledge about how multiple sources of economic opinion can be related.

The economic domain model is fairly straightforward; there are economic quantities such as interest rates, actions over those quantities (increase or decrease), the behavior of those quantities in the short-term and long-term, actors who can affect the economy and their economic goals, and causal relationships between economic factors.

Knowledge about how texts are presented includes how, once a topic has been brought up, subsequent texts can be expected to refer to that topic. The knowledge which bears directly upon the opinion formation task is the knowledge of how multiple opinions are interrelated. Drawing on the work of [Birnbaum *et al.*, 1980], this knowledge is reflected in support and attack structures. These have similar structures; both organize a point and a basis for supporting or attacking that point.

The processing leading up to the example has the effect of modifying memory by the inclusion of several specialized MOPs for new support relationships. All of these support the opinion that interest rates will rise, and the multiplicity of supports causes the system to construct an internal support for this opinion, representing the concept that there are multiple external supports which are in *concord.*

This is by way of preamble, as the presence of these memory structures and their influence on parsing will be noted in the program trace described in the next section.

10.8.3 Program Trace

This section presents a detailed example of how DMAP runs on the input,

DONALD REGAN: ON A LONG TERM BASIS, INTEREST
RATES ARE HEADED DOWN.

The example presents successive words as they are seen by the parser. Following each word are the index patterns whose expectations have been satisfied
by the reference to the input word. With the index pattern is the associated
concept in memory. An asterisk (*) indicates what remains of the pattern to
be recognized. When a pattern is complete, the concept is noted as *referenced*,
and expectations which it satisfies will follow with their index patterns and
associated concepts follow.

Program annotations include:

- Specialization failures, which report which relationship failed and what
  new structure was built or used.

- Refinement failures, which report what new structure was built or used,
  the source of the failure, and any repairs which were able to be performed.

- Repairs, which report new memory structures built to record the repair
  and what the content of those concepts are.

For clarity, all structures built during this input phase, and none of the structures built during previous phases, are given names such as `IR-INCREASE.2`
or `ATTACK-POINT.6`.

```
Reading DONALD
   { DONALD * REGAN } = REGAN

Reading REGAN
   { DONALD REGAN * } = REGAN referenced
   { (actor) * (mtrans) (mobject) } = IR-UP-COMMUNICATION
       Specialization Failure: (actor) REGAN
       Built: IR-UP-COMMUNICATION.1
```

This demonstrates the parsing of a simple lexical phrase. Recognition of the
index pattern results in the reference of the `REGAN` concept, which in turn
satisfies an expectation from `IR-COMMUNICATION`. There is no refinement which
is specific to Regan, so a new specialization is built.

```
Reading :
   { : * } = MTRANS referenced
   { (actor) (mtrans) * (mobject) } = IR-UP-COMMUNICATION.1
```

```
Reading ON
    { ON * A (horizon) BASIS } = BEHAVIOR

Reading A
    { ON A * (horizon) BASIS } = BEHAVIOR

Reading LONG
    { LONG * TERM } = LONG-RUN

Reading TERM
    { LONG TERM * } = LONG-RUN referenced
    { ON A (horizon) * BASIS } = BEHAVIOR = TRUE-BEHAVIOR
```

This is the normal refinement process; the associated concept for this index pattern was BEHAVIOR, but the reference in the input to a LONG-RUN (horizon) caused refinement of the concept to that of TRUE-BEHAVIOR. (The underlying model of economic reasoning being that the long-term action of an economic quantity reflects its true behavior, rather than its (uncertain) short-term activity.)

It is worth noting here that the concept for "long" was expected because the higher-level index pattern for BEHAVIOR was looking for its horizon relationship. "Long term" was connected to this concept because of the presence of the higher-level expectation.

```
Reading BASIS
    { ON A (horizon) BASIS * } = TRUE-BEHAVIOR referenced
    { (behavior) * (event) } = TRUE-TREND
    { (behavior) * (quantity) (action) } = IR-INCREASE
        Specialization Failure:
            (behavior) TRUE-BEHAVIOR
        Built: IR-INCREASE.2

Reading RATES
    { RATES * } = RATES referenced
    { (topic) (reference) * } = INTEREST-RATES referenced
    { (behavior) (quantity) * (action) }
        = IR-INCREASE.2
```

"Interest rates" is the topic of the entire sequence of newspaper texts, and the parser has already represented this from its prior processing. Interest rates are often referred to simply as "rates," and the second index pattern in the immediately preceding trace captures the connection between the topic concept and its corresponding reference concept. Recognition of this sequence from the `reference` results in the `topic` concept being referenced. (Note that `reference` is a packaging relationship, while "referenced" is a fundamental operation of a case-based parser.)

```
Reading ARE
  { ARE * HEADED (direction) } = INCREASE

Reading HEADED
  { ARE HEADED * (direction) } = INCREASE

Reading DOWN
  { DOWN * } = DOWN referenced
  { ARE HEADED * (direction) } = INCREASE
      Refinement Failure: (direction) is DOWN not UP
      Using: DECREASE
      Source: IR-INCREASE.2 no repair
```

This is the first refinement failure so far. The expectations from the previous texts have generated an expectation at this level for another argument supporting a future increase in interest rates. The text does not support this interpretation, and so the (already constructed) text-supported interpretation DECREASE is referenced. The parser attempts to *repair* the failure by recovering the source of the expectation. Unfortunately, no repair structures are able to be found from this failed refinement.

```
  { (behavior) (quantity) (action) * }
      = IR-INCREASE.2
      Refinement Failure:
          (action) is DECREASE not INCREASE
      Built: IR-DECREASE.3
      Source: IR-UP-COMMUNICATION.1 no repair
```

This index pattern recognizes the argument for a particular economic event. Once again, the prior expectations have failed, but no repair is possible.

It should be stressed that the lack of repairs is a function of the knowledge of the system; in other words, there is no *a priori* reason why sensible repairs for this failure might not be present.

```
  { (behavior) (event) * } = TRUE-TREND
      Specialization Failure:
          (event) IR-DECREASE.3
      Built: TRUE-TREND.4
```

The TRUE-TREND structure essentially represents the concept mentioned in passing in the annotations following the word "long," above. Regan's argument results in the recognition of this index pattern and the reference of this concept. There is no refinement failure here, but a new specialization must be built.

```
{ (actor) (mtrans) (mobject) * }
    = IR-UP-COMMUNICATION.1
    Refinement Failure:
        (mobject) is IR-DECREASE.3
                  not IR-INCREASE.2
    Built: IR-COMMUNICATION.5
    Source: SUPPORT-IR-UP (argument)
            found REPAIR:FAILED-SUPPORT
    Repair: ATTACK-POINT
    Built: ATTACK-POINT.6
        (point) IR-INCREASE
        (basis) TRUE-TREND.4
    Built: SUPPORT.8
        (argument) IR-COMMUNICATION.5
    Built: REPAIR.7
        (source) SUPPORT.8
        (expected) IR-INCREASE
        (reference) IR-DECREASE.3
        (repair) ATTACK-POINT.6
```

The failure of the argument communicated by Regan to match the expectations from prior texts finds a suitable repair, REPAIR:FAILED-SUPPORT, that represents knowledge about how to argue: to challenge a point, you may attack it directly. In this case, since the parser is trying to come to a conclusion about the behavior of interest rates, challenging the previous texts' main point may be done by asserting that interest rates will decrease.

The repair is to modify memory to include a new attack structure, which contains packaging relationships to the point attacked and the basis for the attack. Since the TRUE-TREND structure is now part of memory, it is seized upon as a reasonable part of the attack structure. In paraphrase, this new concept represents "interest rates will not increase because decreasing interest rates reflect the true long-term behavior of the quantity."

```
{ (support) (attack) * } = DISPUTED-IR
    Specialization Failure: (attack) ATTACK-POINT.6
    Built: DISPUTED-IR.9
```

The fact that previous texts supported the opinion that interest rates would rise means that the current attack on that opinion indicates that the opinion is disputed. A new specialization must be built to record this interpretation.

```
{ (concord) (attack) * (basis) } = ATTACK-POINT
{ (concord) (attack) * (basis) } = ATTACK-BASIS
{ (concord) (attack) * (basis) } = ATTACK-ATTACK
```

Finally, the fact that the system had already come to an internal conclusion about interest rates based on its previous understanding provokes an internal response to the attack. Although the notion that there is concord about the behavior of interest rates is not necessarily the final decision of the system, it prompts index patterns which can be used to discredit the attack to generate expectations looking for some basis for an attack on the attack.

11

Micro DMAP

11.1 Introduction

In this chapter, we present a miniature version of the DMAP parser. This miniature has Lisp code not only for retrieving cases, but also for creating and handling predictions. The case library and lexicon are set up to parse two sentences: "Milton Friedman says interest rates will rise because of the monetary explosion," and "Arthur Laffer says interest rates will drop." The sentences are deliberately similar, to make things harder for micro DMAP. Micro DMAP has to determine that the object of the first sentence is a causal, whose antecedent looks almost, but not exactly, like the object of the second sentence, which has just a predicted event. If either sentence is parsed again, no new memory structures are created, because DMAP finds the result of the first parsing.

Unlike the real DMAP, micro DMAP does not use marker passing to search memory. There are two reasons for this. First, marker passing requires a number of additional bookkeeping functions that we felt would obscure the basic flow of control. Second, while DMAP has always been implemented with marker passing, marker passing is not an essential aspect of the theory. Any mechanism that parses by searching memory for references to predicted concepts will do. Micro DMAP is simply another way to do things. We would not be at all surprised to see yet other means for accomplishing the same goals.

One issue in both DMAPs is controlling the interactions between index patterns. Basically, DMAP has to pay attention to syntactic constraints on how text can refer to concepts.

First, let's define two terms. *Advancing* an index pattern means seeing a reference to the currently expected item in the pattern and predicting the next item. An *active* pattern is one that has been advanced at least once. Even in a small memory like micro DMAP's, there will be many index patterns active at any one time, for several reasons.

- Many words and MOPs appear in more than one index pattern, so reading a word or referencing a MOP will advance more than one index pattern.

- Most MOPs have many index pattern attached to them, either directly or inherited from abstractions. During parsing, several of those pattern may become active and eventually complete, though not necessarily at the same time.

Consider some of the patterns that are active when parsing "Milton Friedman says interest rates will rise because of the monetary explosion." There are the patterns attached to the MOP M-MTRANS, which represents communication events. These patterns look for an object of the communication, found in the INFO slot of the M-MTRANS. The filler of INFO in M-MTRANS is the MOP for any event or state, including another M-MTRANS. One bug to avoid when micro DMAP parses the Milton Friedman sentence is putting the M-MTRANS instance referenced by the sentence into its own INFO slot!

Another bug to avoid is "premature termination" of active index patterns. For example, the Milton Friedman sentence, up to but not including the "because," completes the index pattern for a prediction. In this example, it might be acceptable to interpret Friedman's argument as both a causal argument and a prediction, but suppose the "because" were replaced with "until." In that case, we would definitely not want DMAP to say that Milton Friedman predicted that interest rates would rise. This is one reason why our index patterns for M-MTRANS insist on seeing PERIOD before completing.

Another bug is "overlapping patterns." The causal MOP M-CAUSAL in micro DMAP's memory has the following index patterns:

- *state change* as a consequence of *state change*

- *state change* because of *state change*

- if *state change* then *state change*

- *state change* can cause *state change*

If micro DMAP reads "Interest rates will rise because of an increase in the money supply; what can cause interest rates to rise?" We don't want DMAP to "see" "an increase in the money supply ... can cause interest rates to rise ...." Although patterns can nest inside each other, and even interleave with each other, this kind of overlapping, where the same piece of text is grabbed by several patterns, is not desirable.

To help control index patterns, micro DMAP keeps track of when particular activations of index patterns start and stop in a sentence. The pattern "Milton Friedman" in the example sentence starts at 1 and ends at 2, while the pattern "*actor* says that *info*" starts at 1 and ends at 13 (counting the period as a position). Each word and MOP in an index pattern must appear at the appropriate position after the starting point of the pattern. Thus, if "Milton" is seen in position 1 of the sentence, "Friedman" must be seen in position 2. If it is, then an *actor* has been seen in positions 1 through 2 of the sentence. This means that the "says that" must be seen in the positions 3 and 4 and that the index pattern referencing the *info* must be start in position 5. Micro DMAP builds *prediction structures* to keep track of things. In this case, after "Milton Friedman" has been read, the prediction structure for "*actor* says that *info*" would record that the pattern started at position 1 and that the *actor* was filled with the MOP for "Milton Friedman." The structure would also predict that "says that" will appear in position 3.

There is an initial static set of *default predictions*, one for each index pattern that has been defined. As index patterns are advanced, *dynamic predictions* are created by copying default or dynamic predictions, updating the slot and index pattern information.

11.2   Implementing Micro DMAP

The top-level function to run DMAP appears in Listing 11.1.

(DMAP *word-list*) reads the words in *word-list* from left to right, triggering whatever predictions apply. If no predictions are triggered by a word, it is ignored, and the sentence position variable *SENT-POS* is not advanced. Trace messages are printed, indicating what MOPs are activated, and, at the end of processing, any predictions waiting for the next input word are shown.

DMAP picks up where the last call to DMAP left off, using any predictions set up previously. This is in keeping with the idea that DMAP should be a text parser, not a sentence parser. It also makes debugging easier. You can DMAP part of sentence, turn on whatever tracing features your version of Lisp has, and then DMAP some more. Use DMAP-INIT in Listing 11.2 to clear the current set of predictions. This does not remove any memory structures that have been built. To do that, you need to clear memory and reload your MOP definition files.

Listing 11.2 defines several global variables and tables, primarily for holding predictions generated by index patterns.

```
(DEFUN DMAP (WORD-LIST)
  (FOR (WORD :IN WORD-LIST)
    :DO (FORMAT T "~&~%Reading ~S" WORD)
        (LET ((PREDS (GET-TRIGGERED-PREDS WORD *SENT-POS*)))
          (COND (PREDS
                  (FOR (PRED :IN PREDS)
                    :DO (ADVANCE-PRED PRED WORD))
                  (SETF *SENT-POS* (+ *SENT-POS* 1))))))
  (DP (+ *SENT-POS* 1)))
```

Listing 11.1: Micro DMAP Top-Level Function

(MOP-PREDS *mop*) returns a list of the default index pattern predictions whose first elements predict *mop*.

(PREDICTED-MOPS) returns a list of all MOPs that are currently being predicted.

(PRED-SLOTS *prediction*) returns the slots of *prediction*.

The variable *PREDICTIONS* is a table of the dynamic predictions.

(POS-PREDS *position*) returns the predictions looking at *position* in the current sentence, where *position* is an integer greater than or equal to 1.

(DMAP-INIT) initializes the globals variables and tables.

Listing 11.3 defines functions for accessing prediction information. Predictions are represented as lists, of the form (*target phrase base start*), where *target* is the MOP or word being predicted, *phrase* is the part of the original index pattern waiting to be recognized, *base* is the MOP that will be activated when the index pattern is finished, and *start* is the position in the sentence where the index pattern first started being recognized.

(PRED-FILLER *role prediction*) gets the filler of *role* in *prediction*.

(ADD-PRED-FILLER *role prediction filler*) adds the slot (*role filler*) to the slots of *prediction*. *prediction* is returned.

(PRED-TARGET *prediction*) returns the target MOP of *prediction*.

(PRED-PHRASE *prediction*) returns the index pattern of *prediction*.

(PRED-BASE *prediction*) returns the base MOP of *prediction*.

(PRED-START *prediction*) returns the starting position of *prediction*.

Listing 11.4 defines the functions for making prediction structures.

(MAKE-PRED *phrase base slots position*) constructs and returns a prediction with the given information. The target of the prediction is calculated from *phrase* and the *base* MOP.

(GET-TARGET *phrase base*) finds the target of the index pattern *phrase*,

```
(DEFINE-TABLE MOP-PREDS (MOP) (MOP-TABLE 'PREDS))

(DEFUN PREDICTED-MOPS ()
 (TABLE-KEYS (MOP-TABLE 'PREDS)))

(SETF *PRED-SLOTS-TABLE* NIL)
(DEFINE-TABLE PRED-SLOTS (PRED) *PRED-SLOTS-TABLE*)

(SETF *PREDICTIONS* NIL)
(DEFINE-TABLE POS-PREDS (POS) *PREDICTIONS*)

(DEFUN DMAP-INIT ()
 (SETF *PREDICTIONS* NIL)
 (SETF *PRED-SLOTS-TABLE* NIL)
 (SETF *SENT-POS* 1))
```

Listing 11.2: Micro DMAP Global Variables and Tables

```
(DEFUN PRED-FILLER (ROLE PRED)
 (ROLE-FILLER ROLE (PRED-SLOTS PRED)))

(DEFUN ADD-PRED-FILLER (ROLE PRED VALUE)
 (INSIST ADD-PRED-FILLER
         (MOPP VALUE) (NULL (PRED-FILLER ROLE PRED)))
 (SETF (PRED-SLOTS PRED)
       (CONS (MAKE-SLOT ROLE VALUE)
             (PRED-SLOTS PRED)))
 PRED)

(DEFUN PRED-TARGET (PRED) (CAR PRED))
(DEFUN PRED-PHRASE (PRED) (CAR (CDR PRED)))
(DEFUN PRED-BASE (PRED) (CAR (CDR (CDR PRED))))
(DEFUN PRED-START (PRED) (CAR (CDR (CDR (CDR PRED)))))
```

Listing 11.3: Micro DMAP Prediction Role Access Functions

```
(DEFUN MAKE-PRED (PHRASE BASE SLOTS START)
 (LET ((TARGET (GET-TARGET PHRASE BASE)))
  (INSIST MAKE-PRED (OR (NULL PHRASE) TARGET))
  (LET ((PRED (LIST TARGET PHRASE BASE START)))
   (SETF (PRED-SLOTS PRED) SLOTS)
   PRED)))

(DEFUN GET-TARGET (PHRASE BASE)
 (COND ((NULL PHRASE) NIL)
       ((ROLE-SPECIFIERP (CAR PHRASE))
        (GET-FILLER (ROLE-SPECIFIER-ROLE (CAR PHRASE))
                    BASE))
       (T (CAR PHRASE))))

(DEFUN ROLE-SPECIFIERP (X) (LISTP X))
(DEFUN ROLE-SPECIFIER-ROLE (X) (CAR X))
```

Listing 11.4: Micro DMAP Prediction Construction Functions

given *base*. Index patterns in micro DMAP contain words and *role specifiers*. A role specifier is represented as a list of one MOP role name. For example, the index pattern ((ACTOR) SAYS (INFO) PERIOD) has two role specifiers and two words. The target of a word is the word itself. The target of a role specifier is the filler of that role in *base*.

Listing 11.5 defines the functions that find the predictions triggered by an input word or newly activated MOP. All default predictions are checked, plus those dynamic predictions looking at the position in the sentence where the word or MOP started. An input word triggers a prediction if the word equals the target of the prediction. An activated MOP triggers a dynamic prediction if the MOP is either a specialization or abstraction of the target. For example, a dynamic prediction whose target was the MOP for "economist" would be triggered both by the MOP for "Milton Friedman" and the MOP for "human." A default prediction, however, is triggered only by specializations of its target.

(GET-TRIGGERED-PREDS *mop position*) returns a list of those predictions triggered by a MOP or word that started at *position* in the sentence.

(MOP-DYNAMIC-PREDICTIONS *mop position*) returns a list of the dynamic predictions looking at *position* triggered by *mop*.

(MOP-DEFAULT-PREDICTIONS *mop*) returns a list of those default predictions triggered by *mop*.

```
(DEFUN GET-TRIGGERED-PREDS (MOP START)
  (APPEND (MOP-DYNAMIC-PREDICTIONS MOP START)
          (MOP-DEFAULT-PREDICTIONS MOP)))

(DEFUN MOP-DYNAMIC-PREDICTIONS (MOP START)
  (FOR (PRED :IN (POS-PREDS START))
    :WHEN (REFERSP (PRED-TARGET PRED) MOP)
    :SAVE PRED))

(DEFUN REFERSP (MOP1 MOP2)
  (OR (ABSTP MOP1 MOP2) (ABSTP MOP2 MOP1)))

(DEFUN MOP-DEFAULT-PREDICTIONS (MOP)
  (FOR (TARGET :IN (PREDICTED-MOPS))
    :WHEN (ABSTP TARGET MOP)
    :SPLICE (FOR (PRED :IN (MOP-PREDS TARGET))
              :SAVE PRED)))
```

Listing 11.5: Micro DMAP Triggering Functions

Listing 11.6 defines the functions for advancing triggered predictions. If there is more index pattern to be recognized, a new prediction is created to recognize it. If the index pattern has been completely recognized, then the slots of the prediction are used to find or create a MOP in memory. This MOP is then activated, perhaps to trigger other predictions.

(ADVANCE-PRED *prediction mop*) advances *prediction* which has been triggered by *mop*. A copy of *prediction* is created, with the index pattern advanced to its next element. (Note that the index pattern in *prediction* itself is not affected). If *mop* matched a role specifier, a slot binding the role and *mop* together is added to the copied prediction. If the copied prediction's index pattern is finished, we get the MOP associated with it. Otherwise, the prediction is added to prediction table, indexed on the next position in the sentence.

(PRED->MOP *prediction*) finds or creates the MOP in memory with the slots in *prediction* and activates it.

Listing 11.7 defines the top-level function for defining new index patterns.

(DEFPHRASE *mop item₁ item₂* ...) attaches a default prediction with the index pattern ($item_1$ $item_2$ ...) to *mop*. $item_i$ can be either a lexical item such as MILTON or a role specifier such as (ACTOR). The prediction is stored

```
(DEFUN ADVANCE-PRED (PRED MOP)
 (LET ((PHRASE (PRED-PHRASE PRED)))
  (LET ((NEW-PRED (MAKE-PRED (CDR PHRASE)
                            (PRED-BASE PRED)
                            (PRED-SLOTS PRED)
                            (OR (PRED-START PRED)
                                *SENT-POS*))))
   (COND ((ROLE-SPECIFIERP (CAR PHRASE))
          (ADD-PRED-FILLER
              (ROLE-SPECIFIER-ROLE (CAR PHRASE))
              NEW-PRED MOP)))
   (COND ((NULL (CDR PHRASE))
          (PRED->MOP NEW-PRED))
         (T (LET ((NEXT-POS (+ *SENT-POS* 1)))
              (SETF (POS-PREDS NEXT-POS)
                    (CONS NEW-PRED
                          (POS-PREDS NEXT-POS)))))))))

(DEFUN PRED->MOP (PRED)
 (LET ((MOP (SLOTS->MOP (PRED-SLOTS PRED)
                       (LIST (PRED-BASE PRED))
                       T))
       (START (PRED-START PRED)))
  (FORMAT T "~&Activating ~S" MOP)
  (FOR (NEXT-PRED :IN (GET-TRIGGERED-PREDS MOP START))
       :DO (ADVANCE-PRED NEXT-PRED MOP))))
```

Listing 11.6: Micro DMAP Prediction Triggering Functions

```
(DEFMACRO DEFPHRASE (MOP &REST PHRASE)
 '(LET ((PRED (MAKE-PRED ',PHRASE ',MOP NIL NIL)))
   (LET ((TARGET (PRED-TARGET PRED)))
    (SETF (MOP-PREDS TARGET)
          (CONS PRED (MOP-PREDS TARGET)))
    ',PHRASE)))
```

Listing 11.7: Micro DMAP Top-Level Functions

in the MOP-PREDS table under the initial target of the prediction. The index pattern is returned.

Listing 11.8 defines some functions for printing the predictions in a readable format. The functions are given short but cryptic names to make them easier to type interactively.

(DP *position*) prints the dynamic predictions looking at the given position in the sentence. The name is short for "display predictions."

(DAP) prints all the dynamic predictions. The name is short for "display all predictions."

(DDP) prints all the default predictions. The name is short for "display default predictions."

(DISPLAY-PREDS *prediction-list*) prints the predictions in *prediction-list*.

Listing 11.9 defines the basic MOPs for micro DMAP, including actions, actors, economic variables, and variable behaviors.

Listing 11.10 defines DMAP's economic event and causal MOPs. M-VTRANS is used to represent changes in economic variables, such as interest rates rising. These state changes are divided into good and bad, so that we can crudely characterize monetarist arguments as "increasing money supply has bad effects."

The apparently redundant VAR slots in the definitions of M-GOOD-VTRANS and M-BAD-VTRANS are included so that these two MOPs are not treated as slotless abstractions. (Slotless abstractions are discussed in Chapter 3.)

Listing 11.11 defines DMAP's MOPs for M-MTRANS communication events. The M-MOBJECT MOP organizes objects of M-MTRANS events to include simple state changes and causals.

Listing 11.12 defines the index patterns for DMAP's MOPs.

Listing 11.13 defines the demo function for DMAP. It parses the two sentences "Milton Friedman says interest rates will rise because of the monetary explosion," and "Arthur Laffer says interest rates will drop." If DMAP-DEMO is

```
(DEFUN DP (N)
  (DISPLAY-PREDS (POS-PREDS N))
  NIL)

(DEFUN DAP ()
  (FOR (N :IN (TABLE-KEYS *PREDICTIONS*))
    :DO (FORMAT T "~&Predictions on Position ~S" N)
        (DISPLAY-PREDS (POS-PREDS N)))
  NIL)

(DEFUN DDP ()
  (FOR (MOP :IN (PREDICTED-MOPS))
    :DO (DISPLAY-PREDS (MOP-PREDS MOP)))
  NIL)

(DEFUN DISPLAY-PREDS (PREDS)
  (LET ((I 0))
    (FOR (PRED :IN PREDS)
      :DO (FORMAT T "~&~S: ~S ==> ~S in ~S"
                  (SETF I (+ I 1))
                  (PRED-TARGET PRED)
                  (CAR (PRED-PHRASE PRED))
                  (PRED-BASE PRED)))))
```

Listing 11.8: Micro DMAP Display Functions

```
(DEFMOP M-ACTOR (M-ROOT))
(DEFMOP M-ECONOMIST (M-ACTOR))
(DEFMOP M-MONETARIST (M-ECONOMIST))
(DEFMOP I-M-FRIEDMAN (M-MONETARIST) INSTANCE)
(DEFMOP M-SUPPLY-SIDER (M-ECONOMIST))
(DEFMOP I-M-LAFFER (M-SUPPLY-SIDER) INSTANCE)

(DEFMOP M-ACT (M-ROOT))
(DEFMOP I-M-MTRANS-ACT (M-ACT) INSTANCE)

(DEFMOP M-VARIABLE (M-ROOT))
(DEFMOP M-BAD-VAR (M-VARIABLE))
(DEFMOP M-NEUTRAL-VAR (M-VARIABLE))
(DEFMOP I-M-INTEREST-RATES (M-BAD-VAR) INSTANCE)
(DEFMOP I-M-MONEY-SUPPLY (M-NEUTRAL-VAR) INSTANCE)

(DEFMOP M-BEHAVIOR (M-ROOT))
(DEFMOP I-M-INCREASE (M-BEHAVIOR) INSTANCE)
(DEFMOP I-M-DECREASE (M-BEHAVIOR) INSTANCE)

(DEFMOP M-STATE-CHANGE (M-ROOT))
```

Listing 11.9: Micro DMAP Basic MOPs

```
(DEFMOP M-VTRANS (M-STATE-CHANGE)
    (VAR M-VARIABLE) (BEH M-BEHAVIOR)))

(DEFMOP M-GOOD-VTRANS (M-VTRANS) (VAR M-VARIABLE)))
(DEFMOP M-BAD-VTRANS (M-VTRANS) (VAR M-VARIABLE)))
(DEFMOP M-NEUTRAL-VTRANS (M-VTRANS)
    (VAR M-NEUTRAL-VAR)))

(DEFMOP M-BAD-DOWN (M-GOOD-VTRANS)
    (VAR M-BAD-VAR) (BEH I-M-DECREASE)))
(DEFMOP M-BAD-UP (M-BAD-VTRANS)
    (VAR M-BAD-VAR) (BEH I-M-INCREASE)))

(DEFMOP I-M-MS-UP (M-NEUTRAL-VTRANS)
    (VAR I-M-MONEY-SUPPLY)))

(DEFMOP M-CAUSAL (M-ROOT)
    (ANTE M-STATE-CHANGE) (CNSQ M-STATE-CHANGE)))
(DEFMOP M-CAUSAL/ECON (M-CAUSAL)
    (ANTE M-VTRANS) (CNSQ M-VTRANS)))
(DEFMOP M-CAUSAL/MON (M-CAUSAL/ECON)
    (ANTE I-M-MS-UP) (CNSQ M-BAD-VTRANS)))
```

Listing 11.10: Micro DMAP Event and State Change MOPs

```
(DEFMOP M-MOBJECT (M-ROOT) (CONTENT NIL))
(DEFMOP M-MOBJECT/STATE-CHANGE (M-MOBJECT)
    (CONTENT M-STATE-CHANGE))
(DEFMOP M-ARG (M-MOBJECT) (CONTENT M-CAUSAL))
(DEFMOP M-ARG/ECON (M-ARG) (CONTENT M-CAUSAL/ECON))
(DEFMOP M-ARG/MON (M-ARG/ECON) (CONTENT M-CAUSAL/MON))

(DEFMOP M-MTRANS (M-EVENT)
    (ACTION I-M-MTRANS-ACT) (ACTOR M-ACTOR)
    (INFO M-MOBJECT))

(DEFMOP M-MTRANS/STATE-CHANGE (M-MTRANS)
    (INFO M-MOBJECT/STATE-CHANGE))

(DEFMOP M-MTRANS/ECON (M-MTRANS)
    (ACTOR M-ECONOMIST)
    (INFO M-ARG (CONTENT M-CAUSAL/ECON)))
```

Listing 11.11: Micro DMAP Event and State Change MOPs

run a second time, the MOPs constructed during the first run will be activated, but no new MOPs will be created.

11.3   Running the DMAP Demo

To run the micro DMAP demo, you need the code in the Listings in Chapter 3 and this chapter. Follow these steps:

1. Load all DEFUN, DEFMACRO, SETF, DEFINE-FOR-KEY and DEFINE-TABLE forms, in the order in which they appear in the Listings.

2. Execute the function calls (CLEAR-MEMORY).

3. Load all the DEFMOP and DEFPHRASE forms, in the order in which they appear in the Listings.

4. Execute the function call (DMAP-DEMO).

After Step 3, the abstraction hierarchy printed by (DAH 'M-ROOT) should look like the following, except for the numbers on the MOPs.

```
(DEFPHRASE I-M-FRIEDMAN MILTON FRIEDMAN)
(DEFPHRASE I-M-LAFFER ARTHUR LAFFER)

(DEFPHRASE I-M-INTEREST-RATES INTEREST RATES)
(DEFPHRASE I-M-MONEY-SUPPLY MONEY SUPPLY)

(DEFPHRASE I-M-INCREASE RISE)
(DEFPHRASE I-M-INCREASE INCREASE)
(DEFPHRASE I-M-INCREASE GO UP)
(DEFPHRASE I-M-DECREASE DROP)
(DEFPHRASE I-M-DECREASE DECREASE)
(DEFPHRASE I-M-DECREASE GO DOWN)

(DEFPHRASE M-VTRANS (VAR) WILL (BEH))

(DEFPHRASE I-M-MS-UP MONETARY EXPLOSION)

(DEFPHRASE M-CAUSAL (CNSQ) AS A CONSEQUENCE OF (ANTE))
(DEFPHRASE M-CAUSAL (CNSQ) BECAUSE OF (ANTE))
(DEFPHRASE M-CAUSAL (ANTE) CAN CAUSE (CNSQ))
(DEFPHRASE M-CAUSAL IF (ANTE) THEN (CNSQ))

(DEFPHRASE M-MOBJECT/STATE-CHANGE (CONTENT))
(DEFPHRASE M-ARG (CONTENT))

(DEFPHRASE M-MTRANS (ACTOR) SAYS (INFO) PERIOD)
```

Listing 11.12: Micro DMAP Phrases

```
(DEFUN DMAP-DEMO ()
  (FORMAT T "~&---------------")
  (DMAP-INIT)
  (SETF *SENT1*
    '(MILTON FRIEDMAN SAYS INTEREST RATES WILL RISE
      BECAUSE OF THE MONETARY EXPLOSION PERIOD))
  (FORMAT T "~&Parsing ~S" *SENT1*)
  (DMAP *SENT1*)
  (FORMAT T "~&---------------")
  (DMAP-INIT)
  (SETF *SENT2*
    '(ARTHUR LAFFER SAYS INTEREST RATES WILL DROP
      PERIOD))
  (FORMAT T "~&Parsing ~S" *SENT2*)
  (DMAP *SENT2*)
  NIL)
```

Listing 11.13: Micro DMAP Demo

```
(M-ROOT
  (M-MOBJECT
    (M-ARG (M-ARG/ECON (M-ARG/MON)))
    (M-MOBJECT/STATE-CHANGE))
  (M-CAUSAL (M-CAUSAL/ECON (M-CAUSAL/MON)))
  (M-STATE-CHANGE
    (M-VTRANS
      (M-NEUTRAL-VTRANS (I-M-MS-UP))
      (M-BAD-VTRANS (M-BAD-UP))
      (M-GOOD-VTRANS (M-BAD-DOWN))))
  (M-BEHAVIOR (I-M-DECREASE) (I-M-INCREASE))
  (M-VARIABLE
    (M-NEUTRAL-VAR (I-M-MONEY-SUPPLY))
    (M-BAD-VAR (I-M-INTEREST-RATES)))
  (M-FAILED-SOLUTION)
  (M-ROLE)
  (M-CASE)
  (M-PATTERN (M-NOT) (M-PATTERN.21))
  (M-FUNCTION
    (GET-SIBLING)
```

```
        (CONSTRAINT-FN (NOT-CONSTRAINT)))
    (M-GROUP (M-EMPTY-GROUP (I-M-EMPTY-GROUP)))
    (M-ACTOR
        (M-ECONOMIST
            (M-SUPPLY-SIDER (I-M-LAFFER))
            (M-MONETARIST (I-M-FRIEDMAN))))
    (M-ACT (I-M-MTRANS-ACT))
    (M-STATE)
    (M-EVENT
        (M-MTRANS
            (M-MTRANS/ECON)
            (M-MTRANS/STATE-CHANGE))))
```

After Step 4, you should see something very close to the output that follows, except for the numbers on the MOPs:

```
----------------

Parsing (MILTON FRIEDMAN SAYS INTEREST RATES WILL
RISE BECAUSE OF THE MONETARY EXPLOSION PERIOD)

Reading MILTON

Reading FRIEDMAN
Activating I-M-FRIEDMAN

Reading SAYS

Reading INTEREST

Reading RATES
Activating I-M-INTEREST-RATES

Reading WILL

Reading RISE
Activating I-M-INCREASE
Activating I-M-VTRANS.23
Activating I-M-MOBJECT/STATE-CHANGE.24

Reading BECAUSE
```

Reading OF

Reading THE

Reading MONETARY

Reading EXPLOSION
Activating I-M-MS-UP
Activating I-M-CAUSAL.25
Activating I-M-ARG.26
Activating I-M-MOBJECT/STATE-CHANGE.27

Reading PERIOD
Activating I-M-MTRANS.28

Parsing (ARTHUR LAFFER SAYS INTEREST RATES WILL
DROP PERIOD)

Reading ARTHUR

Reading LAFFER
Activating I-M-LAFFER

Reading SAYS

Reading INTEREST

Reading RATES
Activating I-M-INTEREST-RATES

Reading WILL

Reading DROP
Activating I-M-DECREASE
Activating I-M-VTRANS.29
Activating I-M-MOBJECT/STATE-CHANGE.30

Reading PERIOD
Activating I-M-MTRANS.31

If you run DMAP-DEMO again, you should get exactly the same output. In particular, the numbers on the MOPs should be the same, because no new MOPs are needed when reading texts that have been read before.

11.4   Extensions

11.4.1   Extending memory

Add more examples of economists and the kinds of things they talk about, such as unemployment and inflation. As always, the first step is to get the memory representations in shape, before trying to parse into them.

11.4.2   Parsing for Other Domains

Use DMAP to parse fights for micro JUDGE, recipes for micro CHEF, and plays for micro COACH.

11.4.3   Pruning Predictions

Micro DMAP does not prune the set of active index patterns. It never decides that some pattern is no longer capable of being advanced. If a pattern is looking for a word in some position, and that position has already been read, then the pattern can clearly be removed if the word was not seen. If a pattern is looking for a MOP, then it is harder to prove that there is no pattern waiting to be completed that might reference the MOP. Fix micro DMAP to prune out patterns looking for words that never appear. Explore ways of pruning patterns looking for MOPs that can never be referenced. Note that if your parser has to scan all of memory to rule a MOP out, it is probably costing more to get rid of the pattern than to leave it there.

11.4.4   Handling Near Misses

An important issue in the real DMAP is dealing with "near misses," that is, with inputs that are almost but not quite the same as existing memory structures. These near-miss remindings can be a rich source for inferencing. For example, one of the examples handled by the real DMAP involves reading a monetarist argument about interest rates by Milton Friedman, followed by a hypothetical instance of Lester Thurow saying basically the same thing. When reading the Thurow argument, DMAP finds the "near miss" Milton Friedman argument MOP, but does not find any prior instance of Thurow giving this argument. In DMAP, there are patterns for near miss situations, and these patterns index MOPs that infer connections between the input and its near miss. For example, if an unknown economist says the same thing as a member of a particular economic camp, then DMAP infers that the unknown economist a member of that camp. If DMAP did not know who Thurow was, it would infer he was a monetarist like Friedman. This fails in this case because DMAP knows that Thurow is not a monetarist. Another pattern says that if economists from opposing camps say the same thing, then infer that the thing said is an accepted "truth" in economics.

Experiment with having micro DMAP notice near misses. Be careful though. In a small memory, almost everything is a near miss, because there are so little information, i.e., slots, to compare.

11.4.5 Representing Index Patterns

Make the index patterns into real memory structures. That is, define an appropriate set of abstraction and packaging relationships to capture the notion of patterns referring to MOPs. These kinds of relationships are probably useful for more than just language. The real DMAP, for example, uses patterns to represent inferential and indexing knowledge.

11.4.6 Generation

The simplicity of DMAP's linguistic representation makes it a natural for application to generation as well as parsing. We'll ignore the most important problem of deciding what to say and focus instead on the problem of how to say it. Given a MOP or instance in memory, we want to express that MOP in English. The basic algorithm for expressing a MOP is simple. First, pick an index pattern attached to the MOP or to one of its abstractions. Replace every role specifier in the pattern with the filler (perhaps inherited) of that role in the MOP, and recursively express the filler. Define EXPRESS-MOP so that (EXPRESS-MOP *mop*) will return a sentence, in the form of a list of symbols, describing *mop*. If a phrase for a MOP can't be found, use its name.

Unfortunately, this algorithm won't work once the number and variety of index patterns starts to grow, because micro DMAP's linguistic knowledge is too limited. One problem is that the same MOP can be expressed in many different syntactic forms. A prediction for example can be expressed as a clause ("Interest rates will fall") or a noun phrase ("the coming fall in interest rates"). It is acceptable to generate "Arthur Laffer says interest rates will fall," but not "Arthur Laffer says the coming fall in interest rates." The simplest solution is to change our notation for index patterns so that

- every index patterns is tagged with its syntactic type, e.g., clause, noun phrase, and so on, and,

- every role specifier in an index pattern is tagged with the type of nested index pattern it requires.

Thus, the index pattern for "interest rates" might look like (NP INTEREST RATES) and the index pattern for M-MTRANS might look like ((NP ACTOR) SAYS (CLAUSE INFO) PERIOD).

11.4.7 Adding Syntactic Knowledge

Ignoring the previous exercise, the only syntactic knowledge micro DMAP has is word order and adjacency. The former knowledge is captured by the fact that index patterns are invoked left to right, and the latter knowledge is captured by the fact that predictions from index patterns are sensitive to where index patterns start and stop.

But natural language is not so rigidly ordered. Different word orders are often available ("John said 'Mary left,' " versus " 'Mary left,' John said") and things like adverbs and prepositional phrases can appear in many places.

To incorporate this knowledge, micro DMAP's index patterns need to be made more complex. Besides including simple syntactic categories, as discussed in the previous exercise, they also need to have the ability to specify optional and "floating" elements. Rather than go into detail here, we refer the interested reader to the work of Jacobs [1987] on representing linguistic knowledge in memory structures. Although his particular knowledge formalism is not identical to ours, it is similar enough to be of obvious applicability.

However, we also want to warn the reader about the dangers of falling into the black hole of syntax. It's all too tempting to try creating an index pattern specification language and interpreter that is really just another syntactic parser in disguise. Don't assume that just because some linguistic generalization is true of a set of index patterns that there must be an abstract index pattern in memory equivalent to that generalization. As a rule of thumb, every pattern, no matter how abstract, should be attached to some meaningful non-linguistic memory structure.

12

Cases and Intelligence

Intelligence is more likely to be a continuum than a "now you have it, now you don't" affair. People differ in intelligence for reasons other than that one person has a property that another is lacking. Similarly, a machine is unlikely to be missing some quality or other that would keep it from being as intelligent as a person. Rather, an intelligent machine probably needs to have certain basic capabilities. The extent of its intelligence would reflect how well it exploited those capabilities. What might those capabilities be?

The abilities that characterize very intelligent people are really a set of processes that these people execute, and they are the very same processes that average people execute. It isn't the case that smart people have some property that dull people are missing. It isn't even true that humans have something that animals don't have. It isn't the presence or absence of a process, but how that process is used that determines how intelligent someone is. The processes of intelligence are what they are and everybody has all of them. What differentiates smart from stupid is the way in which the processes are run.

Below, I have characterized some dimensions of intelligence along which these processes operate. For each of them, there is a normal way in which they are employed, which I call the *normal task*. In addition, there is the extended, more intelligent, use of these processes, which I call the *extended task*.

Dimension1: data finding
normal task: Reminding
extended task: Search

Intelligence is characterized by the ability to get reminded. Why is reminding so important? Quite obviously, if you don't get reminded of stories, you can't tell them, nor can you find old solutions to apply to new problems. Reminding is the means by which our memories present us with data for our consideration. Since reminding depends how we label our experiences, one measure of the intelligence of a system is how well it labels its experiences. No experience has just one label. We might want to recall an experience because of who was involved in it, where it took place, an unusual feature related to it, or one of many conclusions that were derived from it. But, in order to do this, we must either consider all the aspects of that experience at the time of processing and storage of that experience, which is unlikely, or else we must be able to retrieve that experience again in order to reconsider and add more labels to it.

Labeling is not a conscious process, though thinking about an experience is. When mulling over an event in which we have participated, we are not aware of exactly why we are mulling over it, but the mulling is critical to intelligence, because it creates labels for events in myriad ways so that they can be seen again in memory.

It also follows therefore, that the process of searching memory for those events is an intelligent process, dependent upon a knowledge of the labels that have previously been used and also dependent upon an ability to look at an experience in a novel enough way so as to be able to create new labels to consider.

We cannot say for sure if higher level animals get reminded, but it is reasonable to assume that they do. They do not rediscover each day where the best sources of food are for example. They remember them at just the right time. It is certainly safe to say that all people get reminded of past experiences from time to time. Thus, the intelligence in this process is not in the reminding itself. It is a natural phenomenon, not a remarkably intelligent one.

But finding those experiences when they are not obviously connected to what you are now processing is a special kind of reminding. When search requires thinking it is a more conscious type of search than the search that the normal reminding process entails. What makes one person's memory better than another's? The answer has to be two things: labeling and search techniques.

Let's consider labeling first. Imagine two people undergoing the same experience. Let's say they both attend a baseball game and somebody next to them gets hit by a batted ball, is taken to a first aid room and returns to watch the game an inning later. Now, let's imagine that it is two years later. What might our hypothetical experiencers of this day remember of it? Obviously, the possibilities are myriad. Would they remember the score of the game? Who won? Where they were sitting? What the person who was hurt looked like? What the attendants who took the person away were wearing? What inning this occurred in? What they thought about it all?

In some sense, it is the last question that is most important here. What they remember depends heavily on what they thought about the incident. One person could, after all, see this incident in a variety of ways: as an annoying interruption of the game for example, or as an indication of the potential violence of sport, or as an example of how badly fans want to see a game — even if they are injured they come back to watch, or as an example of God's will in keeping the ball from hitting them, or all of the above.

An incident is remembered in terms of how it is seen in the first place. Labeling is in many respects an arbitrary process. Of course, both viewers would label this as something that happened at a baseball game. But, one might see it as having relevance with respect to any sporting event, while the other might see it as being worthy of calling up any time that one is seated next to someone who looks like the victim in this incident looked. And, of course, even that last categorization is arbitrary since one person might characterize the victim as being blond, while the other might characterize him as being fat.

Is it possible that one of the viewers might easily recall this incident while the other might forget it? Of course. Would one then have a good memory while the other was seen as forgetful? Naturally, those characterizations are easy to make. What is actually happening, however, has nothing to do with how many brain cells either person has allocated for this particular experience. The difference between the two viewers is a function of how they labeled the event. If the first viewer was very taken by this incident, seeing it as relevant to his views of sports, religion, health, and whatever, he would of course recall it often and reinforce the memory with each recall. To do this, he has to have labeled the event extensively at the time it happened, or have mulled it over later, relating it to other things he has thought about. For him, this event would be easily recalled later, because of how many labels he has given it.

But, for a viewer for whom this event had little significance in a day otherwise occupied with an exciting and significant baseball game, it is likely that the game would be remembered and the accident would be almost forgotten. In other words, if you don't think about something you aren't likely to remember much,

A variable that affects all this is the number of baseball games attended prior to, and after, this event. If this game were the only game a viewer had attended, it is likely that this incident would be recalled any time that baseball were brought up, because the incident would have become part of the prototype for the baseball-attending script. It is almost as if, were this person to attend another game, they would expect a patron near them to be hit with a ball.

A good memory then, means an attentive labeling facility during processing, or, to put this another way, you aren't going to remember what you don't find interesting, so the more that interests you the better memory you are likely to have. Search, obviously, depends upon labeling. You can't find what you have failed to label or have mislabeled in the first place.

Obviously all higher animals, and certainly all humans, label experiences and store them away in memory. Intelligence in this arena manifests itself before the retrieval process even starts. You can remember better what you have understood more competely, that is, what you have seen from many different vantage points. This mulling process occurs prior to storage. In other words, what you haven't thought about sufficiently is less likely to be available to you in situations later in life where it might be relevant.

In sum, then, we can say that it is normal part of intelligence to be able to find, without looking for it, a story do in a new situation. It is an exceptional aspect of intelligence to be able to find stories that are superficially not so obviously connected to the current situation. If you have labeled a story in a complex fashion prior to storage, it will be available in a large variety of ways in the future. Higher intelligence depends upon complex perception and labeling.

But, how do you know what events to store away as stories worth remembering? It seems obvious that we can't make a story out of everything. Simply walking down a busy street for an hour could supply you with enough different things to think about to occupy you for the rest of your mental life. Intelligence requires you to forget many things, and to ignore most things. Learning to ignore and forget effectively enhances our remembering of relevant information. If you are not concerned with the trivial you can focus on the significant. This means, in effect, that you must establish a set of standard cases into which the vast majority of experiences can be remembered in the short term and forgotten in the long term.

Case recognition is a very important process in memory, but, here again, it is also an ability that everybody can be assumed to have. Generic situations, such as a restaurant, are easy to spot, even if we have never seen that particular restaurant before. Similarly, if we encounter a situation that is new to us, a broken leg for example, we can relate it to other similar types of cases, someone else's broken leg, our own broken arm, another illness or injury we may have had, and invoke the appropriate script. The ability to recognize an event as an instance of a previously processed case is very important because we use prior cases to help us process new events. Thus, case recognition is a critical, and quite common, aspect of human intelligence.

Here again, what is a part of normal everyday intelligence is also, in its extended form, an important aspect of what we consider to be highly intelligent behavior. It is one thing to recognize a restaurant as a restaurant when you've never been there before, but it seems qualitatively different to recognize a new piece of music as being by Beethoven, a newly encountered painting as being by Picasso, a new legal case as being like another, or a new situation in business as being like a superficially dissimilar case. Of course, these are all aspects of the same process of case recognition.

Knowing that you have seen an analogous case before means knowing what you know, which of course means knowing what labels you have employed before. You must have a consistency to your labeling algorithm in the long-term. This consistency is very relevant for being able to make comparisons and generalizations. Intelligence depends upon finding what you have previously labeled which in turn depends on labeling things the same way each time. This is actually not so easy to do and is one reason why some people are smarter than others. The smarter people label more coherently as well as more complexly.

Dimension 2: data manipulation
normal task: Do Partial Matching
extended task: Adapt Cases

It is a part of everyday intelligence to do partial matching. This means that you will not fail to recognize somebody who has shaved off his moustache although you may realize that there is something different about him without knowing exactly what. A total match between your memory of that person and what he looks like now may not occur, but this does not cause you to fail to recognize the person. A partial match suffices.

The same phenomenon occurs in matching stories. Here the problem of matching is different, however. We match new events to stories we already know that are not exactly like those stories. We might, for example, recall an earlier attempt to get a teacher to change a grade while thinking about getting our boss to change his salary decision. Partial matching of one story onto another is a critical aspect of human intelligence.

The extension of this capability shows itself in the extent to which *very* partial matches can be made useful in a new situation. It is all too easy to reject a partial match when the match is very superficial or improbable. More difficult is to keep a very unlikely match alive, to think about it enough to find a way in which it could be helpful.

The tricky part comes when you have to adapt an old story that you've found in such a way as to make it useful for understanding a new story. The more successfully you adapt old stories, the more creative you are. Adaptation of old theorems helps mathematicians prove new ones; adaptation of old programs helps programmers write new programs; adaptation of old cases helps lawyers argue new cases and helps doctors prescribe treatment. The better you can adapt an old case to a new situation, the more able you are to cope with the unforeseen.

When you decide to purchase a stock, you want to recall other stock purchases and how they turned out. The other purchases that you recall may not match on very many features. The name, the date, the price, the state of the economy, just to name a few are likely to be different. But what if the business the company engages in, its price-earnings ratio, its selling price relative to its historical low, its position in its industry and such are different as well? Which of these criteria are normally different and which, if they are different, make the comparison absurd?

In fact, individual decision makers have theories about which features are criterial and which are irrelevant. Partial matching is an art. We must guess what we can ignore because no match is ever really a complete match. The intelligence problem is one of finding effective theories of partial matches. We must know when stories are relevant enough to tell, when cases are paradigmatic enough to base future actions upon. There are no hard and fast rules for doing this correctly. The making and testing of new theories of usefulness of a partial match is thus another hallmark of intelligence.

Any intelligent being can recognize that a partial match is good enough and can learn to treat such matches as if they were complete matches. The high end of this aspect of intelligence requires that you can find a match where there may not obviously be one, and utilize that possibly errant match to help you cope with brand new situations.

Dimension 3: comprehension
normal task: Connect New Cases with Old Cases
extended task: Invent Coherency for New Cases

Part of being intelligent is figuring out where the actions of others fit. Dumb animals perceive everything unknown as a potential threat. It may not be that brilliant a strategy, but, as the guy said who dropped popcorn around himself to keep the elephants away, "See? It works." Consider your own response to the following story:

> TOKYO, SEPT 23, 1985 - A Japan Air Lines official who had been negotiating with relatives of the 520 people killed in last month's Boeing 747 crash has killed himself to apologize for the disaster, the police said.
> They said Saturday that Hiro Tominaga, 59, a manager of JAL's Haneda Airport maintenance shop near Tokyo, stabbed himself in neck and chest.

He left a note saying, "I offer my apology with my life," the police said.

Do this man's actions make sense? In some cultures they do, in some they don't. Interpreting what you see and hear involves referring to established norms. Being intelligent, therefore, requires knowing wide ranges of different norms, so that unusual actions can be interpreted in a context that makes them sensible. Intelligence involves ascertaining what plan the action of another might be part of, what goal that plan was intended to satisfy, and what belief that the actor held would explain why that goal was a goal that he held.

People whom we would characterize as less intelligent than others often also display the property of seeing the behavior of people outside their own social world as being crazy. People from other cultures are crazy because they eat funny foods, or wear funny clothes. We characterize the ambitions of people in other social worlds according to the extent to which we have attempted to invent coherence for them. It sometimes takes a great deal of work to consider the rationale behind other's actions. It is much easier to dismiss their seemingly unusual behavior as incoherent and let it go at that.

This aspect of intelligence is, in a sense, just hard work. You have got to know what goes on in the world and be able to figure out where what you just saw fits. As is often the case with human intelligence, what appears to be a very difficult process can be short-circuited in actual practice by learning some tricks. One of the most common of these tricks is the script, as discussed in Chapter 1. The value of scripts is that they allow us not to think. We either know what a Japanese official must do when something in his charge screws up or we don't. If we don't then we call his action "crazy." If we do, then his action seems obvious and straightforward. Either way we don't have to think too much. Part of normal intelligence is this ability to find a context for actions that makes them either comprehensible to us or allow us to dismiss them as irrelevant.

What makes for the really intelligent behavior here is again a difference in degree rather than in kind. Intelligent people don't easily accept either the answer that a given action fits into a script nor the answer that if it does not fit a script, then the action in question was crazy. In other words, when intelligent people see an action, they try to see it as different from what they know rather than similar to what they know (if they are interested in that action of course, otherwise they can ignore it like everybody else). And, when they see actions that are obviously different and out of the bounds of what they know, they try to find similarities with what they have experienced, in order to render crazy actions comprehensible.

To put this another way, intelligence here means being interested in *ex-*

plaining as much as possible rather than *explaining away* as much as possible. The more you find of interest, that is, the more you need to explain, the more you have to think about, and, the more there is to think about, the more you think.

We can see easily enough why a waitress has brought the food we asked for, but why she has flung it down angrily on the table may be more difficult to understand. We must *invent* a coherent reason for her actions or else we must see her as being crazy in some way. This ability to see the disconnected behaviors of others as part of a coherent plan of action is an important aspect of intelligence.

Intelligence means finding coherence where it isn't obvious that it exists. Humans, in the normal course of processing experiences, must find out why people do what they do. But, intelligence in this arena means doing the extra processing to find coherence where it may not be obvious, or to invent coherence where it actually cannot be found.

Dimension 4: explanation
normal task: Explain Expectation Failure
extended task: Create New Expectations

Often we fail to find a coherent explanation for what has happened. The usual signal that this has happened is an *expectation* failure. Something didn't happen that we thought would, or something happened that we didn't expect. As just discussed, one part of intelligence is to look for an explanation of the event. Another part, though, is to explain why we failed to explain the event in the first place. That is, there are two events of interest. The event that we couldn't explain, and the mental event of having made a bad prediction. Dimension 4 is related to how we handle this mental event.

One part of intelligence then involves explaining why expectation failures have occurred. Often people explain problems in such a way as to make them disappear. We observe someone doing something odd and we attempt to figure a good reason why we need not be concerned with that odd action. "He's just crazy, don't worry about him" is a useful thing to believe after all. If we explain away the event with something like "he's crazy," or "things happen," then we simultaneously relieve ourselves of the burden of figuring out how we should have expected what actually happened. This makes a lot of sense. Every little failure is not worth dwelling on. Intelligence thus involves the ability to know where to spend our intellectual time. We can't go around wondering about everything after all. Or can we?

My daughter, when she was three years old, used to ask me, every time we passed anyone on the street, why that man was doing what he was doing.

Now, sometimes those questions were easy to answer, and sometimes they were completely impossible to answer. But, naturally, my daughter expected me to know and kept on asking. In fact, as I write this, she is fifteen years old, and still asks such questions. These days the questions are a kind of joke between us, but the key point is, she still is wondering why people do what they do. Children have to learn to stop asking such questions. They learn this in several ways, but mostly by their not getting answered. Often those questions are not answered because they are answered by the technique of explaining away. Whatever curiosity the child has, an adult can, and often will, stifle by explaining that the interesting phenomenon is not interesting at all. A child asks for an explanation and two things can happen, he can have the phenomenon explained away for him ("It's nothing to worry about dear. Elephants do that all the time.") or he can have an explanation given to him ("The sky is blue because of way molecules in the atmosphere disperse sunlight.") Either way, the child fails to advance to the next aspect of this dimension of intelligence.

It seems fairly obvious that speculating about what may be going on in an anomalous situation is an important form of thinking. Moreover children who naturally seek explanations can also learn to explain things for themselves. To learn to explain expectation failures, you must practice. Therefore, there is really only one right answer for a child ("Why do you think that man is doing that?"), although it often isn't so simple to answer a child in that fashion. In any case the point is that the more curiosity there is, the more anomalies there are, the more anomalies there are, the more explanations you need, and the more explanations you need, the more explanations you invent.

Learning to explain phenomena in such a way that you continue to be fascinated by the failure of your explanations creates a continuing cycle of thinking which is the crux of intelligence. It isn't that one person knows more than another then. In a sense it is important to know less than the next guy, or at least to be certain of less, thus enabling more curiosity and less explaining away. This is a well-known phenomenon. The less you know the more you can find out about, and finding out for yourself is what intelligence is all about.

From what I said above, it follows that intelligence is intimately connected with failure. Well, then I must be very intelligent because I fail all the time, I hear you saying. Actually that statement is not so very far from the truth. A characteristic of dumb systems is that they never have expectation failures. Every day is like every other for them. They know a limited amount, never venture outside their limits, and never need to grow or change. Change is a product of failure. Learning depends upon a system venturing beyond known borders into places where the rules may not be so clear cut, and where failure may occur.

Failure is valuable because it encourages explanation. You must wonder why you've failed and invent a strategy that will eliminate the failure next time. The more intelligent you are the more you will fail. Ultimately the value of failure and the explanation of failure is to come up with new rules that predict how events will turn out. Of course, these too will fail. This is one of the reasons that you must keep your stories available. If all you recall is the rule, it will be hard to figure out what to do when the rule fails. But, if the story that generated the rule is still available, you can look at the data again, and create a new rule. No story worthy of the name has only one possible rule that can be derived from it. We all see a given story, if it has sufficient complexity, in a variety of ways. Thus, the task for an intelligent system is to be looking for failures that it can use its stories to explain in order to create new rules to be tried and considered again.

Dimension 5: planning
normal task: Execute Plans
extended task: Create Plans

Everybody plans. Cats plan. Dogs plan. Babies plan. Now, planning would seem to be a very complex mental activity. In fact, efforts to simulate human planning behavior by computer in Artificial Intelligence labs have indicated that planning is overwhelmingly complex. How is it then that planning is possible by beings who are not overwhelmingly intelligent?

The answer is that most beings don't create plans, they copy plans. If animals had to figure out how to get fed, by reasoning it out from general principles, there would be a great many starving animals. Fortunately, animals have other animals to copy from. Even so, from time to time, a pet has to have food shoved under its face for it to realize that it is there and that it might consider eating it.

Leaving aside the possibility that some planning is done entirely by instinct, can all human planning behavior be accounted for by the concept of copying? I ask this question because this is the issue that differentiates intelligence along the dimension of planning. Think of how many times you have done something just because you did it that way before, or because that is how your parents did it, or because that is how a friend told you to do it. Reasoning out a plan from first principles can be quite difficult. It is easier to modify old plans. So, when a new plan is needed, a standard human trick is to find a plan that is a lot like the needed plan and satisfies a goal a lot like the new goal, and try and modify the old plan to make it work in the new situation. Cooks do this when they are missing an ingredient from a recipe, drivers do this when they are trying to get to a new destination, and chess players and generals do this when they are trying to find a new strategy for winning. They look for an old strategy that has worked before and see if it will fit somehow in the new situation.

Certainly there are times when even this adaptive planning won't work and genuinely new plans must be created from scratch. The argument is that this kind of planning behavior occurs quite rarely, not because it wouldn't be a good idea, but because it is quite difficult to do.

So, along the dimension of planning, we all use the plans of others, we all can adapt some of these plans to fit new situations. But the extent of our abilities to find plans to adapt is just like the extent of ability to be reminded that was discussed above. It depends upon clever indexing strategies and the accumulation of a great deal of experience.

The ability to create brand new plans is one of the real hallmarks of intelligence. These plans need not be new to society in general, of course, but just to the individual who created them. In gneral then, the more intelligent you are, the more you can create new plans.

Dimension 6: communication/discovery
normal task: Present Cases
extended task: generalize, crystallize, and elaborate

Intelligent beings communicate. It is an interesting property of human beings that the process of communication itself can alter what is being communicated. When an animal communicates something, such as the fact that he is hungry or frightened, the act of communication itself does not lead him to new insights about the situation. People, however, can discuss things, and then notice things about what they say that can cause them to change their view on what they are saying in midstream. This is the process of *communication/discovery*.

Normally, the communication process for humans is very case oriented. People tell about their experiences and these experiences can be considered as cases that illustrate some point that they want to make. The ability to illustrate a point with your own experience is yet another important aspect of intelligence.

The relevant extension here is in being able either to come to new generalizations as a result of the communication process, to summarize or crystallize a complex experience in a simple way. To put this bluntly, dull people tell you what happened to them, leaving no detail out, and putting no point in. Intelligent people quickly find the essence of the experience they are conveying and try and relate it to the topic at hand in a way that sheds light on the generalizations between them.

We all have a desire to communicate. When something happens to us, we want to tell about it. Why this is so is an open question. But it seems that for most people, the telling of an experience makes that experience live again. And, perhaps more importantly, telling about an experience forces us to crystallize that experience in terms of its essence. We cannot relay the entirety of what has occurred of course. Describing a two week trip would take about two weeks, maybe more. So, we eliminate the unessential.

Now, recall that a human's memory cannot be bothered by all the details either. We cannot afford to devote mental resources, storage facilities in the brain so to speak, to every single detail of our two week trip. Some of the details we can reconstruct if necessary. We need not remember the details of the airplane ride unless something unusual occurred. One airplane trip is like another and, if we have traveled often, such things are good candidates for aspects of the trip to forget.

On the other hand, there are some things we would especially like to remember. They were important in some way to us. Further, there are some aspects of the trip that we would like to think about some more. We may not be sure what we think about certain events, what we felt at the time or why, how we behaved in critical events and how we feel we should have behaved.

This is one reason why telling about an experience is important to us. It helps us to understand that experience ourselves. We can see the difference in intelligence along this dimension. Everyone knows how to present a case, to tell about what happened to us, but not everyone knows how to get the event into a few short sentences that convey the most important aspects of that event or the aspects of that event that would be of most interest to the person who we are talking to.

The more ideas are discussed, the more insights you will come to. This seems fairly obvious but how this happens in actual practice is not. The analysis of an experience is critical to understanding. Unexamined experiences may contain many possible lessons for future use, but they remain dormant until they are discussed. The more you examine your experiences, the more you try to crystallize the essence of an experience *for the consumption of another*, the more you can be reminded or remind others of similar experiences which can be compared and contrasted, yielding new generalizations. Good crystallizations enhance discovery, and discovery is at the heart of intelligence.

It is a property of intelligence to be able to tell what has happened to us and to be able to know the extent to which that experience might be relevant to others and to know when to tell it. We have a sense of what people want to hear when, what constitutes communication. The idea of a dialogue, with two people taking part in a kind of mutual story telling is an interesting aspect of intelligence. Other animals don't really do anything like this, yet all human cultures do.

The extension of this ability is seen in the creation of new stories and the elaboration of old ones. To talk about things that didn't happen is, ironically, an important aspect of intelligence. Intelligence here relates to the concept of entertainment. Knowing that it is possible to entertain people in various ways, story tellers hone the skills necessary to be entertaining. Thus, the ability to create new, entertaining stories, is another important aspect of intelligence.

Another side of intelligence in this arena relates to what we discussed above. Knowing what to leave out can be as important as knowing what to add. Dull people bore their listeners by telling every detail of a story. People who are intelligent along this dimension say just what needs to be said, in the right order, and in the right way for maximum impact on the listener.

Certainly, the ability to tell stories is there from the time you learn to speak. Children are asked to relate their experiences of the day and in so doing become story tellers. The extra step along this dimension requires an ability to see yourself as your audience is seeing you and to care about improving. People are not born as fascinating story tellers; they grow into it, if they choose to, by paying attention to their listeners. In the process of doing this they, in this sense, become more intelligent because they learn from the process of talking.

Dimension 7: integration
normal task: Understand Stories
extended task: Be Curious

At the Yale AI lab, in the late 1970's the problem of getting a computer program to understand stories was investigated. What would it mean for a program to understand a story? Below is the input and output of one of those programs (called FRUMP) [DeJong, 1979]:

INPUT: WASHINGTON, MARCH 15 - THE STATE DEPARTMENT ANNOUNCED
TODAY THE SUSPENSION OF DIPLOMATIC RELATIONS WITH EQUATORIAL
GUINEA. THE ANNOUNCEMENT CAME FIVE DAYS AFTER THE DEPARTMENT
RECEIVED A MESSAGE FROM THE FOREIGN MINISTER OF THE WEST
AFRICAN COUNTRY SAYING THAT HIS GOVERNMENT HAD DECLARED TWO
UNITED STATES DIPLOMATS PERSONA NON GRATA.

THE TWO ARE AMBASSADOR HERBERT J. SPIRO AND CONSUL WILLIAM C.
MITHOEFER JR., BOTH STATIONED IN NEIGHBORING CAMEROON BUT
ALSO ACCREDITED TO EQUATORIAL GUINEA.

ROBERT L. FUNSETH, STATE DEPARTMENT SPOKESMAN, SAID MR. SPIRO
AND MR. MITHOEFER SPENT FIVE DAYS IN EQUATORIAL GUINEA EARLIER
THIS MONTH AND WERE GIVEN ''A WARM RECEPTION''.

BUT AT THE CONCLUSION OF THEIR VISIT, MR. FUNSETH SAID,
EQUATORIAL GUINEA'S ACTING CHIEF OF PROTOCOL HANDED THEM A
FIVE-PAGE LETTER THAT CAST ''UNWARRANTED AND INSULTING SLURS''
ON BOTH DIPLOMATS.

======

SELECTED SKETCHY SCRIPT $BREAK-RELATIONS

CPU TIME FOR UNDERSTANDING - 2515 MILLISECONDS

ENGLISH SUMMARY:

    THE US STATE DEPARTMENT AND GUINEA HAVE BROKEN DIPLOMATIC
    RELATIONS.

FRENCH SUMMARY:

    LE DEPARTEMENT D'ETAT DES ETATS-UNIS ET LA GUINEE ONT COUPE
    LEURS RELATIONS DIPLOMATIQUES.

CHINESE SUMMARY:

    MEEIGWO GWOWUHYUANN GEN JIINAHYAH DUANNJYUELE WAY JIAU
    GUANSHIH.

SPANISH SUMMARY:

    EL DEPARTAMENTO DE RELACIONES EXTERIORES DE LOS EE UU Y
    GUINEA CORTARON SUS RELACIONES DIPLOMATICAS.

    It became clear to us, from working on such programs, that while un-
derstanding stories might entail being able to summarize them, some deeper

concept of understanding was also implied when we talked about understanding. For example, we told some Yale graduate students to verbalize questions they had after reading the following newspaper story:

JERUSALEM, April 13 - A 16-year-old Lebanese was captured by Israeli troops hours before he was supposed to get into an explosive-laden car and go on a suicide bombing mission to blow up the Israeli Army headquarters in Lebanon, according to Israeli officials and an account from the youth himself.

The teenager, Mohammed Mohmoud Burro, was captured by Israeli soldiers in a raid on a southern Lebanese village on February 23.

It is believed to be the first time that a trained suicide car-bomber has been seized alive.

=======

Why would someone commit suicide if they are not depressed?

Why does the news tell us only about Lebanese truck bombers? Aren't there any Israeli truck bombers?

These kids remind one of Kamikaze pilots in World War II. Are they motivated in the same way?

Why is it that every Arab seems to be named Mohammed?

How do the Israelis know where to make their raids?

How do Lebanese teenagers compare to US teenagers?

Why hadn't they been caught alive before?

What do the parents of suicide-bombers think of their children's training for this job?

Is there a political group organizing the kids?

This story reminds me of Oliver Twist. Is there a Lebanese Fagan around who organizes homeless kids into suicide bombers?

What property did these students exhibit that our program did not? The simple answer is curiosity. FRUMP wasn't a very intelligent program. It seems safe to say that, but why? The answer is that FRUMP didn't learn anything from what it read. Every story was grist for the mill that chewed up stories and summarized them. FRUMP seemed intelligent because it could summarize stories and thus seemed to understand them, and computers that understand stories were not then, nor are they now, everyday phenomena.

FRUMP didn't learn. Of course it wasn't intended to learn, so that is not a terrible criticism. But people who read stories do learn from them. At least some people learn some things from them sometimes. The variable in all this is curiosity. If you care about a subject enough to speculate about it some, then you are likely to become more interested in what you read. Anomalies present themselves to be explained. If you cannot explain them, you generate questions for later. Later — maybe years later — you see something that reminds you of these questions and perhaps suggests some answers. Fortunately, curiosity is often quite patient.

Intelligence along the dimension of integration means trying to get everything you see and hear to fit into your internal model of how the world works. The problem, of course, is what to do when things don't fit. If you fall apart every time that happens you will be incapable of reading anything for example, because everything you read would have to have the feature of never containing anything new and that seems quite unlikely. So, integration of new material requires you to decide to what extent each unusual thing is worth updating your memory about. In other words, like FRUMP, you can read about an earthquake in Iran, or the breaking of diplomatic relations between two countries, but how much of what you read should you remember?

It might seem that the answer to this question is obvious: all of it. But, in fact, if you really did remember every article you read in one Sunday's *New York Times*, you might never have room in your head for anything else ever again. The trick in reading is knowing what to forget, and of course, that is the trick in the integration of new information into memory as well.

Not everything is worthy of remembering. Go back and look at the news stories that I presented above. How many of the details did you remember? A smart reader would not have paid much attention to any of it since the content was neither germane nor up-to-date. Smart readers learn to ignore a great deal of what they read, partially by never reading it in the first place in any serious sense, and also by quickly forgetting what they find irrelevant to their own needs.

The basics of integration are done by every human being. We all must decide what to retain and what to discard, because we all process tremendous amounts of information every day. The smartest of us becomes curious about certain aspects of what we encounter and it is precisely those aspects that are worth focusing on.

Now, what constitutes a payoff is a question of values and not of fact. There is no law that mandates where mental processing time is best spent. Of course, if what you are curious about and spend time integrating into memory is what has happened on the daily soap operas or what is for sale and in fashion, it is fairly likely that the intelligence that will be developed by this particular domain of curiosity will not earn kudos among those people who evaluate intelligence. Intelligence in the area of integration is a very subjective thing. Being an expert on certain things, or having a curiosity about certain things, implies intelligence in the eyes of the world if those things are in vogue among the intelligentsia. But this is a matter of fashion. For example, children who know a great deal about computers, who are very curious about computers, who spend mental processing time integrating new information about computers into their memories, are not necessarily more intelligent than those who spend the same effort on motorcycles, but they are more in fashion. (They are also likely to be more employable.)

So, the issue with respect to cases is this. We know them, find them, reconsider them, manipulate them, use them to understand the world and to operate in the world, adapt them to new purposes, tell about them in new ways, and, we invent them. We live in a world of cases. Our ability to utilize these cases in novel ways is a hallmark of what we consider to be intelligence.

Bibliography

R. Alterman. (February 1985). A dictionary based on concept coherence. *Artificial Intelligence*, 25(2):153–186.

R. Alterman. (1986). An adaptive planner. In *Proceedings of AAAI-86*, pages 65–69, American Association for Artificial Intelligence, Morgan Kaufmann Publishers, Inc., Los Altos, CA.

J.R. Anderson. (1986). Knowledge compilation: the general learning mechanism. In *Machine Learning: An Artificial Intelligence Approach*, pages 289–310, Morgan Kaufmann Publishers, Inc., Los Altos, CA.

J.R. Anderson, A.T. Corbett, and B.J. Reiser. (1987). *Essential Lisp*. Addison-Wesley Publishing Co., Reading, MA.

Kevin D. Ashley. (1987). Distinguishing – a reasoner's wedge. In *Proceedings of the Ninth Annual Conference of the Cognitive Science Society*, pages 737–747, Cognitive Science Society, Lawrence Erlbaum Associates, Hillsdale, N.J.

Kevin D. Ashley and Edwina L. Rissland. (1987). Compare and contrast, a test of expertise. In *Proceedings of AAAI-87*, pages 273–278, American Association for Artificial Intelligence, Morgan Kaufmann Publishers, Inc., Los Altos, CA.

W.M. Bain. (1986). *Case-Based Reasoning: A Computer Model of Subjective Assessment*. PhD thesis, Yale University.

J.D. Becker. (1975). The phrasal lexicon. In *Theoretical Issues in Natural Language Processing*, pages 60–63, Cambridge, MA.

L. Birnbaum. (1985). A short note on opportunistic planning and memory in arguments. In *Proceedings of the Ninth International Joint Conference on Artificial Intelligence*, pages 281–283, Morgan Kaufmann Publishers, Inc., Los Altos, CA.

L. Birnbaum and M. Selfridge. (1981). Conceptual analysis of natural language. In R.C. Schank and C.K. Riesbeck, editors, *Inside Computer Understanding*, pages 318–353, Lawrence Erlbaum Associates, Hillsdale, N.J.

L. Birnbaum, M. Flowers, and R. McGuire. (1980). Towards an AI model of argumentation. In *Proceedings of AAAI-80*, pages 313–315, American Association for Artificial Intelligence, Morgan Kaufmann Publishers, Inc., Los Altos, CA.

Lawrence A. Birnbaum. (1986). *Integrated Processing in Planning and Understanding*. PhD thesis, Yale University.

D.G Bobrow and J.B. Fraser. (1969). An augmented state transition network analysis procedure. In *Proceedings of the International Joint Conference on Artificial Intelligence*, pages 52–57, The International Joint Conferences on Artificial Intelligence, Morgan Kaufmann Publishers, Inc., Los Altos, CA.

B.G. Buchanan and E.H. Shortliffe, editors. (1984). *Rule-Based Expert Systems*. Addison-Wesley Publishing Co., Reading, MA.

J.G. Carbonell. (1979). *Subjective Understanding: Computer Models of Belief Systems*. Research Report 150, Yale University.

J.G. Carbonell. (1981). Counterplanning: a strategy-based model of adversary planning in real-world situations. *Artificial Intelligence*, 16:295–329.

J.G. Carbonell. (1986). Derivational analogy: a theory of reconstructive problem solving and expertise acquisition. In *Machine Learning: An Artificial Intelligence Approach*, pages 371–392, Morgan Kaufmann Publishers, Inc., Los Altos, CA.

J.S. Carroll and J.W. Payne. (1976). The psychology of the parole decision process: a joint application of attribution theory and information-processing psychology. In J.S. Carroll and J.W. Payne, editors, *Cognition and Social Behavior*, Lawrence Erlbaum Associates, Hillsdale, N.J.

B. Chandrasekaran and S. Mittal. (1982). Deep versus compiled knowledge approaches to diagnostic problem-solving. In *Proceedings of AAAI-82*, pages 349–354, American Association for Artificial Intelligence, Morgan Kaufmann Publishers, Inc., Los Altos, CA.

D. Chapman. (1985). *Planning for conjunctive goals.* Memo AI-802, MIT Artificial Intelligence Laboratory.

E. Charniak. (1986). A neat theory of marker passing. In *Proceedings of AAAI-86*, pages 584–588, American Association for Artificial Intelligence, Morgan Kaufmann Publishers, Inc., Los Altos, CA.

E. Charniak and D. McDermott. (1985). *Introduction to Artificial Intelligence.* Addison-Wesley Publishing Co., Reading, MA.

E. Charniak, C. K. Riesbeck, and D. McDermott. (1980). *Artificial Intelligence Programming Techniques.* Lawrence Erlbaum Associates, Hillsdale, N.J.

E. Charniak, C. K. Riesbeck, D. McDermott, and J.R Meehan. (1987). *Artificial Intelligence Programming Techniques.* Lawrence Erlbaum Associates, Hillsdale, N.J., second edition.

G.C. Collins. (1987). *Plan Creation: Using Strategies as Blueprints.* PhD thesis, Yale University.

G.F. DeJong. (1979). Prediction and substantiation: a new approach to natural language processing. *Cognitive Science*, 3(3):251–273.

G.F. DeJong. (1981). Generalizations based on explanations. In *Proceedings of the Seventh International Joint Conference on Artificial Intelligence*, pages 67–69, The International Joint Conferences on Artificial Intelligence, Morgan Kaufmann Publishers, Inc., Los Altos, CA.

G. DeJong and R. Mooney. (1986). Explanation-based learning: an alternative view. *Machine Learning*, 1(2):145–176.

J. Doyle. (1979). A truth maintenance system. *Artificial Intelligence*, 12(3):231–272.

M.G. Dyer. (1983). *In-Depth Understanding.* The MIT Press, Cambridge, MA.

E.A. Feigenbaum, B.G. Buchanan, and J. Lederberg. (1971). On generality and problem solving: a case study involving the dendral program. In B. Meltzer and D. Michie, editors, *Machine Intelligence*, pages 165–190, American Elsevier, New York.

R. Fikes and N. Nilsson. (1971). STRIPS: a new approach to the application of theorem proving to problem solving. *Artificial Intelligence*, 2:189–208.

R.H. Granger. (1980). *Adaptive Understanding: Correcting Erroneous Inferences.* Technical Report 171, Yale University Department of Computer Science.

R.H. Granger, K.P. Eiselt, and J.K. Holbrook. (1984). The parallel organization of lexical, syntactic, and pragmatic inference processes. In *Proceedings of the First Annual Workshop on Theoretical Issues in Conceptual Information Processing*, pages 97–106, Atlanta, GA.

Kristian J. Hammond. (1989). *Case-based Planning: Viewing Planning as a Memory Task.* Perspectives in Artificial Intelligence, Academic Press, Boston, MA.

Barbara Hayes-Roth and Frederick Hayes-Roth. (1979). A cognitive model of planning. *Cognitive Science*, 3(4):275–310.

F. Hayes-Roth, D. Waterman, and D. Lenat, editors. (1983). *Building Expert Systems.* Addison-Wesley Publishing Co., Reading, MA.

Eduard Hendrik Hovy. (March 1987). *Generating Natural Language Under Pragmatic Constraints.* research report YALEU/CSD/RR #521, Yale University Department of Computer Science.

Paul S. Jacobs. (1987). Knowledge-intensive natural language generation. *Artificial Intelligence*, 33(3):325–378.

R. Kaplan. (1975). On process models for sentence analysis. In D. Norman and D. Rumelhart, editors, *Explorations in Cognition*, pages 117–135, W.H. Freeman and Company, San Francisco.

Alex Kass. (1986). Modifying explanations to understand stories. In *Proceedings of the Eighth Annual Conference of the Cognitive Science Society*, pages 691–696, Cognitive Science Society, Lawrence Erlbaum Associates, Hillsdale, N.J.

J.L. Kolodner. (1984). *Retrieval and Organizational Strategies in Conceptual Memory.* Lawrence Erlbaum Associates, Hillsdale, N.J.

J.L. Kolodner. (1987). Capitalizing on failure through case-based inference. In *Proceedings of the Ninth Annual Conference of the Cognitive Science Society*, pages 715–726, Cognitive Science Society, Lawrence Erlbaum Associates, Hillsdale, N.J.

J.L Kolodner, editor. (1988). *Proceedings of the First Case-Based Reasoning Workshop*, Morgan Kaufmann Publishers, Inc., Los Altos, CA.

J.L. Kolodner and C.K. Riesbeck. (1986). *Experience, Memory and Reasoning.* Lawrence Erlbaum Associates, Hillsdale, N.J.

R. Korf. (1982). A program that learns to solve Rubik's Cube. In *Proceedings of AAAI-82*, pages 164–167, American Association for Artificial Intelligence, Morgan Kaufmann Publishers, Inc., Los Altos, CA.

Phyllis Koton. (1988). Reasoning about evidence in causal explanation. In *Proceedings of AAAI-88*, pages 256–261, American Association for Artificial Intelligence, Morgan Kaufmann Publishers, Inc., Los Altos, CA.

J.E. Laird, P.S. Rosenbloom, and A. Newell. (1986). Chunking in Soar: the anatomy of a general learning mechanism. *Machine Learning*, 1(1):11–46.

David B. Leake and Christopher C. Owens. (1986). Organizing memory for explanations. In *Proceedings of the Eighth Annual Conference of the Cognitive Science Society*, pages 710–715, Cognitive Science Society, Lawrence Erlbaum Associates, Hillsdale, N.J.

M. Lebowitz. (October 1980). *Generalization and Memory in an Integrated Understanding System.* Research Report 186, Yale University.

M. Lebowitz. (1986). Integrated learning: controlling explanation. *Cognitive Science*, 10(2):219–240.

M. Lebowitz. (1986). Not the path to perdition: the utility of similarity-based learning. In *Proceedings of AAAI-86*, pages 533–537, American Association for Artificial Intelligence, Morgan Kaufmann Publishers, Inc., Los Altos, CA.

S. Lytinen. (November 1984). *The organization of knowledge in a multilingual, integrated parser.* Research Report 340, Yale University.

M.P. Marcus. (1980). *A Theory of Syntactic Recognition for Natural Language.* The MIT Press, Cambridge, MA.

Drew McDermott. (1978). Planning and acting. *Cognitive Science*, 2(2):71–109.

R.S. Michalski. (February 1983). A theory and methodology of inductive learning. *Artificial Intelligence*, 20(2):111–161.

M. Minsky. (1975). A framework for representing knowledge. In P. H. Winston, editor, *The Psychology of Computer Vision*, McGraw-Hill, New York.

T.M. Mitchell, R.M. Keller, and S.T. Kedar-Cabelli. (1986). Explanation-based generalization: a unifying view. *Machine Learning*, 1(1):47–80.

T.M. Mitchell, Paul Utgoff, and Ranan Banerji. (1983). Learning by experimentation: acquiring and refining problem-solving heuristics. In R. Michalski, J. Carbonell, and T. Mitchell, editors, *Machine Learning: An Artificial Intelligence Approach*, pages 163–190, Morgan Kaufmann Publishers, Inc., Los Altos, CA.

A. Newell. (1981). The knowledge level. *AI Magazine*, 2(2):1–20.

A. Newell and H. Simon. (1972). *Human Problem Solving*. Prentice-Hall, Englewood Cliffs, NJ.

P. Norvig. (1987). Inference in text understanding. In *Proceedings of AAAI-87*, pages 2561–565, American Association for Artificial Intelligence, Morgan Kaufmann Publishers, Inc., Los Altos, CA.

N. Pennington and R. Hastie. (August 1981). *Juror Decision Making: Story Structure and Verdict Choice*. Technical Report, American Psychological Association.

F.C.N. Periera and D.H.D. Warren. (May 1980). Definite clause grammars for language analysis–a survey of the formalism and a comparison with augmented transition networks. *Artificial Intelligence*, 13(3):231–278.

M.R. Quillian. (1969). The teachable language comprehender: a simulation program and theory of language. *Communications of the ACM*, 12(8).

J.R. Quinlan. (1983). Learning efficient classification procedures and their application to chess endgames. In R. Michalski, J. Carbonell, and T. Mitchell, editors, *Machine Learning*, Tioga Press, Palo Alto, CA.

C. J. Rieger. (1975). Conceptual memory and inference. In R.C. Schank, editor, *Conceptual Information Processing*, North Holland, Amsterdam.

C.K. Riesbeck. (1974). *Conputational Understanding: Analysis of Sentences and Context*. PhD thesis, Stanford University, Stanford, CA.

C.K. Riesbeck and C.E. Martin. (1985). *Direct Memory Access Parsing*. YALEU/DCS/RR 354, Yale University.

C.K. Riesbeck and R.C. Schank. (1976). Comprehension by computer: expectation-based analysis of sentences in context. In W.J.M Levelt and G.B. Flores d'Arcais, editors, *Studies in the Perception of Language*, John Wiley and Sons, Chichester, England.

Edwina L. Rissland and Kevin D. Ashley. (1986). Hypotheticals as heuristic device. In *Proceedings of AAAI-86*, pages 289–297, American Association for Artificial Intelligence, Morgan Kaufmann Publishers, Inc., Los Altos, CA.

E. Sacerdoti. (1975). The nonlinear nature of plans. In *Advance Papers from the Fourth International Joint Conference on Artificial Intelligence*, pages 206–214, The International Joint Conferences on Artificial Intelligence, Morgan Kaufmann Publishers, Inc., Los Altos, CA.

E. Sacerdoti. (1977). *A Structure for Plans and Behavior*. Elsevier North-Holland, Amsterdam.

R.C. Schank. (1975). *Conceptual Information Processing*. North Holland/American Elsevier, Amsterdam.

R.C. Schank. (1982). *Dynamic Memory: A Theory of Learning in Computers and People*. Cambridge University Press.

R.C. Schank. (1986). *Explanation Patterns: Understanding Mechanically and Creatively*. Lawrence Erlbaum Associates, Hillsdale, N.J.

R. Schank and R. Abelson. (1977). *Scripts, Plans, Goals, and Understanding*. Lawrence Erlbaum Associates, Hillsdale, N.J.

R.C. Schank and R. Wilensky. (1978). A goal-directed production system for story understanding. In D.A. Waterman and F. Hayes-Roth, editors, *Pattern-directed Inference Systems*, pages 415–430, Academic Press, New York.

Reid G. Simmons. (1988). A theory of debugging. In J.L Kolodner, editor, *Proceedings of the First Case-Based Reasoning Workshop*, pages 388–401, Morgan Kaufmann Publishers, Inc., Los Altos, CA.

R.L. Simpson. (1984). *Strategies for retrieval and prediction in an advisory system: A research proposal*. Technical Report GIT-ICS-84/03, Georgia Institute of Technology, School of Information and Computer Science, Atlanta GA.

R.L. Simpson. (1985). *A Computer Model of Case-Based Reasoning in Problem Solving: An Investigation in the Domain of Dispute Mediation.* Technical Report GIT-ICS-85/18, Georgia Institute of Technology, School of Information and Computer Science, Atlanta GA.

E.E. Smith, N. Adams, and D. Schorr. (1978). Fact retrieval and the paradox of interference. *Cognitive Psychology*, 10:438–464.

Jr. Steele, Guy L. (1984). *Common Lisp: The Language.* Digital Press, Billerica, MA.

G. Sussman. (1975). *A computer model of skill acquisition.* Volume 1 of *Artificial Intelligence Series*, American Elsevier, New York.

E.P. Sycara. (1987). *Resolving Adversarial Conflicts: An Approach to Integrating Case-Based and Analytic Methods.* Technical Report GIT-ICS-87/26, Georgia Institute of Technology, School of Information and Computer Science, Atlanta GA.

A. Tate. (1977). Generating project networks. In *Proceedings of the Fifth International Joint Conference on Artificial Intelligence*, pages 888–893, The International Joint Conferences on Artificial Intelligence, Morgan Kaufmann Publishers, Inc., Los Altos, CA.

J. Thorne, P. Bratley, and H. Dewar. (1968). The syntactic analysis of English by machine. In D. Michie, editor, *Machine Intelligence 3*, pages 281–309, Ellis Horwood, Chichester, England.

David L. Waltz. (1975). Understanding line drawings of scenes with shadows. In P. H. Winston, editor, *The Psychology of Computer Vision*, McGraw-Hill, New York.

D.A. Waterman. (1975). Adaptive production systems. In *Advance Papers from the Fourth International Joint Conference on Artificial Intelligence*, pages 296–303, The International Joint Conferences on Artificial Intelligence, Morgan Kaufmann Publishers, Inc., Los Altos, CA.

R. Wilensky. (1978). *Understanding Goal-Based Stories.* Research Report 140, Yale University.

R. Wilensky. (August 1980). *META-PLANNING.* Technical Report M80 33, UCB College of Engineering.

R. Wilensky. (1983). *Planning and Understanding: A Computational Approach To Human Reasoning.* Addison-Wesley Publishing Co., Reading, MA.

R. Wilensky. (1986). *Common LISPcraft.* W.W.Norton & Company, Inc., New York.

David Wilkins. (1984). Domain-independent planning. *Artificial Intelligence,* 22(3):269–302.

Y. Wilks. (1973). An artificial intelligence approach to machine translation. In R.C. Schank and K.M. Colby, editors, *Computer Models of Thought and Language,* pages 114–151, W.H. Freeman and Company, San Francisco.

Y. Wilks. (1975). A preferential, pattern-matching semantics for natural language understanding. *Artificial Intelligence,* 6:53–74.

T. Winograd. (1972). *Understanding Natural Language.* Academic Press, New York.

P.H. Winston. (1975). Learning structural descriptions from examples. In P.H. Winston, editor, *The Psychology of Computer Vision,* McGraw-Hill, New York.

Patrick Henry Winston and Berthold Klaus Paul Horn. (1984). *Lisp.* Addison-Wesley Publishing Co., Reading, MA., second edition.

Ludwig Wittgenstein. (1953). *Philosophical Investigations.* Basil Blackwell, Oxford.

W.A. Woods. (1970). Transition network grammars for natural language analysis. *Communications of the ACM,* 13(10):591–606.

Appendix

A.1 Common Lisp in Other Lisps

For the most part, we have tried to use only the most basic capabilities of Common Lisp, elements that should be available in almost any serious Lisp dialect. However, there are several functions and macros that were simply too useful to avoid that might not be in the Lisp you are using. We define simple versions of these items here. These definitions are solely for pedagogical purposes, to help you get the micro programs to run. They are neither as efficient nor as powerful as the real Common Lisp versions.

A.2 Backquote (`)

The backquote (`) facility in Common Lisp is very handy for creating complex list structures. If your Lisp does not have it, we recommend that you define it, if possible. The code in Listing A.1 defines a simple version of a backquote function, based on the one in [Charniak *et al.*, 1987].

If your Lisp supports "readmacros," i.e., attaching functions to characters to be called whenever those characters are read, then you should attach BACKQUOTE to the character `. In Common Lisp, this would be done by executing the mysterious forms in Listing A.2.

If your Lisp does not have readmacros, but it does have macros, then define the macro BQ:

```
(DEFMACRO BQ (L) (BACKQUOTE L))
```

and replace occurrences of `*exp*, ,*exp* and ,@*exp* with (BQ *exp*), ($ *exp*) and ($$ *exp*), respectively. For example,

```
(LET ((L '(A B C))
      (M NIL))
  `(1 ,L 2 ,@L 3 ,M 4 ,@M 5))
```

```
(DEFUN BACKQUOTE (SKEL)
  (COND ((NULL SKEL) NIL)
        ((ATOM SKEL) (LIST 'QUOTE SKEL))
        ((EQL (CAR SKEL) '$) (CAR (CDR SKEL)))
        ((AND (LISTP (CAR SKEL))
              (EQL (CAR (CAR SKEL)) '$$))
         (LIST 'APPEND (CAR (CDR (CAR SKEL)))
               (BACKQUOTE (CDR SKEL))))
        (T (COMBINE-SKELS (BACKQUOTE (CAR SKEL))
                          (BACKQUOTE (CDR SKEL))))))

(DEFUN COMBINE-SKELS (LEFT RIGHT)
  (COND ((AND (CONSTANTP LEFT) (CONSTANTP RIGHT))
         (LIST 'QUOTE (CONS (CAR (CDR LEFT))
                            (CAR (CDR RIGHT)))))
        ((NULL RIGHT) (LIST 'LIST LEFT))
        ((AND (LISTP RIGHT)
              (EQL (CAR RIGHT) 'LIST))
         (CONS 'LIST (CONS LEFT (CDR RIGHT))))
        (T (LIST 'CONS LEFT RIGHT))))

(DEFUN CONSTANTP (X)     ;only if not in your Lisp
  (OR (NULL X) (NUMBERP X) (STRINGP X)
      (AND (LISTP X) (EQL (CAR X) 'QUOTE))))
```

Listing A.1: Definitions for BACKQUOTE

```
(SET-MACRO-CHARACTER #\'
   #'(LAMBDA (STREAM CHAR)
      (BACKQUOTE (READ STREAM T NIL T))))

(SET-MACRO-CHARACTER #\,
   #'(LAMBDA (STREAM CHAR)
      (LIST (GET-UNQUOTER STREAM)
            (READ STREAM T NIL T))))

(DEFUN GET-UNQUOTER (STREAM)
 (LET ((NEXT-CHAR (READ-CHAR STREAM T NIL T)))
  (COND ((EQL NEXT-CHAR #\@) '$$)
        (T (UNREAD-CHAR NEXT-CHAR STREAM)
           '$))))
```

Listing A.2: Definitions for Backquote (') Readmacro

```
(DEFUN COPY-LIST (L)
 (AND L (CONS (CAR L) (COPY-LIST (CDR L)))))
```

Listing A.3: Definition of COPY-LIST

would be written as

```
(LET ((L '(A B C))
      (M NIL))
 (BQ (1 ($ L) 2 ($$ L) 3 ($ M) 4 ($$ M) 5)))
```

A.3   COPY-LIST

> (COPY-LIST *list*) returns a copy of *list*.

If your Lisp doesn't have COPY-LIST, you can define it very easily with the code in Listing A.3.

A.4   EQL

If your Lisp does not have EQL, replace it with EQUAL.

A.5 ERROR

The function ERROR, called in Listing 3.1, is used to tell Lisp that something
has gone wrong. Depending on your implementation, this may either simply stop your program with a message, or may put you into some kind of
interactive dialog to help you diagnose the source of the error.

Most Lisps have some kind of error-signaling function. Use whatever your
Lisp has. If your Lisp error-signaler does not take a message argument to
print, use your Lisp's printing functions to print messages before calling the
error-signaler.

A.6 #' and FUNCTION

If your Lisp does not recognize #'*exp*, simply replace it with (FUNCTION *exp*),
e.g.,

    (PPRINT (TREE->LIST MOP #'SPECS->LIST NIL))

would become

    (PPRINT (TREE->LIST MOP (FUNCTION SPECS->LIST) NIL)).

If your Lisp does not even know about FUNCTION, use QUOTE instead.

A.7 FORMAT for Output

We used two forms of the FORMAT function in this book.

> (FORMAT T *string* exp_1 exp_2 ...) replaces occurrences of the
> command codes in *string* with the appropriate values and
> prints the result.

A command code of ~S is replaced with the next unprinted exp_i and a code of
~& is replaced with a new line character. This is called "formatted output."

If your Lisp does not have FORMAT, it will certainly have other functions
for printing expressions, strings, and new line characters. A common set of
functions is given in Table A.1 and examples of the output in Table A.2.

You can either define your own version of FORMAT, using whatever functions
your Lisp has for manipulating strings to take *string* apart, or replace every
occurrence of (FORMAT T ...) with the appropriate set of calls to the primitive
printing functions. For example,

    (FORMAT T "~&~S:~S <= ~S" MOP ROLE FILLER)

Calling Format	Effect
(PRIN1 *exp*)	prints *exp*
(PRINC *exp*)	prints *exp*, without the quote (") delimiters
(TERPRI)	prints a new line character

Table A.1: Primitive Printing Functions

Example	Output
(PRIN1 '(A B C))	(A B C)
(PRINC '(A B C))	(A B C)
(PRIN1 "A string")	"A string"
(PRINC "A string")	A string
(TERPRI)	*starts a new line*

Table A.2: Examples of Primitive Printing Functions

would become

```
(TERPRI)
(PRIN1 MOP)
(PRINC ":")
(PRIN1 ROLE)
(PRINC " <= ")
(PRIN1 FILLER)
```

A.8   GENTEMP

The function SPEC-NAME in Listing 3.9 generates names for MOPs. This code uses two functions that may not be available if your Lisp is not Common Lisp.

> (FORMAT NIL *string* *exp*$_1$ *exp*$_2$ ...) replaces occurrences of the command codes in *string* with the appropriate values and returns the resulting string. No printing occurs.

The command codes are the same as those used when FORMAT is used for printing.

If your Lisp does not have this string-making version of FORMAT, then you can either define it yourself, or just change the definition of SPEC-NAME in Listing 3.9 to be

```
(DEFUN SPEC-NAME (ABSTS TYPE)
(GENTEMP (COND ((EQL TYPE 'MOP) "MOP.")
               (T "INST."))))
```

The only effect will be that a MOP's name will no longer include the name of one of its immediate abstractions. Thus, an instance of M-MTRANS will be something like INST.12, rather than I-M-MTRANS.12.

The (FORMAT NIL ...) creates a string. GENTEMP makes a symbol from that string.

> (GENTEMP *string*) creates a new symbol beginning with *string*.

If your Lisp does not have GENTEMP, it probably has GENSYM.

> (GENSYM) creates a new symbol.

With GENSYM you usually have to call another function called INTERN to "install" the symbol into Lisp. We won't go into what "installing" a symbol actually does.

> (INTERN *symbol*) installs *symbol* into your Lisp.

GENSYM is less flexible in how the symbol is constructed. If your Lisp has these functions, a workable definition of SPEC-NAME would be

```
(DEFUN SPEC-NAME (ABSTS TYPE)
(INTERN (GENSYM)))
```

The name of a MOP will probably be something like G0120.

A.9   GETF

> (GETF *plist exp*) returns the value following the first key in *plist* EQL to *exp*, where *plist* is any Lisp expression that returns a (possibly empty) list of the form (key_1 $value_1$ key_2 $value_2$ ...).

If your Lisp doesn't have GETF, the code in Listing A.4 will implement a simple version adequate for the code in this book. To do so, we need to use two primitive functions found in most Lisps.

> - (RPLACA *list exp*) changes *list* so that its CAR is now *exp*, and returns *list*.
> - (RPLACD *list exp*) changes *list* so that its CDR is now *exp*, and returns *list*.

Unlike CONS, RPLACA and RPLACD do not build a new list, leaving the old one alone. *They change the list permanently.* For example,

```
(SETF L '(A B C))
(CONS 1 L)                   ;returns (1 A B C)
L                            ;still (A B C)
(RPLACA L 1)                 ;returns (1 B C)
L                            ;is now (1 B C)
(RPLACA (CDR (CDR L)) 3)    ;returns (3)
L                            ;is now (1 B 3)
(RPLACD (CDR L) NIL)         ;returns (B)
L                            ;is now (1 B)
```

Bugs from inappropriate calls to RPLACA and RPLACD are among the hardest to find. We recommend avoiding these functions if at all possible. Unfortunately, to make GETF do the right thing in all cases, we have to use them in Listing A.4.

If your Lisp has neither GETF nor SETF, see the discussion in Section A.12.

(GETF *plist key*) returns the value attached to *key* in *plist*, if any, otherwise it returns NIL.

(SETF (GETF *plist key*) *value*) attaches *value* to *key* in *plist*. *plist* is either NIL or a list of the form (key_1 $value_1$ key_2 $value_2$ ...).

(GETF-SEARCH *plist key*) returns the tail of *plist* following *key*, if *key* is a key in *plist*.

(SET-GETF *plist key exp*) sets the expression attached to *key* in *plist* to the value of *exp*. If *key* is not already in *plist*, it and its value are added to the front of *plist*, otherwise the existing value for *key* is replaced. SET-GETF returns the value of *exp*.

(REMF *plist key*) removes *key* and its value from *plist*. REMF returns true if *key* was found in *plist*. For reasons which we won't go into here, if *key* is the first key in *plist*, we have to set the form *plist* to the appropriately truncated list. Otherwise, REM-KEY can modify *plist* directly.

(REM-KEY *list plist key*) removes *key* and its value from *plist*. *list* is that part of the original GETF list whose CDR is *plist*. That is, if the original list was (A 1 B 2 C 3), then when *plist* is (B 2 C 3), *list* is (1 B 2 C 3), and when *plist* is (C 3), *list* is (2 C 3). In this way, setting the CDR of *list* to the double-CDR of *plist* will effectively remove the first two elements of *plist*.

```
(DEFUN GETF (PLIST KEY)
 (LET ((ENTRY (GETF-SEARCH PLIST KEY)))
  (AND ENTRY (CAR ENTRY))))

(DEFUN GETF-SEARCH (PLIST KEY)
 (COND ((NULL PLIST) NIL)
       ((EQL (CAR PLIST) KEY) (CDR PLIST))
       (T (GETF-SEARCH (CDR (CDR PLIST)) KEY))))

(DEFMACRO SET-GETF (PLIST KEY VAL)
 '(LET ((P ,PLIST) (K ,KEY) (V ,VAL))
   (LET ((ENTRY (GETF-SEARCH P K)))
    (COND ((NULL ENTRY)
           (SETF ,PLIST (CONS K (CONS V P))))
          (T (RPLACA ENTRY V)))
    V)))

(DEFSETF GETF SET-GETF)

(DEFMACRO REMF (PLIST KEY)
 '(LET ((P ,PLIST) (K ,KEY))
   (AND P
    (LET ((R (CDR (CDR P))))
     (COND ((EQL (CAR P) K)
            (SETF ,PLIST R))
           (T (REM-KEY (CDR P) R K)))
     T))))

(DEFUN REM-KEY (L P K)
 (COND ((NULL P) NIL)
       ((EQL (CAR P) K)
        (RPLACD L (CDR (CDR P)))
        T)
       (T (REM-KEY (CDR (CDR L)) (CDR (CDR P)) K))))
```

Listing A.4: Definitions of GETF and REMF

```
(DEFUN REMOVE-DUPLICATES (L)
 (AND L
  (LET ((X (CAR L))
        (R (REMOVE-DUPLICATES (CDR L))))
   (COND ((MEMBER X R) R)
         (T (CONS X R)))))))
```

Listing A.5: Definition of REMOVE-DUPLICATES

A.10   REMOVE-DUPLICATES

> (REMOVE-DUPLICATES *list*) returns a copy of *list* with any duplicate elements removed. If an element appears more than once in *list*, the earlier appearances are removed.

If your Lisp doesn't have REMOVE-DUPLICATES, you can define a simple version with the code in Listing A.5.

A.11   &REST

In several macro definitions, we took advantage of the &REST feature in Common Lisp, e.g., in Listing 3.1 we wrote

```
(DEFMACRO INSIST (FNNAME &REST EXPS)
 '(AND ,@(MAKE-INSIST-FORMS FNNAME EXPS)))
```

The &REST in the parameter list for INSIST means that when INSIST is called, FNNAME is assigned the the first argument, and EXPS is assigned a list of the remaining arguments.

If your Lisp does not have &REST, it may allow the following equivalent notation:

```
(DEFMACRO INSIST (FNNAME . EXPS)
 '(AND ,@(MAKE-INSIST-FORMS FNNAME EXPS)))
```

The period (.) serves the same function here as the &REST.

If your Lisp does not allow this either, then it is probably set up so that all macros are defined with only one parameter, but this parameter is bound to the entire macro call. If this is the case with your Lisp, you'll have to add code to each definition to "take the argument apart." For example, in some Lisps, the proper definition of INSIST would be:

```
(DEFMACRO INSIST (L)
 (LET ((FNNAME (CAR (CDR L))) (EXPS (CDR (CDR L))))
   '(AND ,@(MAKE-INSIST-FORMS FNNAME EXPS))))
```

In such Lisps, if the form

```
(INSIST FOR
        (NOT (NULL VAR-FORMS))
        (NOT (NULL BODY-FORMS)))
```

is expanded, L will be assigned the entire form, so `(CAR (CDR L))` will return `FOR` and `(CDR (CDR L))` will return the list 'code`((NOT (NULL VAR-FORMS)) (NOT (NULL BODY-FORMS)))`.

Similar changes will fix the other macro definitions that use `&REST`.

A.12   SETF and DEFSETF

> (SETF *form value*) assigns *value* to *form*. *form* should be either the name of a variable or a function call of the form (*fname expression₁ expression₂* ...), where *fname* is the name of a function.

When we define a new function, we can also tell SETF how to "set" calls to that function. We used this ability extensively in micro MOPS. For example, the function MOP-ABSTS is defined so that (MOP-ABSTS *mop*) returns the immediate abstractions of *mop*. Furthermore, (SETF (MOP-ABSTS *mop*) *mop-list*) sets the immediate abstractions of *mop* to be the MOPs in *mop-list*

> (DEFSETF *fname₁ fname₂*) tells SETF that something of the form
>
> (SETF (*fname₁ expression₁ expression₂* ...) *value*)
>
> should be evaluated by evaluating
>
> (*fname₂ expression₁ expression₂* ... *value*)
>
> *fname₂* should return the value of *value*.

```
(SETQ *SETF-FNS* NIL)

(DEFMACRO SETF (PLACE VAL)
  (COND ((SYMBOLP PLACE) '(SETQ ,PLACE ,VAL))
        (T (LET ((SETF-FN (GETF *SETF-FNS* (CAR PLACE))))
             '(,SETF-FN ,@(CDR PLACE) ,VAL)))))

(DEFMACRO DEFSETF (FN1 FN2)
  '(SET-GETF *SETF-FNS* ',FN1 ',FN2))    ;see text!
```

Listing A.6: Definitions of SETF and DEFSETF

SETF is a macro. A call to SETF expands into some more primitive assignment function, depending on what *form* is. For example, if *form* is a variable name, the primitive Lisp assignment function SETQ is used.

> (SETQ *variable* *value*) resets *variable* to the value of *value*.

DEFSETF modifies a table linking functions to their "setters" and SETF uses this table when expanding itself. If your Lisp does not have SETF and DEFSETF then the simple version in Listing A.6 will support the code in this book.

The function SET-GETF in the definition of DEFSETF is not a standard Common Lisp function. You should replace it with the function that adds entries to GETF-style plists in your Lisp. If your Lisp does not have GETF, then you'll also need Listing A.4, which defines GETF and SET-GETF. The definitions in Listing A.6 should be evaluated before those in Listing A.4.

If your Lisp has GETF and SETF but not DEFSETF, use Listing A.7 instead of Listing A.6, and change all occurrences of SETF in all listings *except Listing A.7* to ESETF.

```
(SETQ *SETF-FNS* NIL)

(DEFMACRO ESETF (PLACE VAL)
 (COND ((SYMBOLP PLACE) '(SETQ ,PLACE ,VAL))
       (T (LET ((SETF-FN (GETF *SETF-FNS* (CAR PLACE))))
          '(,SETF-FN ,@(CDR PLACE) ,VAL)))))

(DEFMACRO DEFSETF (FN1 FN2)
 '(SETF (GETF *SETF-FNS* ',FN1) ',FN2))
```

Listing A.7: Definitions of ESETF and DEFSETF

Author Index

Abelson, R., 20, 34, 277, 279, 284, 289, 333, 397
Adams, N., 31, 398
Alterman, R., 29, 31, 47, 343, 391
Anderson, J.R., 55, 391
Ashley, K.D., 29, 391, 397

Bain, W.M., 27, 93, 161, 162, 391
Banerji, R., 271, 396
Becker, J.D., 330, 391
Birnbaum, L., 108, 254, 273, 319, 323, 328, 338, 347, 391, 392
Bobrow, D.G, 319, 392
Bratley, P., 319, 398
Buchanan, B.G., 2, 17, 392, 393

Carbonell, J.G., 20, 43, 262, 392
Carroll, J.S., 99, 392
Chandrasekaran, B., 31, 392
Chapman, D., 257, 393
Charniak, E., 35, 55, 88, 137, 199, 252, 343, 393, 401
Collins, G.C., 28, 249, 271, 393
Corbett, A.T., 55, 391

DeJong, G.F., 37, 170, 202, 254, 385, 393
Dewar, H., 319, 398
Doyle, J., 270, 393
Dyer, M.G., 319, 393

Eiselt, K.P., 343, 394

Feigenbaum, E.A., 2, 393
Fikes, R., 167, 393

Flowers, M., 347, 392
Fraser, J.B., 319, 392

Granger, R.H., 332, 343, 394

Hammond, K.J., 28, 42, 248, 394
Hastie, R., 99, 396
Hayes-Roth, B., 108, 394
Hayes-Roth, F., 17, 108, 394
Holbrook, J.K., 343, 394
Horn, B.K.P., 55, 399
Hovy, E.H., 117, 394

Jacobs, P.S., 372, 394

Kaplan, R., 319, 394
Kass, A., 30, 47, 52, 394
Kedar-Cabelli, S.T., 37, 170, 202, 396
Keller, R.M., 37, 170, 202, 396
Kolodner, J.L., 9, 27, 50, 87, 328, 394, 395
Korf, R., 167, 395
Koton, P., 30, 395

Laird, J.E., 31, 395
Leake, D.B., 30, 52, 395
Lebowitz, M., 27, 87, 91, 169, 328, 341, 395
Lederberg, J., 2, 393
Lenat, D., 17, 394
Lytinen, S., 319, 328, 395

Marcus, M.P., 319, 395
Martin, C.E., 326, 396

413

McDermott, D., 35, 55, 88, 137, 199, 252, 257, 393, 395, 401
McGuire, R., 347, 392
Meehan, J.R, 35, 55, 137, 199, 393, 401
Michalski, R.S., 169, 395
Minsky, M., 61, 395
Mitchell, T.M., 37, 170, 202, 271, 396
Mittal, S., 31, 392
Mooney, R., 37, 170, 202, 393

Newell, A., 2, 31, 256, 395, 396
Nilsson, N., 167, 393
Norvig, P., 343, 396

Owens, C.C., 30, 52, 395

Payne, J.W., 99, 392
Pennington, N., 99, 396
Periera, F.C.N., 319, 396

Quillian, M.R., 329, 341, 343, 396
Quinlan, J.R., 40, 396

Reiser, B.J., 55, 391
Rieger, C.J., 270, 396
Riesbeck, C.K., 9, 35, 55, 88, 137, 199, 319, 326, 341, 393, 395–397, 401
Rissland, E.L., 29, 45, 391, 397
Rosenbloom, P.S., 31, 395

Sacerdoti, E., 167, 168, 190, 252, 257, 397
Schank, R.C., 9, 19, 20, 27, 30, 33–35, 40, 52, 61, 169, 189, 253, 255, 269, 277, 279, 284, 285, 288, 289, 328, 332, 333, 341, 397
Schorr, D., 31, 398
Selfridge, M., 319, 323, 392
Shortliffe, E.H., 17, 392

Simmons, R.G., 49, 397
Simon, H., 2, 396
Simpson, R.L., 29, 38, 43, 107, 397, 398
Smith, E.E., 31, 398
Steele, G.L., Jr., 55, 88, 398
Sussman, G., 49, 167, 190, 398
Sycara, E.P., 29, 38, 46, 398

Tate, A., 167, 252, 398
Thorne, J., 319, 398

Utgoff, P., 271, 396

Waltz, D.L., 260, 398
Warren, D.H.D., 319, 396
Waterman, D.A., 17, 31, 394, 398
Wilensky, R., 20, 55, 167, 168, 275, 397–399
Wilkins, D., 252, 399
Wilks, Y., 319, 399
Winograd, T., 319, 399
Winston, P.H., 55, 169, 399
Wittgenstein, L., 260, 399
Woods, W.A., 319, 337, 399

Lisp Index

BAD-STEP, 232
FOR-KEYS, 61
MOP-TABLES, 67
PREDICTIONS, 356
:ALWAYS, 60
:DO, 59
:FIRST, 60
:SAVE, 59
:WHEN, 59, 60
<, 150
#', 404
', 401

ABST-FN, 76
ABST-MOPP, 68
ABSTP, 68, 90, 318
ACTOR, 84
ADAPT-SENTENCE, 148, 150
ADAPT-STEPS, 222, 244
ADD-PRECONS, 221
ADD-PRED-FILLER, 356
ADD-ROLE-FILLER, 70, 227
ADJUST-FN, 148
ADJUST-SENTENCE, 147, 151, 163
ADVANCE-PRED, 359
ALL-MOPS, 74
ALWAYS, 222
APPEND, 90
APPLY-REPAIR, 229

BACKQUOTE, 401
BACKQUOTE, 402

CALC-ALL-ABSTS, 70

CALC-DECEPTION, 307
CALC-ESCALATIONS, 143, 162
CALC-FN, 74
CALC-MOTIVES, 143
CALC-TYPE, 73, 232
CALC-TYPES, 80
CHEF, 213, 232
CHEF-DEMO, 232, 233
CHEF-EXPLAIN, 232, 247, 248
CHEF-REPAIR, 226
CHEF1, 232
CHEF2, 232, 246, 248
CHEF3, 233
CHEF4, 233
CHEF5, 233
CHEF6, 233
CLEAR-MEMORY, 74, 158, 233, 309, 365
COACH, 292
COACH-DEMO, 309
COMPARE-CONSTRAINT, 150, 294
CONS, 90, 407
CONSTRAINT-FN, 84, 86
COPY-LIST, 61, 403
COPY-LIST, 404
CRIME-COMPARE-SLOTS, 148
CYCLE-EXCLUSION-P, 300

DAH, 83, 84, 89, 158, 233, 309, 365
DAP, 361
DDP, 361
DEFENSIVE-DETECT-INFO, 303, 318

DEFINE-FOR-KEY, 61, 158, 233, 309, 365
DEFINE-TABLE, 57, 158, 233, 309, 365
DEFMACRO, 158, 233, 309, 365
DEFMOP, 76, 80, 81, 158, 233, 309, 365
DEFPHRASE, 359, 365
DEFSETF, 411
DEFSTRUCT, 88
DEFUN, 158, 233, 309, 365
DELAY-STEP, 303
DELAYABLEP, 306
DELAYED-INSERT, 303
DELETE-KEY, 57
DISPLAY-PREDS, 361
DMAP, 355
DMAP-DEMO, 361, 365
DMAP-INIT, 355, 356
DP, 361
DPH, 83, 84, 213, 243, 292

EMPTY-MOPS, 89
ENABLESP, 303
EQL, 150, 294, 403
EQUAL, 403
ERROR, 404
EVENT-EXCLUSION-P, 300, 318
EVERY, 59
EXPRESS-MOP, 371

FOR, 59, 222
FOR-BODY), 61
FOR-EXPANDER, 61
FOR-KEY, 61
FOR-VAR-FORMS, 61
FORMAT, 404–406
FORMAT, 405
FORMS->SLOTS, 81
FUNCTION, 404

GENERALIZE-MOP, 230

GENERALIZE-REPAIR, 230
GENERALIZE-SLOT, 230
GENERALIZE-SLOTS, 230
GENSYM, 406
GENTEMP, 73, 405, 406
GET-ABST-IN-GROUP, 307
GET-DETECTED-EVENT, 303
GET-FILLER, 74, 141, 213, 292
GET-PRECONS, 217
GET-SIBLING, 84, 87, 162, 245
GET-TARGET, 356
GET-TRIGGERED-PREDS, 358
GET-TWIN, 76
GETF, 407, 412
GETF, 407
GETF-SEARCH, 407
GROUP->LIST, 82
GROUP-INSERT, 221
GROUP-MEMBER, 217
GROUP-SIZE, 82
GROUP-SPLICE, 217
GROUPP, 68

HAS-LEGAL-ABSTS-P, 79

I-M-EMPTY-GROUP, 82, 84
INDIRECT-FILLER, 150, 294
INHERIT-FILLER, 74, 90
INSIST, 56, 408, 410
INSTALL-ABSTRACTION, 80
INSTALL-INSTANCE, 79
INSTANCE-MOPP, 68
INTERN, 406
ISA-CONSTRAINT, 227

JUDGE, 141
JUDGE-DEMO, 153, 158

LEGAL-ABSTP, 79, 84
LINK-ABST, 70, 81
LIST->GROUP, 83, 217

M-BAD-STATE, 299

M-CASE, 84
M-COMPARE, 150, 294
M-CRIME, 141, 142
M-EMPTY-GROUP, 84
M-EQUAL, 150, 294
M-EXPLANATION, 299
M-FAILED-SOLUTION, 86
M-FAILURE, 299
M-FUNCTION, 84
M-GROUP, 82, 84, 300
M-INGRED, 64
M-LESS-THAN, 150
M-MOBJECT, 65
M-MTRANS, 65
M-NOT, 84, 86
M-NOT-EQUAL, 294
M-PATH, 247, 294
M-PATTERN, 84
M-RANGE, 142
M-RECIPE, 222
M-REPAIR, 226
M-ROLE, 84
M-ROOT, 64, 74
M-SIDE-EFFECT-EXPLANATION, 226
MAKE-DECEPTION, 307
MAKE-M-N, 83
MAKE-MOP, 217
MAKE-PRED, 356
MAKE-SLOT, 70
MAPC, 59
MAPCAN, 59, 61
MAPCAR, 59
MERGE-PLAYS, 306, 307
MERGE-STEP, 221
MERGE-STEPS, 306
MIXED-MOPS, 89
MOP->FORM, 84
MOP-ABSTS, 67, 411
MOP-ALL-ABSTS, 68
MOP-CALC, 143, 151
MOP-DEFAULT-PREDICTIONS, 358

MOP-DYNAMIC-PREDICTIONS, 358
MOP-EQUALP, 76
MOP-INCLUDESP, 76
MOP-INDEXES, 90
MOP-PREDS, 356
MOP-SLOTS, 68
MOP-SPECS, 68, 90
MOP-SUBST, 217
MOP-TABLE, 67
MOP-TYPE, 68
MOPP, 68
MOPS-ABSTP, 76

NAME->MOP, 88
NEW-MOP, 70, 76, 81, 88
NEXT-EVENTS, 306
NIL, 91
NON-EMPTY-INSTANCES, 89
NOT-CONSTRAINT, 84, 86
NOT-EQL, 294

OBJECT, 84

PATH-FILLER, 75
PATTERNP, 68
POS-PREDS, 356
PRED->MOP, 359
PRED-BASE, 356
PRED-FILLER, 356
PRED-PHRASE, 356
PRED-SLOTS, 356
PRED-START, 356
PRED-TARGET, 356
PREDICTED-MOPS, 356
PROGN, 61

QUOTE, 404

RAISE-ABST, 217
REDO-ALL-ABSTS, 70
REFINE-INSTANCE, 76
REINDEX-SIBLINGS, 80
REM-KEY, 408

REMF, 408
REMOVE-DUPLICATES, 70
REMOVE-DUPLICATES, 408
REMOVE-GOAL-STEP, 306, 318
REMOVE-MOP, 74
REPAIR-1-EXCLUSION-P, 300
REPLACE-SLOTS, 217, 247
RESET-ROLE-FILLER, 227
REST, 408, 410
ROLE-FILLER, 70, 74
ROLE-SLOT, 70
RPLACA, 407
RPLACA, 407
RPLACD, 407
RPLACD, 407
RUN-CHEF, 232

SATISFIEDP, 76
SET-GETF, 408, 411
SETF, 57, 88, 158, 233, 309, 365, 411
SETF, 410
SETQ, 411
SEVERITY, 142
SLOT-FILLER, 70
SLOT-ROLE, 70
SLOTS->FORMS, 84
SLOTS->MOP, 80, 81, 88
SLOTS-ABSTP, 75
SLOTS-SUBST, 217
SPEC-NAME, 73, 405, 406
SPECS->LIST, 84
SPLIT-STEP, 227
SUBST, 214
SUBST-INGRED, 222
SUM-SQUARES, 56

T, 91
TABLE-KEYS, 57
TREE->LIST, 84

UNLINK-ABST, 70

Index

abstraction
  functions, 76, 84, 86, 142, 149,
    292
  hierarchy, 35, 64, 173, 331, 336
  immediate, 64, 67, 70
abstractions
  slotless, 67, 76, 79, 82, 294
adaptation, 5, 7, 13, 24, 25, 28–30,
    33, 38, 41–50, 53, 75, 84, 86,
    107, 108, 114, 129–136, 147,
    148, 210, 213, 214, 222, 226,
    230, 233, 245, 250, 252, 289,
    291, 377
  abstraction and respecialization,
    47–48
  critc-based, 49–50
  derivational, 43–44
  functions, 75, 148
  in CHEF, 174–176
  in DMAP, 337
  in JUDGE, 135
  in micro CHEF, 221
  in micro JUDGE, 151
  null, 44–45
  parameterized solutions, 45–47
  structural, 43
assignment functions, 411
attribute-value pairs, 34, 90

business
  case-based, 6

calculation
  functions, 74, 86, 143

MOPs, 143, 150
case
  library, 25, 42
  recognition, 376
  representation, 34, 40, 61, 214,
    244, 316, 318, 326
cases
  comparing, 122–124, 131–134, 149
  ossified, 12
  paradigmatic, 11–13, 16, 378
  uses of, 110, 166
CASEY, 30
categories, 17
causal knowledge, 37
CHEF, 26, 28, 38, 40, 41, 43, 46,
    47, 49, 50, 52, 53, 184–209,
    291, 337, 338
  output, 184–209
COACH, 26, 28, 41, 52, 338
Common Lisp, 55, 214
communication, 383–385
concept refinement, 325, 328, 337,
    341, 349
conceptual analysis, 319, 321, 323,
    328, 330, 332, 338, 339
Conceptual Dependency, 35, 292, 328
conjunctive plans, 275
constraints, 76, 86
  in MOPs, 300
counterplanning, 262
creativity, 14, 289
credit assignment, 248

CYRUS, 27, 36, 37, 39, 40, 87, 91, 328

data dependencies, 270
debugging, 88, 167
deductive systems, 30
deep domain knowledge, 31
delta agency plan, 279
delta functions, 277
DENDRAL, 2
design domains, 28
Direct Memory Access Parsing, see DMAP
disambiguation, 338–341
discrimination net, 35
DMAP, 27, 65, 67, 319–352
    input, 346, 347
    output, 326, 348–352
domain experts, 26
domain knowledge, 2

error-signaling functions, 404
expectation, 181–182, 323, 329, 342, 348
    failures, 35, 168, 255, 285, 380
    scriptal, 340, 341
expert systems, 2, 9, 17
experts, 16–17
explanation, 3, 5, 26, 30, 52, 99, 137–138, 168, 177, 246, 248, 269, 380, 381
    not in micro CHEF, 232

failures
    avoiding, 167
    expectation, 168
football
    rules of, 263–264
FOR-keyword, 60
forced choice, 262, 263
form tests, 329, 343
frame, 33, 61

FRUMP, 385, 387, 388

garbage collection, 90
general problem solver, 1, 2, 9, 10
generalization, 7, 23, 36–40, 54, 91, 124–125
    explanation-based, 37
    in micro CHEF, 230
    similarity-based, 36
generation of natural language , 371
goal subsumption, 275
GPS, 2, 9

HACKER, 190
hillclimbing, 252
HYPO, 29, 45, 47

idiosyncratic criteriality, 11
implicit decisions, 259
    taxonomy, 260
implicit knowledge, 260
index patterns, 331, 340, 348, 350, 353
    active, 353
    advancing, 353
    controlling, 355
indexing, 6, 17, 18, 24, 33, 110, 169, 179–180, 374–376
    problem, 33
input analysis, 117–118
instances, 64, 73, 76
integration, 385–389
intelligence, 9, 373–389
interpretation, see input analysis
IPP, 27, 36, 87, 91, 328, 341
isa-plateaus, 343

JUDGE, 26–28, 32, 33, 43, 45, 46, 113–140, 162
    case base, 113
    output, 117
    stages of operation, 114

JULIA, 50

labelling, *see* indexing
law
    case-based, 6
learning, 17, 36–40, 138–139, 166,
    169, 249, 261, 387
    by remembering, 169
    concept, 169
    critics, 170
    expectations, 170
    explanation-based, 169, 271
    failure-driven, 38, 255, 382
        steps in, 255
    in CHEF, 36, 176
    in CYRUS, 36
    in IPP, 36
    in MEDIATOR, 36
    in planning, 209–212
    plans, 170
legal reasoning, 93
lexicons
    scriptal, 328, 339–341
librarian, 8–9
Lisp, 55
logarithms, 42

macros, 401, 410, 411
man in the street, 5
mapping functions, 59
marker passing, 329, 341, 343–345
    in DMAP, 344–345
    in TLC, 343–344
    not in micro DMAP, 353
markers
    activation, 341–342
        passing rules, 342
    prediction, 341–343
        passing rules, 342
matching, 33, 118–121, 171
    partial, 24, 172, 377, 378
    pattern, 66–67

mathematics
    case-based, 7
MEDIATOR, 29, 38, 43, 50
memory
    dynamic, 27, 33–34, 209, 210,
        328, 329, 332–333, 347
    episodic, 18
memory organization, 33–40
Memory Organization Packages, *see*
    MOPs
micro CHEF, 90, 213–248
    abstraction hierarchy, 233
    output, 238
    running, 233
micro COACH, 291–318
    abstraction hierarchy, 309
    output, 314
    running, 309
micro DMAP, 353–372
    abstraction hierarchy, 365
    output, 368
    running, 365
micro JUDGE, 141–163, 245
    abstraction hierarchy, 158
    MOPS, 142
    output, 160
    running, 158
MOPs, 27, 33–36, 61, 253, 321, 323–
    326, 328, 332, 338, 341
    abstractions, 34
    exemplars, 34
    failures, 35
    filler, 64
    fillers, 70
    group, 68, 82
    indexes, 34
    norms, 34, 35
    pattern, 68, 74, 76, 84, 87
    roles, 64, 70
    scenes, 34
    slots, 70

specializations, 34
MOPTRANS, 328
motive rules
  in JUDGE, 115
  in micro JUDGE, 143
MTRANS, 65

NOAH, 190

opportunism, 254
  execution-time, 275
  plan-time, 275
option play, 281–289

packaging hierarchy, 35
parsing
  case-based, 319
    features of, 330
patterns, 7
PERSUADER, 29, 36, 38, 45, 47,
  50
plan
  creation, 249
  repair, 261
  strategies, 250
    features of, 252
  tranformation rules
    vs. planning rules, 258
  transformation
    purpose of, 259
  transformation rules, 252, 254,
    256
    aggressive counterplan, 266
    applying, 268–269
    be unpredictable, 266–267
    beat them to the punch, 267–
      268
    delegate, 278–280
    factor precondition, 254, 273–
      274, 278
    find middle path, 276–277
    fork, 284, 286–289

hedge your bets, 268
hold the fort, 267
information processing transformations, 277–281
merge conjuncts, 274–276
reduce variance, 277–278, 284
reschedule, 272–273
scheduling transformations, 272–
  277
successive approximation, 280–
  281
plan repair, 291
planning, 5, 165, 382–383
  case-based, 165
    features of, 166–171
  conservatism in, 290
  Generate and Store Model, 252
  non-linear, 252, 257
  Notice Opportunites Model, 254
  problems, 256
    analysis, 269
    features of, 253
    problem description, 269
    taxonomy, 256–257
  Response to Problems Model, 253,
    255
  rule-based, 165
  Serendipity Model, 254
PLEXUS, 29, 47
plists, 56
points, 13
prediction structures, 355
predictions
  default, 355, 358, 361
  dynamic, 355, 358, 361
  representation in micro DMAP,
    356
production systems, 30
property lists, 56
proverbs, 13

rationalization, 108–109
readmacros
in Common Lisp, 401
reasoning
case-based, 6, 7, 9–11, 16, 24–
54, 107, 109
analysis phase, 33
flow chart, 32
vs. rule-based, 9–11, 26
rule-based, 2, 9, 25–26, 30–31
refinement, 66, 76
failures, 348, 350
reinstantiation, 50
reminding, 15–24, 373
cross-contextual, 21–22
goal-based, 19–20
intentional, 22–23
morals, 22
near-miss, 370
plan-based, 20–21
repair, 41, 52, 53, 177–179
in DMAP, 337–338, 348
in micro CHEF, 226, 227
strategies, 49, 53
replanning
requirements, 289
retrieval, 7, 42, 118–121, 171–174
in CHEF, 172–174
role specifiers, 358
rule
base, 30
differentiation, 125–129
interpreter, 30
mappings, 226
memory, 30
rules, 7, 11, 12, 26, 124
additivity of, 31
plan transformation, *see* plan,
transformation rules

scripts, 4–5, 7, 18, 34, 253, 333, 379

selectional restrictions, 328, 339
sentencing
examples of, 94–98, 101–102
features of, 98–100, 103–111
specialization failures, 336–337, 348
specializations, 64
stories, 12–14, 99, 376, 377, 384–385
structures
in Common Lisp, 88
subjective appraisal, 28
substitution
in Lisp, 214
in MOPs, 214
successive approximation, 251, 262
SWALE, 30, 48, 52

tables, 56
Teachable Language Comprehender,
see TLC
Thematic Organization Packages, *see*
TOPs
time cycles, 294
TLC, 329
TOPs, 40, 53, 189–193, 199

value hierarchy, 173

weak method, 40